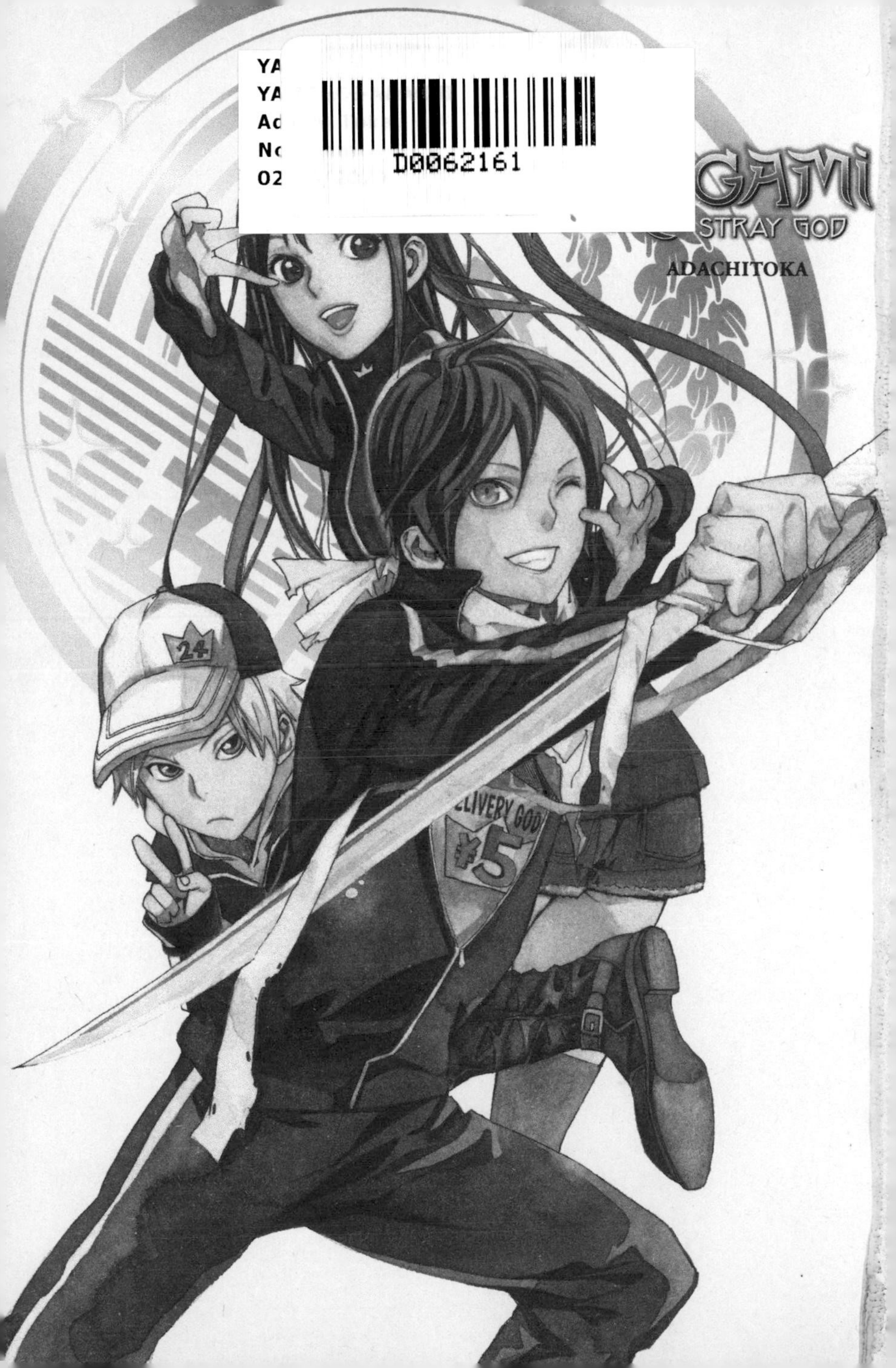
GAMI
STRAY GOD
ADACHITOKA
24
ELIVERY GOD
¥5

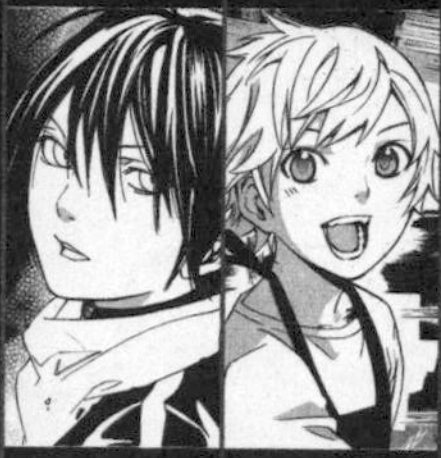

YATO

A minor deity who always wears a sweatsuit.

YUKINÉ

Yato's shinki who turns into swords.

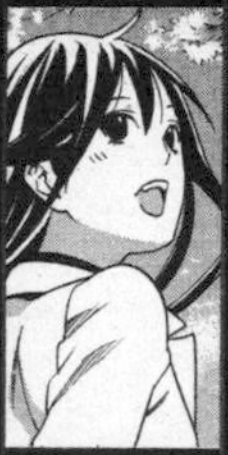

HIYORI IKI

A high school student who has become half ayakashi.

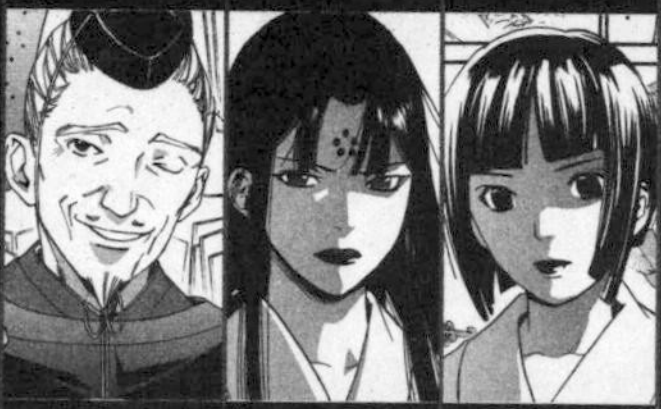

TENJIN

The god of learning, Sugawara no Michizane.

TSUYU

Tenjin's attendant.

MAYU

Formerly Yato's shinki, now Tenjin's shinki.

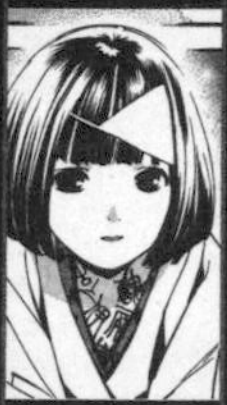

STRAY

A shinki who serves an unspecified number of deities.

characters

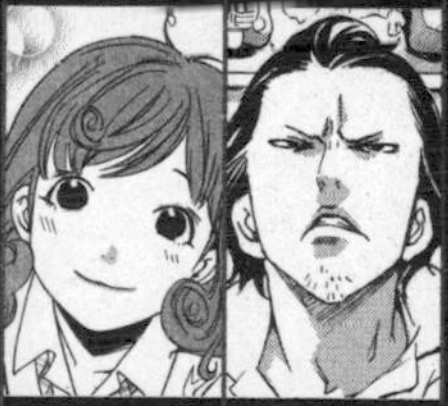

KOFUKU

A goddess of poverty who calls herself Ebisu after the god of fortune.

DAIKOKU

Kofuku's shinki who summons storms.

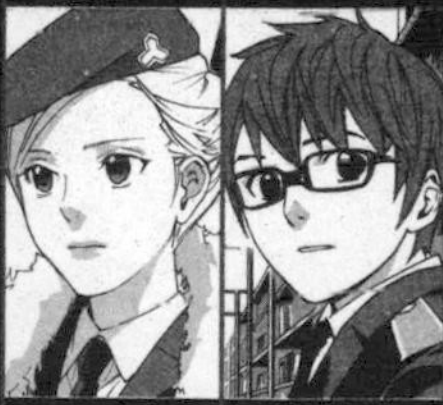

BISHAMONTEN

A powerful warrior god, one of the Seven Gods of Fortune.

KAZUMA

A navigational shinki who serves as guide to Bishamon.

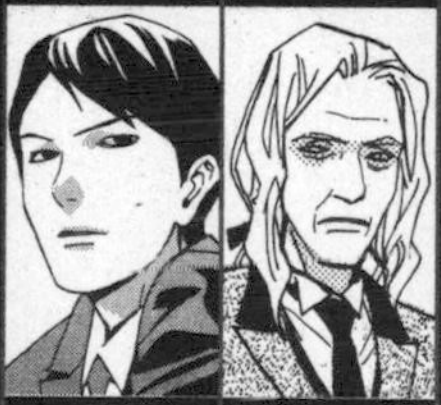

EBISU

A no-nonsense business-god, one of the Seven Gods of Fortune.

IWAMI

Ebisu's shinki and guide.

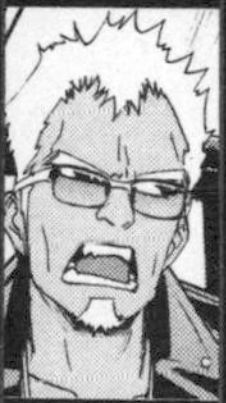

ÔKUNINUSHI (DAIKOKUTEN)

Number one of the Seven Gods of Fortune.

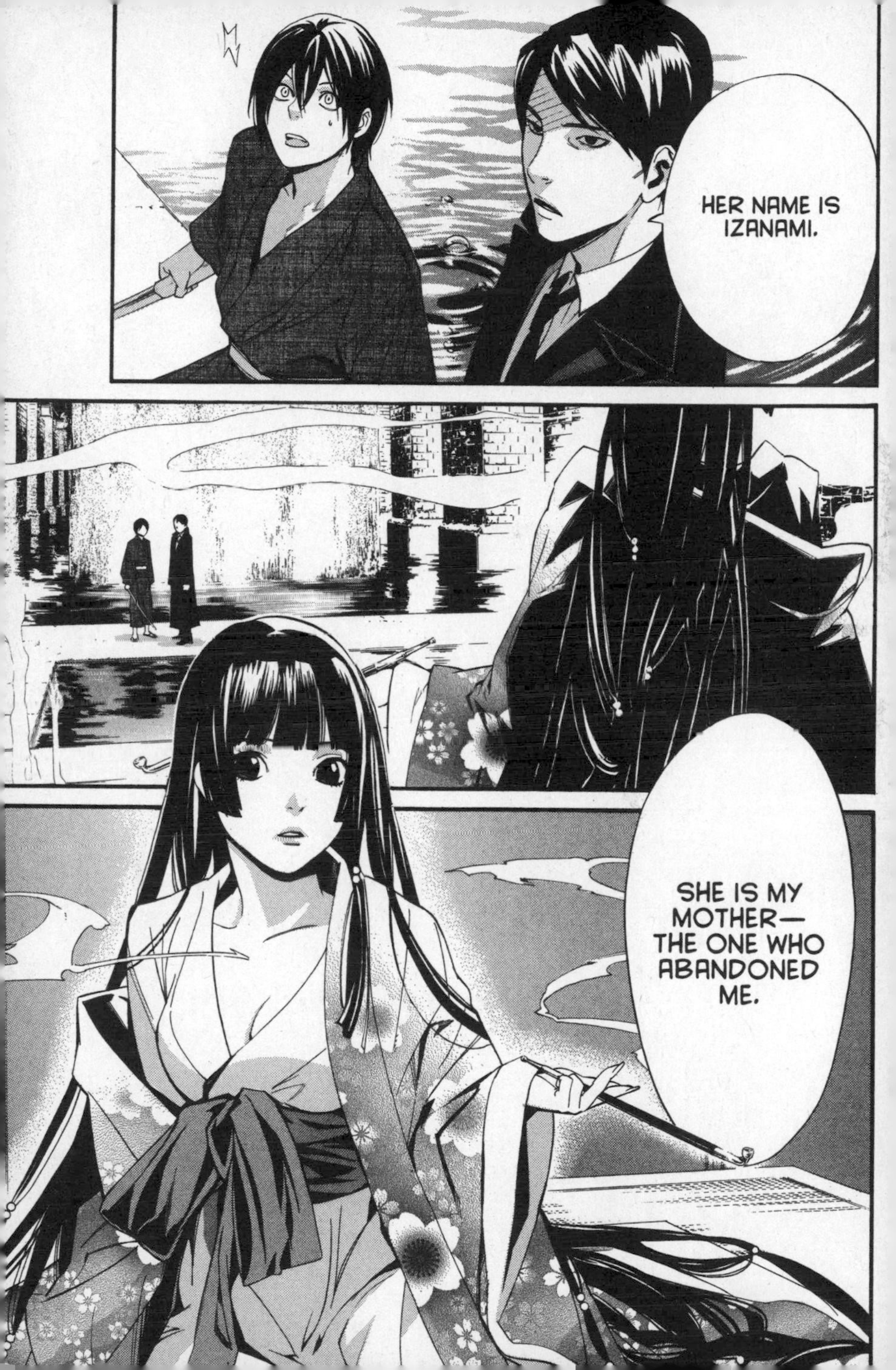
HER NAME IS IZANAMI.
SHE IS MY MOTHER— THE ONE WHO ABANDONED ME.

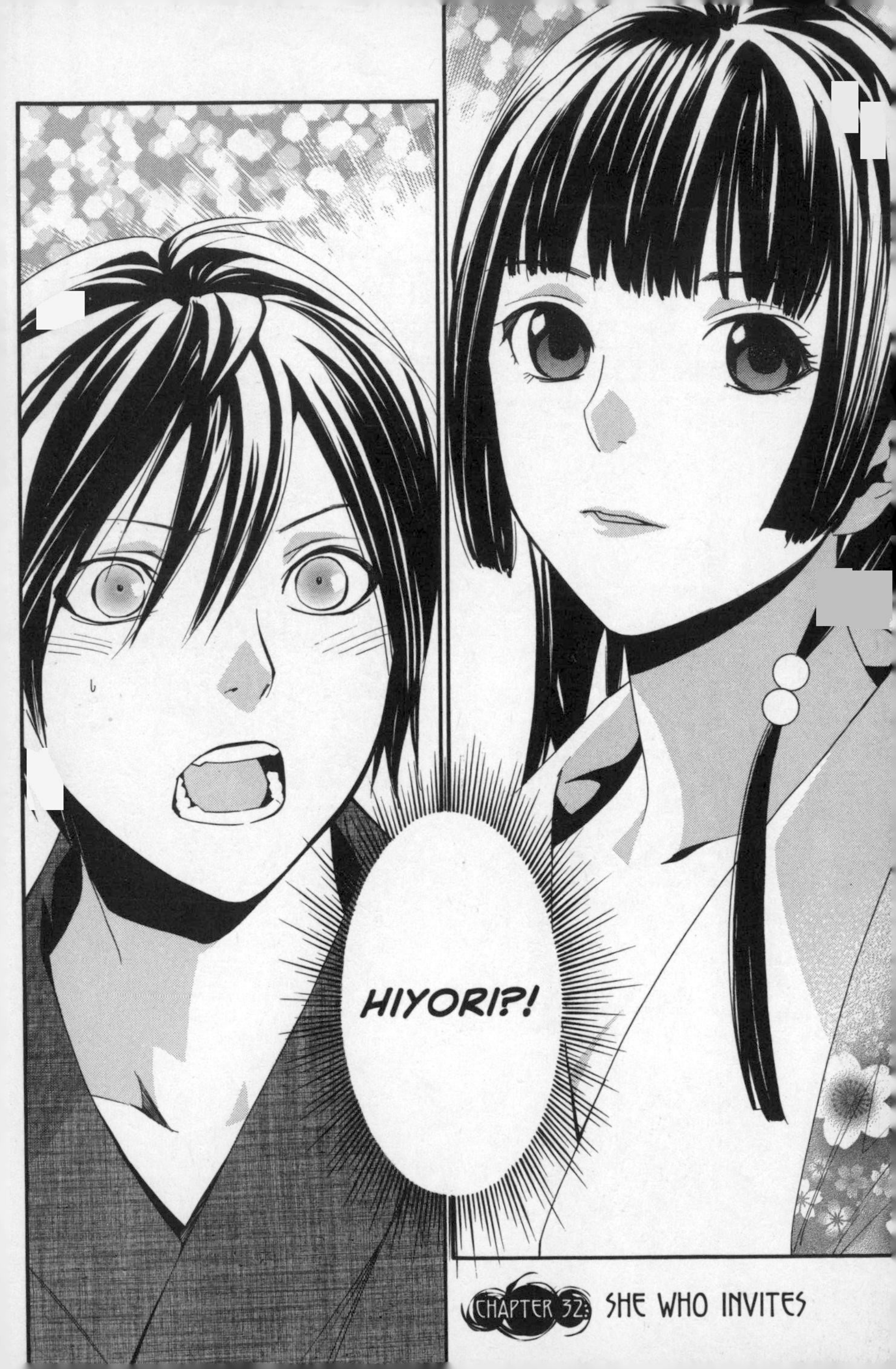
HIYORI?!

CHAPTER 32: SHE WHO INVITES

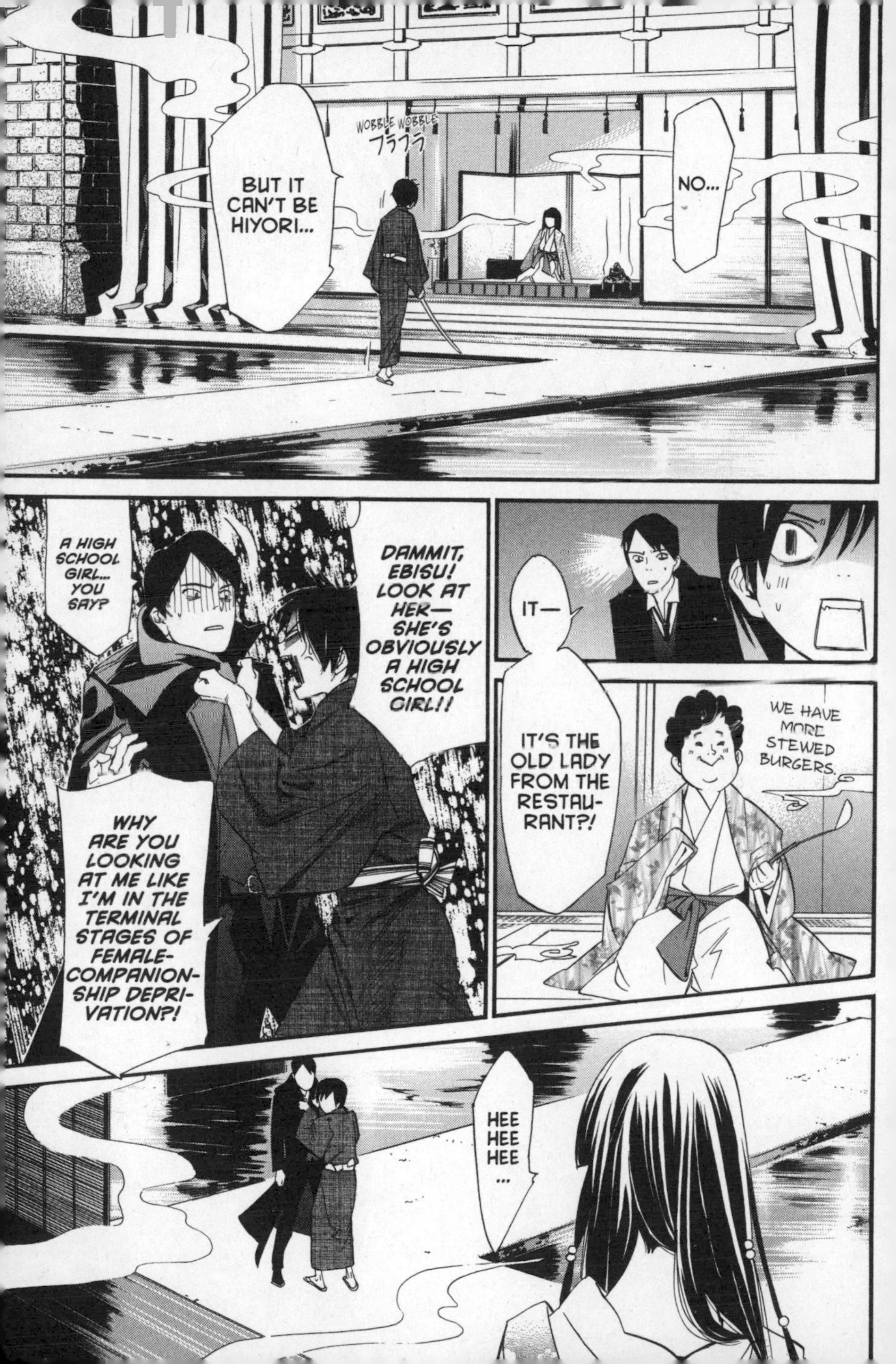
NO...
WOBBLE WOBBLE
フラフラ
BUT IT CAN'T BE HIYORI...
IT—
IT'S THE OLD LADY FROM THE RESTAU-RANT?!
WE HAVE MORE STEWED BURGERS.
DAMMIT, EBISU! LOOK AT HER—SHE'S OBVIOUSLY A HIGH SCHOOL GIRL!!
A HIGH SCHOOL GIRL... YOU SAY?
WHY ARE YOU LOOKING AT ME LIKE I'M IN THE TERMINAL STAGES OF FEMALE-COMPANION-SHIP DEPRI-VATION?!
HEE HEE HEE ...

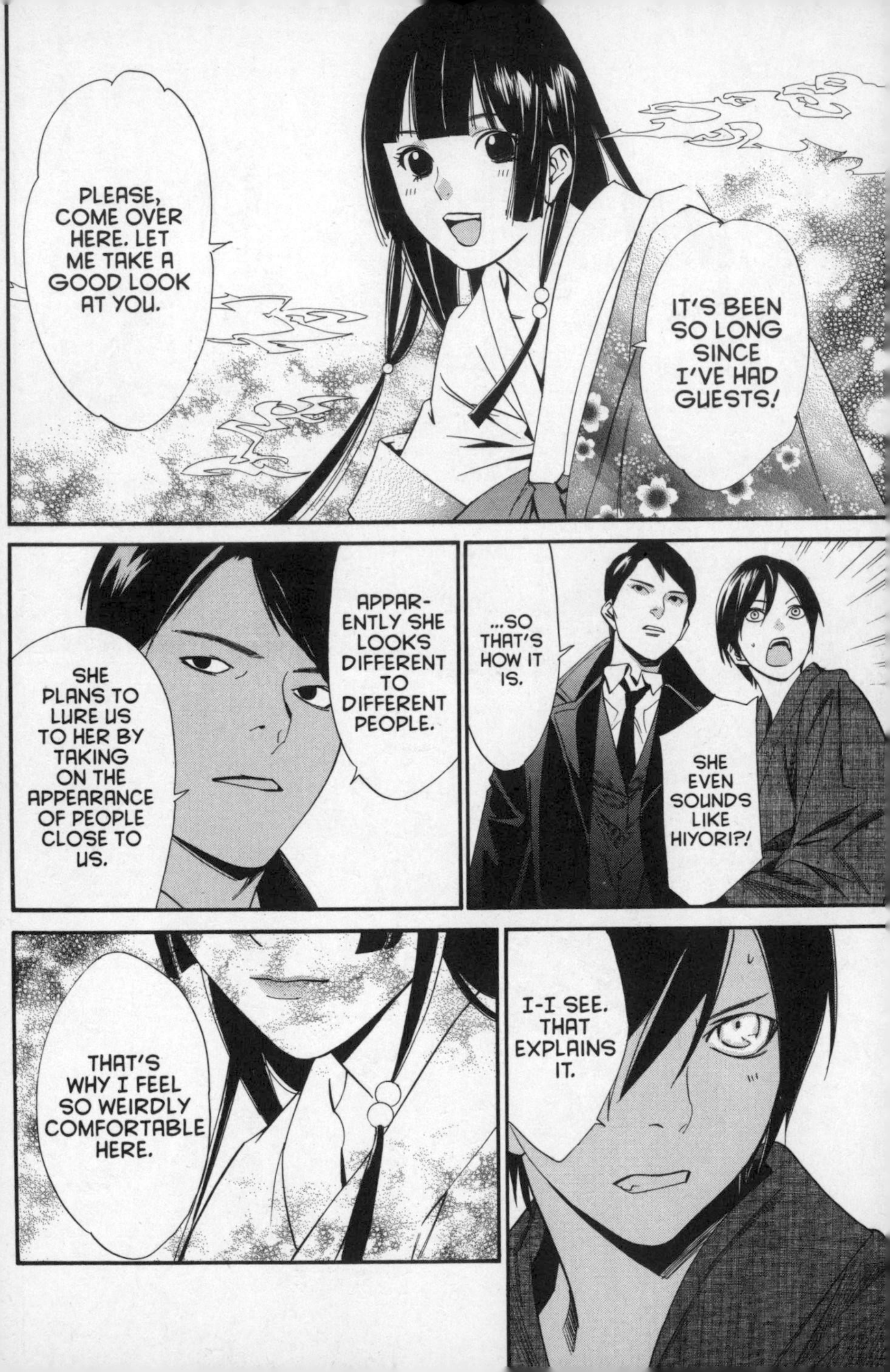
IT'S BEEN SO LONG SINCE I'VE HAD GUESTS!
PLEASE, COME OVER HERE. LET ME TAKE A GOOD LOOK AT YOU.
...SO THAT'S HOW IT IS.
SHE EVEN SOUNDS LIKE HIYORI?!
APPAR-ENTLY SHE LOOKS DIFFERENT TO DIFFERENT PEOPLE.
SHE PLANS TO LURE US TO HER BY TAKING ON THE APPEARANCE OF PEOPLE CLOSE TO US.
I-I SEE. THAT EXPLAINS IT.
THAT'S WHY I FEEL SO WEIRDLY COMFORTABLE HERE.

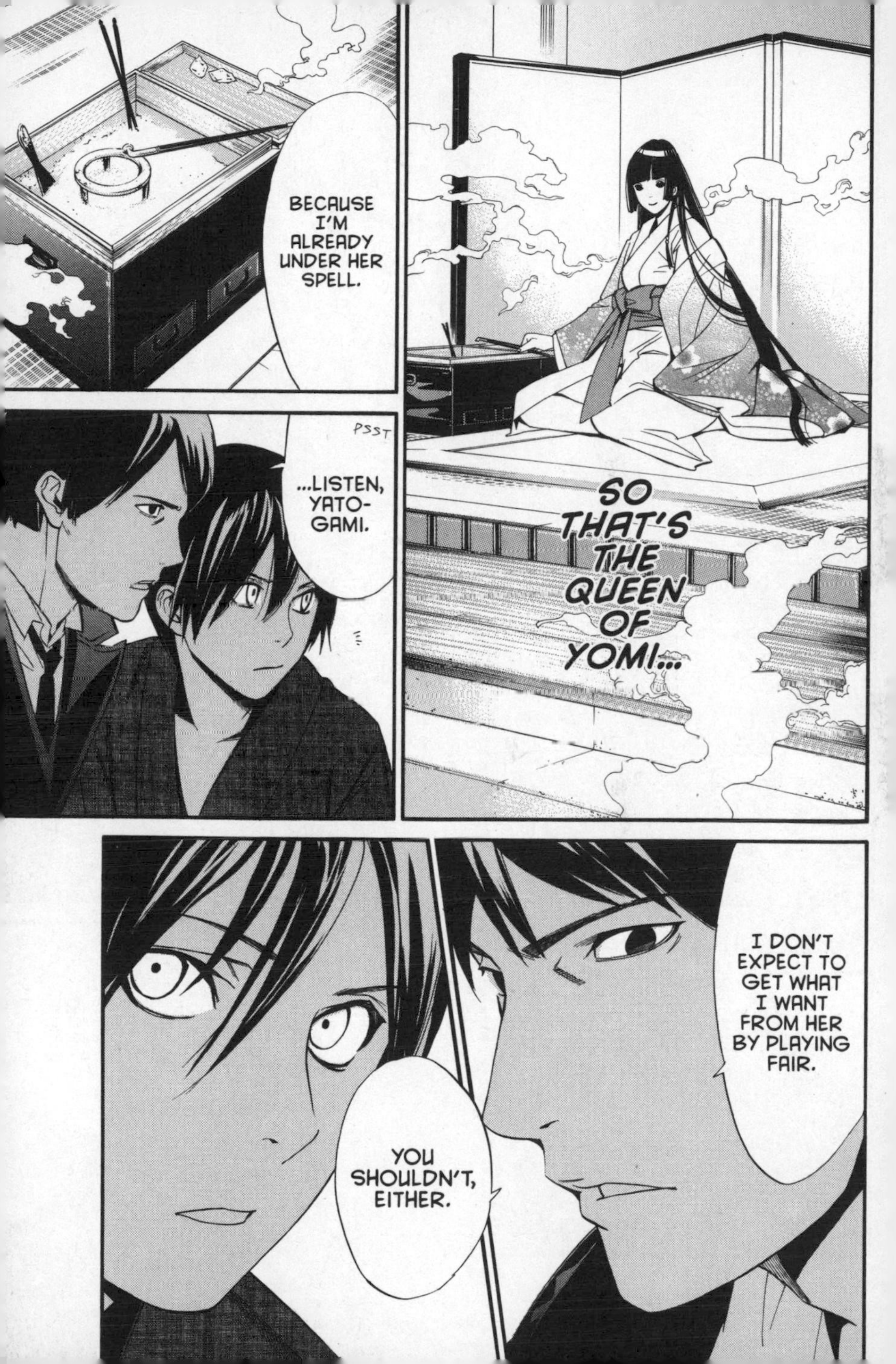
SO THAT'S THE QUEEN OF YOMI...
BECAUSE I'M ALREADY UNDER HER SPELL.
PSST
...LISTEN, YATO-GAMI.
I DON'T EXPECT TO GET WHAT I WANT FROM HER BY PLAYING FAIR.
YOU SHOULDN'T, EITHER.

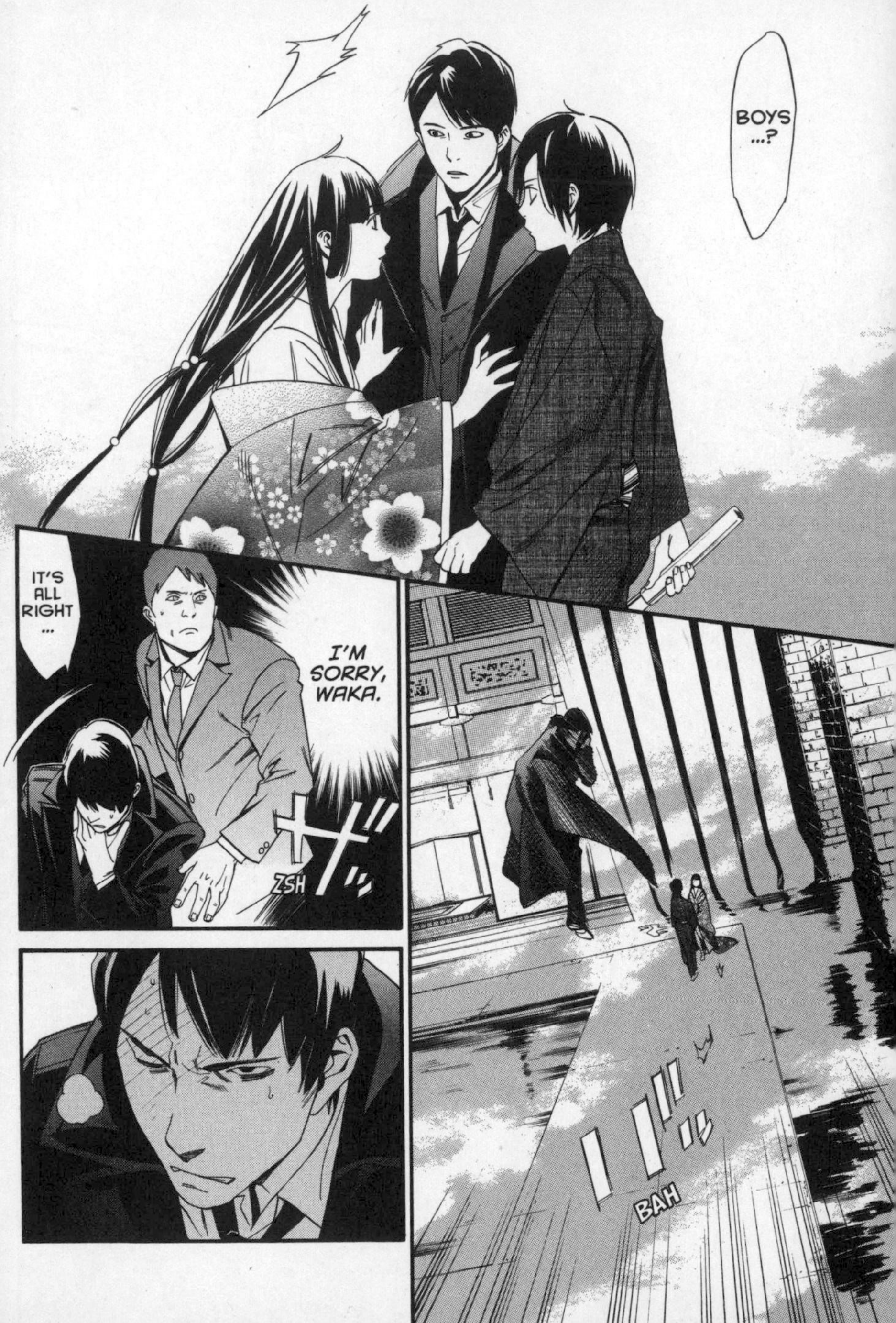
BOYS ...?
BAH
I'M SORRY, WAKA.
IT'S ALL RIGHT ...
ZSH

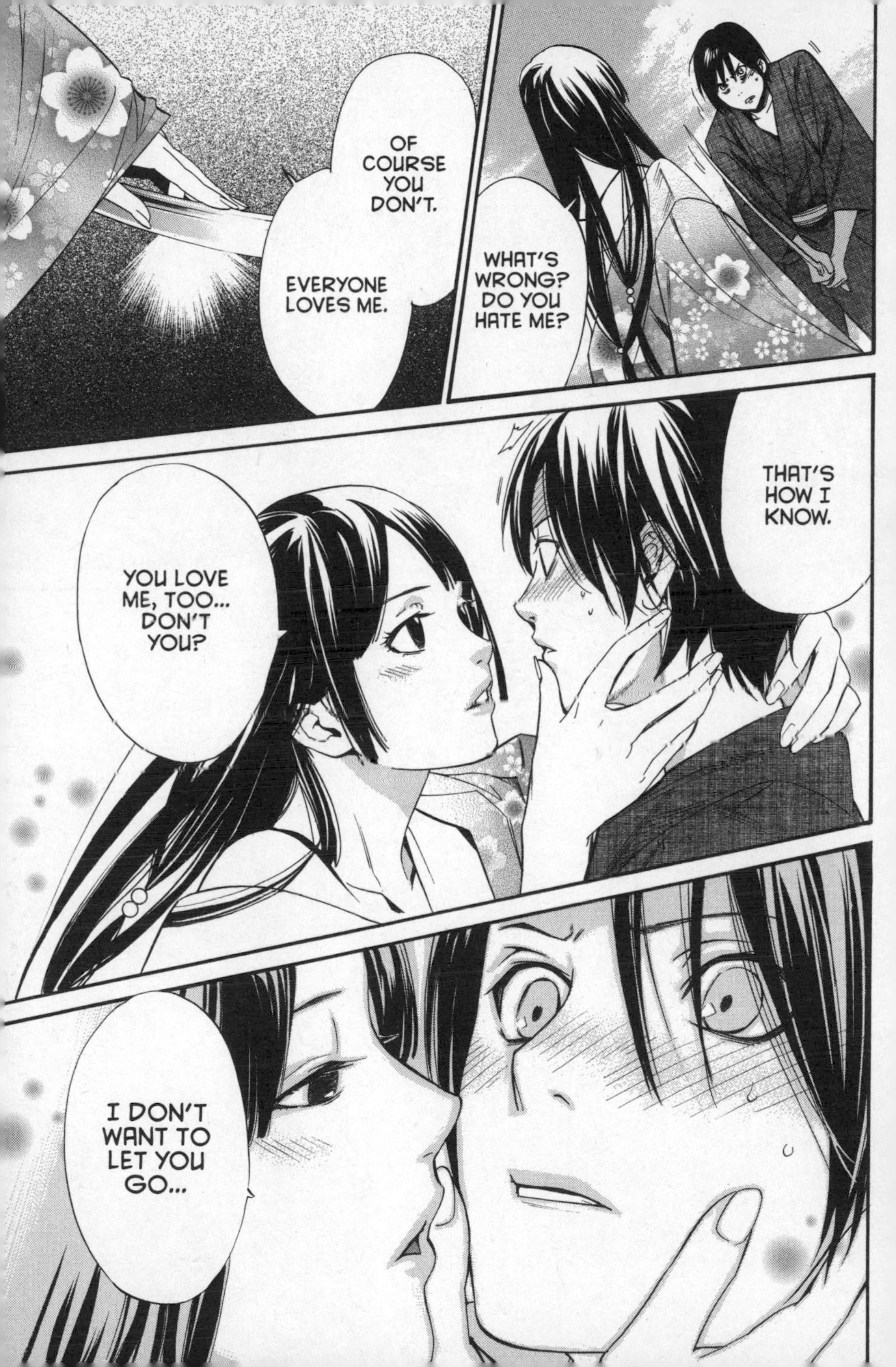
WHAT'S WRONG? DO YOU HATE ME?
OF COURSE YOU DON'T.
EVERYONE LOVES ME.
THAT'S HOW I KNOW.
YOU LOVE ME, TOO... DON'T YOU?
I DON'T WANT TO LET YOU GO...

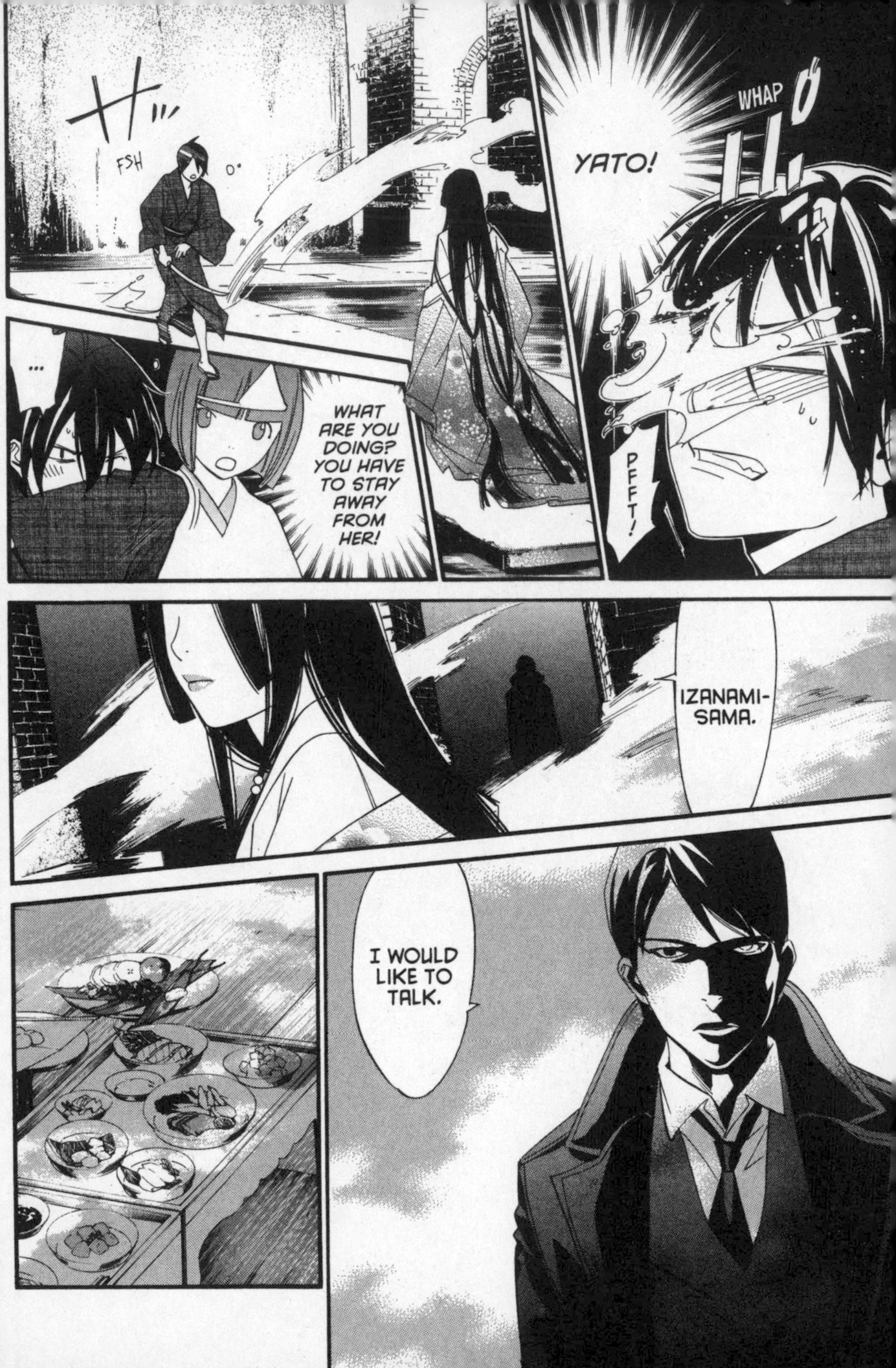
YATO!
WHAP
PFFT!
FSH
...
WHAT ARE YOU DOING? YOU HAVE TO STAY AWAY FROM HER!
IZANAMI-SAMA.
I WOULD LIKE TO TALK.

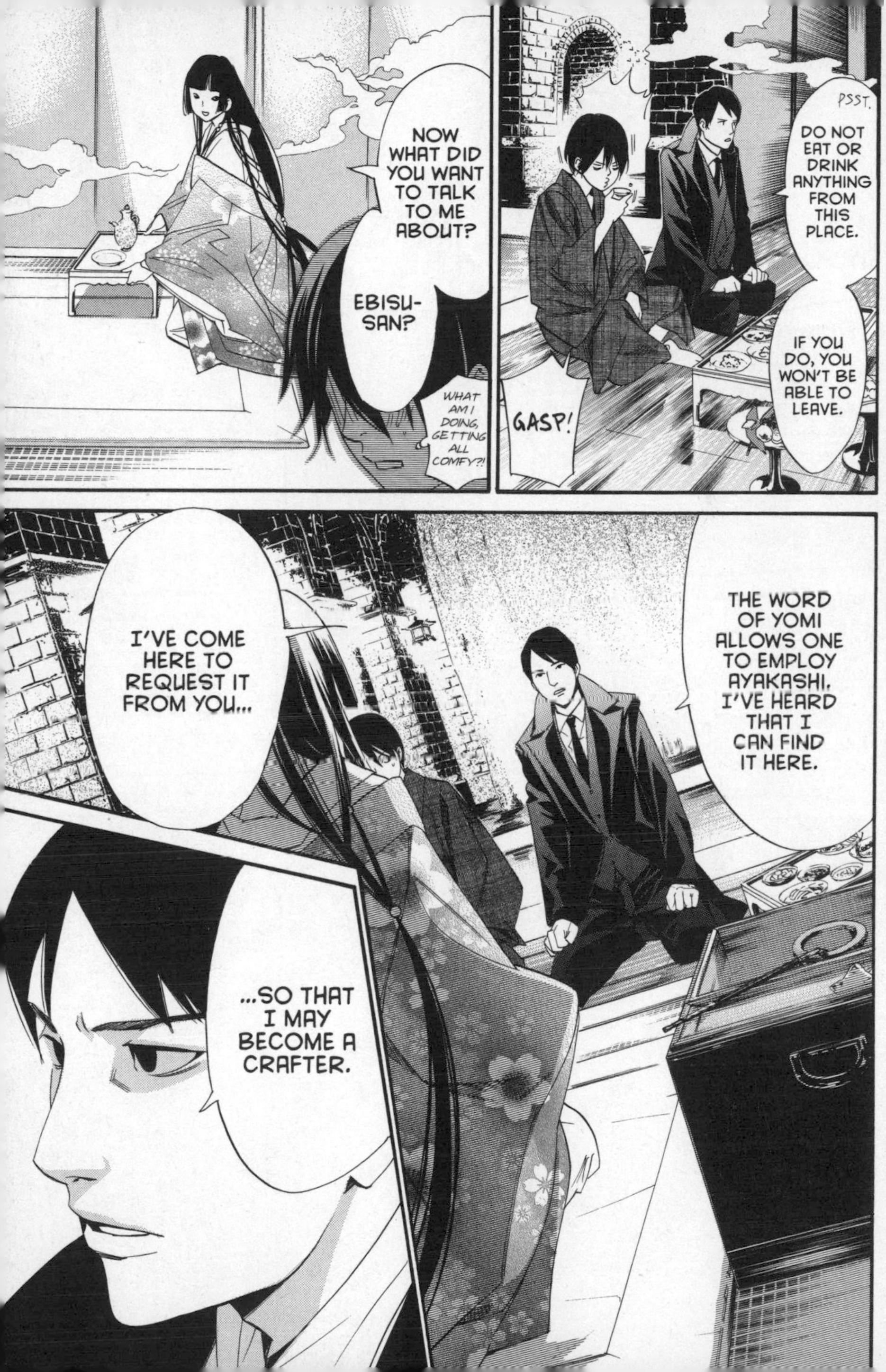
PSST.
DO NOT EAT OR DRINK ANYTHING FROM THIS PLACE.
IF YOU DO, YOU WON'T BE ABLE TO LEAVE.
GASP!
NOW WHAT DID YOU WANT TO TALK TO ME ABOUT?
EBISU-SAN?
WHAT AM I DOING, GETTING ALL COMFY?!
THE WORD OF YOMI ALLOWS ONE TO EMPLOY AYAKASHI. I'VE HEARD THAT I CAN FIND IT HERE.
I'VE COME HERE TO REQUEST IT FROM YOU...
...SO THAT I MAY BECOME A CRAFTER.

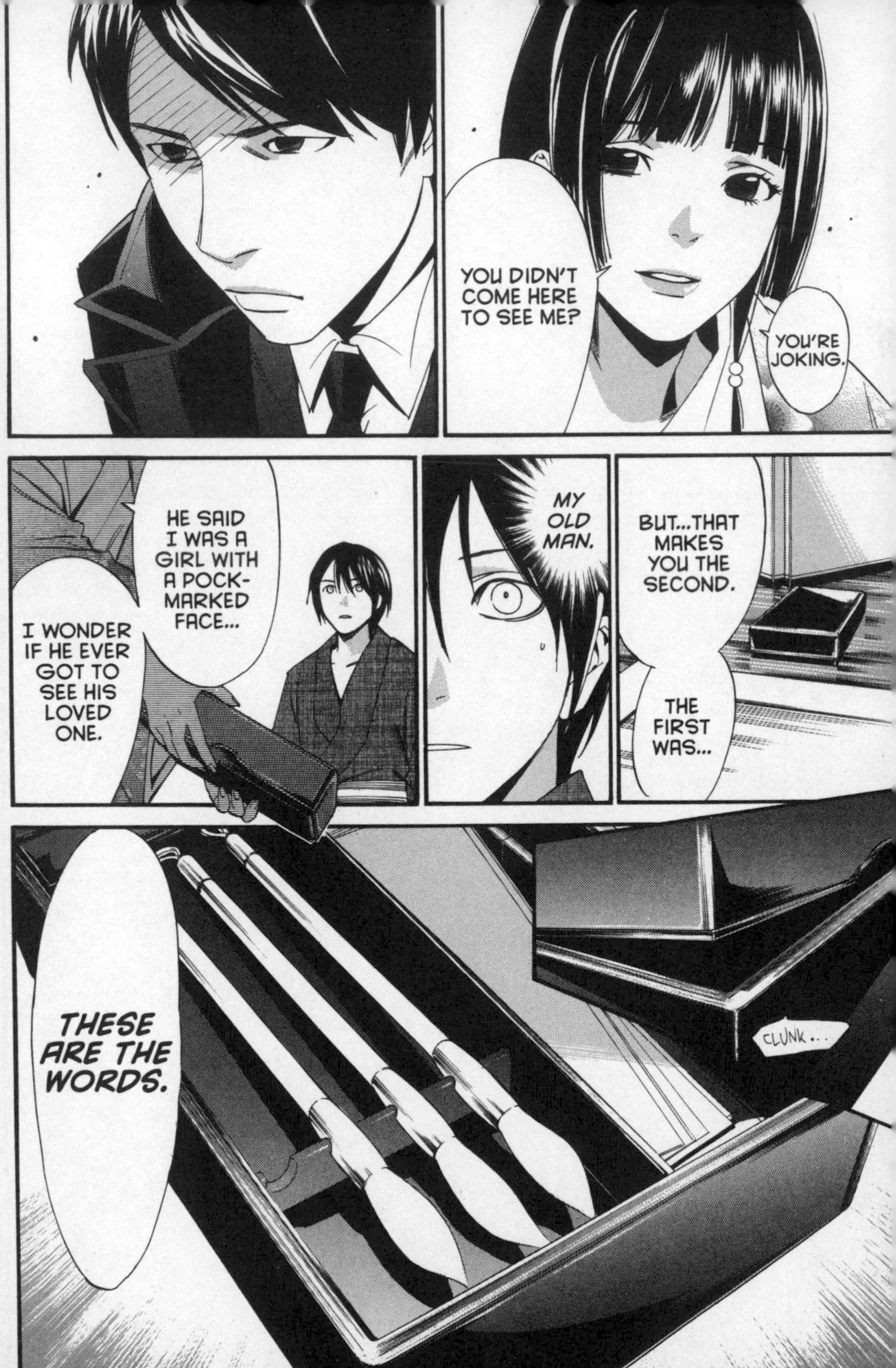
YOU DIDN'T COME HERE TO SEE ME?
YOU'RE JOKING.
BUT...THAT MAKES YOU THE SECOND.
THE FIRST WAS...
MY OLD MAN.
HE SAID I WAS A GIRL WITH A POCK-MARKED FACE...
I WONDER IF HE EVER GOT TO SEE HIS LOVED ONE.
CLUNK...
THESE ARE THE WORDS.

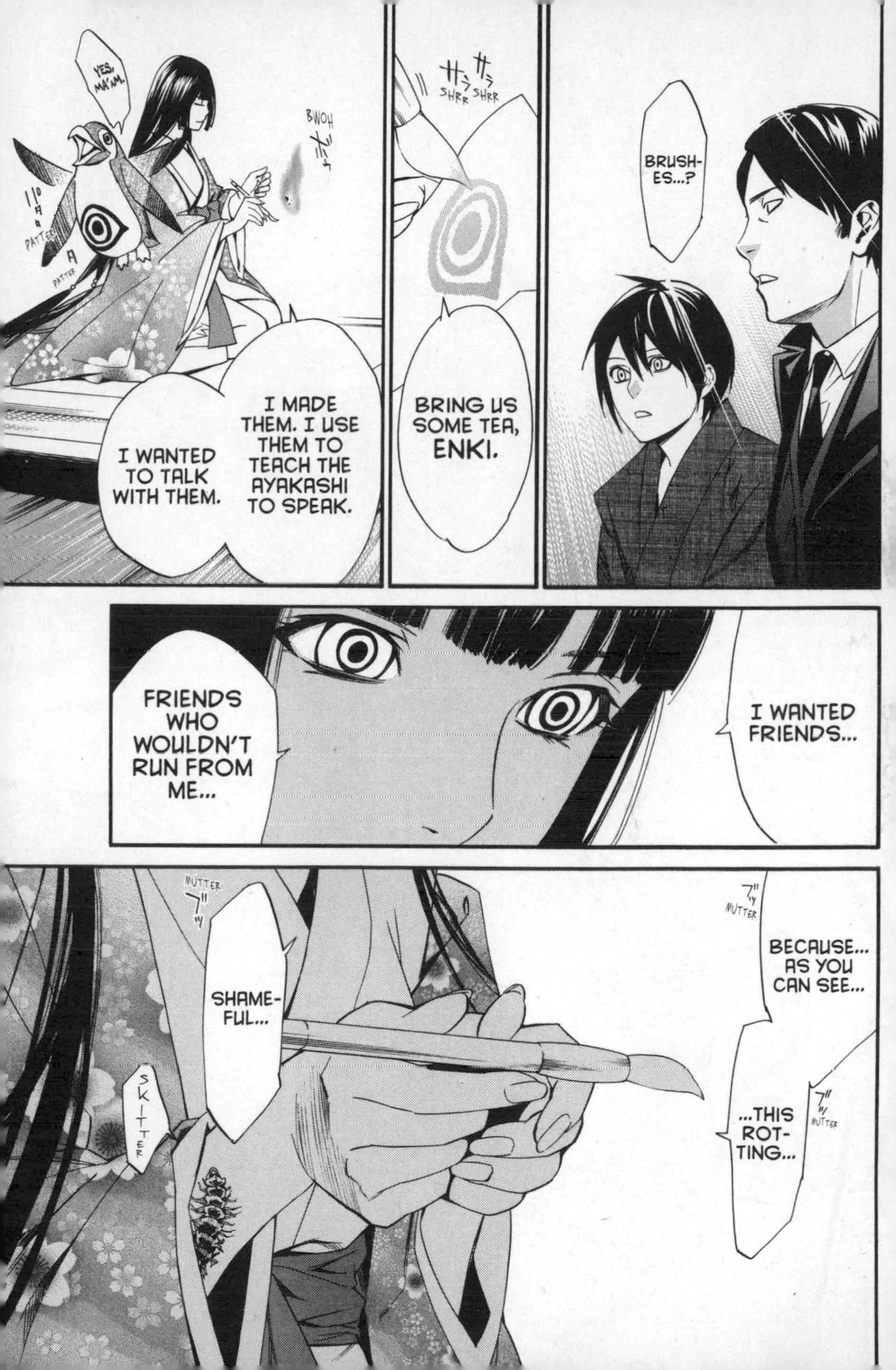
BRUSH-ES...?
SHRR SHRR
BRING US SOME TEA, ENKI.
BWOH
YES, MA'AM.
I MADE THEM. I USE THEM TO TEACH THE AYAKASHI TO SPEAK.
I WANTED TO TALK WITH THEM.
PATTER
PATTER
I WANTED FRIENDS...
FRIENDS WHO WOULDN'T RUN FROM ME...
MUTTER
BECAUSE... AS YOU CAN SEE...
MUTTER
...THIS ROT-TING...
MUTTER
SHAME-FUL...
SKITTER

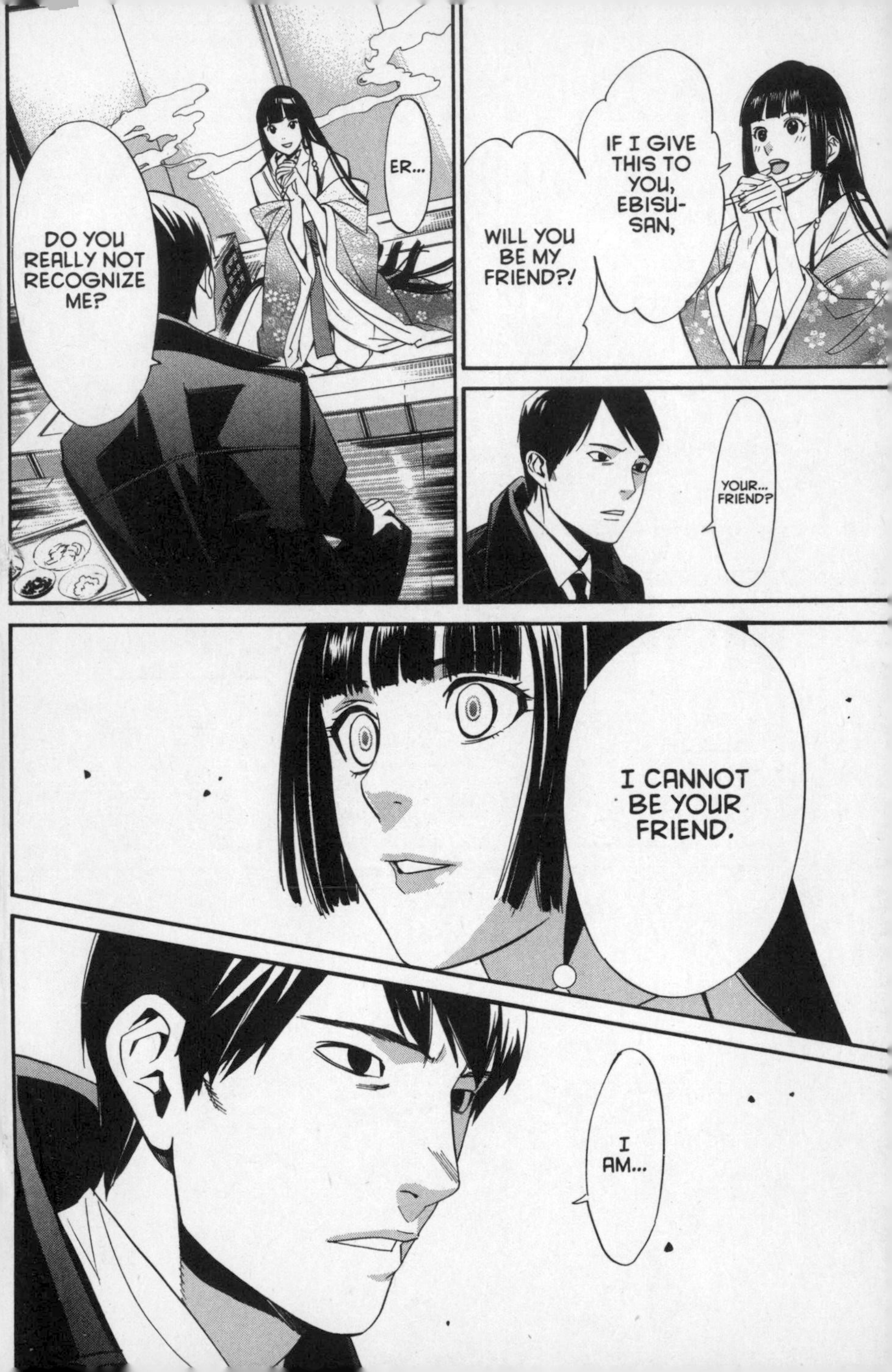
IF I GIVE THIS TO YOU, EBISU-SAN,
WILL YOU BE MY FRIEND?!
YOUR... FRIEND?
ER...
DO YOU REALLY NOT RECOGNIZE ME?
I CANNOT BE YOUR FRIEND.
I AM...

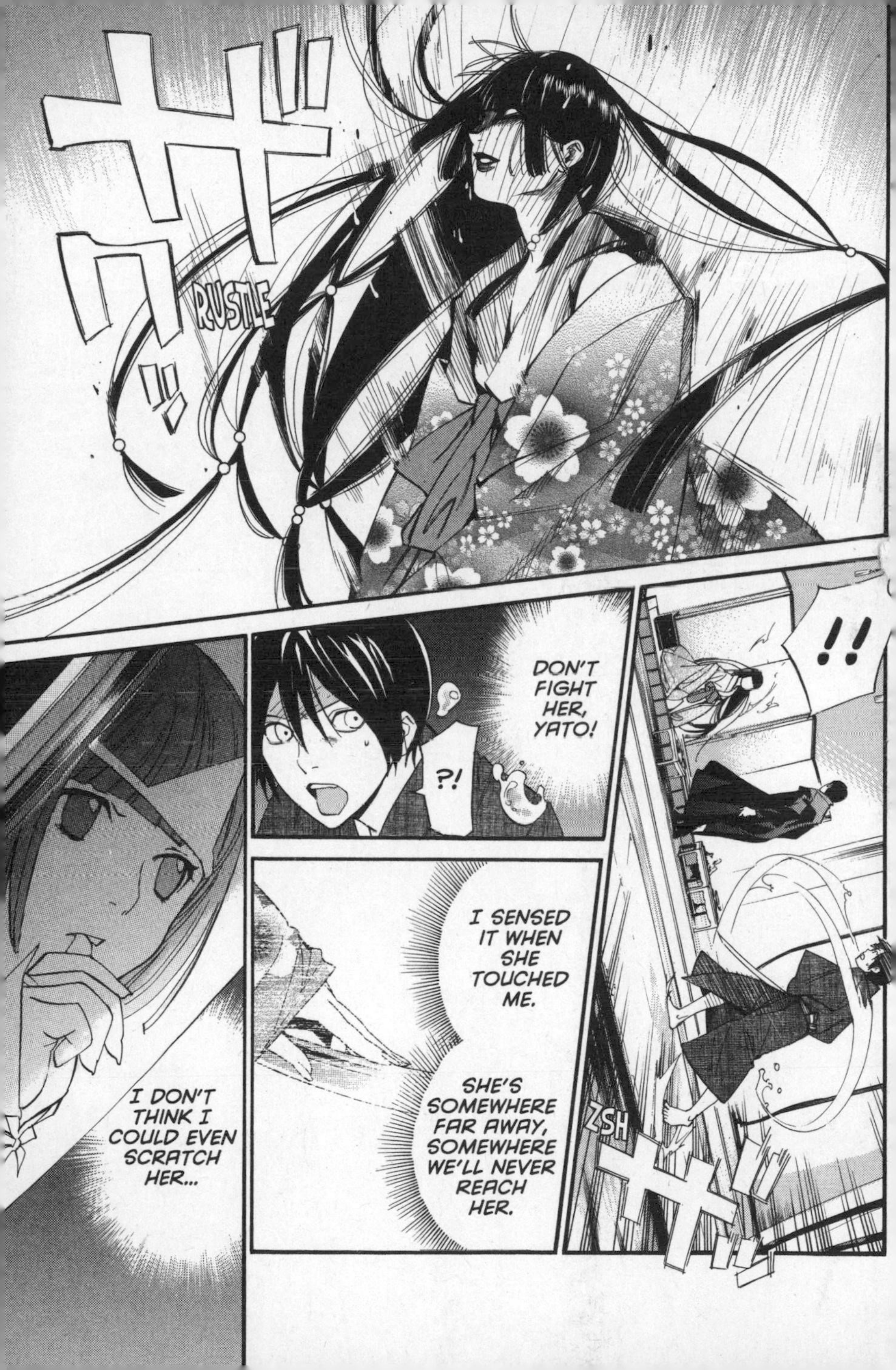
RUSTLE
!!
ZSH
DON'T FIGHT HER, YATO!
?!
I SENSED IT WHEN SHE TOUCHED ME.
SHE'S SOMEWHERE FAR AWAY, SOMEWHERE WE'LL NEVER REACH HER.
I DON'T THINK I COULD EVEN SCRATCH HER...

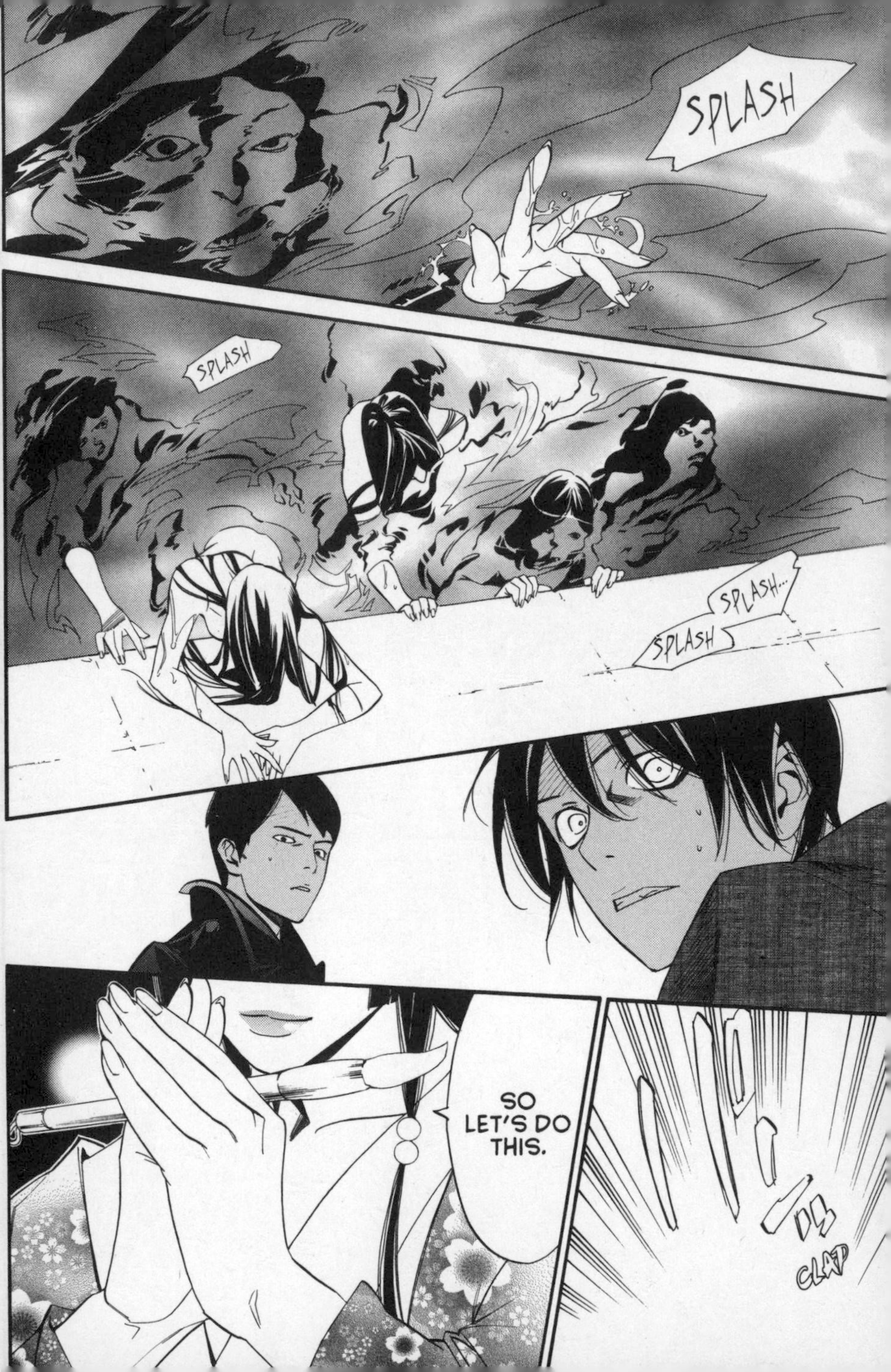
SPLASH
SPLASH...
SPLASH
SPLASH
CLAP
SO LET'S DO THIS.

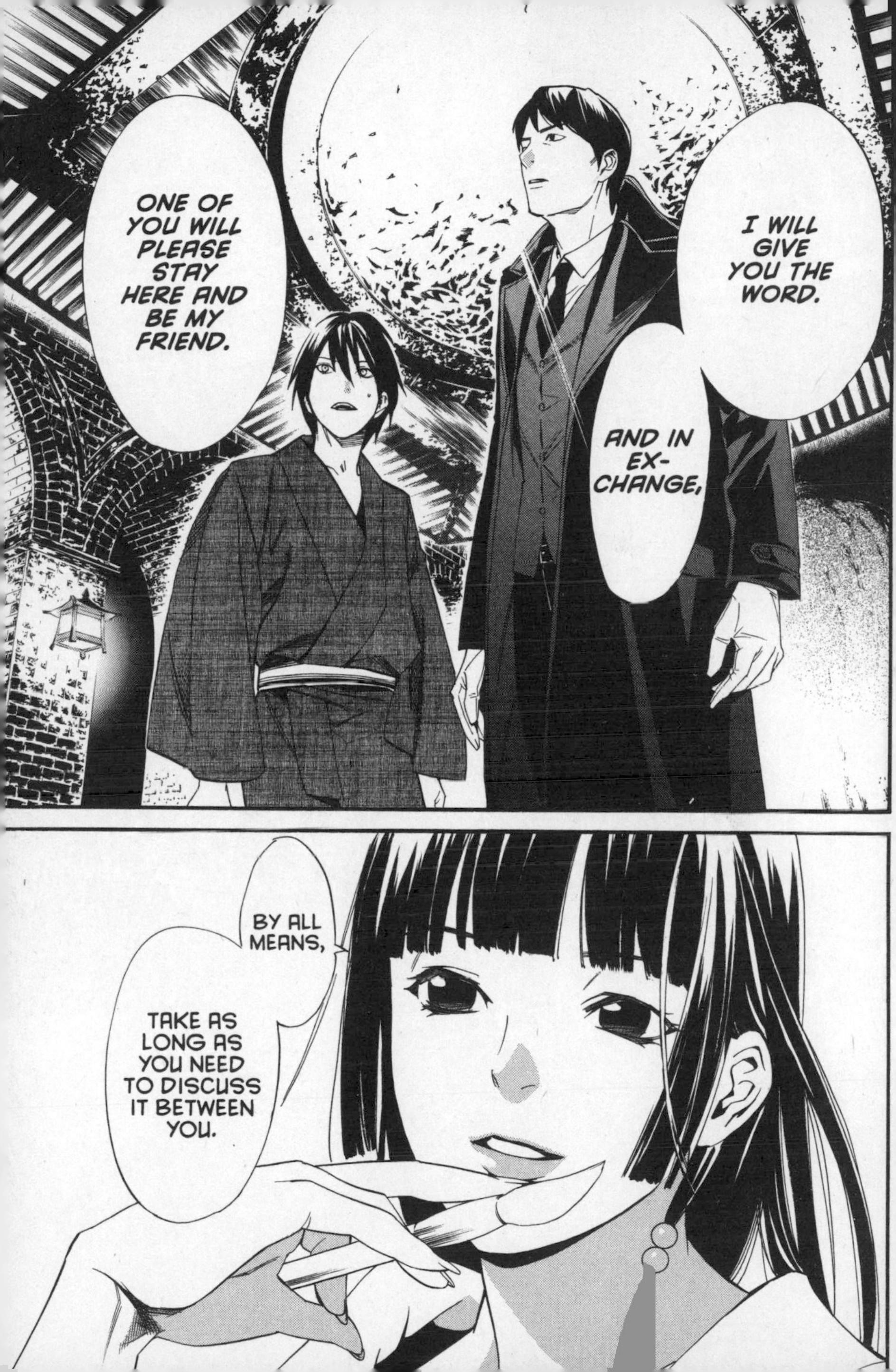
I WILL GIVE YOU THE WORD.
AND IN EX-CHANGE,
ONE OF YOU WILL PLEASE STAY HERE AND BE MY FRIEND.
BY ALL MEANS,
TAKE AS LONG AS YOU NEED TO DISCUSS IT BETWEEN YOU.

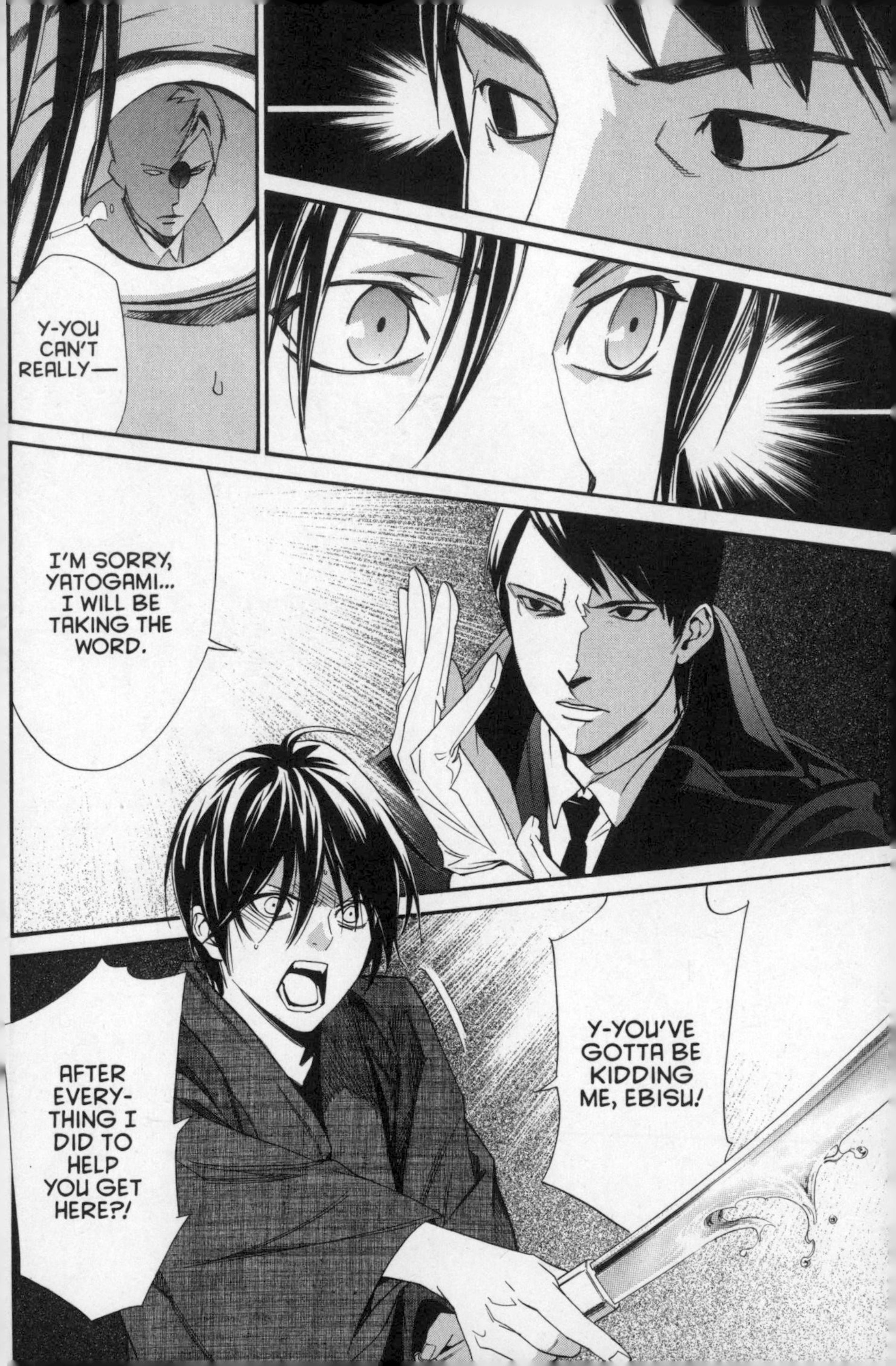
Y-YOU CAN'T REALLY—
I'M SORRY, YATOGAMI... I WILL BE TAKING THE WORD.
Y-YOU'VE GOTTA BE KIDDING ME, EBISU!
AFTER EVERY-THING I DID TO HELP YOU GET HERE?!

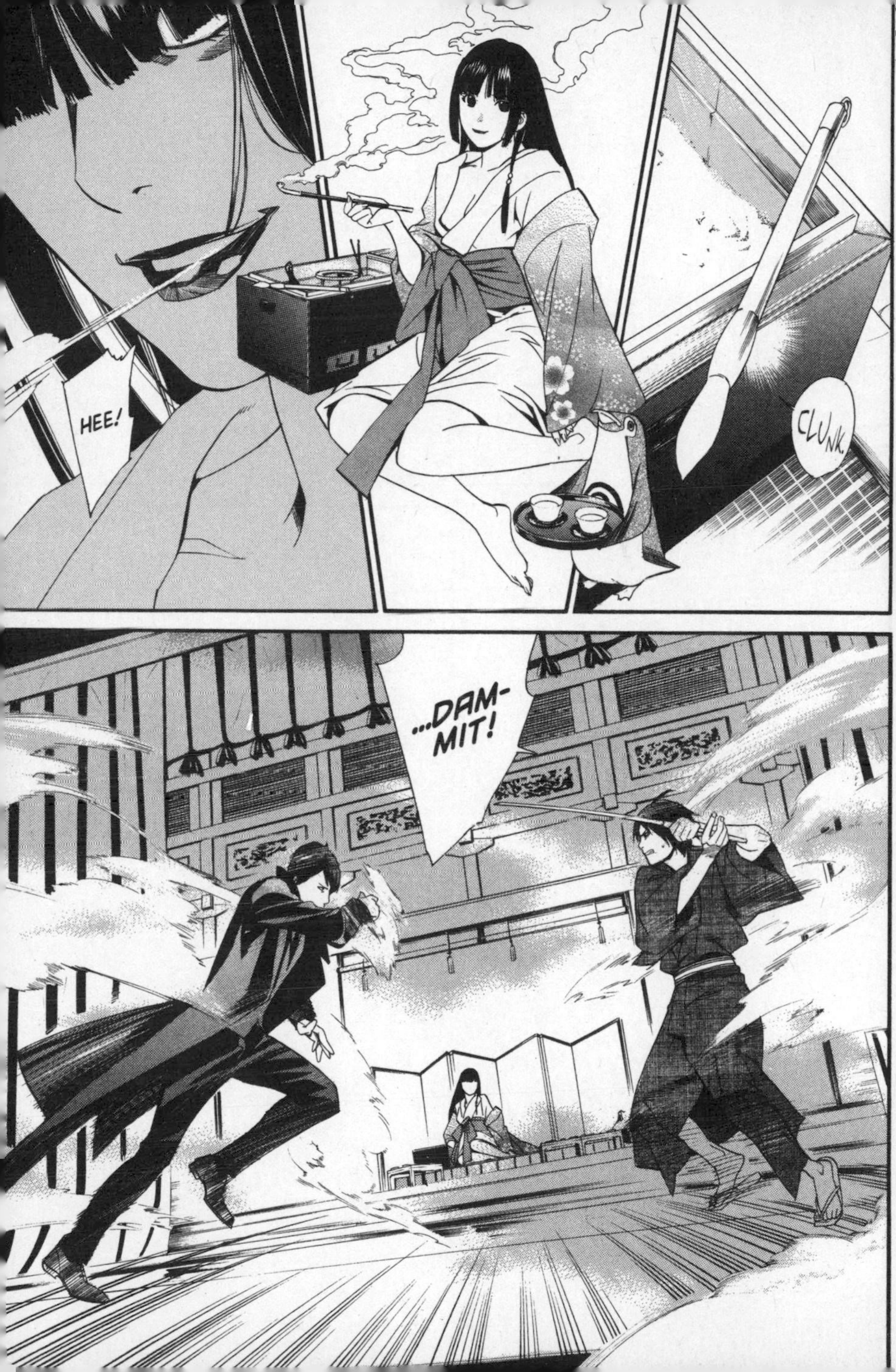
CLUNK.
HEE!
...DAM-
MIT!

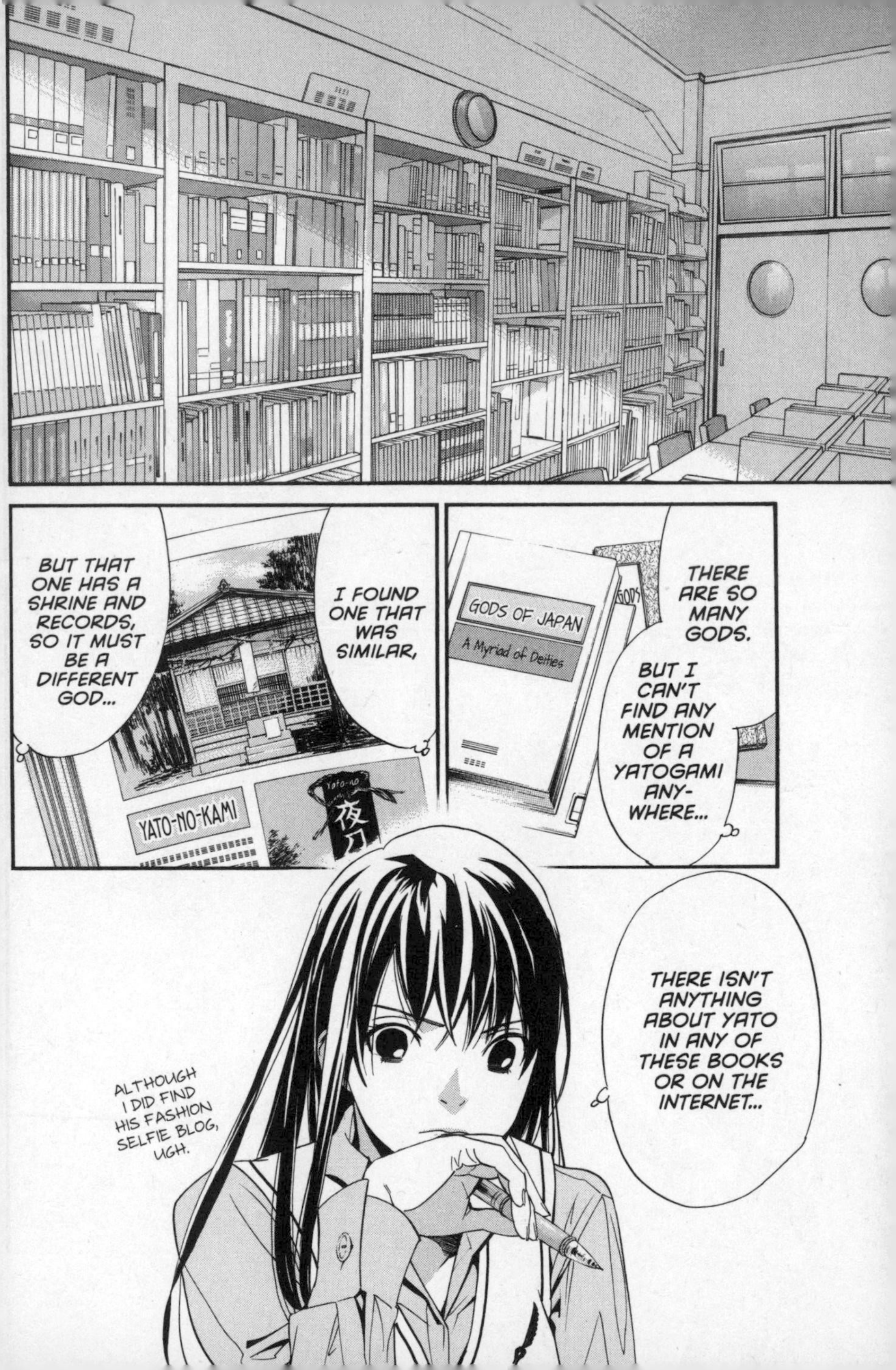
GODS OF JAPAN
A Myriad of Deities
THERE ARE SO MANY GODS.
BUT I CAN'T FIND ANY MENTION OF A YATOGAMI ANYWHERE...
I FOUND ONE THAT WAS SIMILAR,
BUT THAT ONE HAS A SHRINE AND RECORDS, SO IT MUST BE A DIFFERENT GOD...
YATO-NO-KAMI
THERE ISN'T ANYTHING ABOUT YATO IN ANY OF THESE BOOKS OR ON THE INTERNET...
ALTHOUGH I DID FIND HIS FASHION SELFIE BLOG, UGH.

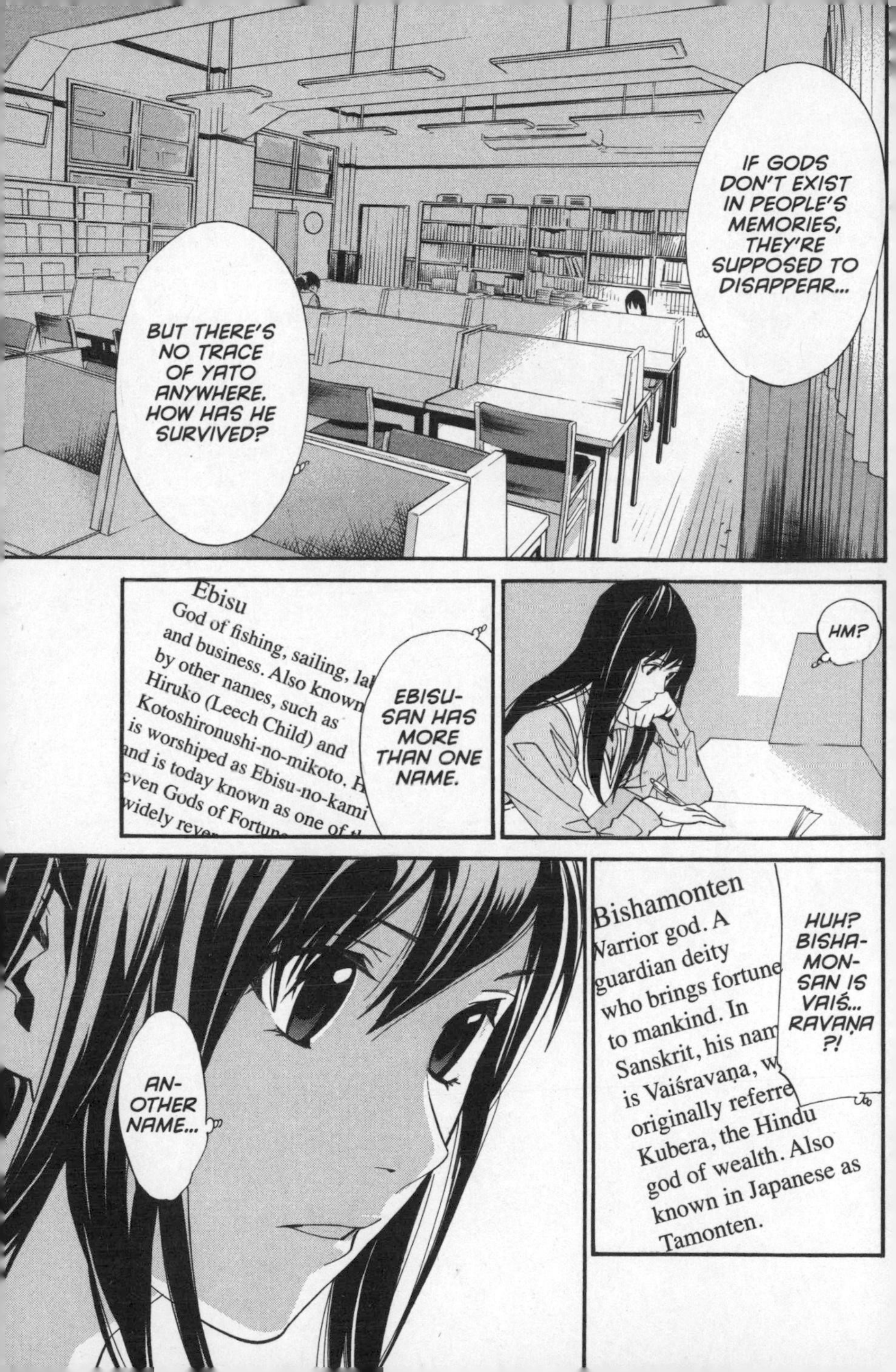
IF GODS DON'T EXIST IN PEOPLE'S MEMORIES, THEY'RE SUPPOSED TO DISAPPEAR...
BUT THERE'S NO TRACE OF YATO ANYWHERE. HOW HAS HE SURVIVED?
HM?
Ebisu
God of fishing, sailing, la
and business. Also known
by other names, such as
Hiruko (Leech Child) and
Kotoshironushi-no-mikoto.
is worshiped as Ebisu-no-kami
and is today known as one of
even Gods of Fortun
widely rever
EBISU-SAN HAS MORE THAN ONE NAME.
Bishamonten
Warrior god. A
guardian deity
who brings fortune
to mankind. In
Sanskrit, his nam
is Vaiśravaṇa, w
originally referre
Kubera, the Hindu
god of wealth. Also
known in Japanese as
Tamonten.
HUH? BISHAMON-SAN IS VAIŚ... RAVAṆA?!
AN-OTHER NAME...

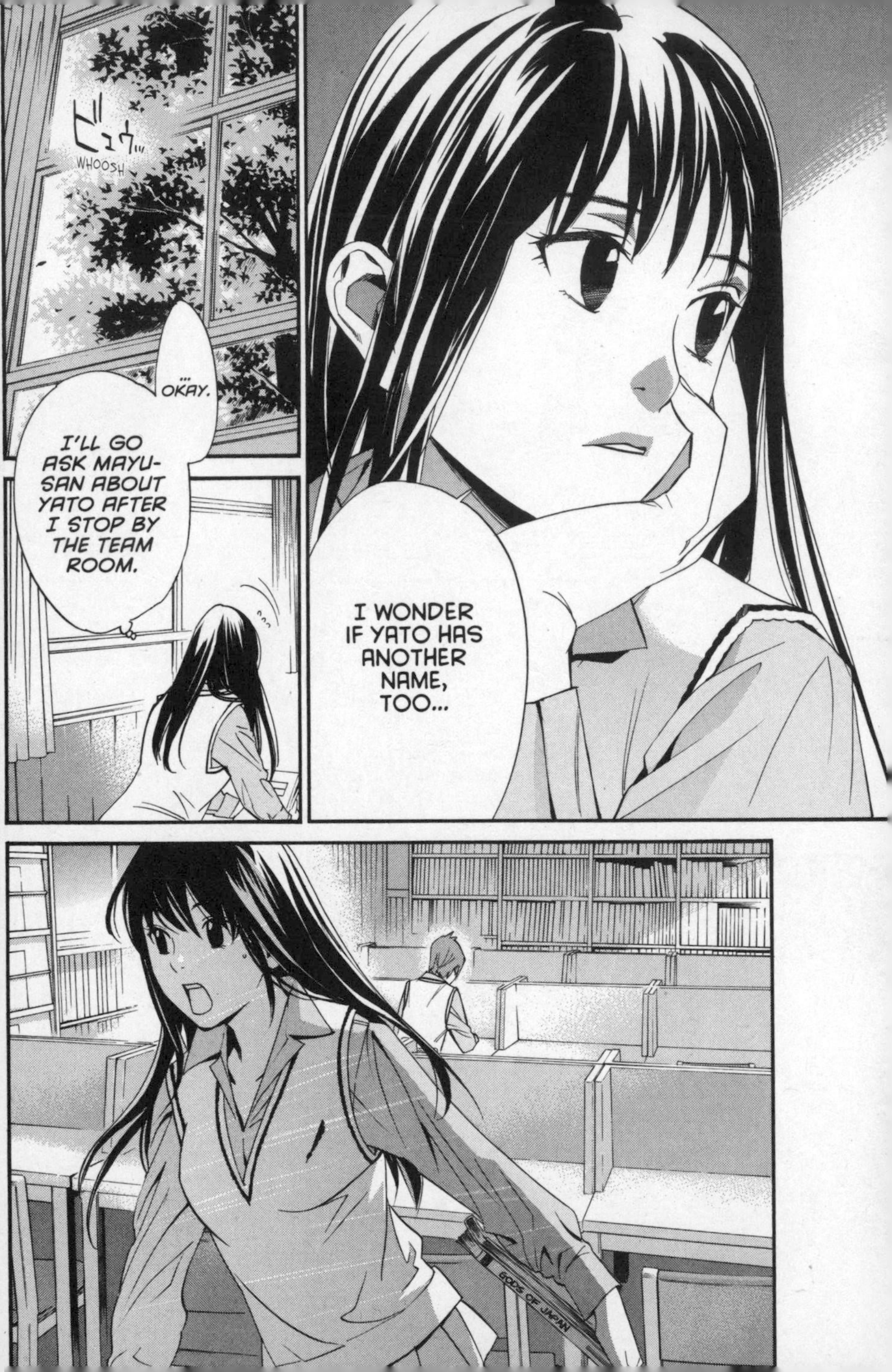
I WONDER IF YATO HAS ANOTHER NAME, TOO...
ビュゥ...
WHOOSH
...OKAY.
I'LL GO ASK MAYU-SAN ABOUT YATO AFTER I STOP BY THE TEAM ROOM.
GODS OF JAPAN

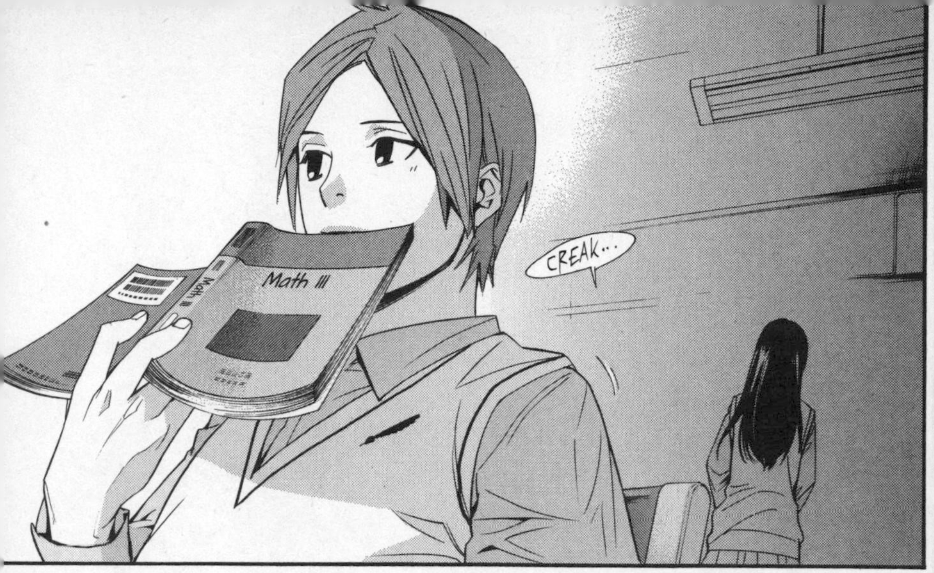
Math III
CREAK...

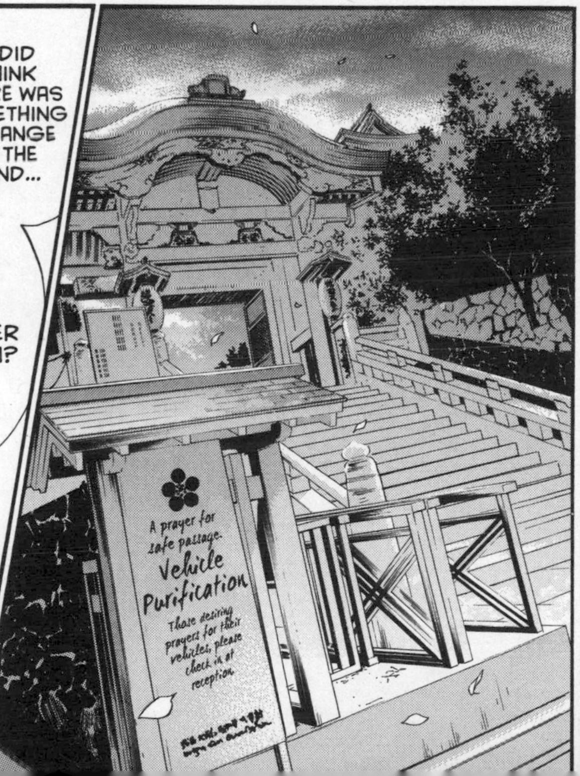
A prayer for safe passage.
Vehicle Purification
Those desiring prayers for their vehicles, please check in at reception.

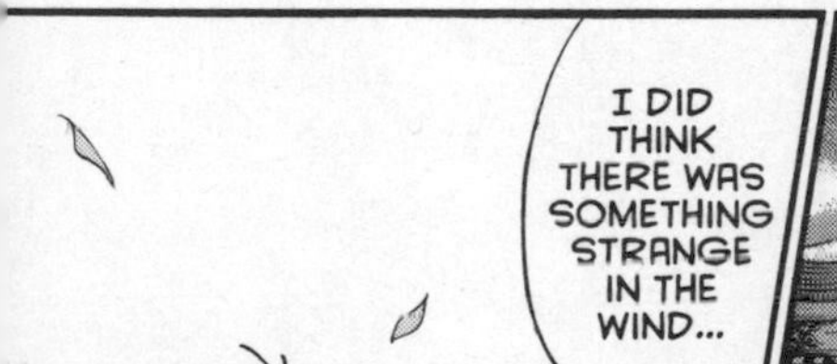
I DID THINK THERE WAS SOMETHING STRANGE IN THE WIND...
IS IT ANOTHER STORM?

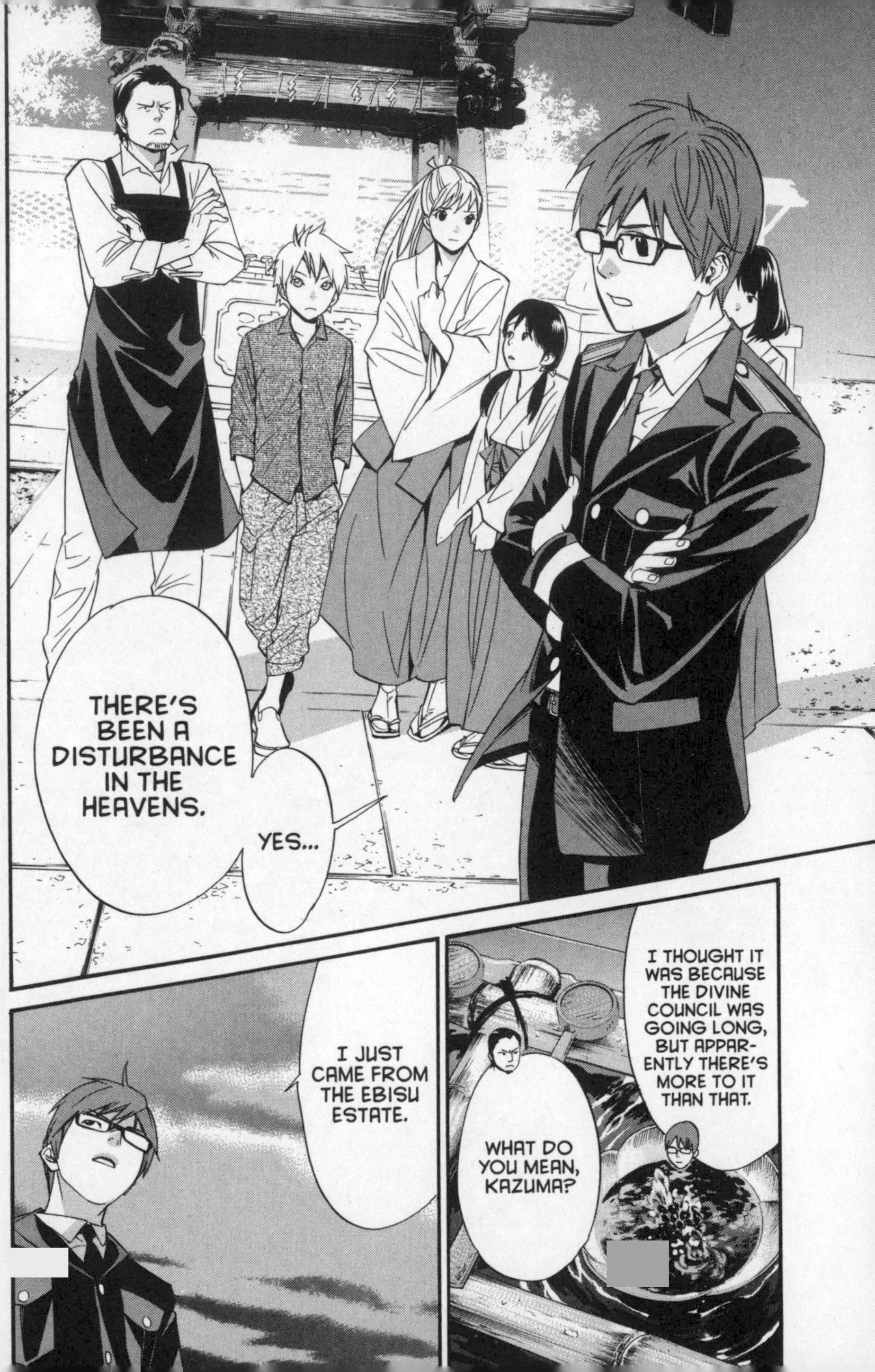
THERE'S BEEN A DISTURBANCE IN THE HEAVENS.
YES...
I THOUGHT IT WAS BECAUSE THE DIVINE COUNCIL WAS GOING LONG, BUT APPARENTLY THERE'S MORE TO IT THAN THAT.
WHAT DO YOU MEAN, KAZUMA?
I JUST CAME FROM THE EBISU ESTATE.

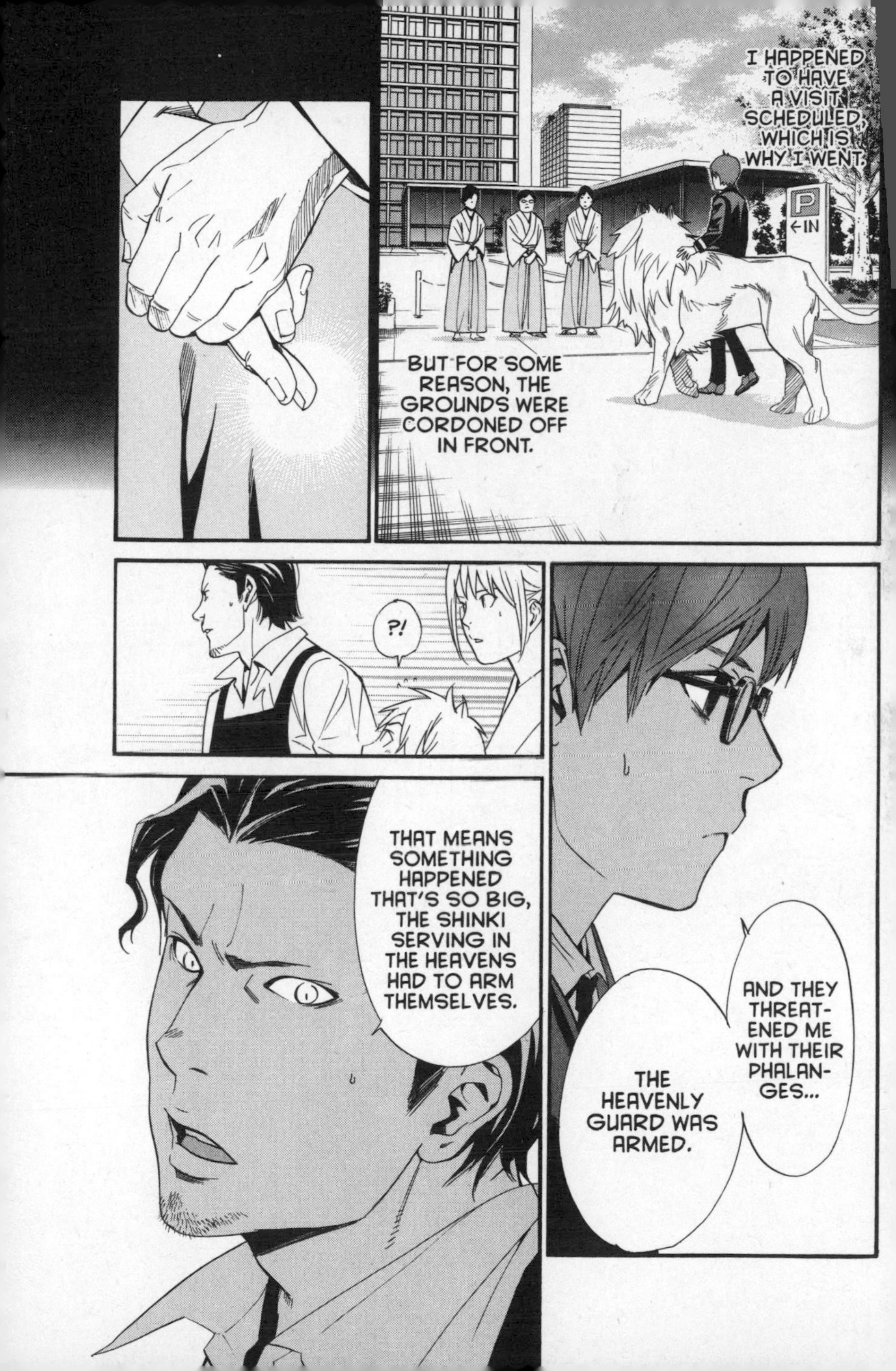
I HAPPENED TO HAVE A VISIT SCHEDULED, WHICH IS WHY I WENT.
P
←IN
BUT FOR SOME REASON, THE GROUNDS WERE CORDONED OFF IN FRONT.
AND THEY THREAT-ENED ME WITH THEIR PHALAN-GES...
THE HEAVENLY GUARD WAS ARMED.
?!
THAT MEANS SOMETHING HAPPENED THAT'S SO BIG, THE SHINKI SERVING IN THE HEAVENS HAD TO ARM THEMSELVES.

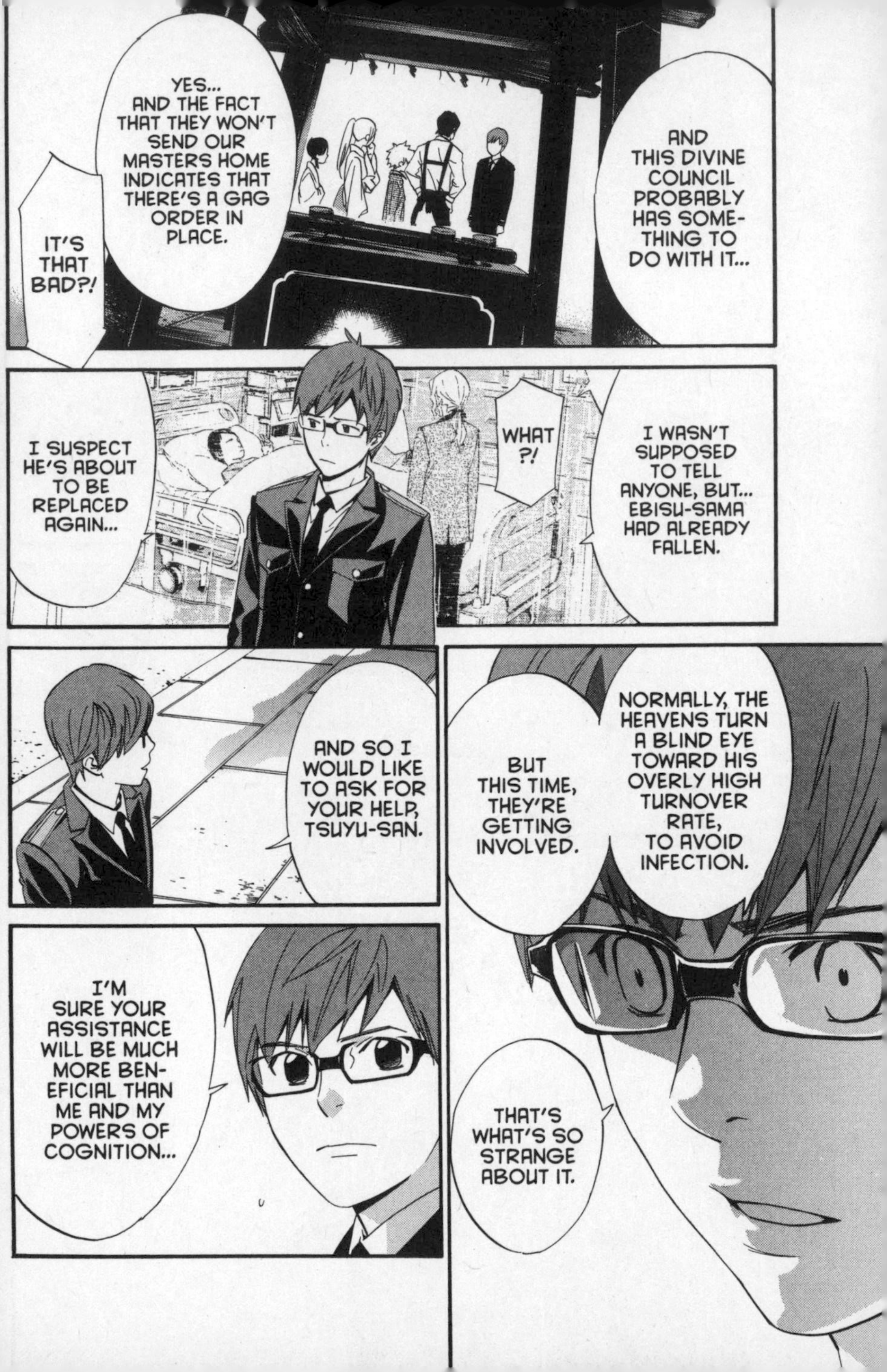
AND THIS DIVINE COUNCIL PROBABLY HAS SOME-THING TO DO WITH IT...
YES... AND THE FACT THAT THEY WON'T SEND OUR MASTERS HOME INDICATES THAT THERE'S A GAG ORDER IN PLACE.
IT'S THAT BAD?!
I WASN'T SUPPOSED TO TELL ANYONE, BUT... EBISU-SAMA HAD ALREADY FALLEN.
WHAT ?!
I SUSPECT HE'S ABOUT TO BE REPLACED AGAIN...
NORMALLY, THE HEAVENS TURN A BLIND EYE TOWARD HIS OVERLY HIGH TURNOVER RATE, TO AVOID INFECTION.
BUT THIS TIME, THEY'RE GETTING INVOLVED.
THAT'S WHAT'S SO STRANGE ABOUT IT.
AND SO I WOULD LIKE TO ASK FOR YOUR HELP, TSUYU-SAN.
I'M SURE YOUR ASSISTANCE WILL BE MUCH MORE BEN-EFICIAL THAN ME AND MY POWERS OF COGNITION...

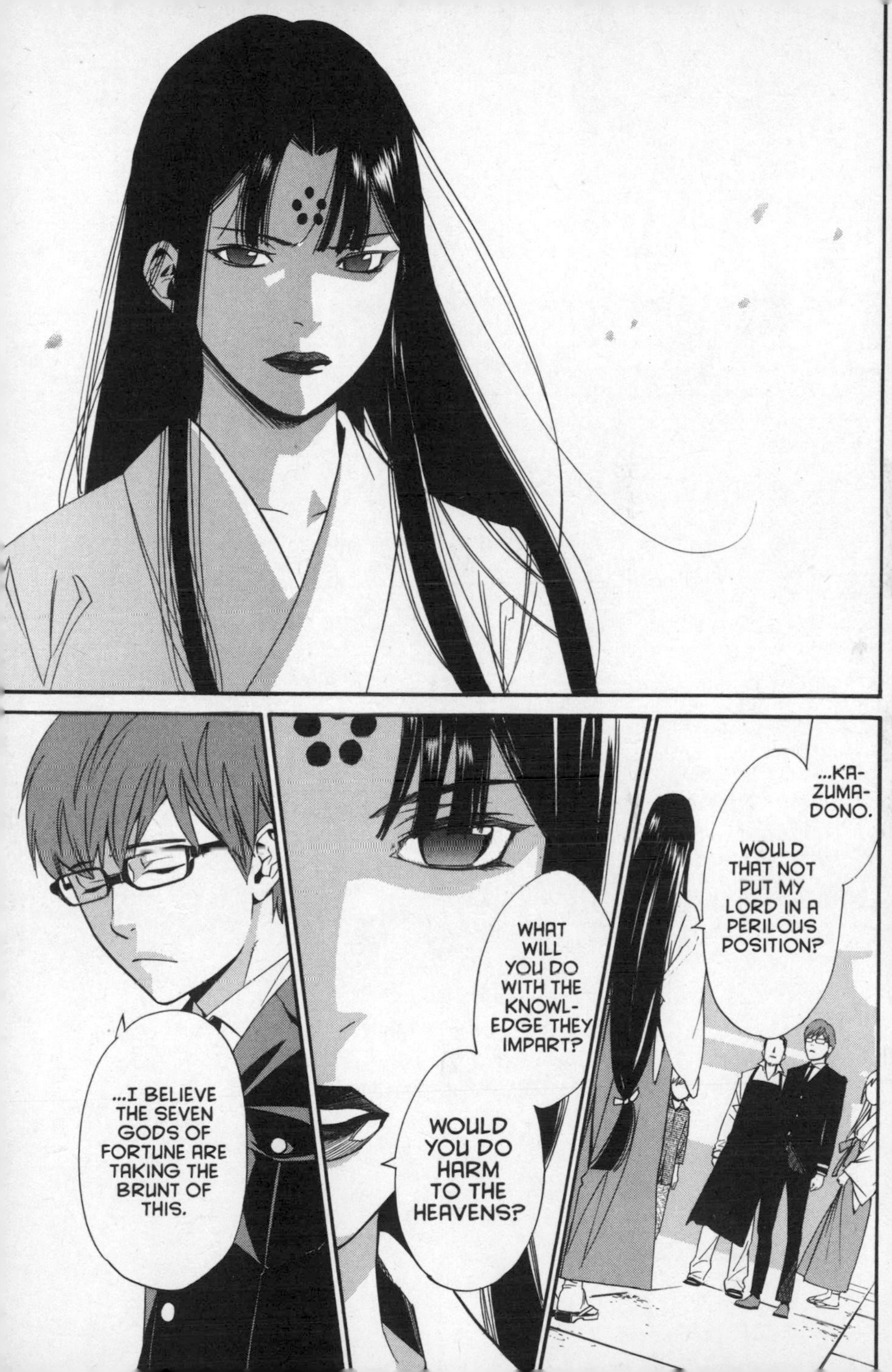
...KA-ZUMA-DONO.
WOULD THAT NOT PUT MY LORD IN A PERILOUS POSITION?
WHAT WILL YOU DO WITH THE KNOWLEDGE THEY IMPART?
WOULD YOU DO HARM TO THE HEAVENS?
...I BELIEVE THE SEVEN GODS OF FORTUNE ARE TAKING THE BRUNT OF THIS.

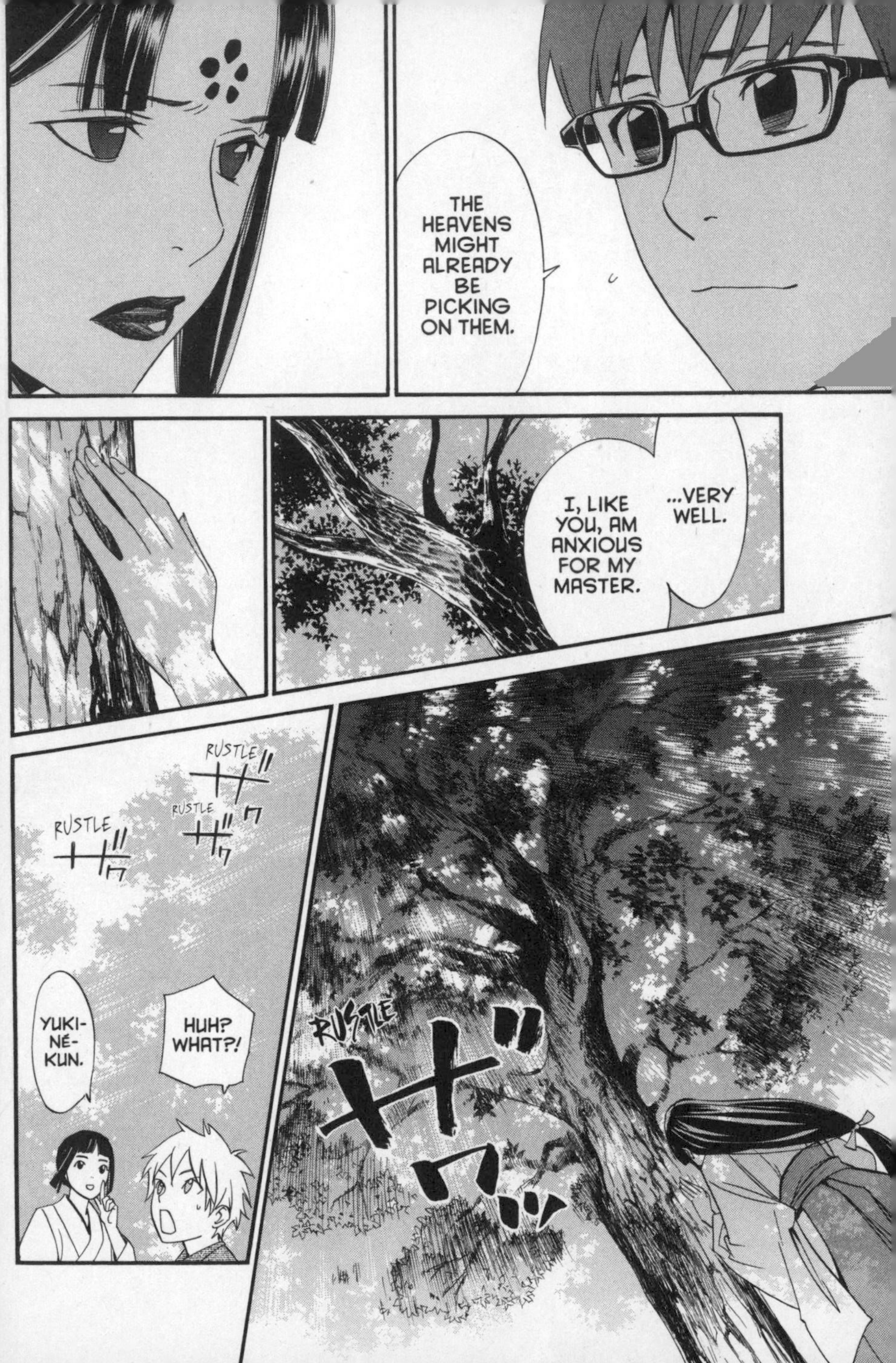
THE HEAVENS MIGHT ALREADY BE PICKING ON THEM.
...VERY WELL.
I, LIKE YOU, AM ANXIOUS FOR MY MASTER.
RUSTLE
RUSTLE
RUSTLE
RUSTLE
YUKI-NÉ-KUN.
HUH? WHAT?!

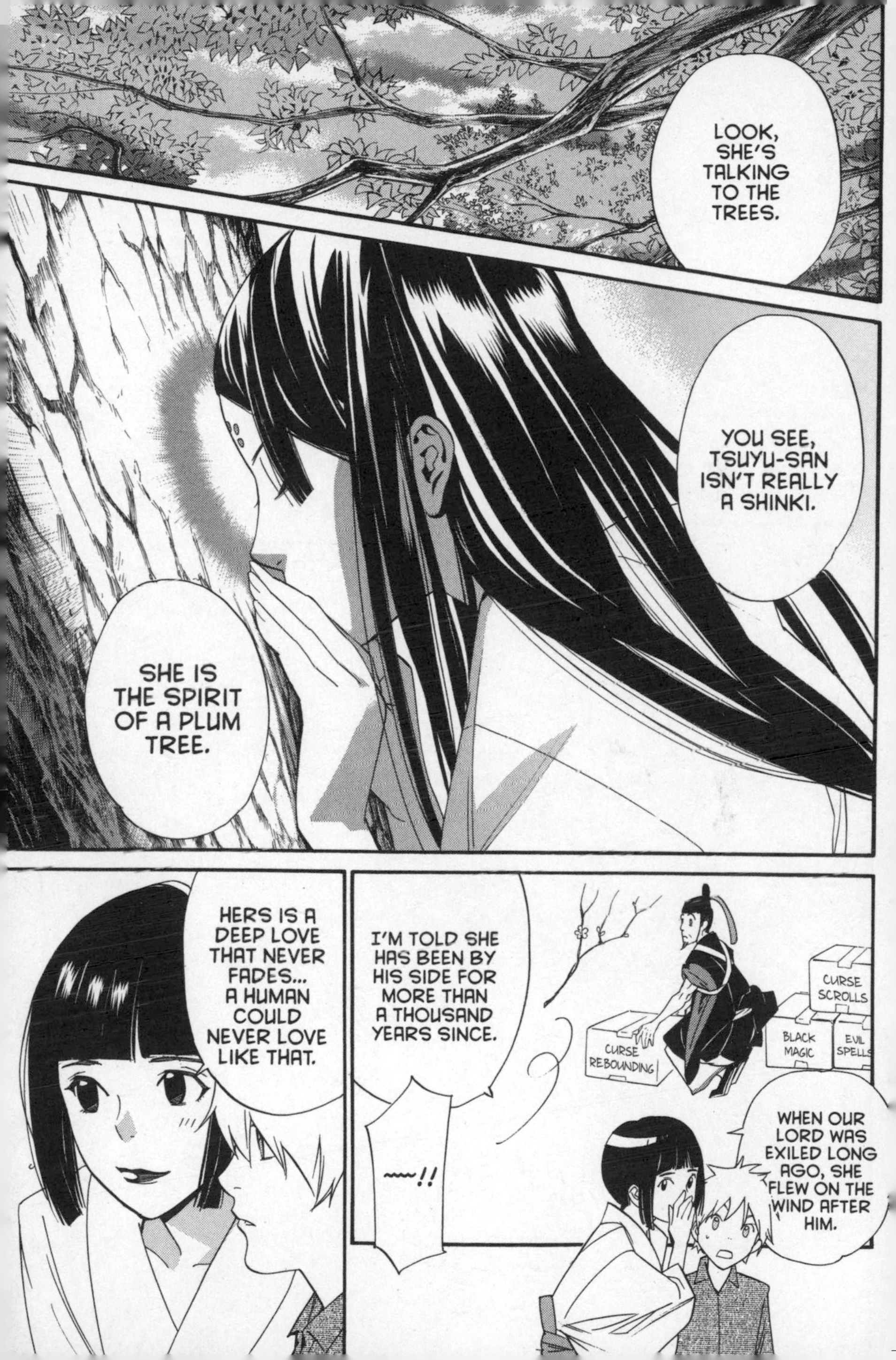
LOOK, SHE'S TALKING TO THE TREES.
YOU SEE, TSUYU-SAN ISN'T REALLY A SHINKI.
SHE IS THE SPIRIT OF A PLUM TREE.
CURSE SCROLLS
EVIL SPELLS
BLACK MAGIC
CURSE REBOUNDING
WHEN OUR LORD WAS EXILED LONG AGO, SHE FLEW ON THE WIND AFTER HIM.
I'M TOLD SHE HAS BEEN BY HIS SIDE FOR MORE THAN A THOUSAND YEARS SINCE.
~~!!
HERS IS A DEEP LOVE THAT NEVER FADES... A HUMAN COULD NEVER LOVE LIKE THAT.

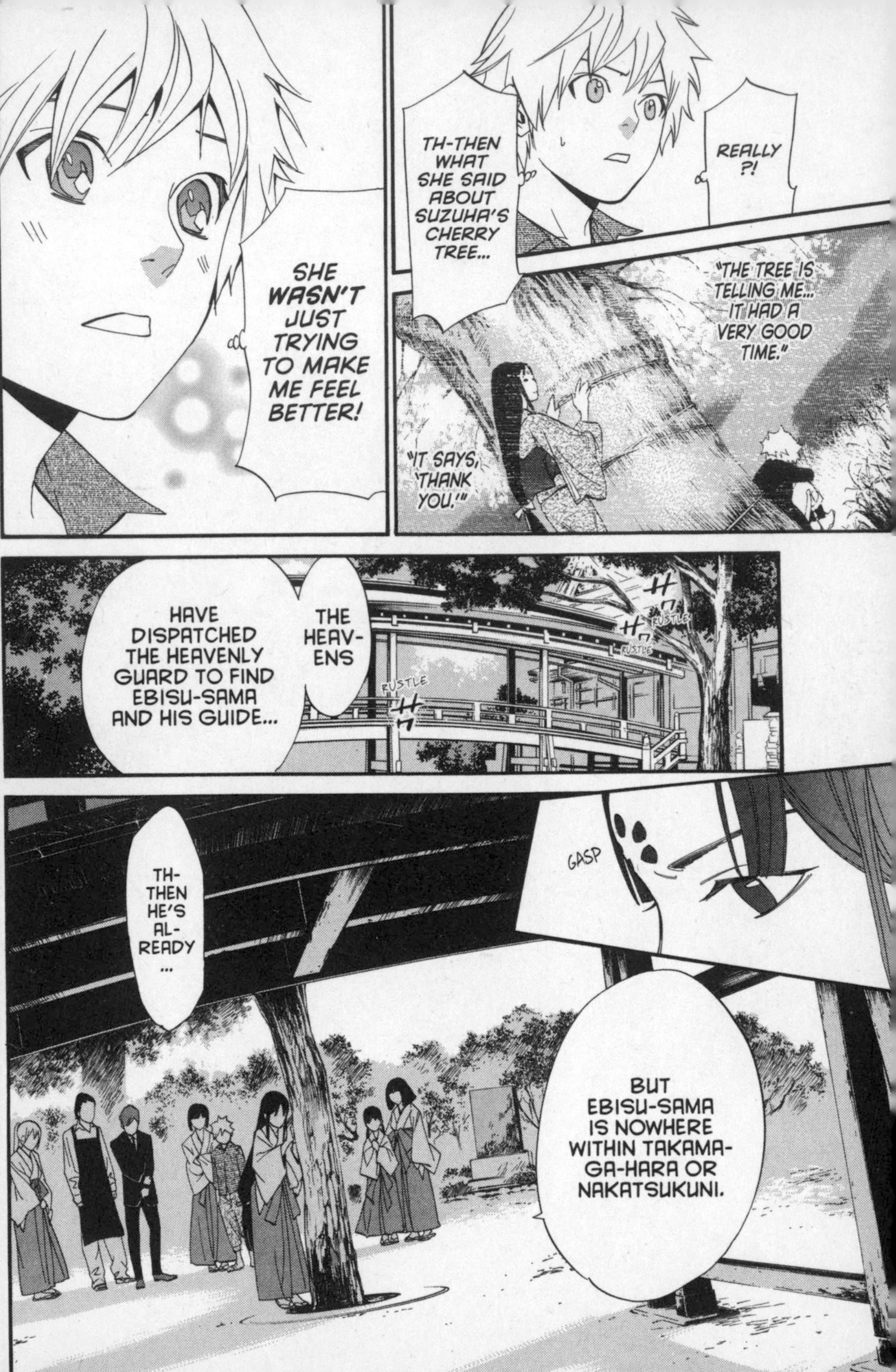
REALLY ?!
TH-THEN WHAT SHE SAID ABOUT SUZUHA'S CHERRY TREE...
"THE TREE IS TELLING ME... IT HAD A VERY GOOD TIME."
"IT SAYS, 'THANK YOU.'"
SHE WASN'T JUST TRYING TO MAKE ME FEEL BETTER!
THE HEAVENS
HAVE DISPATCHED THE HEAVENLY GUARD TO FIND EBISU-SAMA AND HIS GUIDE...
RUSTLE
RUSTLE
RUSTLE
GASP
BUT EBISU-SAMA IS NOWHERE WITHIN TAKAMA-GA-HARA OR NAKATSUKUNI.
TH-THEN HE'S AL-READY ...

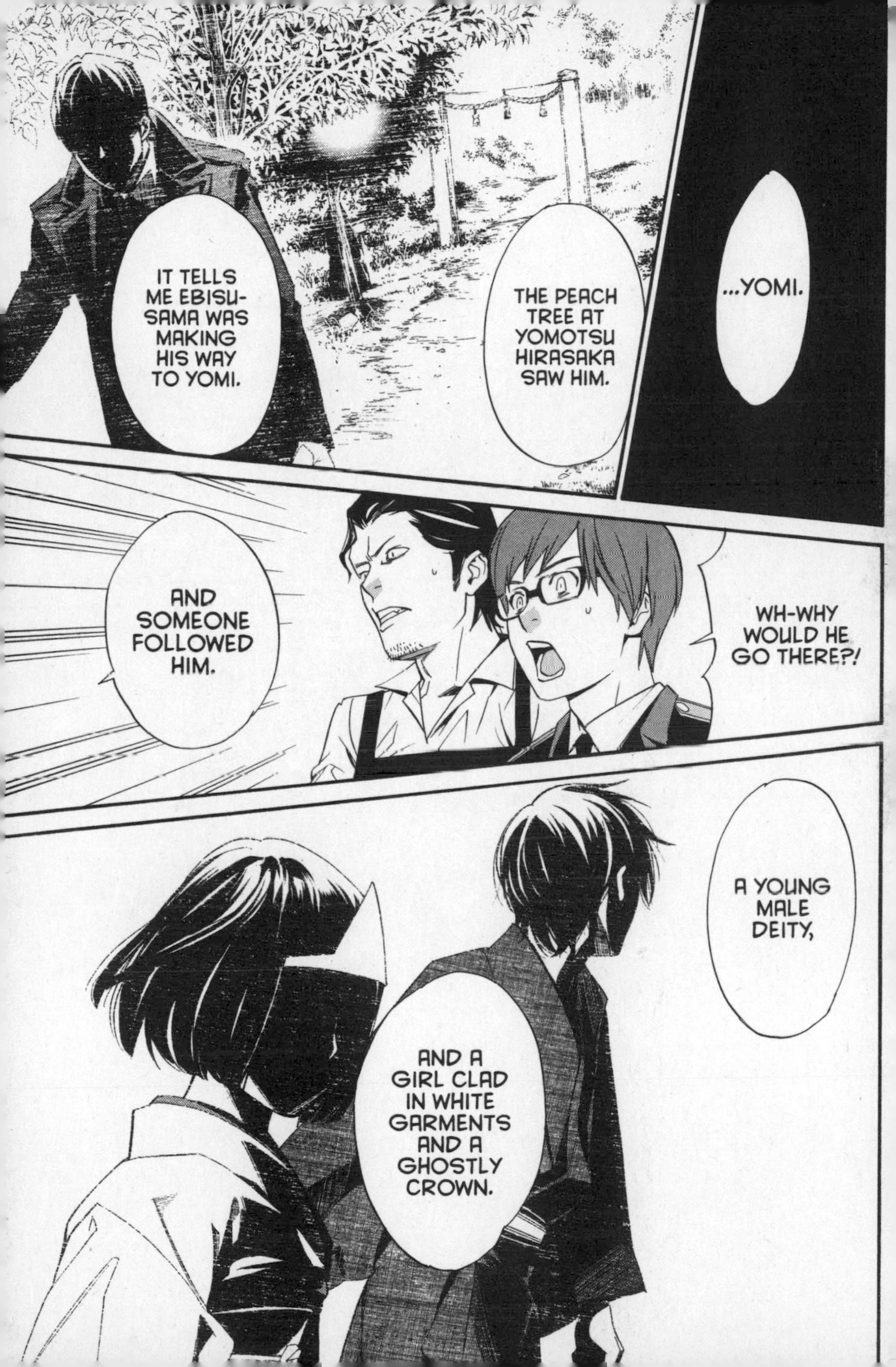
...YOMI.
THE PEACH TREE AT YOMOTSU HIRASAKA SAW HIM.
IT TELLS ME EBISU-SAMA WAS MAKING HIS WAY TO YOMI.
WH-WHY WOULD HE GO THERE?!
AND SOMEONE FOLLOWED HIM.
A YOUNG MALE DEITY,
AND A GIRL CLAD IN WHITE GARMENTS AND A GHOSTLY CROWN.

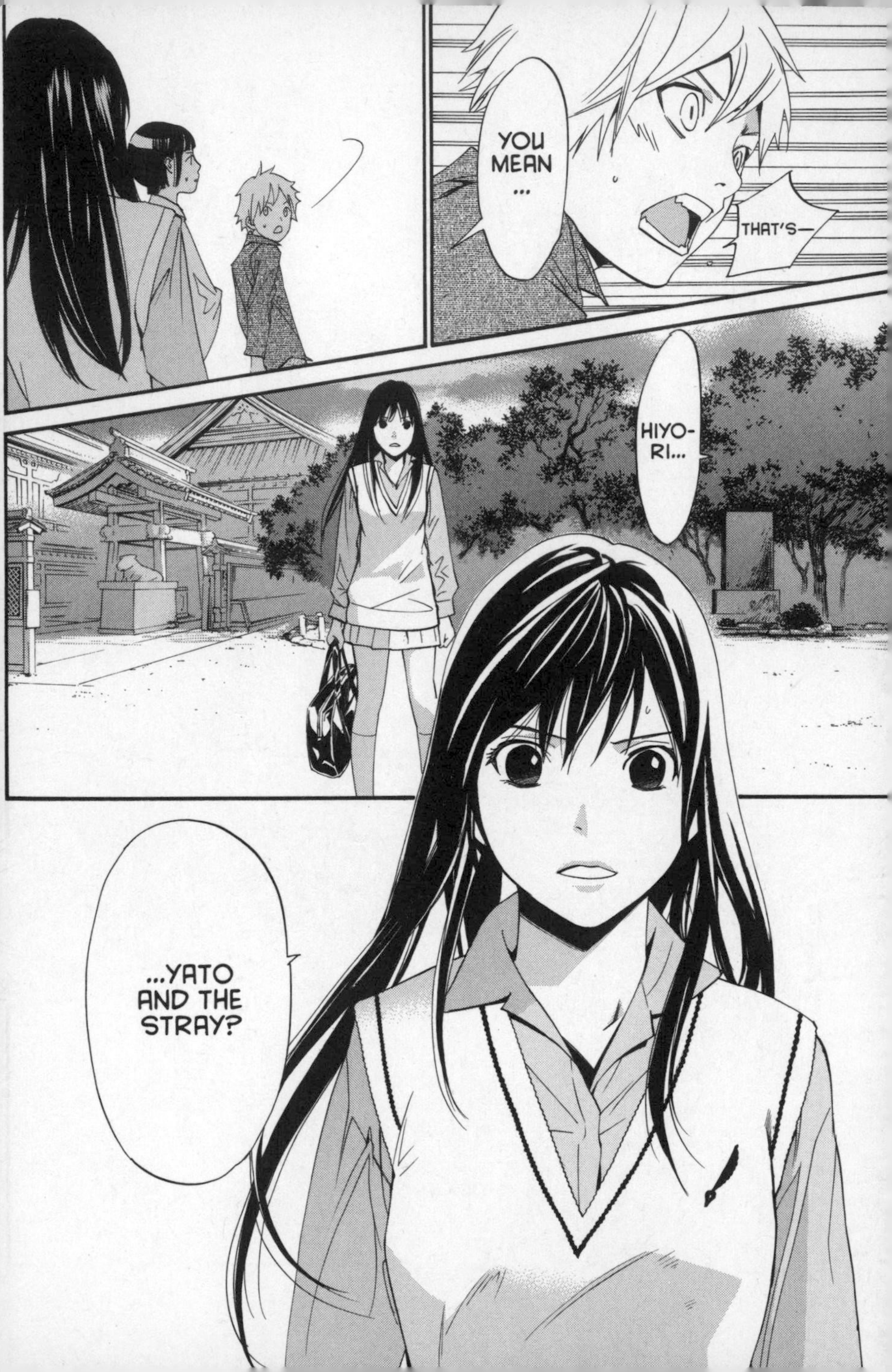
YOU MEAN ...
THAT'S—
HIYO-RI...
...YATO AND THE STRAY?

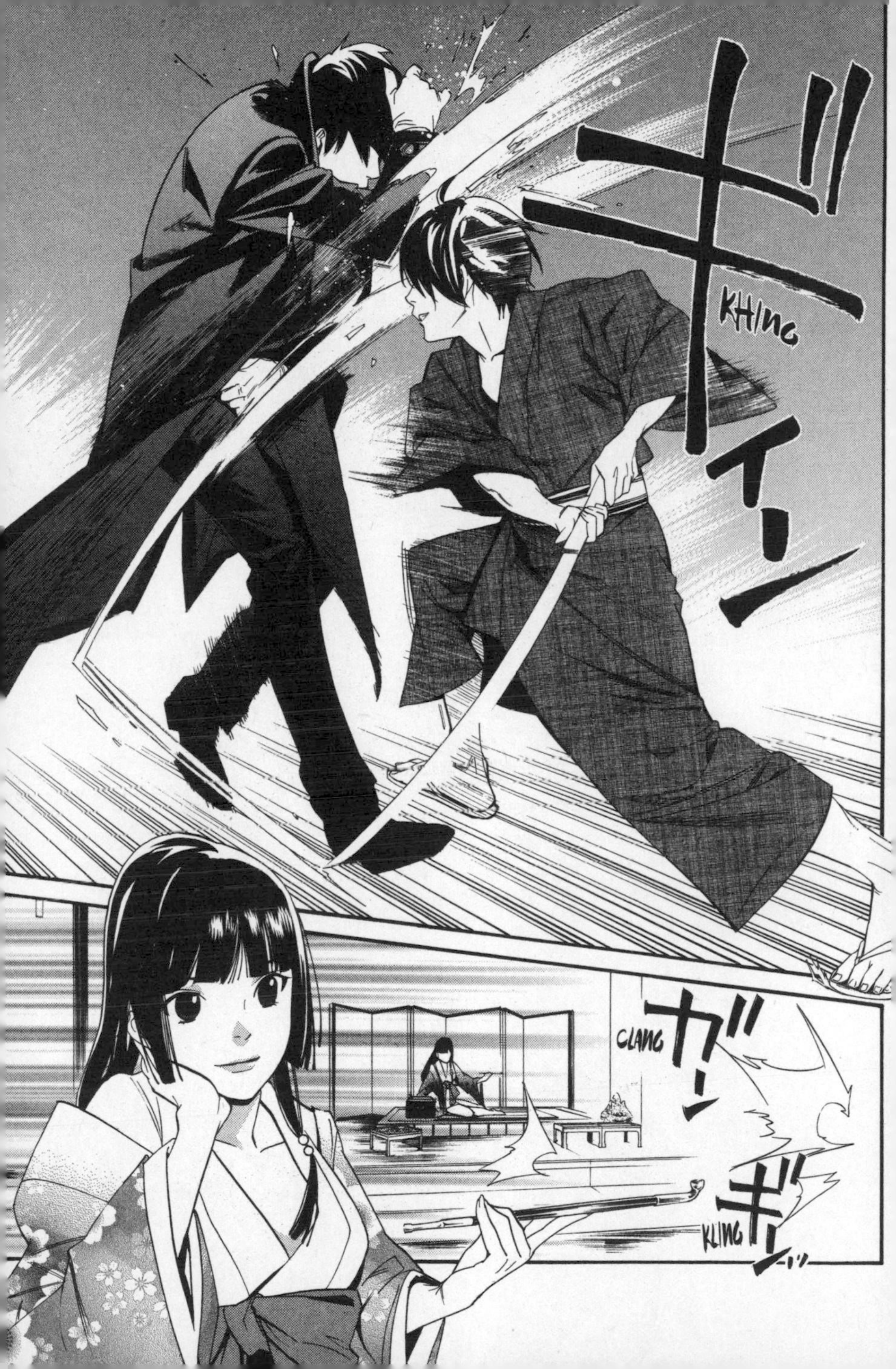
ギィーン
KHING
ガッ
CLANG
ギッ
KLING

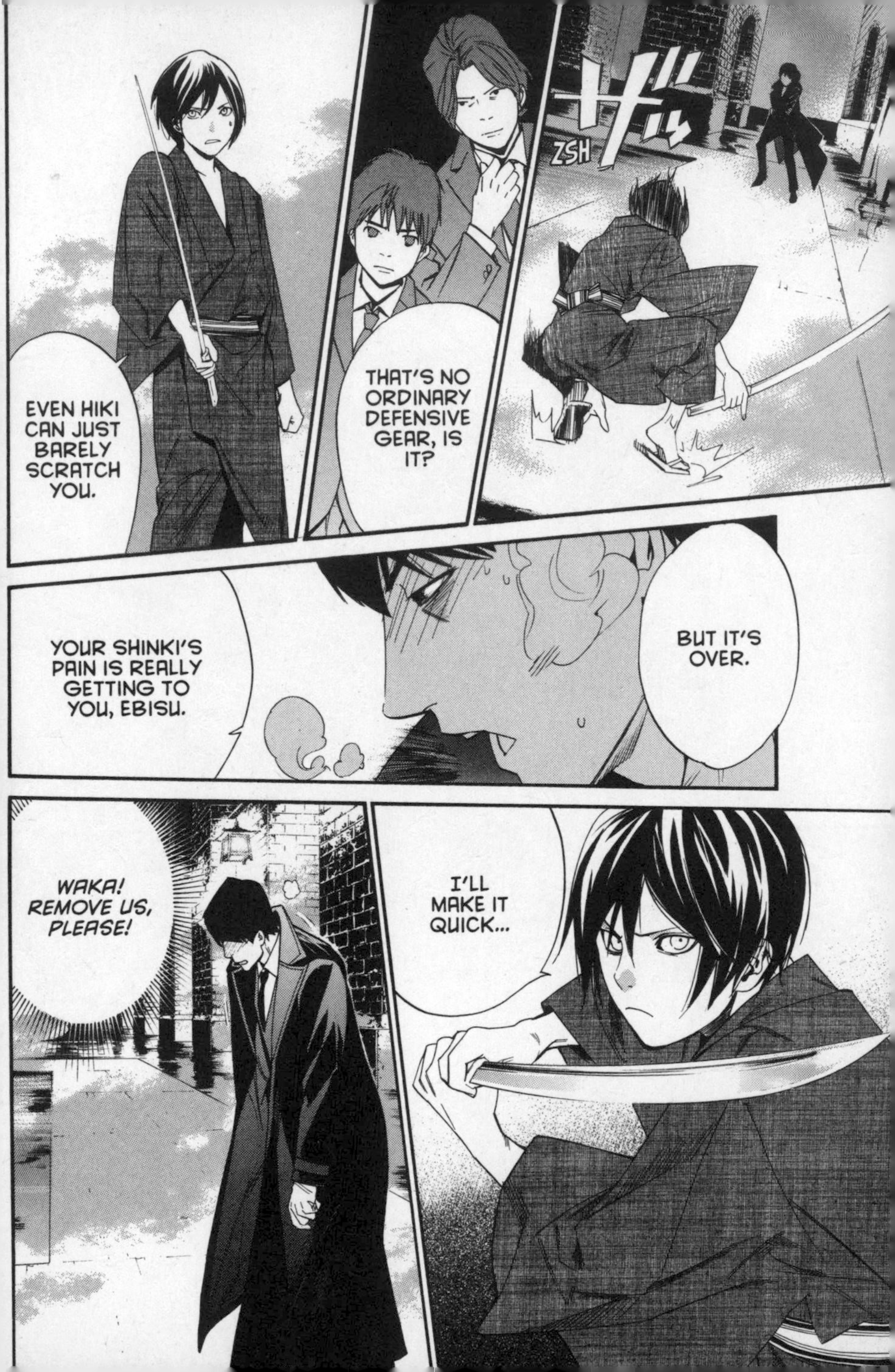
ZSH
THAT'S NO ORDINARY DEFENSIVE GEAR, IS IT?
EVEN HIKI CAN JUST BARELY SCRATCH YOU.
YOUR SHINKI'S PAIN IS REALLY GETTING TO YOU, EBISU.
BUT IT'S OVER.
I'LL MAKE IT QUICK...
WAKA! REMOVE US, PLEASE!

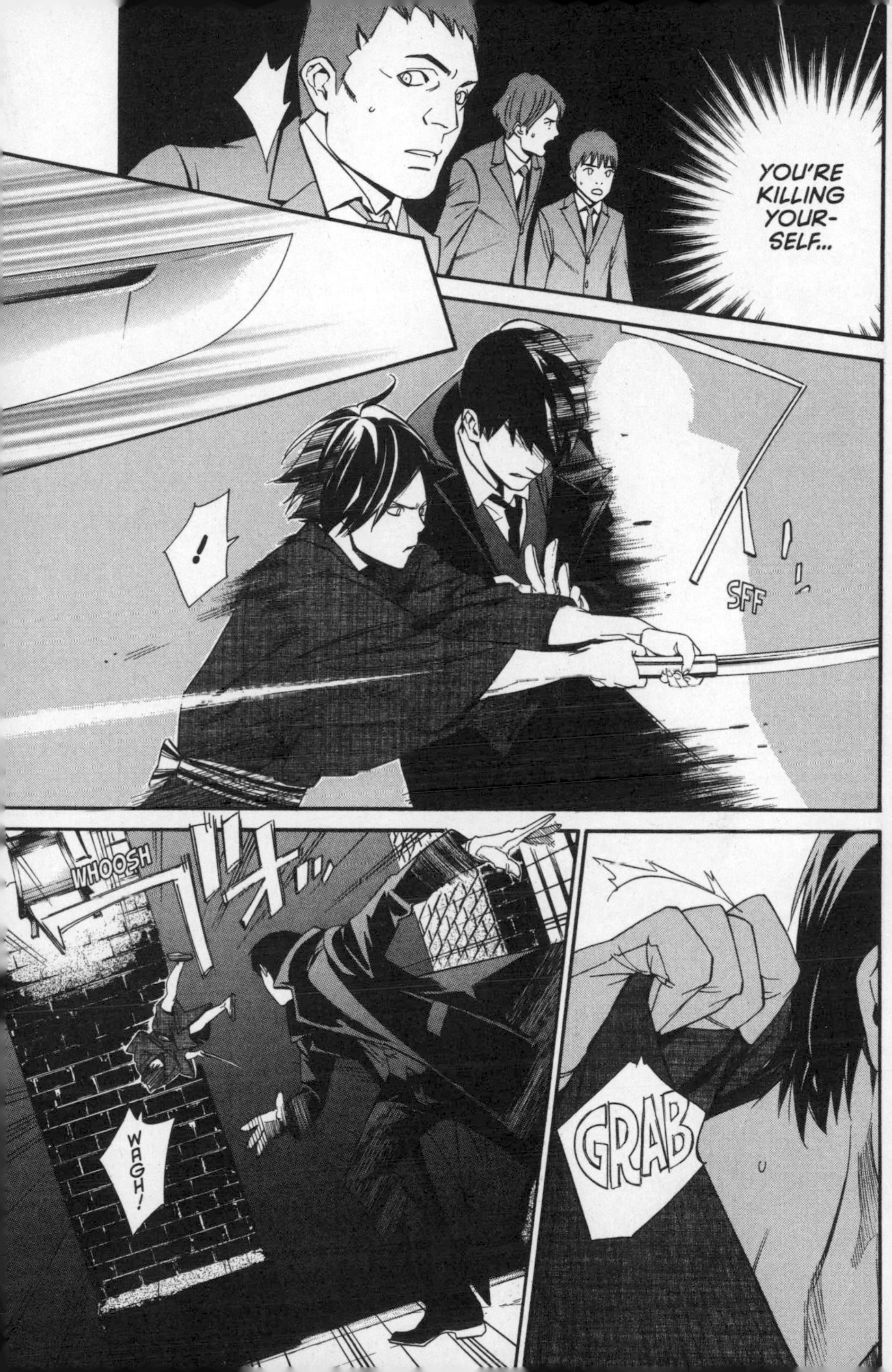
YOU'RE KILLING YOUR-SELF...
SFF
!
GRAB
WHOOSH
WAGH!

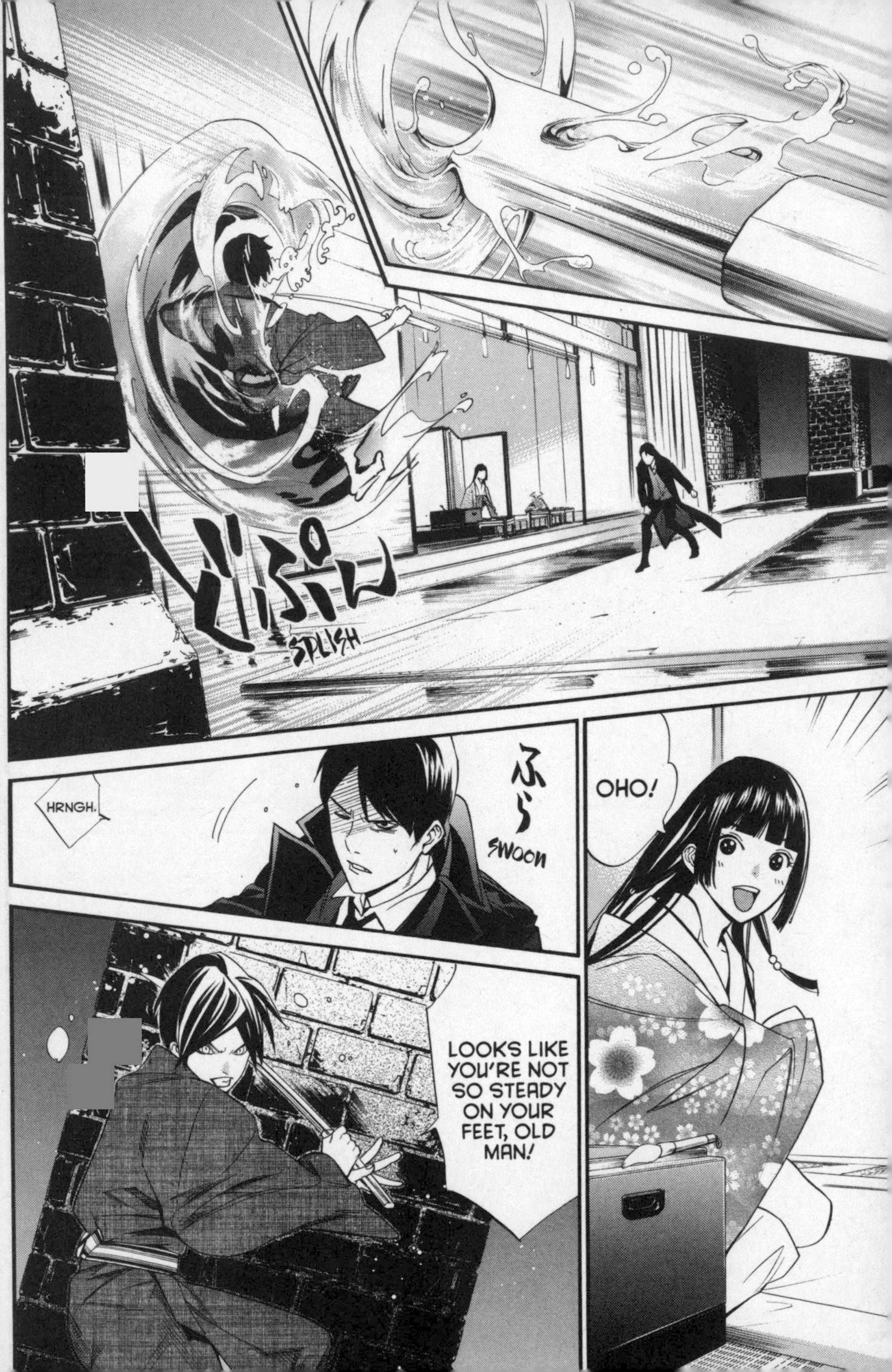
どぷん
SPLISH
OHO!
ふら
SWOON
HRNGH.
LOOKS LIKE YOU'RE NOT SO STEADY ON YOUR FEET, OLD MAN!

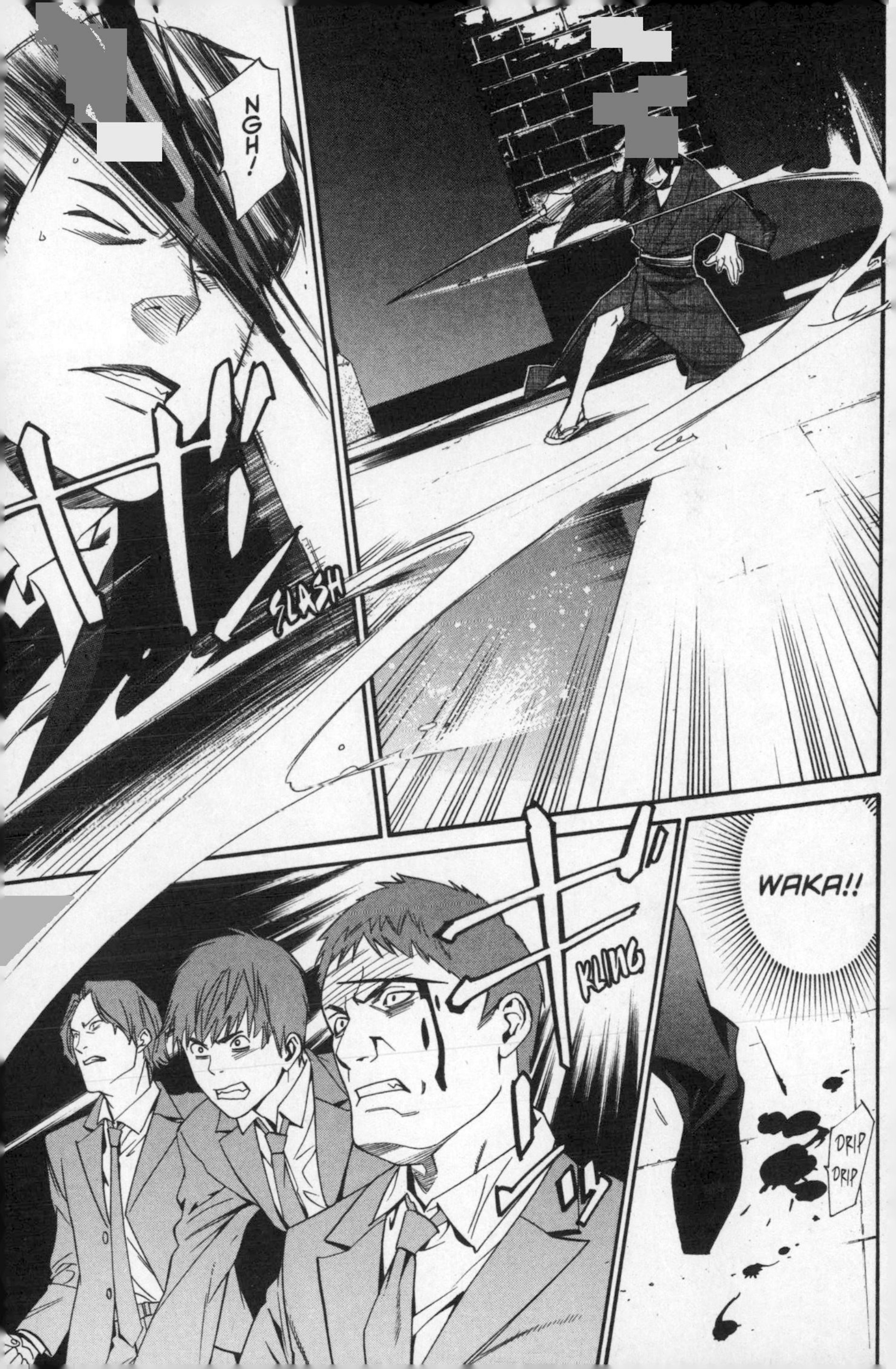
NGH!
SLASH
WAKA!!
DRIP
DRIP
KLING

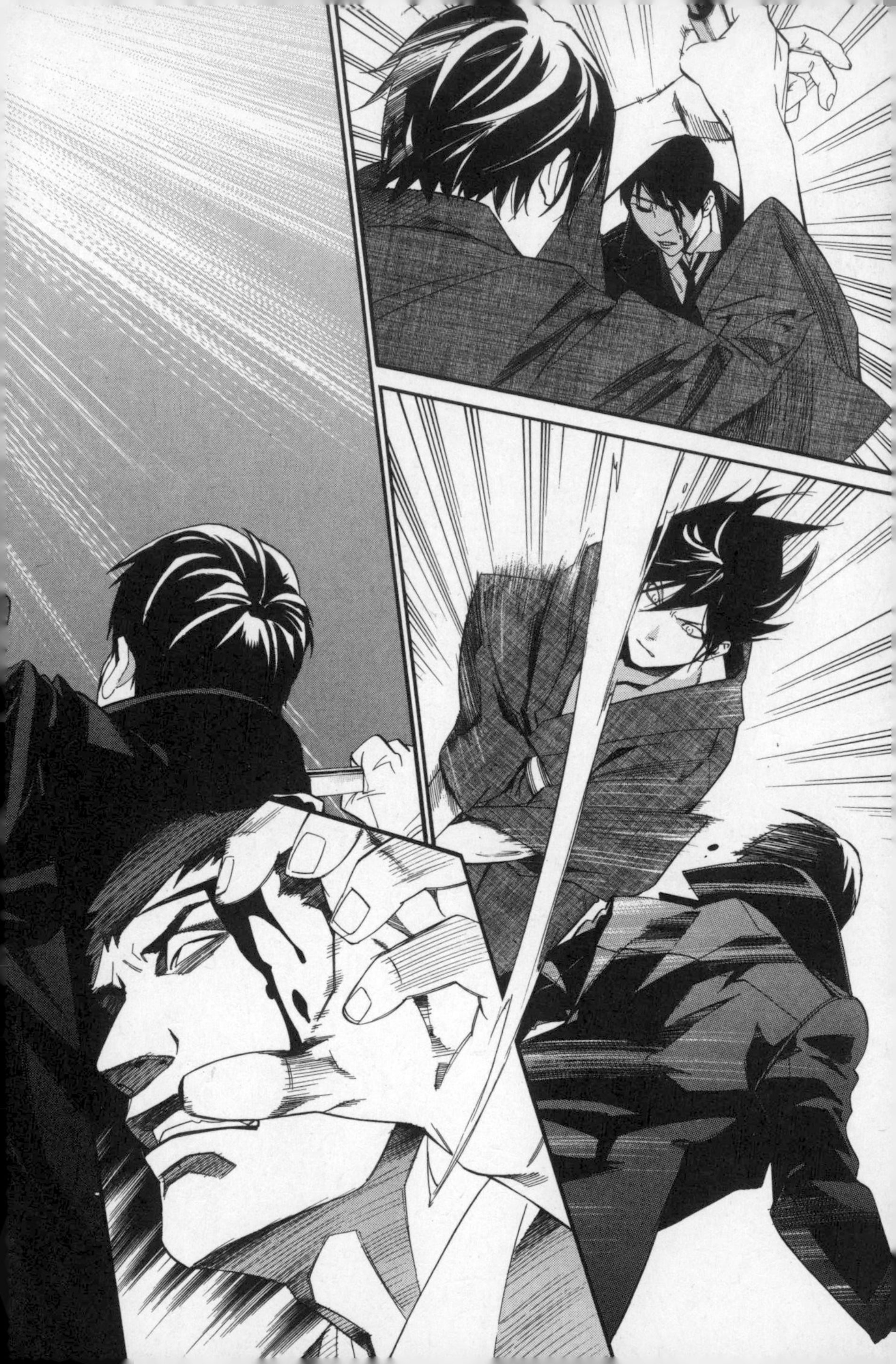

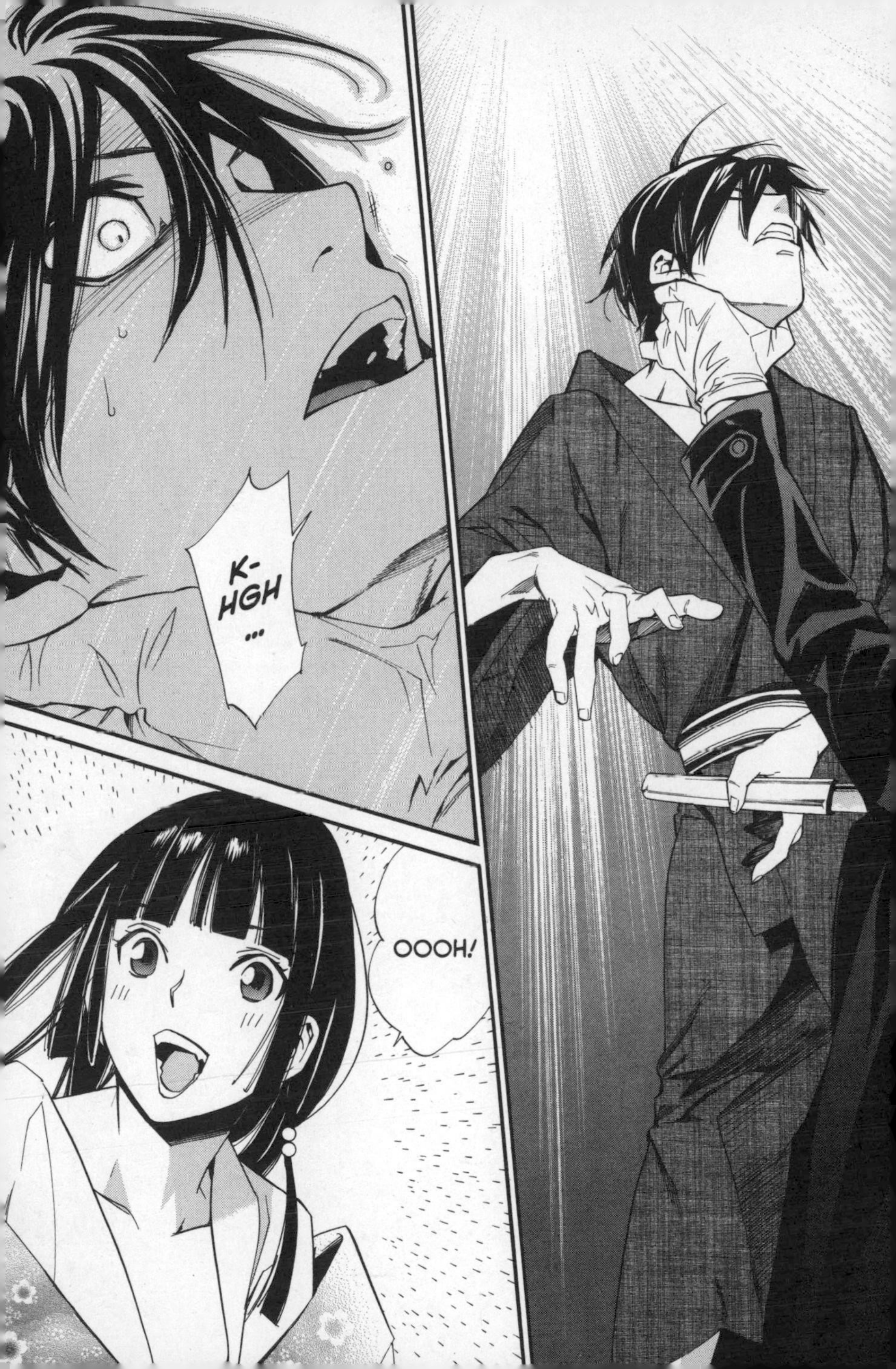
K-HGH...
OOOH!

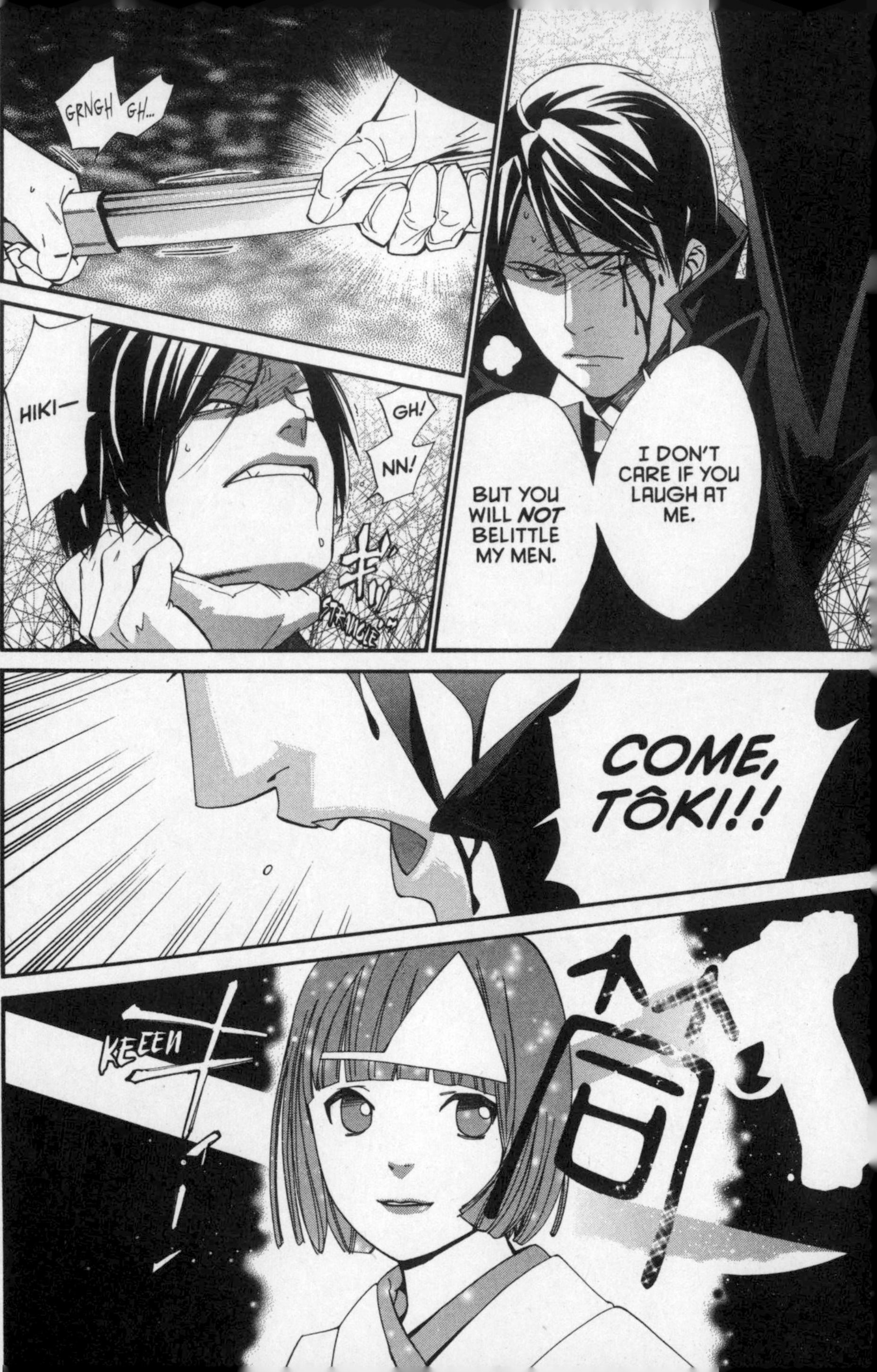
I DON'T CARE IF YOU LAUGH AT ME.
BUT YOU WILL *NOT* BELITTLE MY MEN.
GRNGH GH...
GH!
NN!
HIKI—
STRANGLE
COME, TÔKI!!
KEEEN

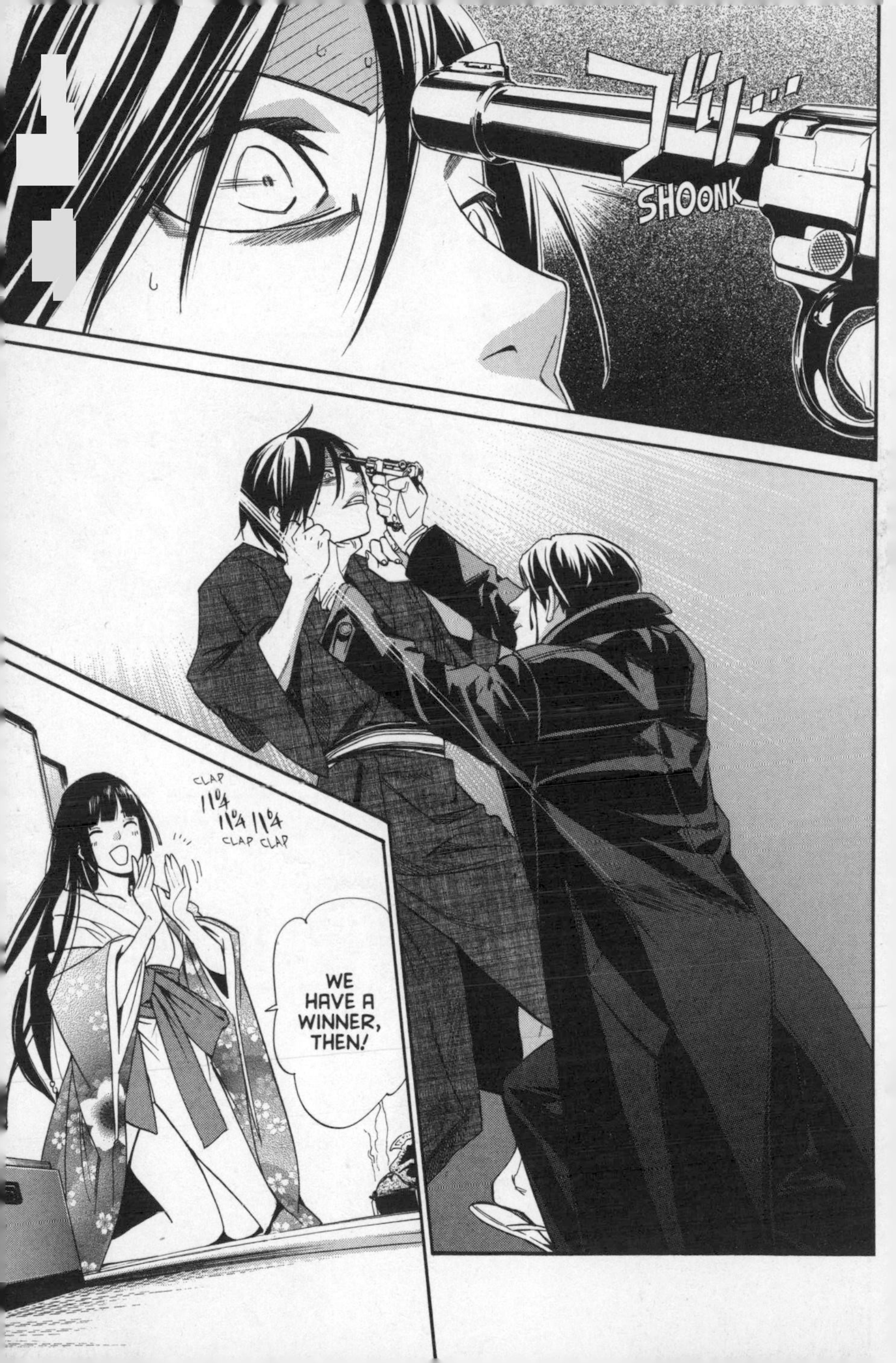
SHOONK
CLAP
CLAP CLAP
WE HAVE A WINNER, THEN!

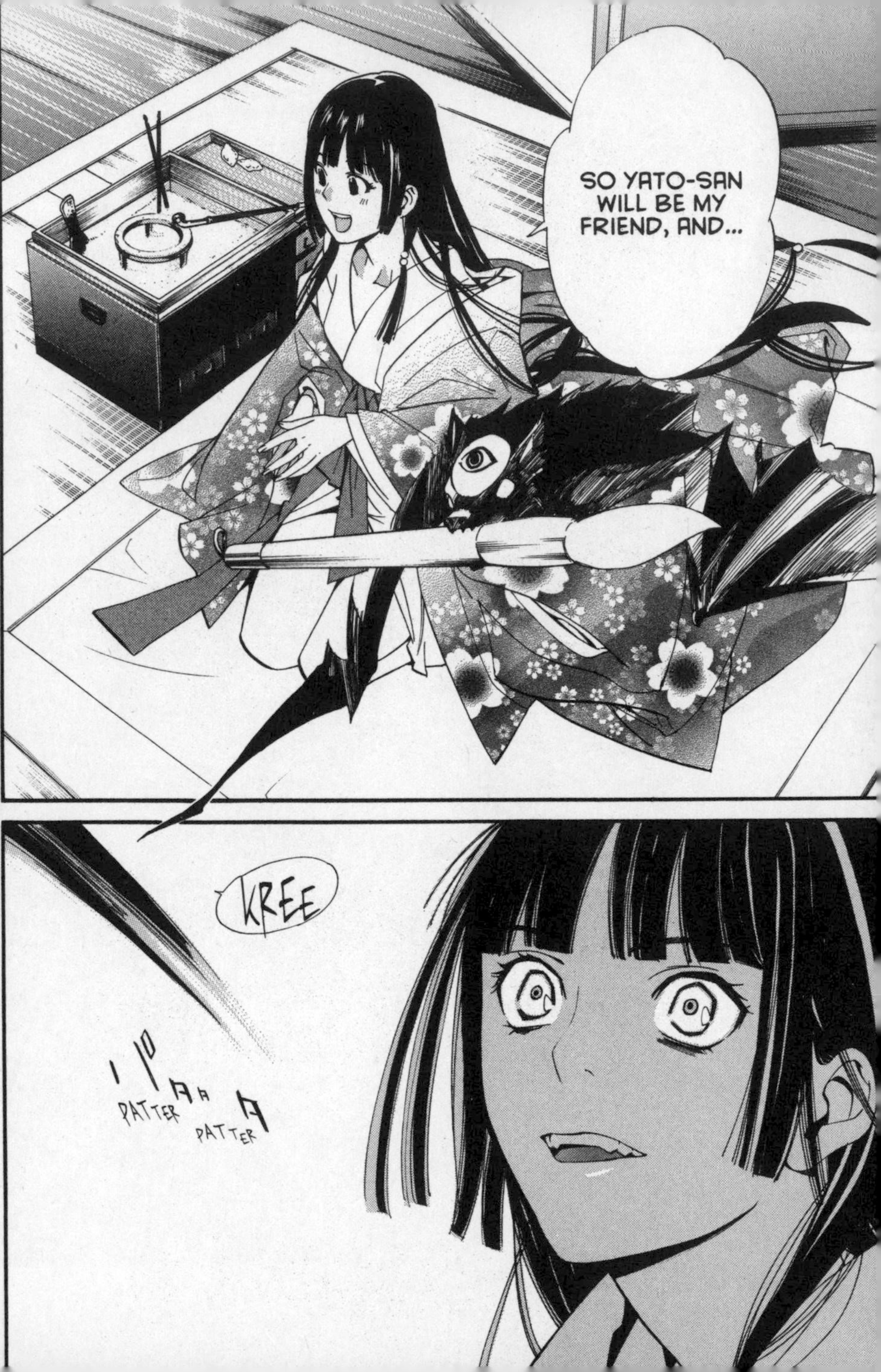
SO YATO-SAN WILL BE MY FRIEND, AND...
KREE
PATTER PATTER

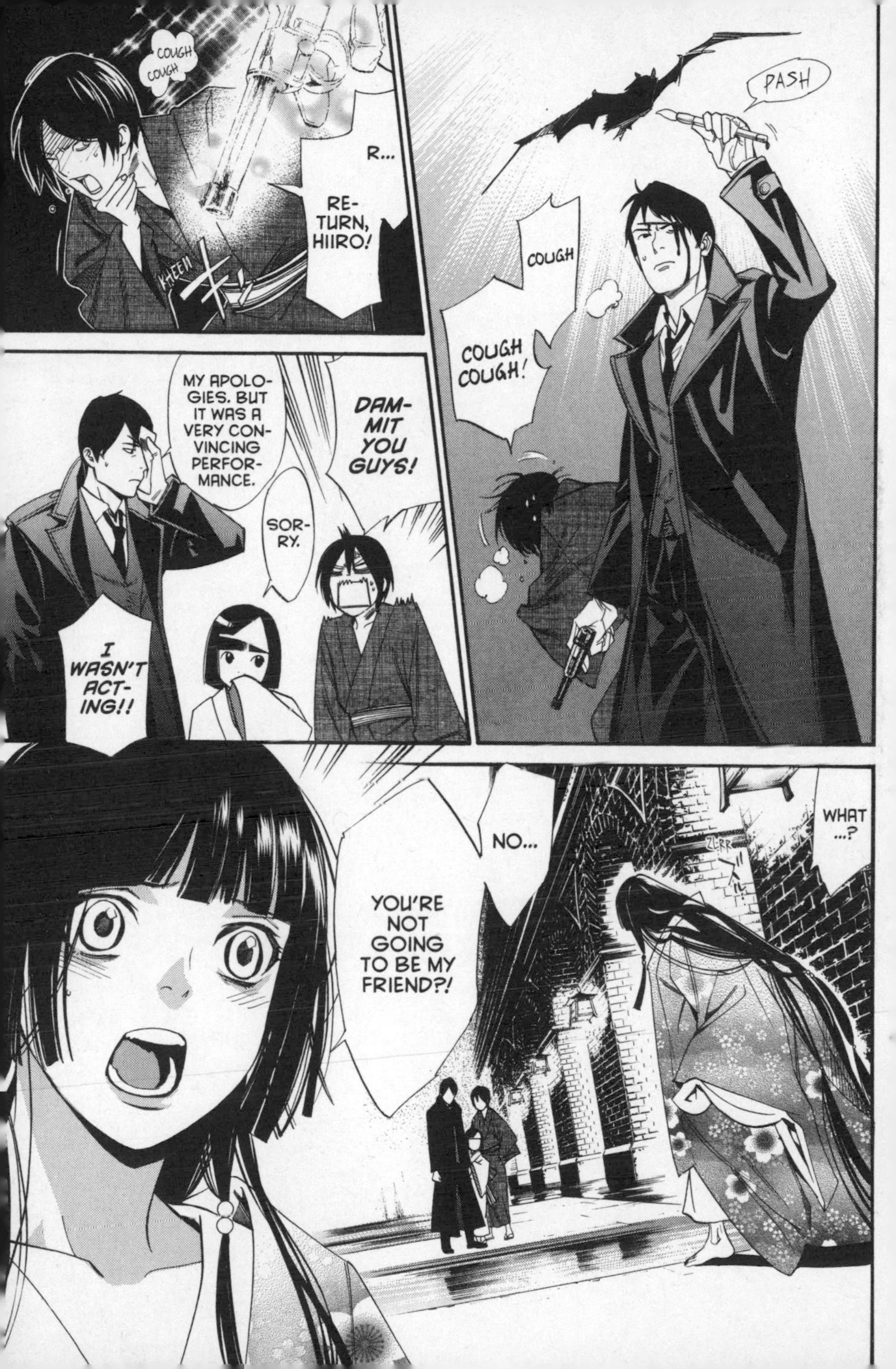
PASH
COUGH
COUGH COUGH!
COUGH COUGH
R...
RE-TURN, HIIRO!
DAM-MIT YOU GUYS!
MY APOLO-GIES. BUT IT WAS A VERY CON-VINCING PERFOR-MANCE.
SORRY.
I WASN'T ACT-ING!!
WHAT ...?
NO...
YOU'RE NOT GOING TO BE MY FRIEND?!

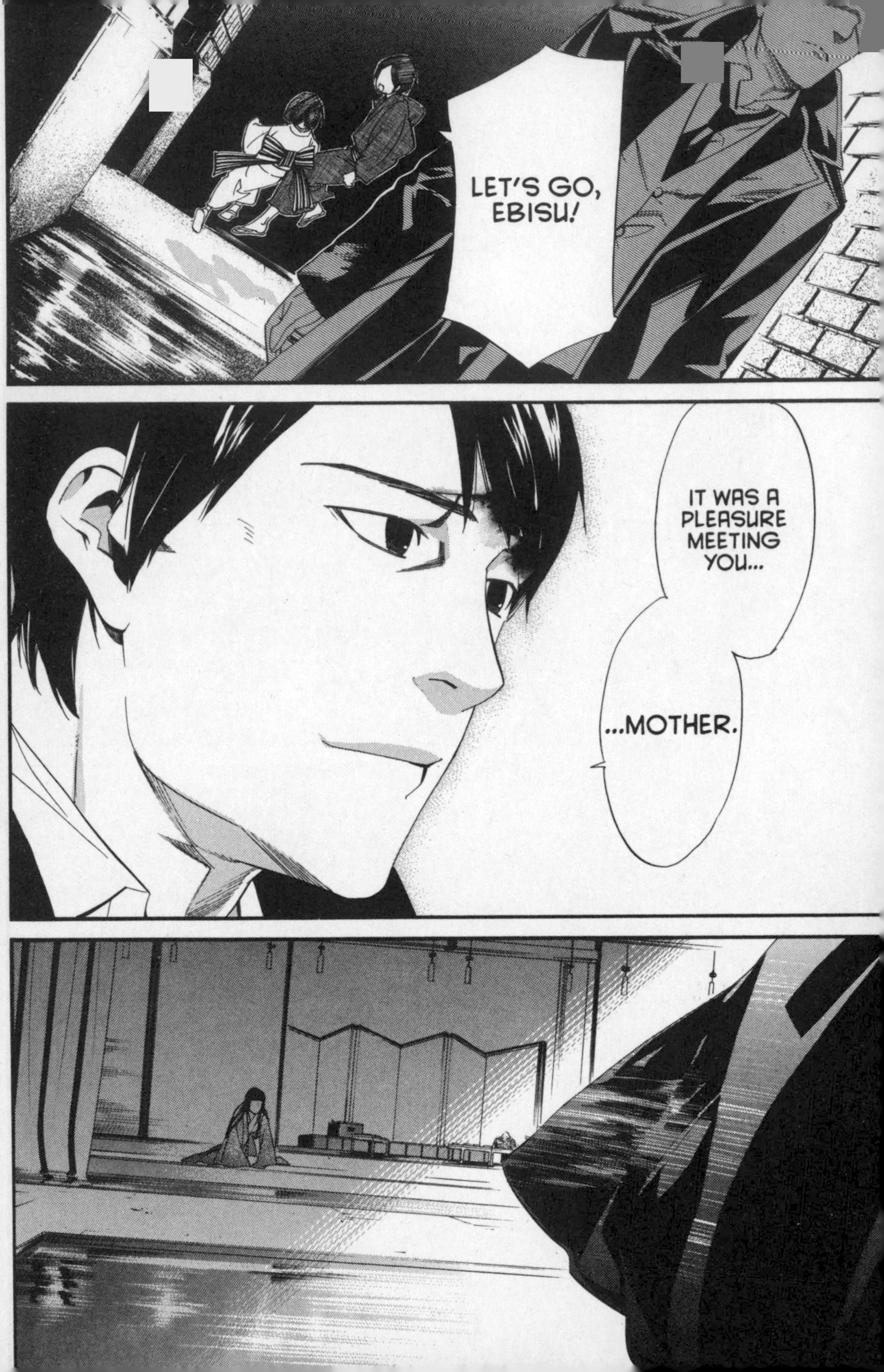
LET'S GO, EBISU!
IT WAS A PLEASURE MEETING YOU...
...MOTHER.

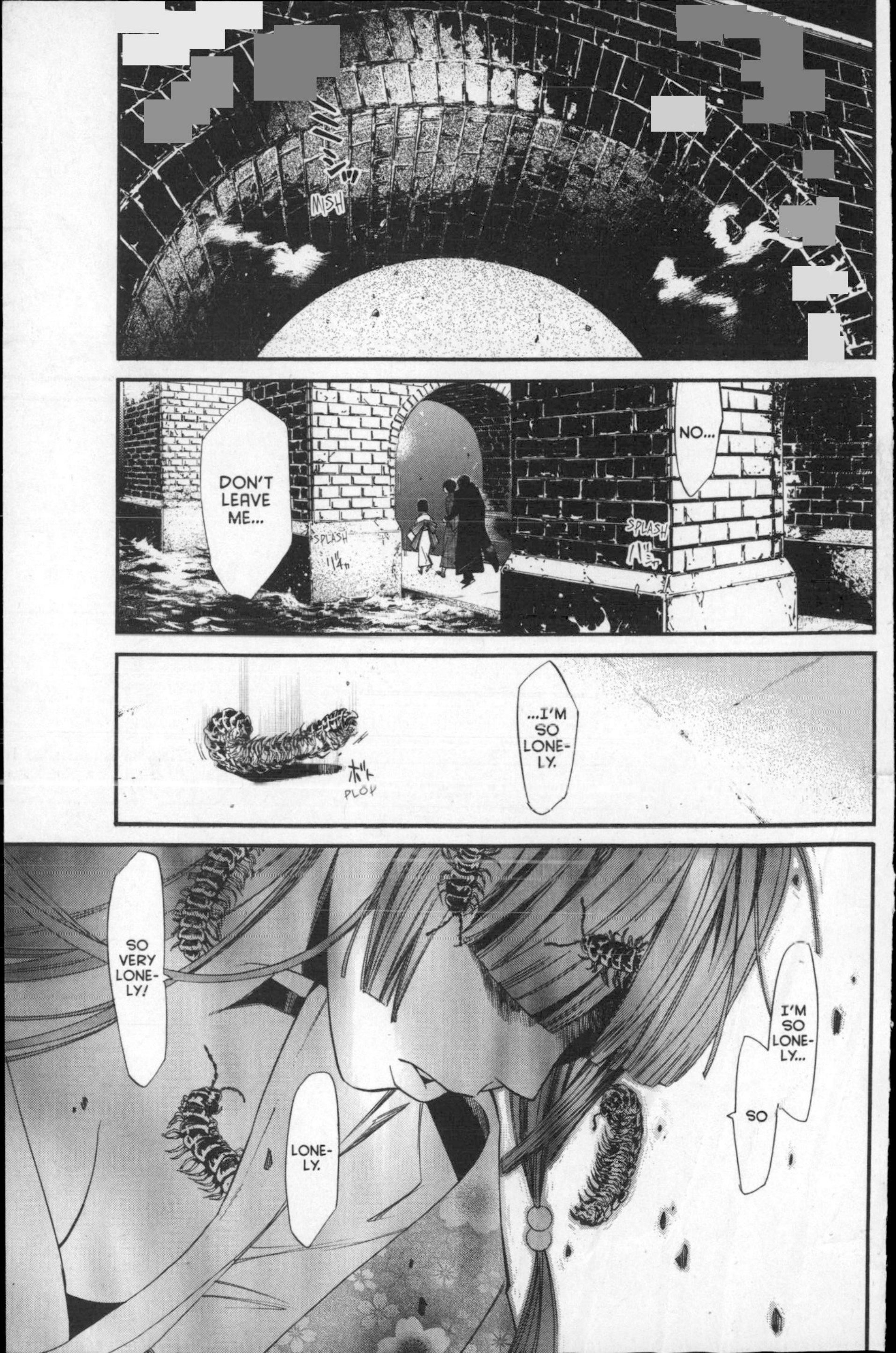
MISH
NO...
SPLASH
DON'T LEAVE ME...
SPLASH
...I'M SO LONE-LY.
PLOP
I'M SO LONE-LY...
SO
LONE-LY.
SO VERY LONE-LY!

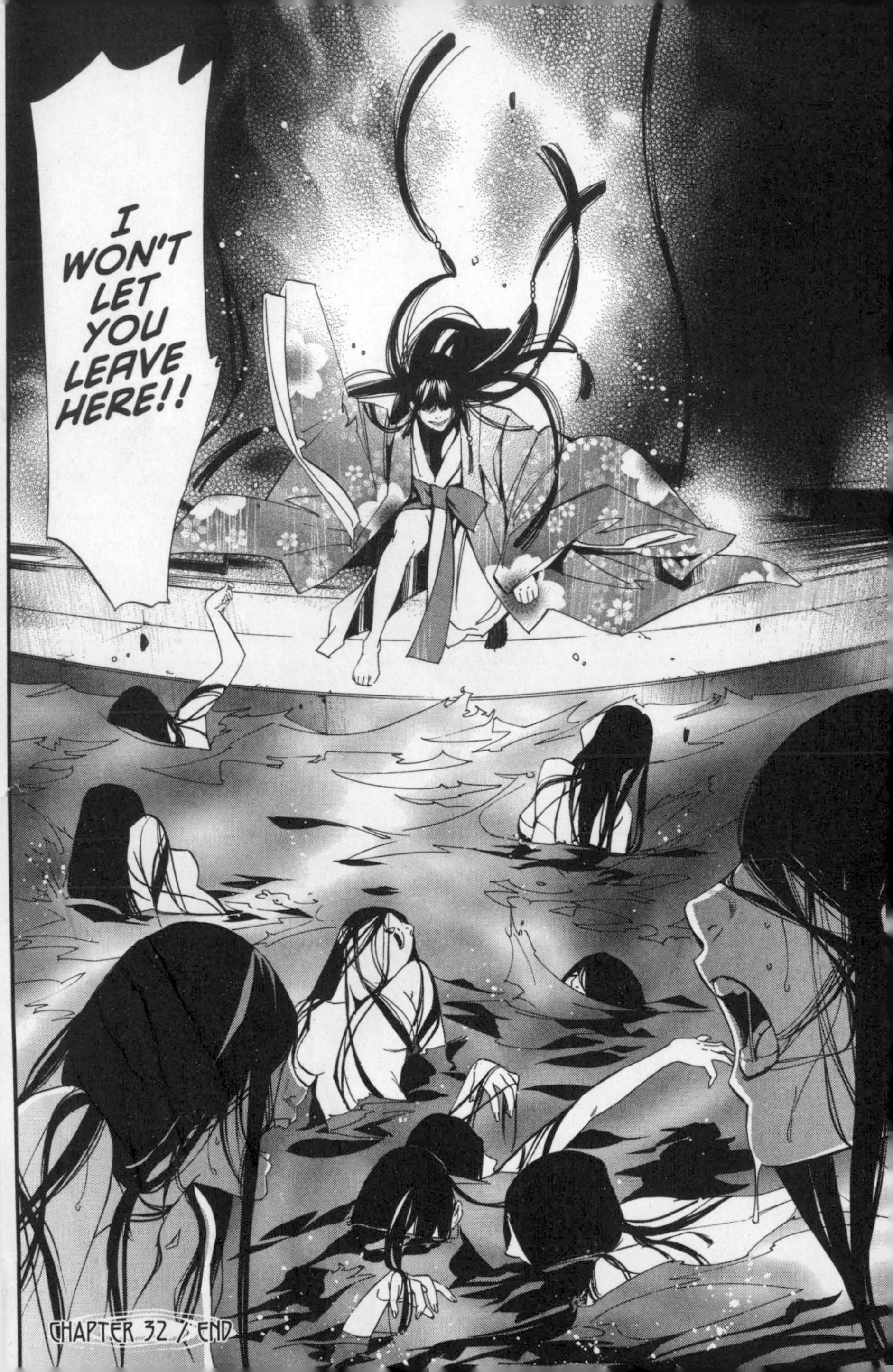
I WON'T LET YOU LEAVE HERE!!
CHAPTER 32 / END

野

[illegible]

神

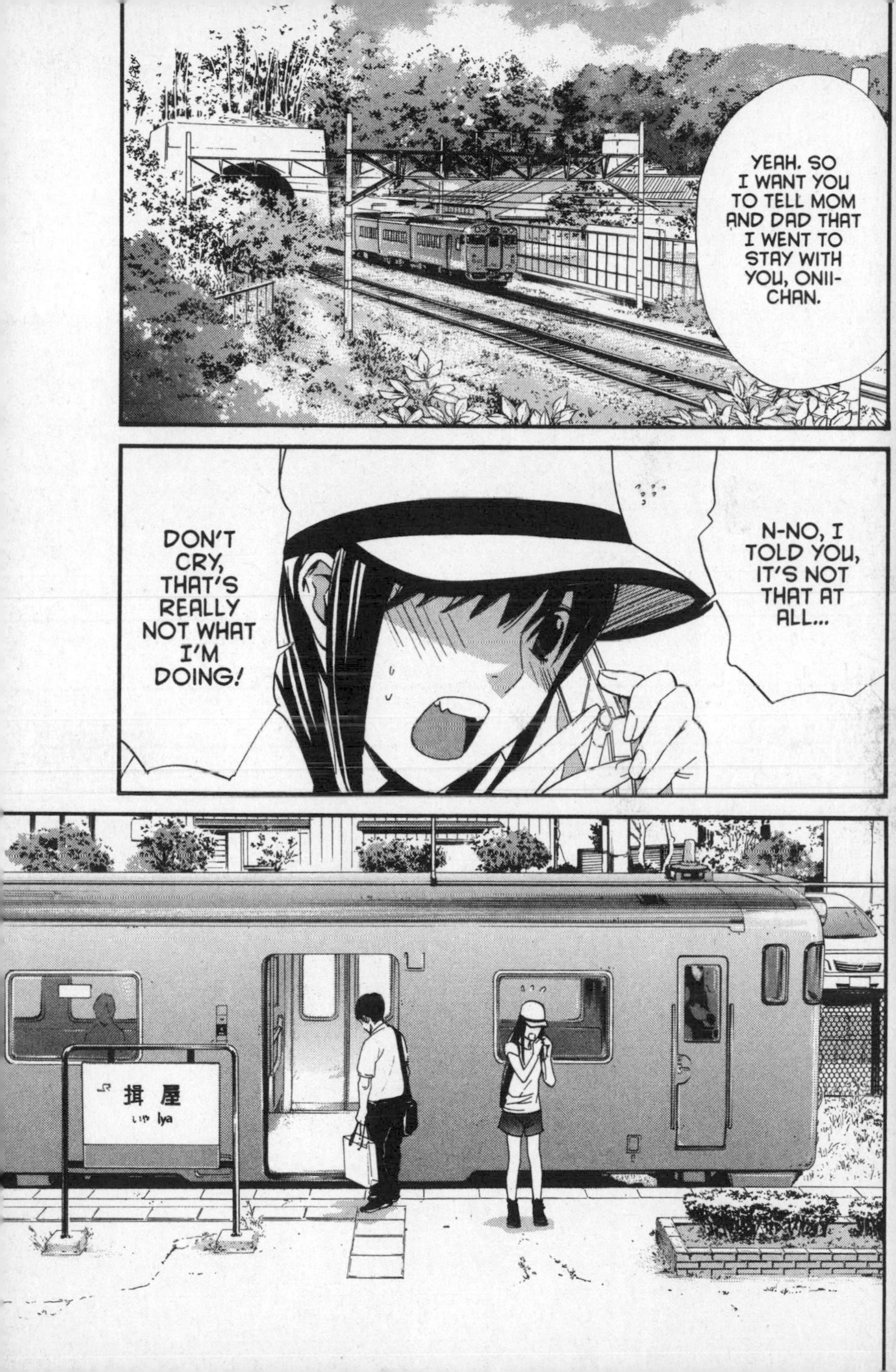
YEAH. SO I WANT YOU TO TELL MOM AND DAD THAT I WENT TO STAY WITH YOU, ONII-CHAN.
N-NO, I TOLD YOU, IT'S NOT THAT AT ALL...
DON'T CRY, THAT'S REALLY NOT WHAT I'M DOING!
揖屋
いや Iya

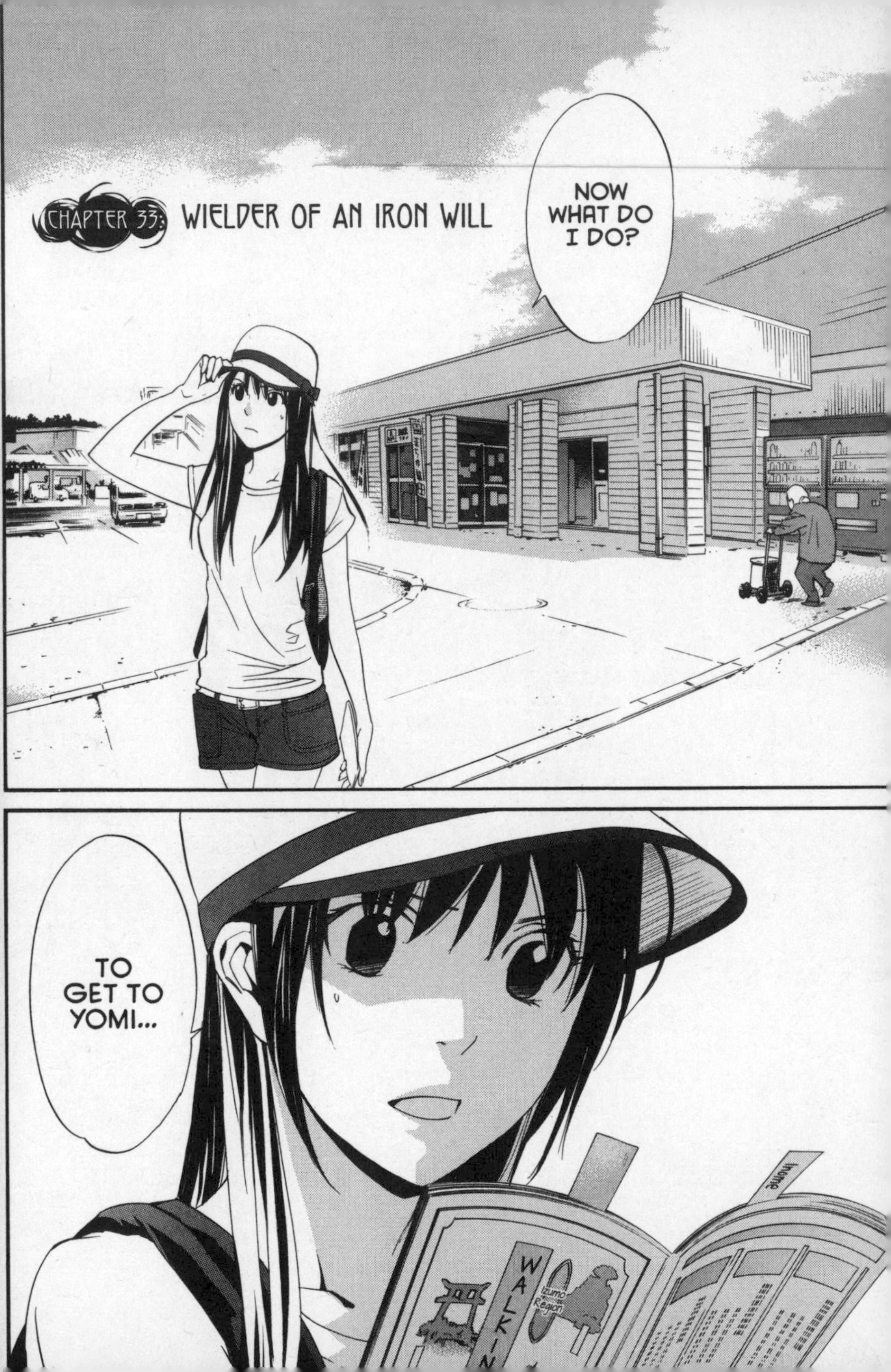
CHAPTER 33: WIELDER OF AN IRON WILL
NOW WHAT DO I DO?
TO GET TO YOMI...
WALKIN
Izumo Region

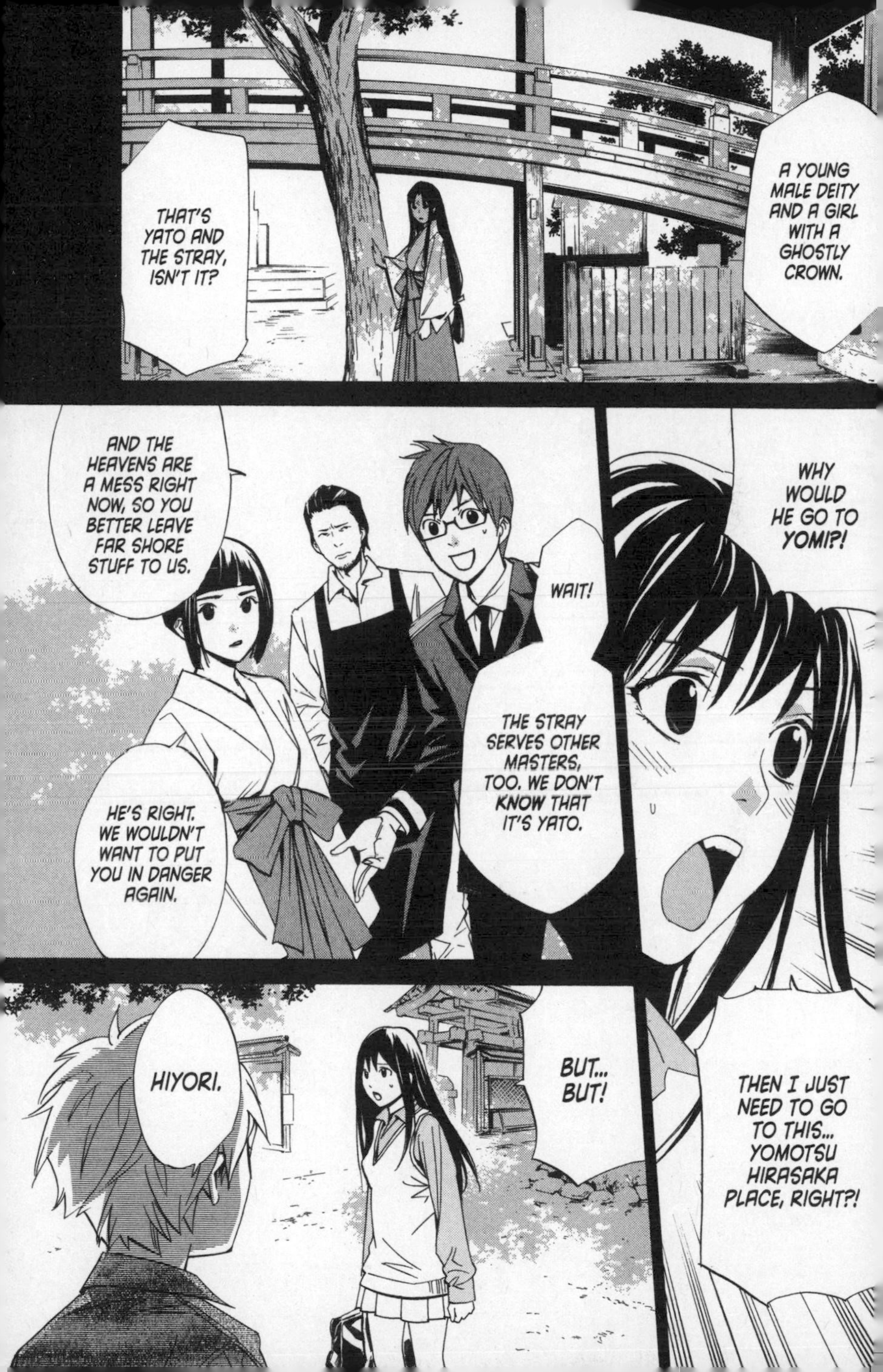
A YOUNG MALE DEITY AND A GIRL WITH A GHOSTLY CROWN.
THAT'S YATO AND THE STRAY, ISN'T IT?
WHY WOULD HE GO TO YOMI?!
THEN I JUST NEED TO GO TO THIS... YOMOTSU HIRASAKA PLACE, RIGHT?!
WAIT!
THE STRAY SERVES OTHER MASTERS, TOO. WE DON'T KNOW THAT IT'S YATO.
AND THE HEAVENS ARE A MESS RIGHT NOW, SO YOU BETTER LEAVE FAR SHORE STUFF TO US.
HE'S RIGHT. WE WOULDN'T WANT TO PUT YOU IN DANGER AGAIN.
BUT... BUT!
HIYORI.

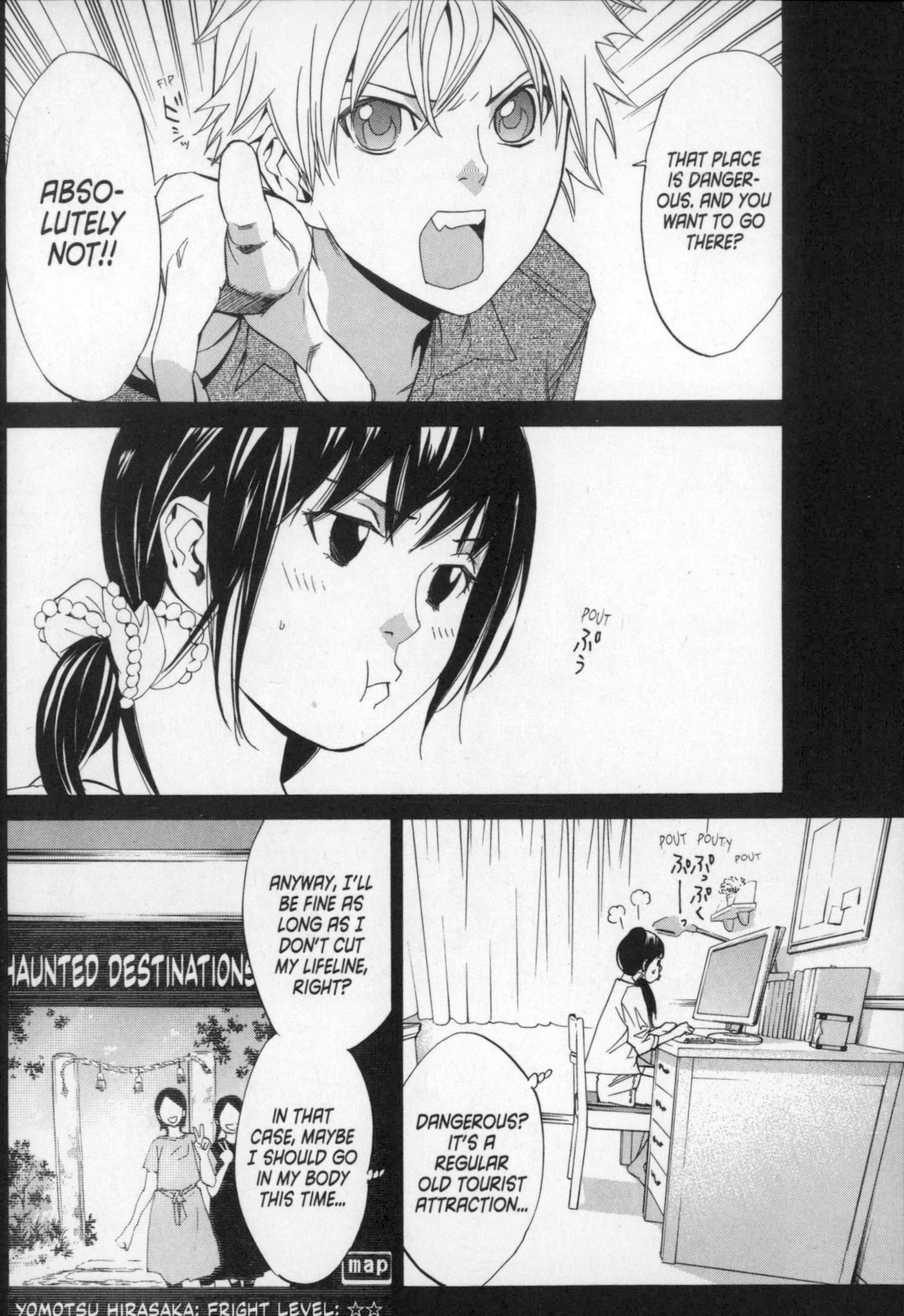
THAT PLACE IS DANGER-OUS. AND YOU WANT TO GO THERE?
FIP
ABSO-LUTELY NOT!!
POUT
POUT POUTY POUT
DANGEROUS? IT'S A REGULAR OLD TOURIST ATTRACTION...
ANYWAY, I'LL BE FINE AS LONG AS I DON'T CUT MY LIFELINE, RIGHT?
IN THAT CASE, MAYBE I SHOULD GO IN MY BODY THIS TIME...
HAUNTED DESTINATIONS
map
YOMOTSU HIRASAKA: FRIGHT LEVEL: ☆☆

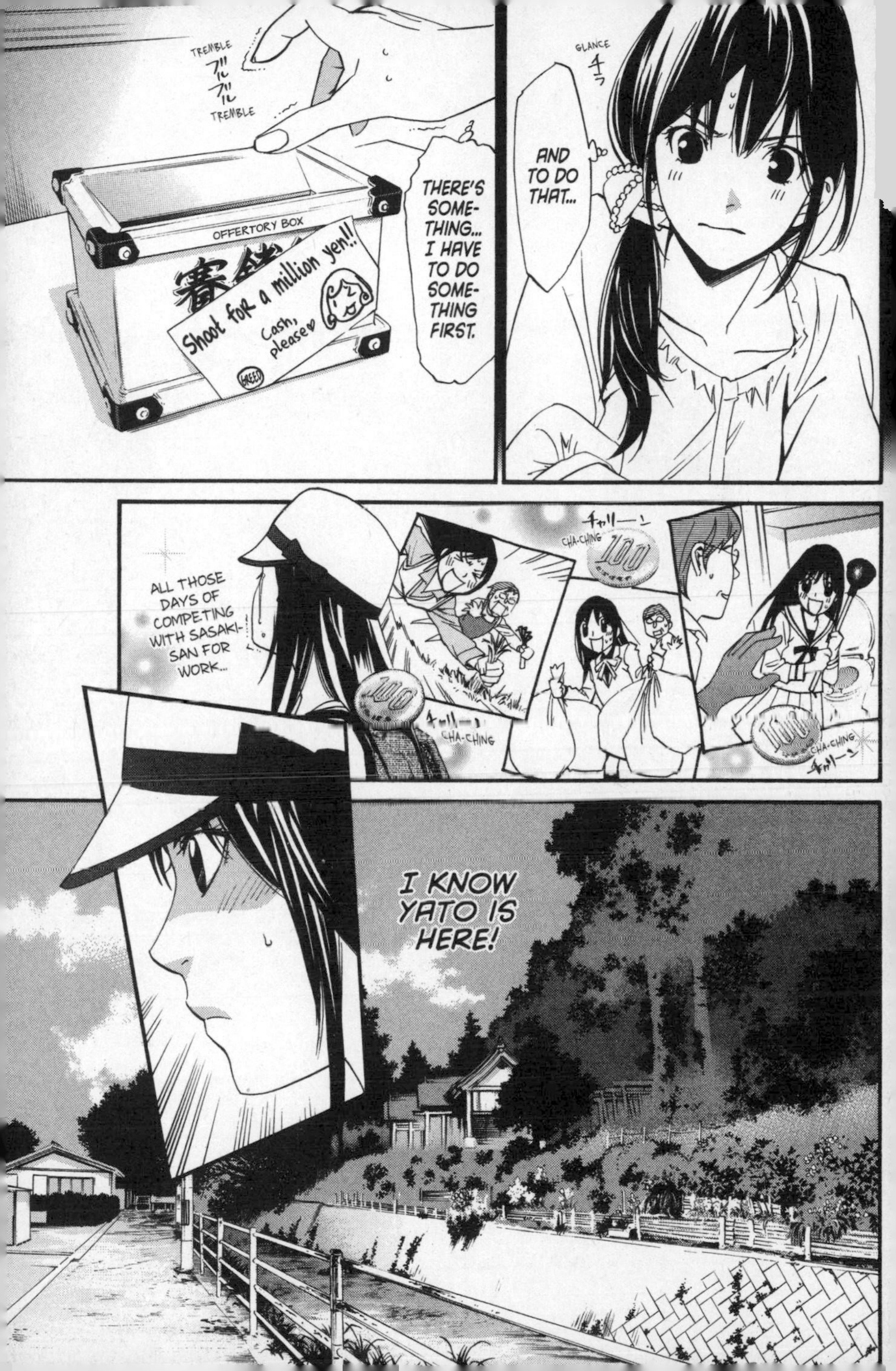

GLANCE
チラ
AND TO DO THAT...
TREMBLE
ブル
ブル
TREMBLE
THERE'S SOMETHING... I HAVE TO DO SOMETHING FIRST.
OFFERTORY BOX
賽銭
Shoot for a million yen!!
Cash, please♥
GREED
チャリーン
CHA-CHING
ALL THOSE DAYS OF COMPETING WITH SASAKI-SAN FOR WORK...
チャリーン
CHA-CHING
CHA-CHING
チャリーン
I KNOW YATO IS HERE!

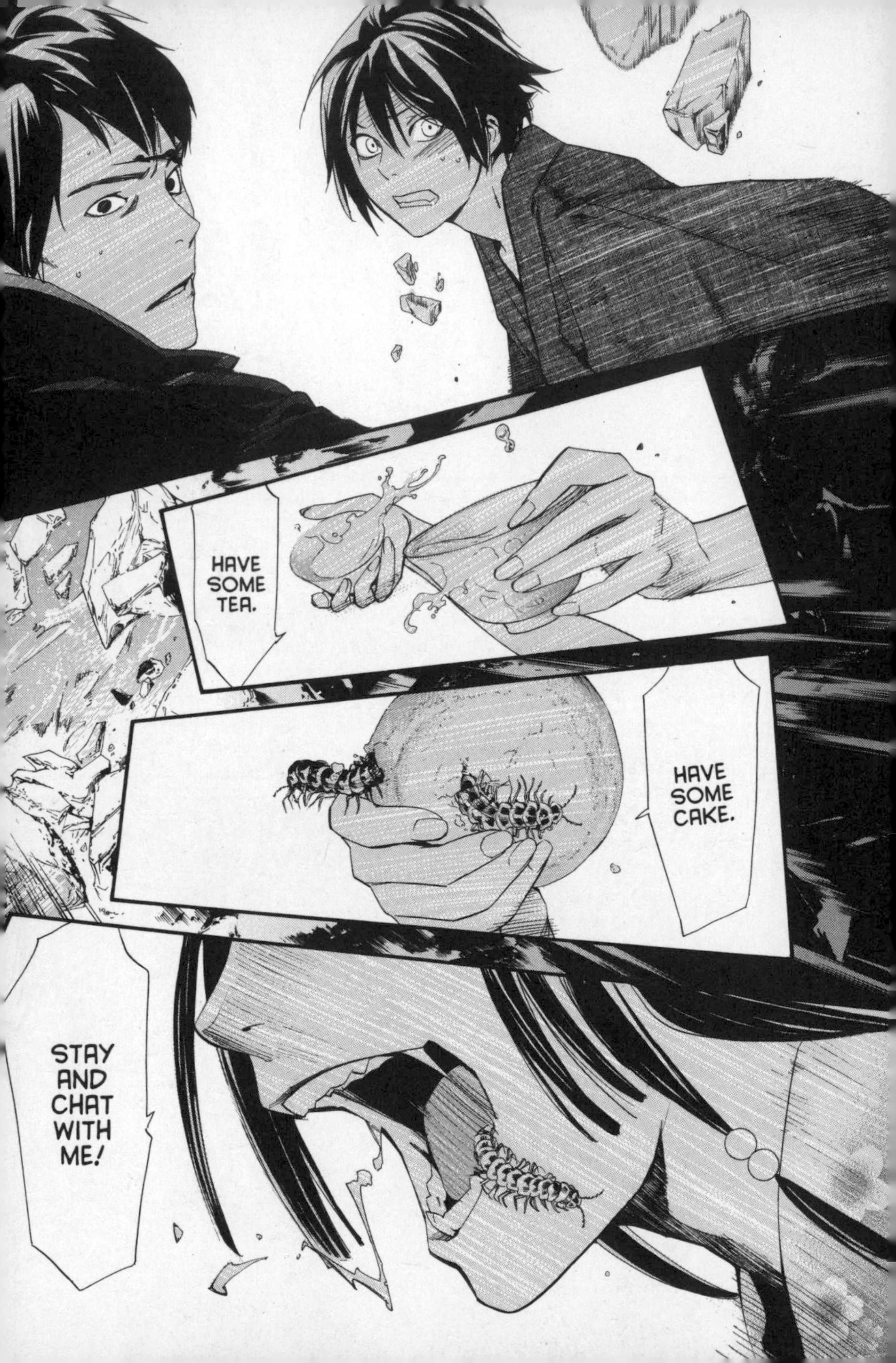
HAVE SOME TEA.
HAVE SOME CAKE.
STAY AND CHAT WITH ME!

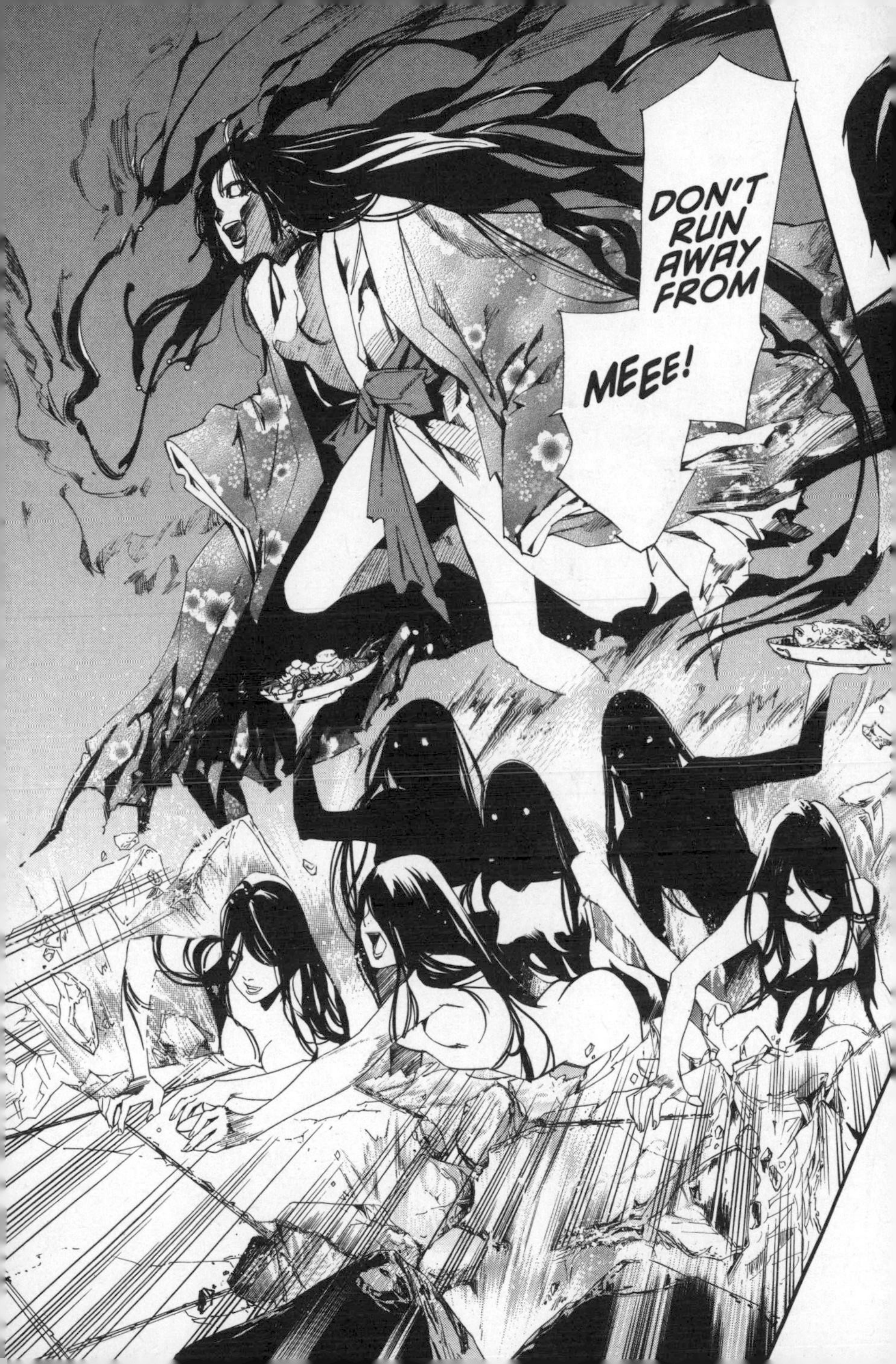
DON'T RUN AWAY FROM
MEEE!

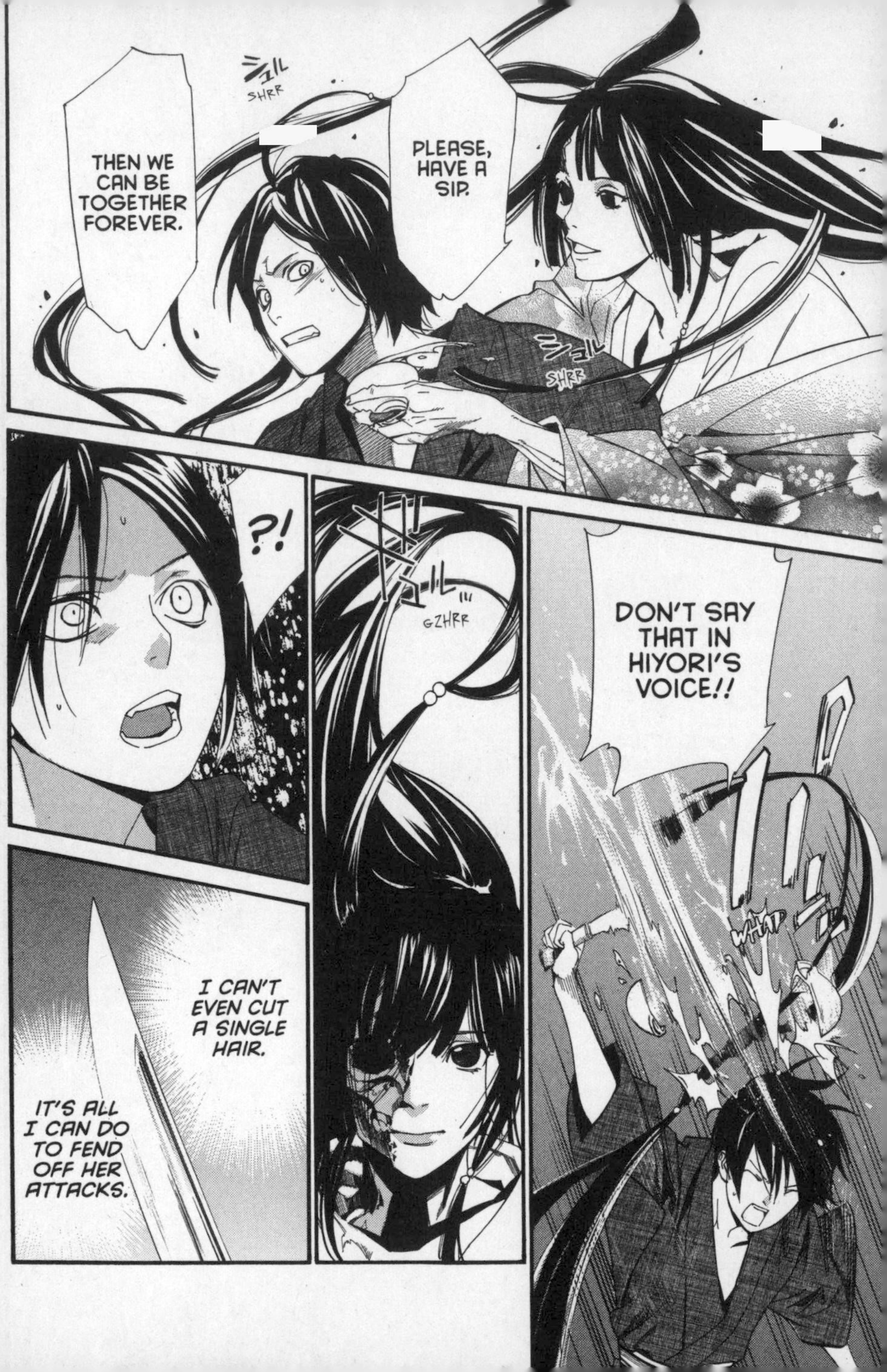
SHRR
PLEASE, HAVE A SIP.
SHRR
THEN WE CAN BE TOGETHER FOREVER.
DON'T SAY THAT IN HIYORI'S VOICE!!
WHAP
GZHRR
?!
I CAN'T EVEN CUT A SINGLE HAIR.
IT'S ALL I CAN DO TO FEND OFF HER ATTACKS.

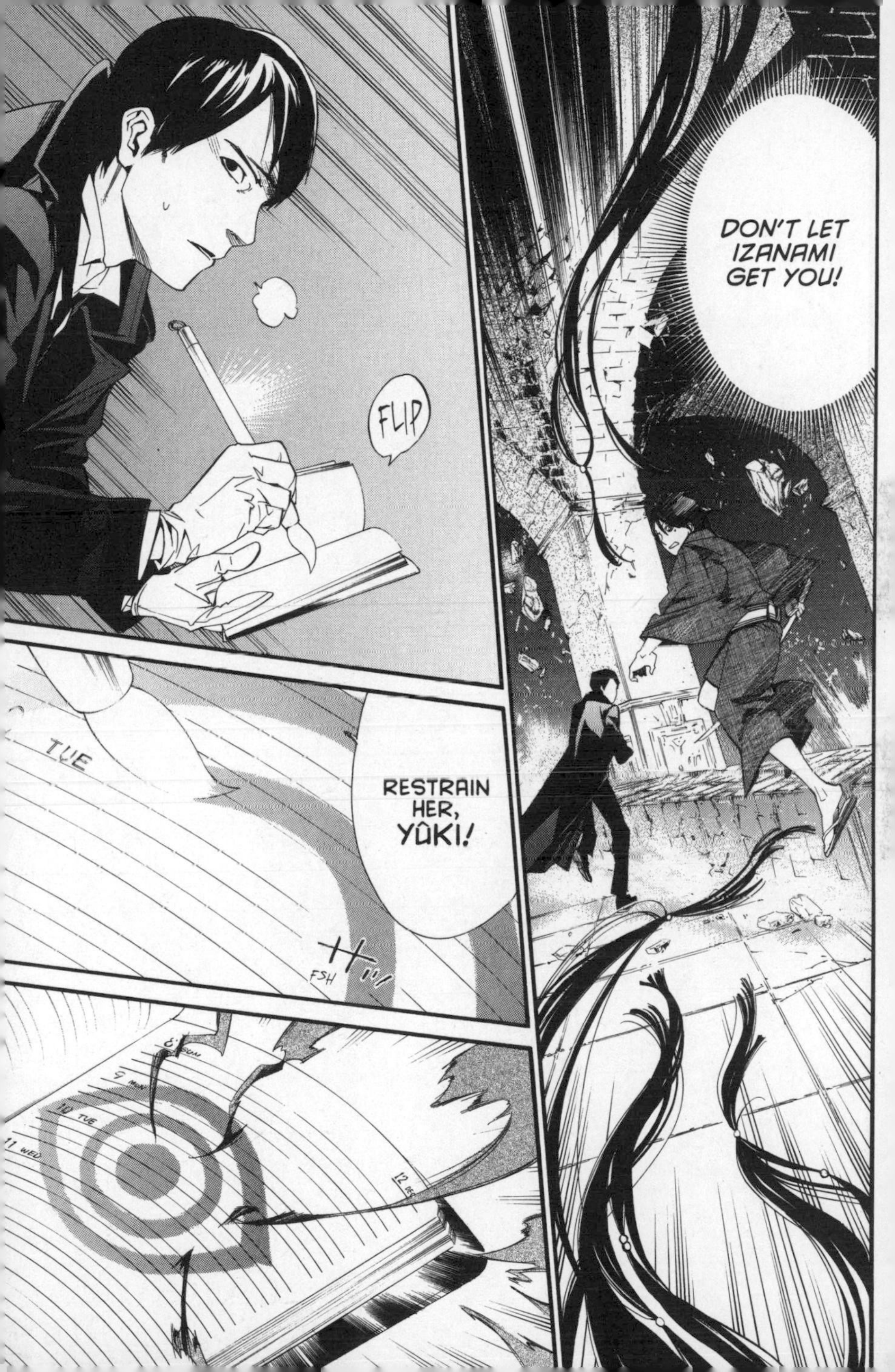
DON'T LET IZANAMI GET YOU!
FLIP
TUE
RESTRAIN HER, YÛKI!
FSH

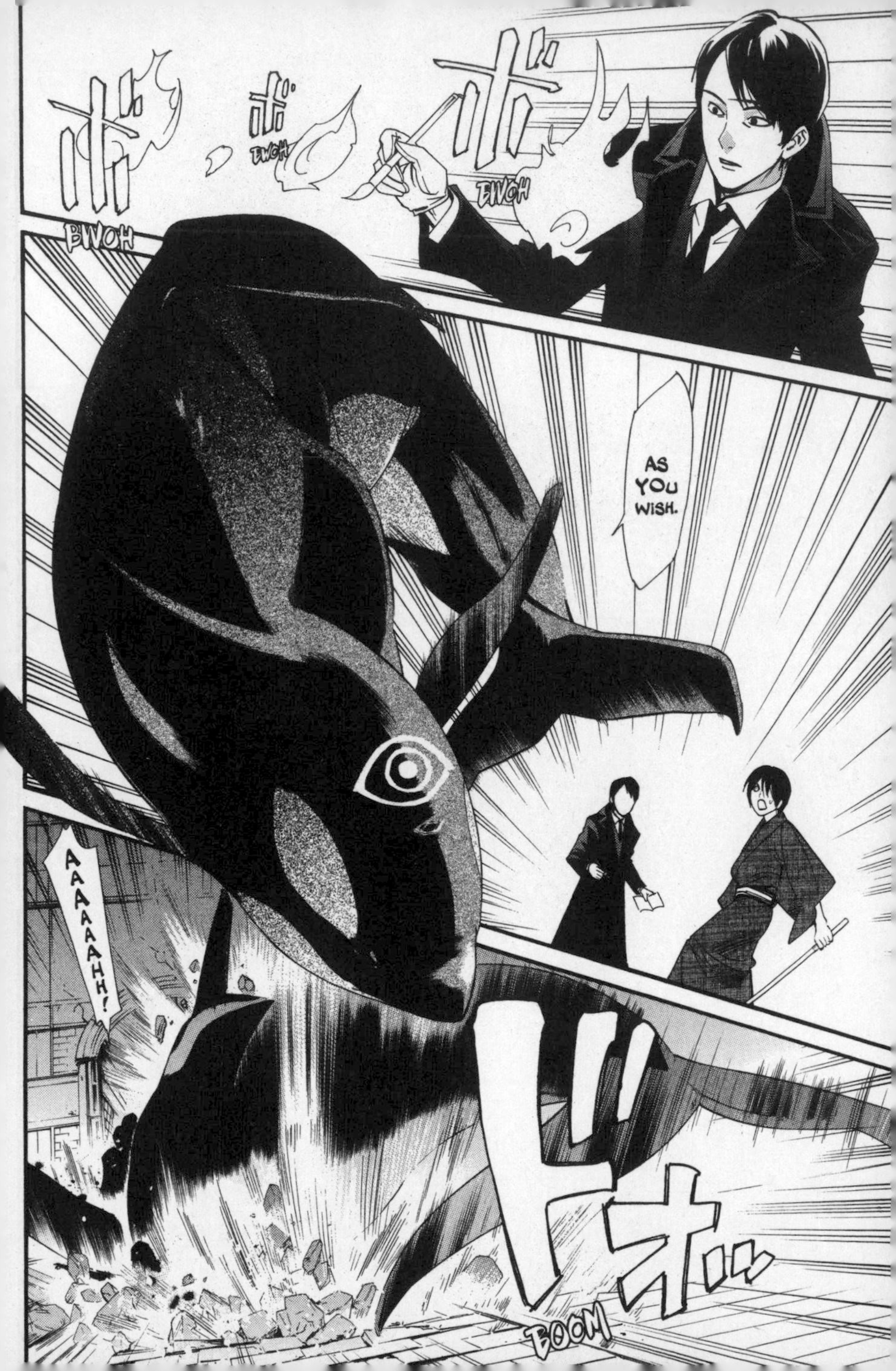

ボ
BWOH
ぼ
BWOH
ボ
BWOH
AS YOU WISH.
AAAAAAAHH!
ドォ
BOOM

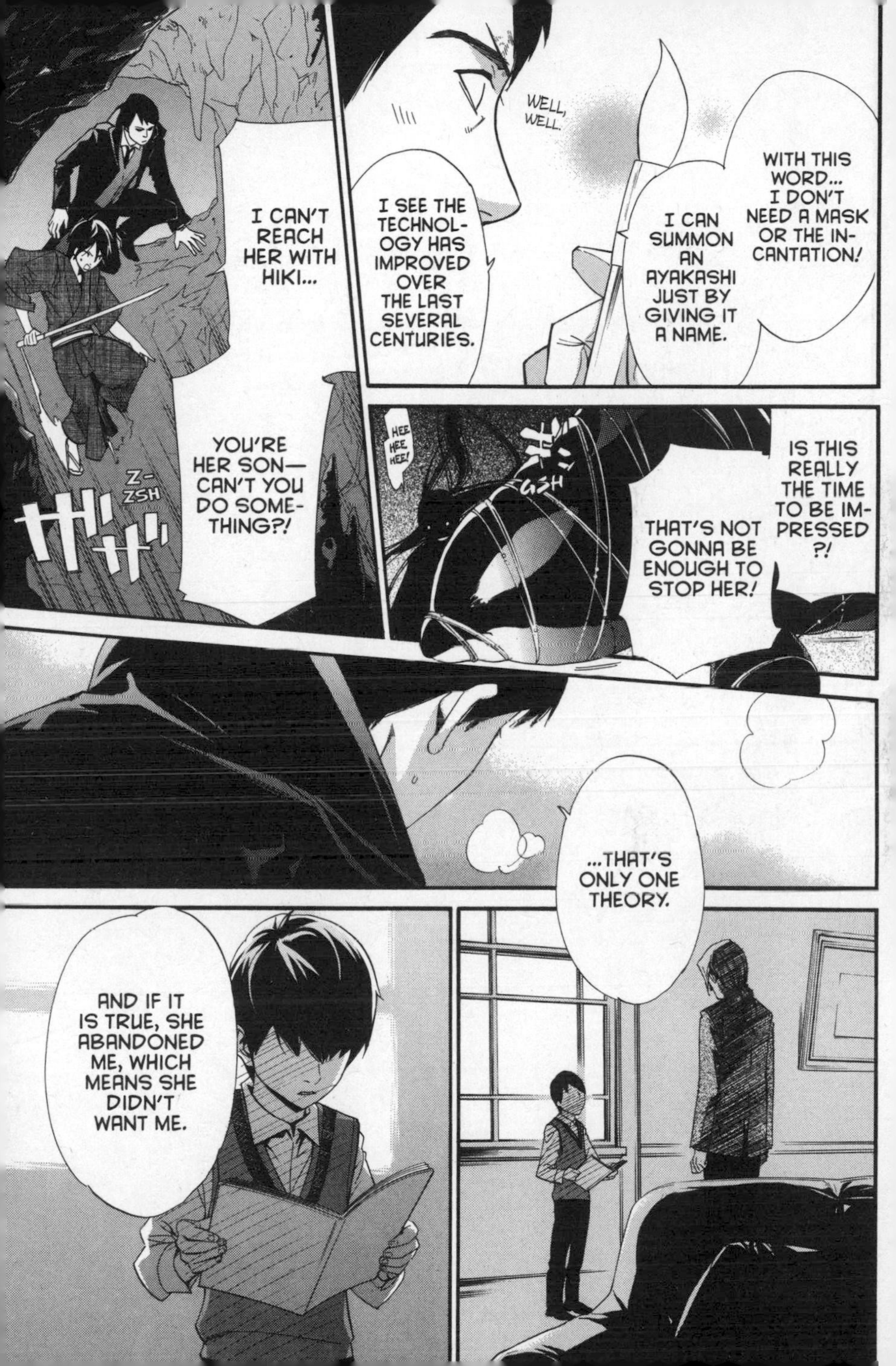
WITH THIS WORD... I DON'T NEED A MASK OR THE IN-CANTATION!
I CAN SUMMON AN AYAKASHI JUST BY GIVING IT A NAME.
WELL, WELL.
I SEE THE TECHNOL-OGY HAS IMPROVED OVER THE LAST SEVERAL CENTURIES.
IS THIS REALLY THE TIME TO BE IM-PRESSED?!
THAT'S NOT GONNA BE ENOUGH TO STOP HER!
GSH
HEE HEE HEE!
I CAN'T REACH HER WITH HIKI...
YOU'RE HER SON—CAN'T YOU DO SOME-THING?!
Z-ZSH
...THAT'S ONLY ONE THEORY.
AND IF IT IS TRUE, SHE ABANDONED ME, WHICH MEANS SHE DIDN'T WANT ME.

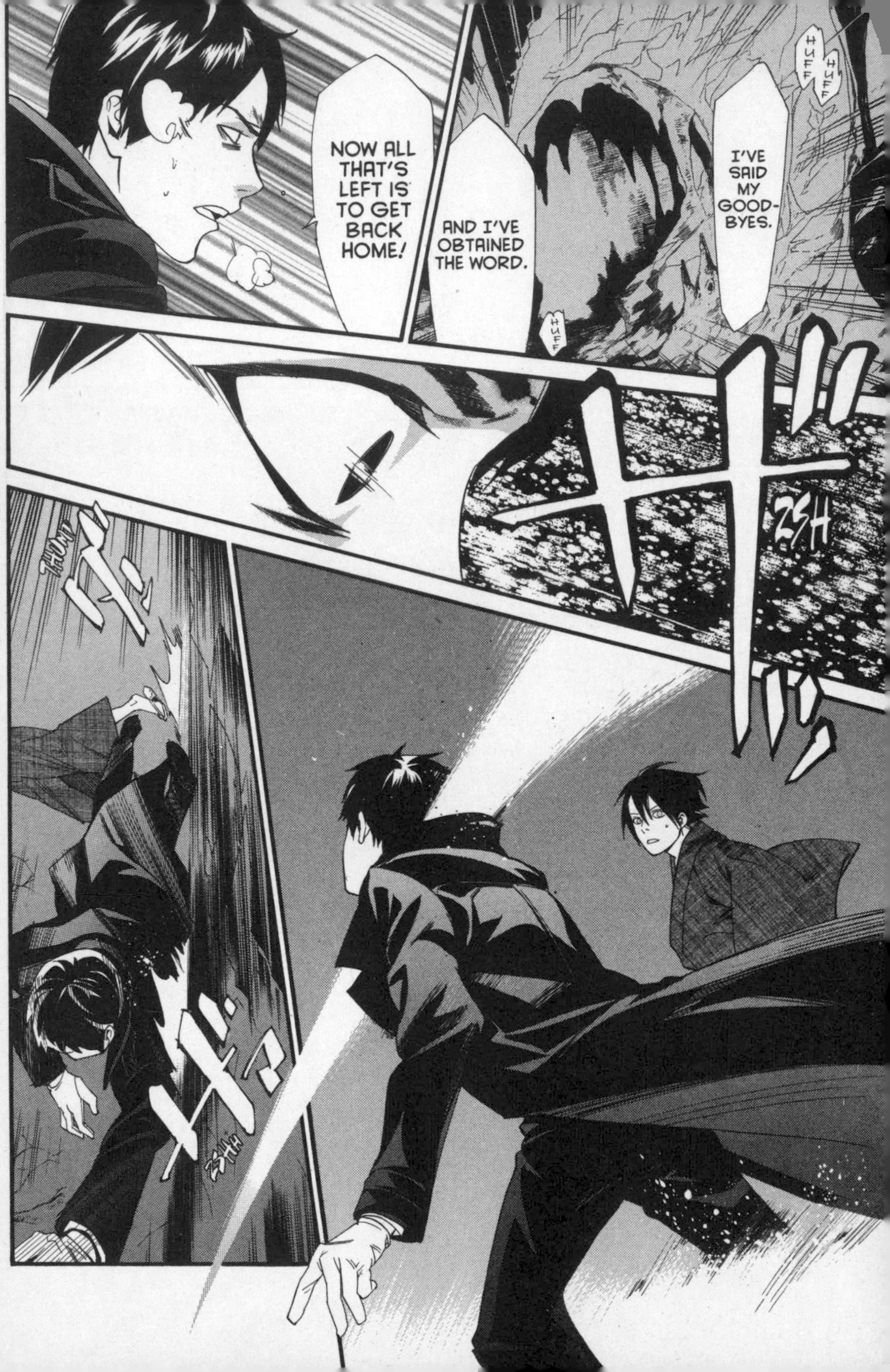
HUFF
HUFF
I'VE SAID MY GOOD-BYES.
HUFF
AND I'VE OBTAINED THE WORD.
NOW ALL THAT'S LEFT IS TO GET BACK HOME!
ZSH
THUMP
ZSHH

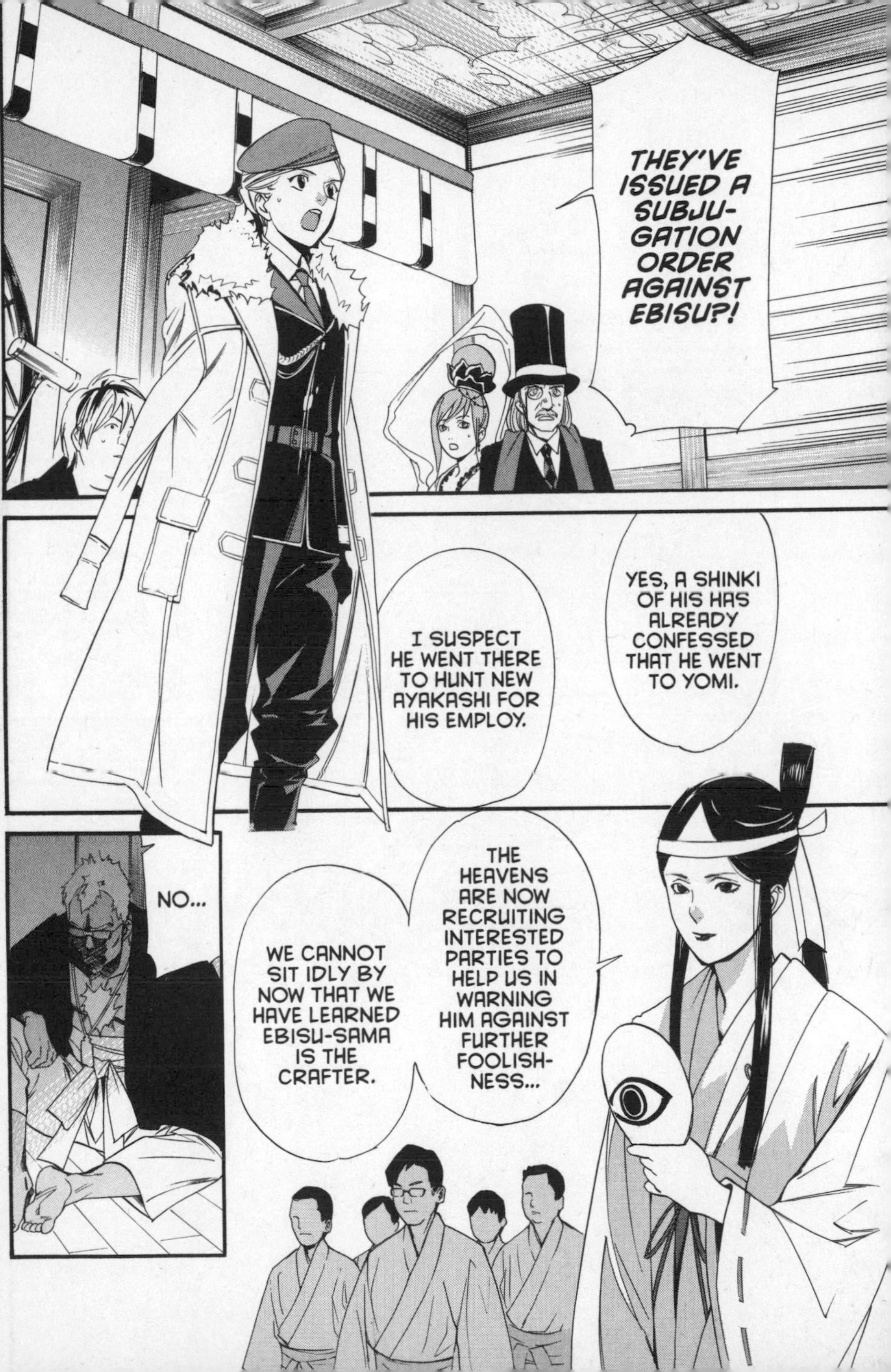
THEY'VE ISSUED A SUBJU-GATION ORDER AGAINST EBISU?!
YES, A SHINKI OF HIS HAS ALREADY CONFESSED THAT HE WENT TO YOMI.
I SUSPECT HE WENT THERE TO HUNT NEW AYAKASHI FOR HIS EMPLOY.
THE HEAVENS ARE NOW RECRUITING INTERESTED PARTIES TO HELP US IN WARNING HIM AGAINST FURTHER FOOLISH-NESS...
WE CANNOT SIT IDLY BY NOW THAT WE HAVE LEARNED EBISU-SAMA IS THE CRAFTER.
NO...

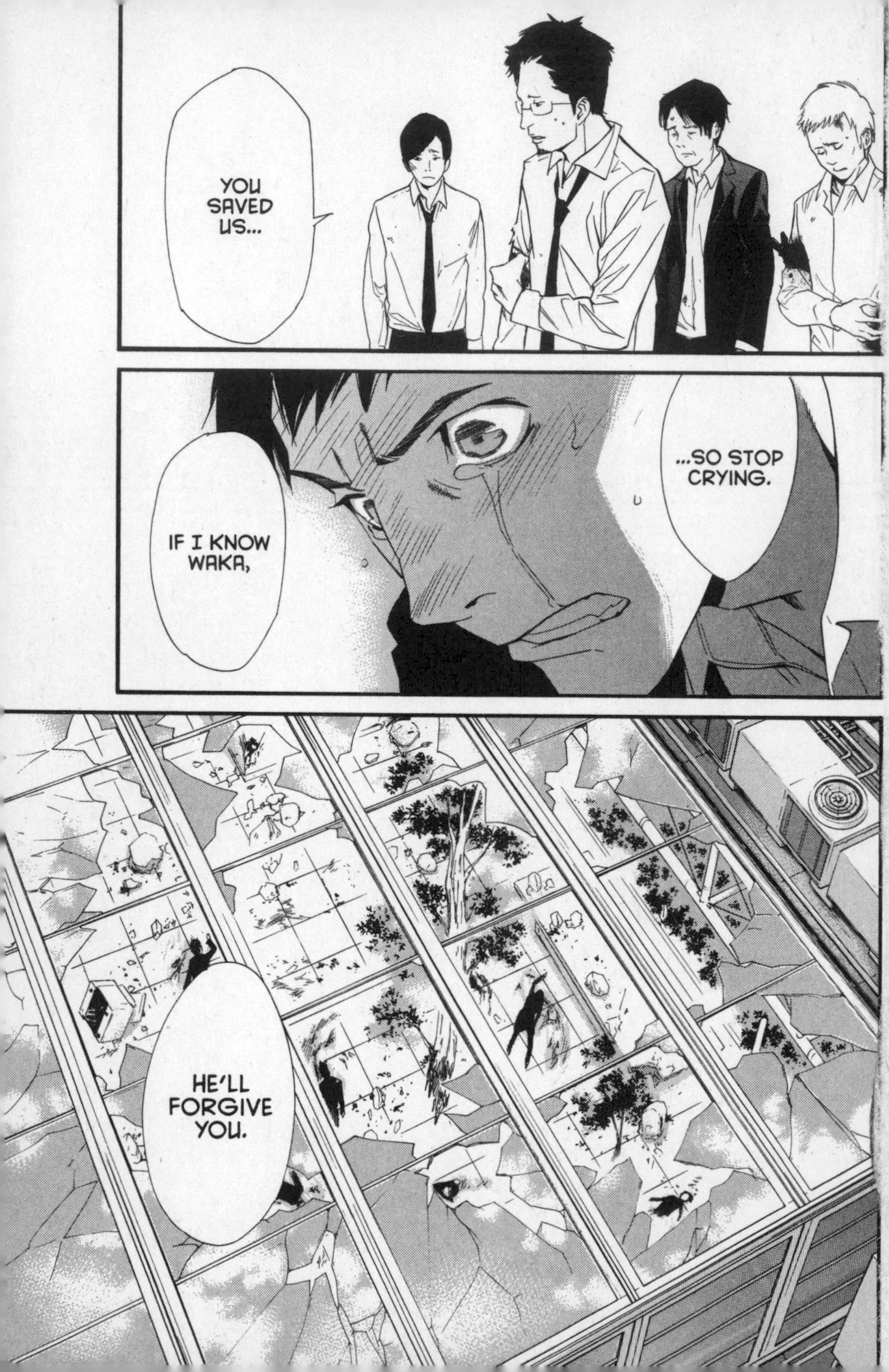
YOU SAVED US...
...SO STOP CRYING.
IF I KNOW WAKA,
HE'LL FORGIVE YOU.

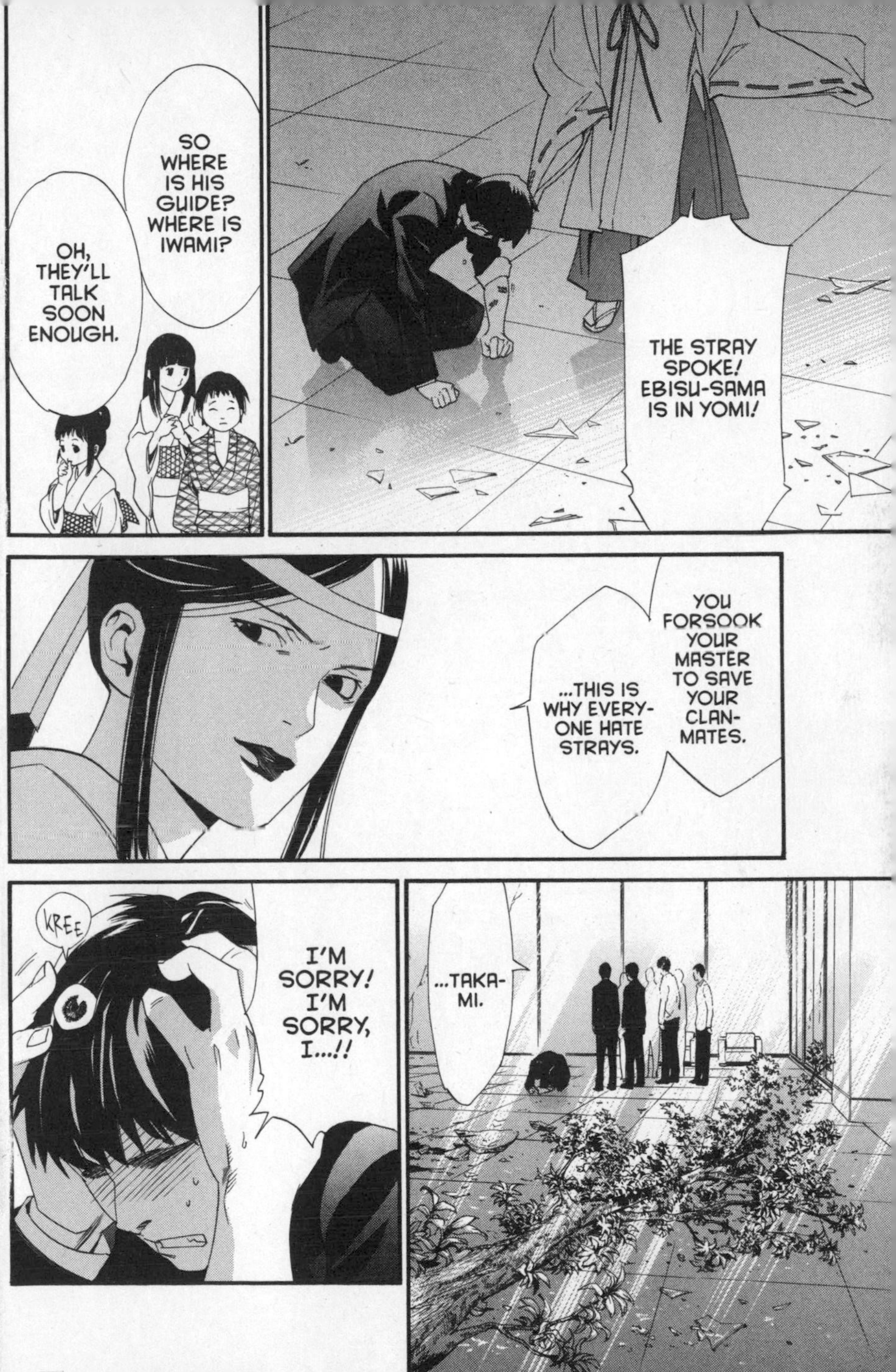
THE STRAY SPOKE! EBISU-SAMA IS IN YOMI!
SO WHERE IS HIS GUIDE? WHERE IS IWAMI?
OH, THEY'LL TALK SOON ENOUGH.
YOU FORSOOK YOUR MASTER TO SAVE YOUR CLAN-MATES.
...THIS IS WHY EVERY-ONE HATE STRAYS.
...TAKA-MI.
I'M SORRY! I'M SORRY, I...!!
KREE

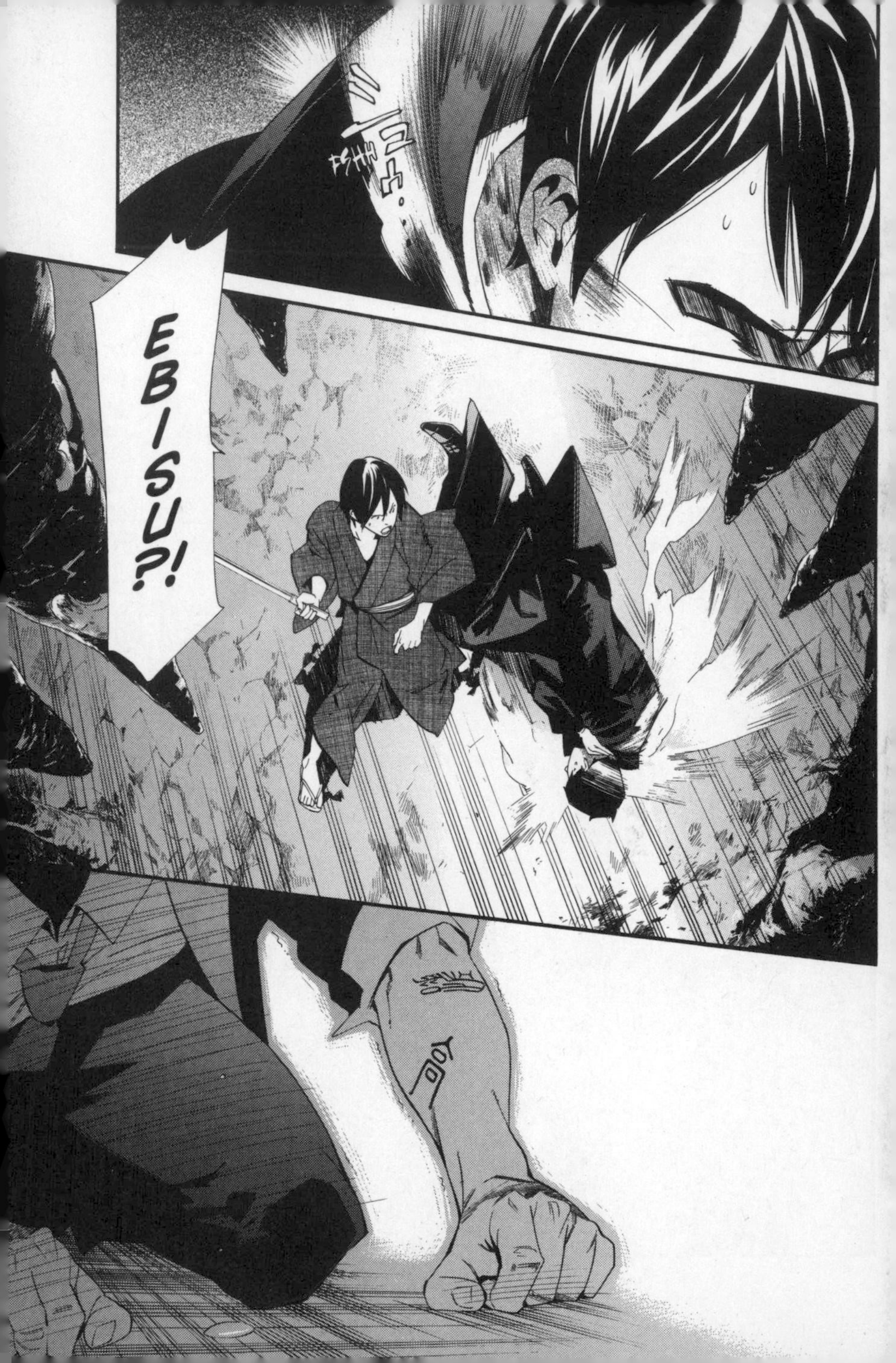
FSHH
EBISU?!

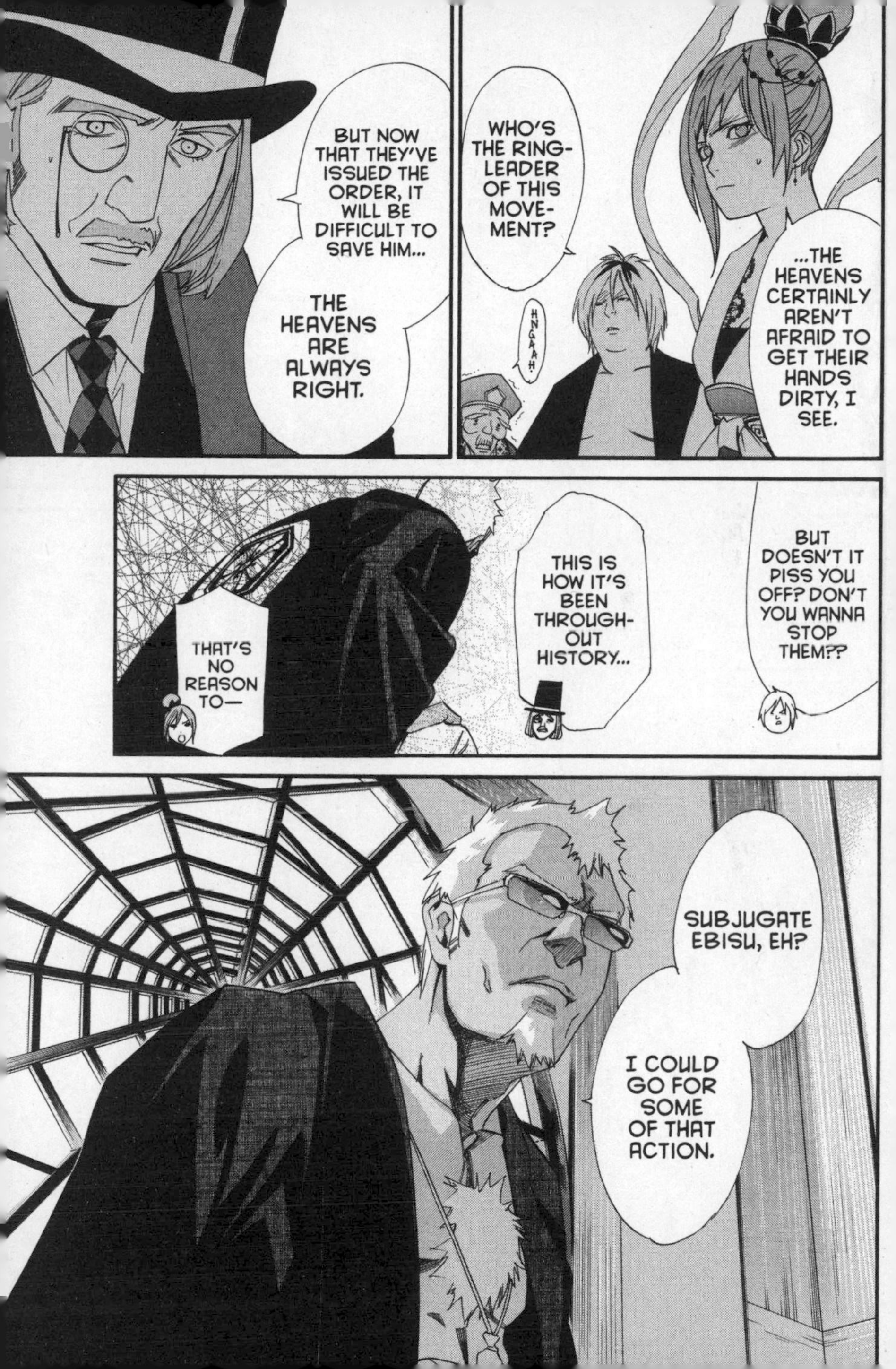
WHO'S THE RING-LEADER OF THIS MOVEMENT?
HNGAAH
...THE HEAVENS CERTAINLY AREN'T AFRAID TO GET THEIR HANDS DIRTY, I SEE.
BUT NOW THAT THEY'VE ISSUED THE ORDER, IT WILL BE DIFFICULT TO SAVE HIM...
THE HEAVENS ARE ALWAYS RIGHT.
BUT DOESN'T IT PISS YOU OFF? DON'T YOU WANNA STOP THEM??
THIS IS HOW IT'S BEEN THROUGH-OUT HISTORY...
THAT'S NO REASON TO—
SUBJUGATE EBISU, EH?
I COULD GO FOR SOME OF THAT ACTION.

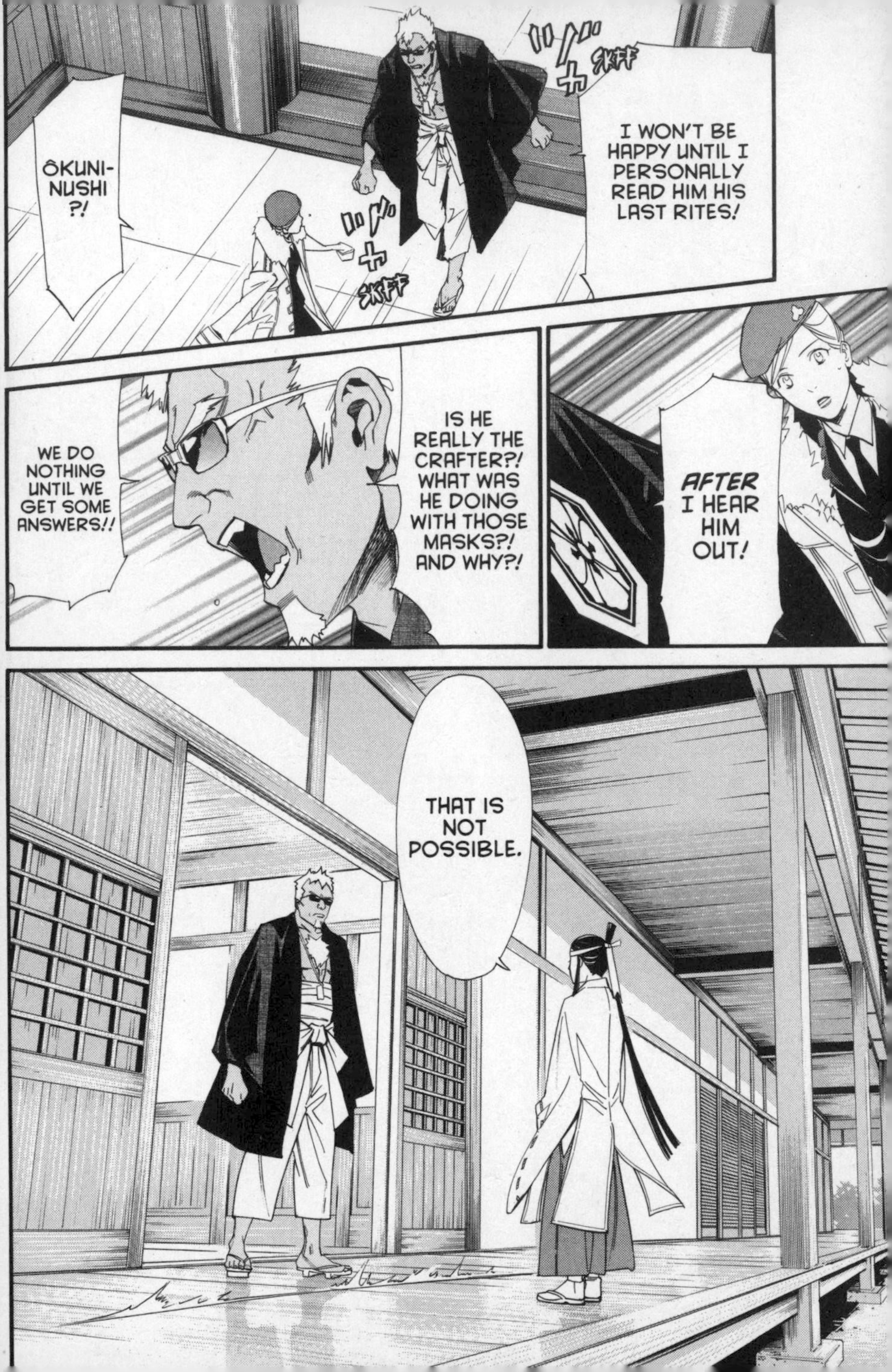
SKFF
I WON'T BE HAPPY UNTIL I PERSONALLY READ HIM HIS LAST RITES!
SKFF
ÔKUNI-NUSHI?!
AFTER I HEAR HIM OUT!
IS HE REALLY THE CRAFTER?! WHAT WAS HE DOING WITH THOSE MASKS?! AND WHY?!
WE DO NOTHING UNTIL WE GET SOME ANSWERS!!
THAT IS NOT POSSIBLE.

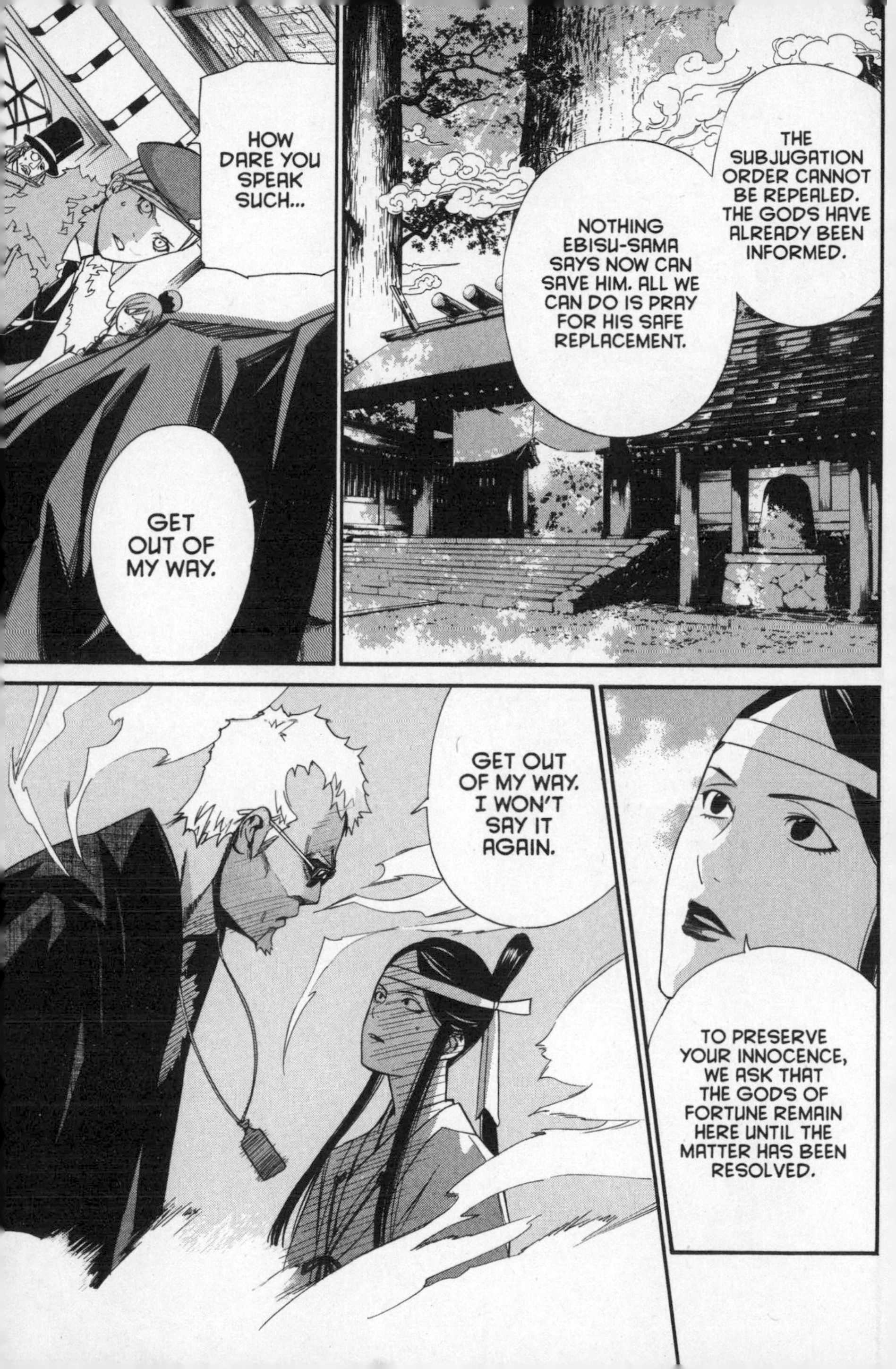
THE SUBJUGATION ORDER CANNOT BE REPEALED. THE GODS HAVE ALREADY BEEN INFORMED.
NOTHING EBISU-SAMA SAYS NOW CAN SAVE HIM. ALL WE CAN DO IS PRAY FOR HIS SAFE REPLACEMENT.
HOW DARE YOU SPEAK SUCH...
GET OUT OF MY WAY.
TO PRESERVE YOUR INNOCENCE, WE ASK THAT THE GODS OF FORTUNE REMAIN HERE UNTIL THE MATTER HAS BEEN RESOLVED.
GET OUT OF MY WAY. I WON'T SAY IT AGAIN.

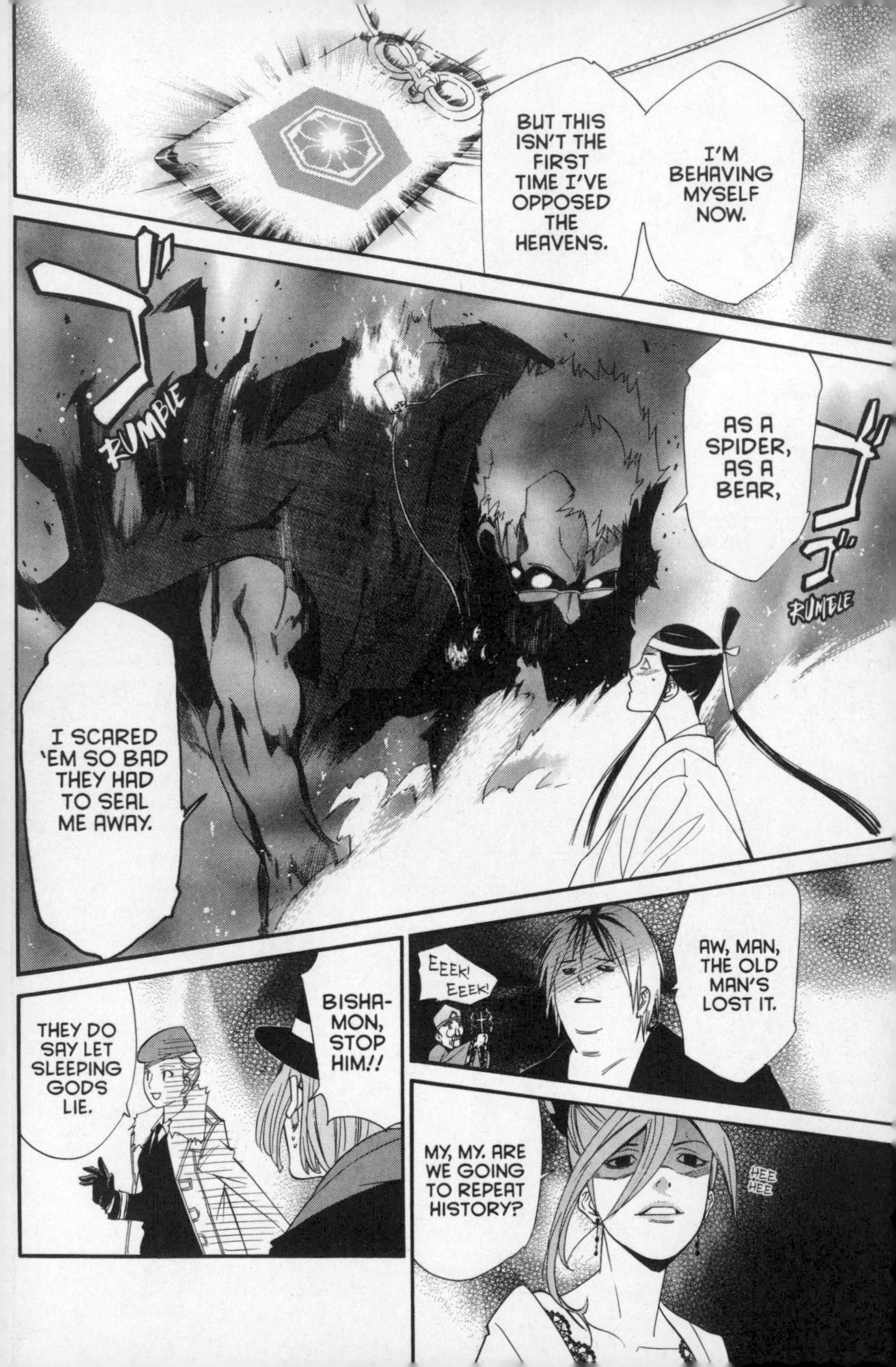
I'M BEHAVING MYSELF NOW.
BUT THIS ISN'T THE FIRST TIME I'VE OPPOSED THE HEAVENS.
AS A SPIDER, AS A BEAR,
RUMBLE
RUMBLE
I SCARED 'EM SO BAD THEY HAD TO SEAL ME AWAY.
AW, MAN, THE OLD MAN'S LOST IT.
EEEK! EEEK!
MY, MY. ARE WE GOING TO REPEAT HISTORY?
HEE HEE
BISHAMON, STOP HIM!!
THEY DO SAY LET SLEEPING GODS LIE.

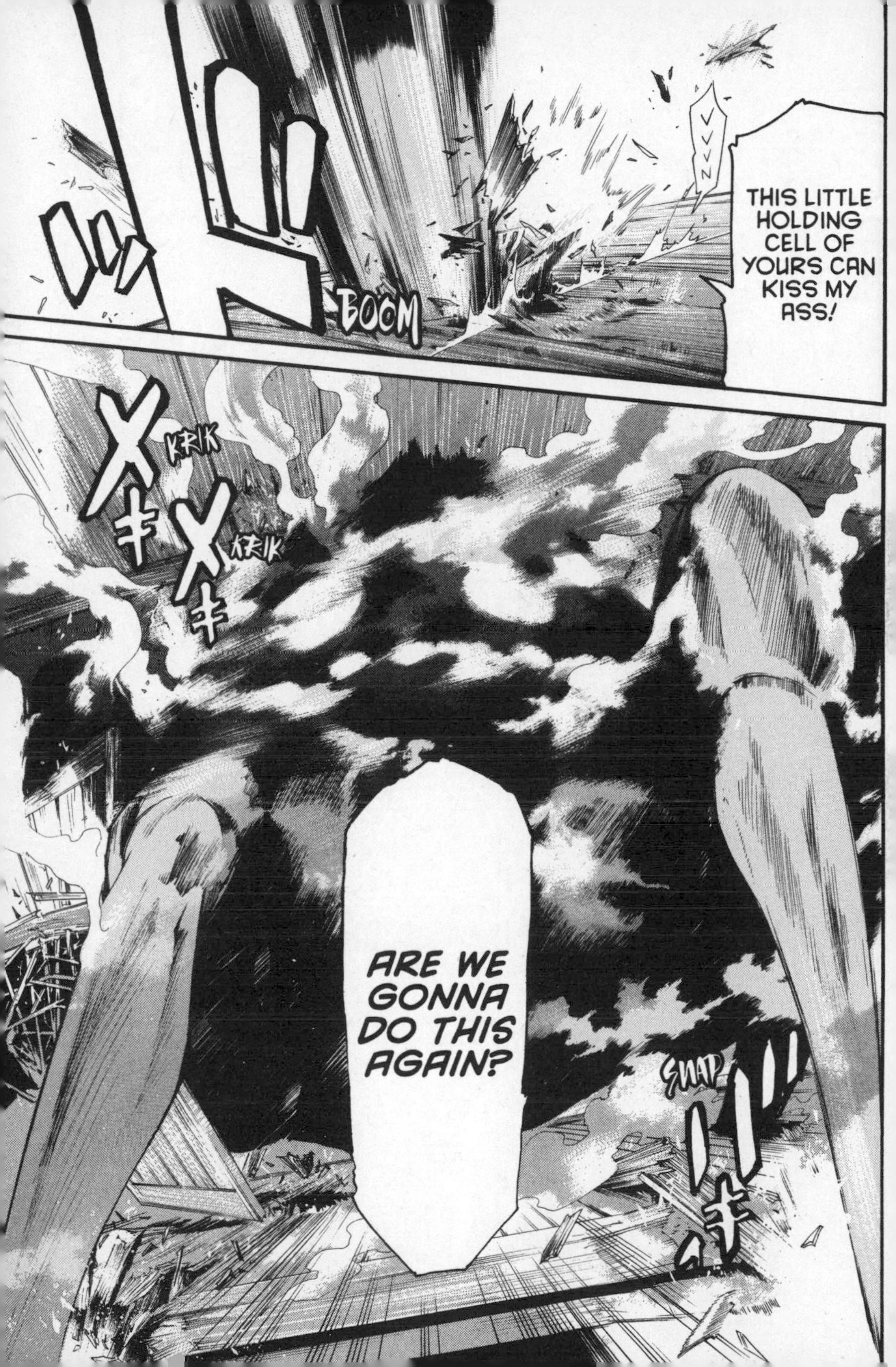
THIS LITTLE HOLDING CELL OF YOURS CAN KISS MY ASS!
VVVN
BOOM
ARE WE GONNA DO THIS AGAIN?
SNAP
KRIK
KRIK

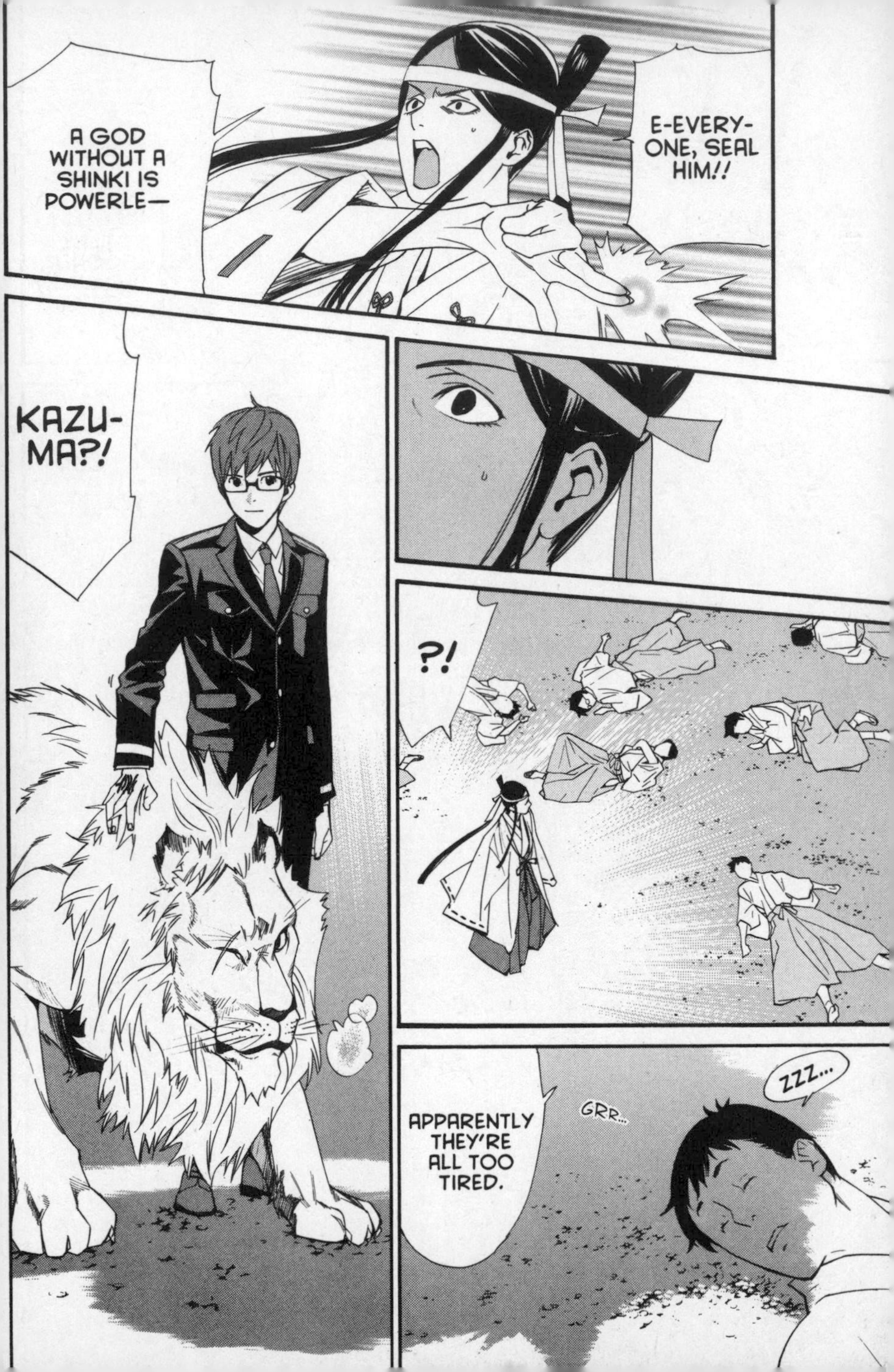
E-EVERY-ONE, SEAL HIM!!
A GOD WITHOUT A SHINKI IS POWERLE—
?!
ZZZ...
GRR...
APPARENTLY THEY'RE ALL TOO TIRED.
KAZU-MA?!

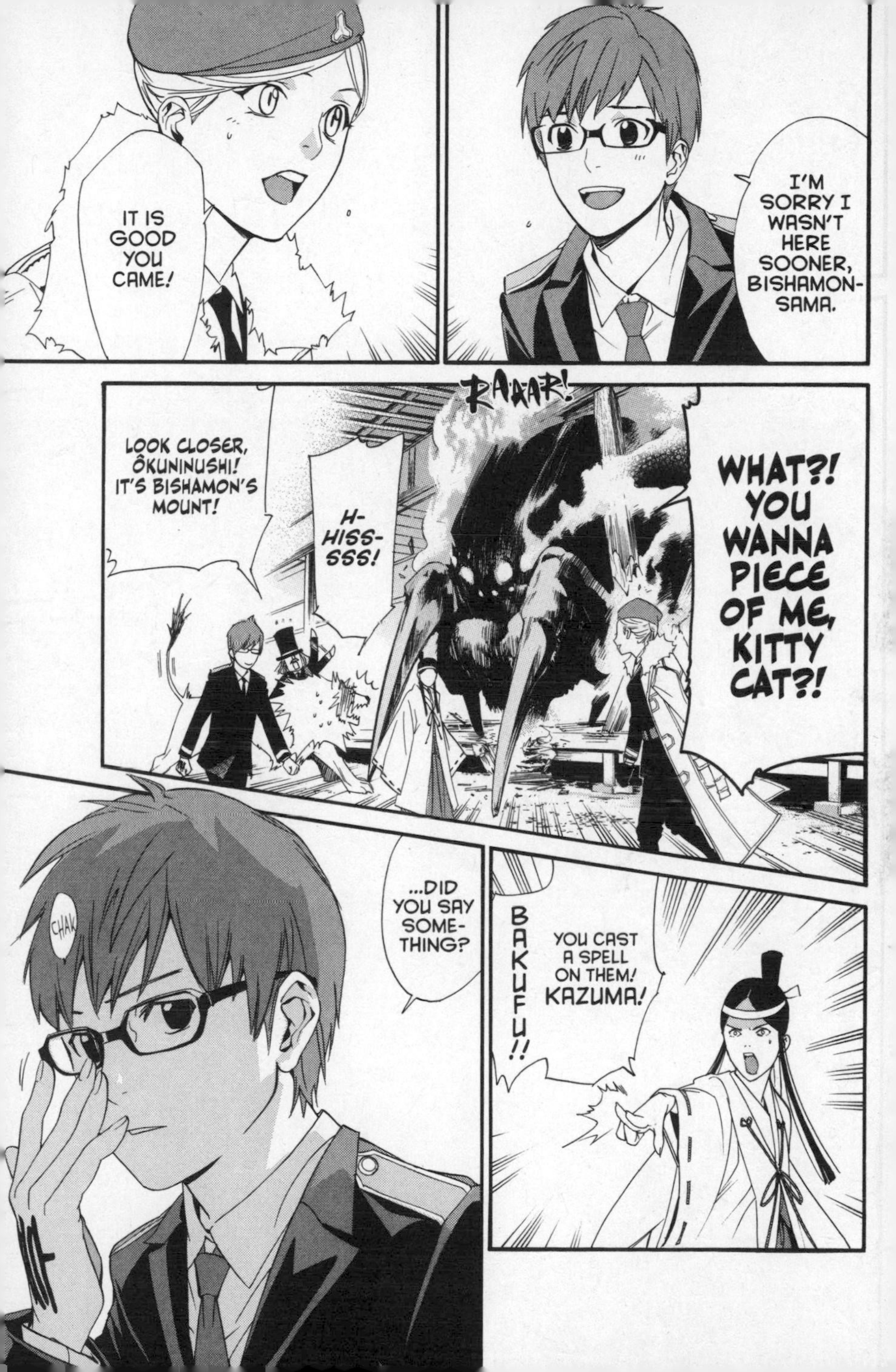
I'M SORRY I WASN'T HERE SOONER, BISHAMON-SAMA.
IT IS GOOD YOU CAME!
RAAAR!
WHAT?! YOU WANNA PIECE OF ME, KITTY CAT?!
H-HISS-SSS!
LOOK CLOSER, ÔKUNINUSHI! IT'S BISHAMON'S MOUNT!
BAKUFU!!
YOU CAST A SPELL ON THEM! KAZUMA!
...DID YOU SAY SOME-THING?
CHAK

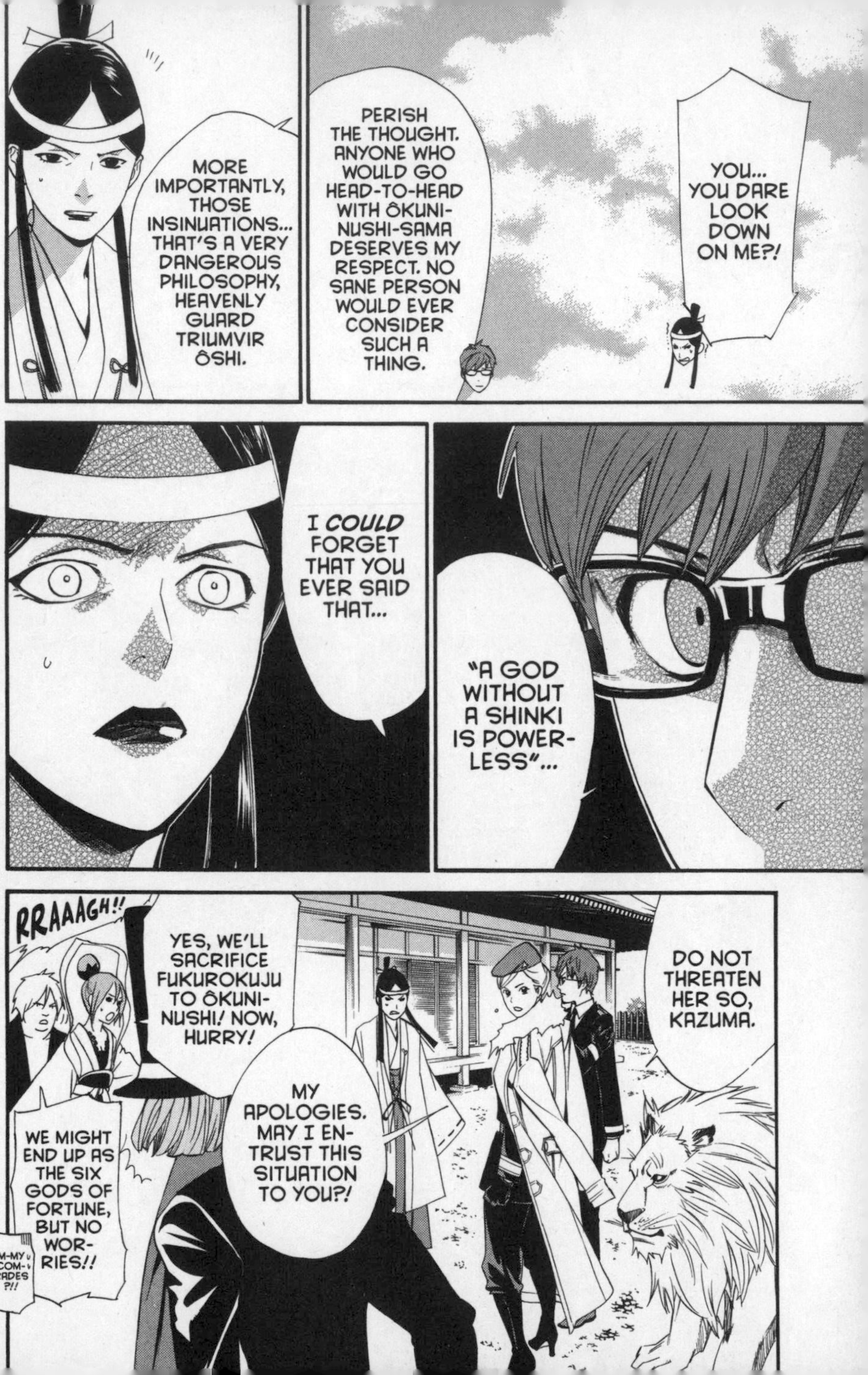
YOU... YOU DARE LOOK DOWN ON ME?!
PERISH THE THOUGHT. ANYONE WHO WOULD GO HEAD-TO-HEAD WITH ÔKUNI-NUSHI-SAMA DESERVES MY RESPECT. NO SANE PERSON WOULD EVER CONSIDER SUCH A THING.
MORE IMPORTANTLY, THOSE INSINUATIONS... THAT'S A VERY DANGEROUS PHILOSOPHY, HEAVENLY GUARD TRIUMVIR ÔSHI.
"A GOD WITHOUT A SHINKI IS POWER-LESS"...
I *COULD* FORGET THAT YOU EVER SAID THAT...
DO NOT THREATEN HER SO, KAZUMA.
YES, WE'LL SACRIFICE FUKUROKUJU TO ÔKUNI-NUSHI! NOW, HURRY!
RRAAAGH!!
MY APOLOGIES. MAY I EN-TRUST THIS SITUATION TO YOU?!
WE MIGHT END UP AS THE SIX GODS OF FORTUNE, BUT NO WOR-RIES!!
M-MY COM-RADES?!!

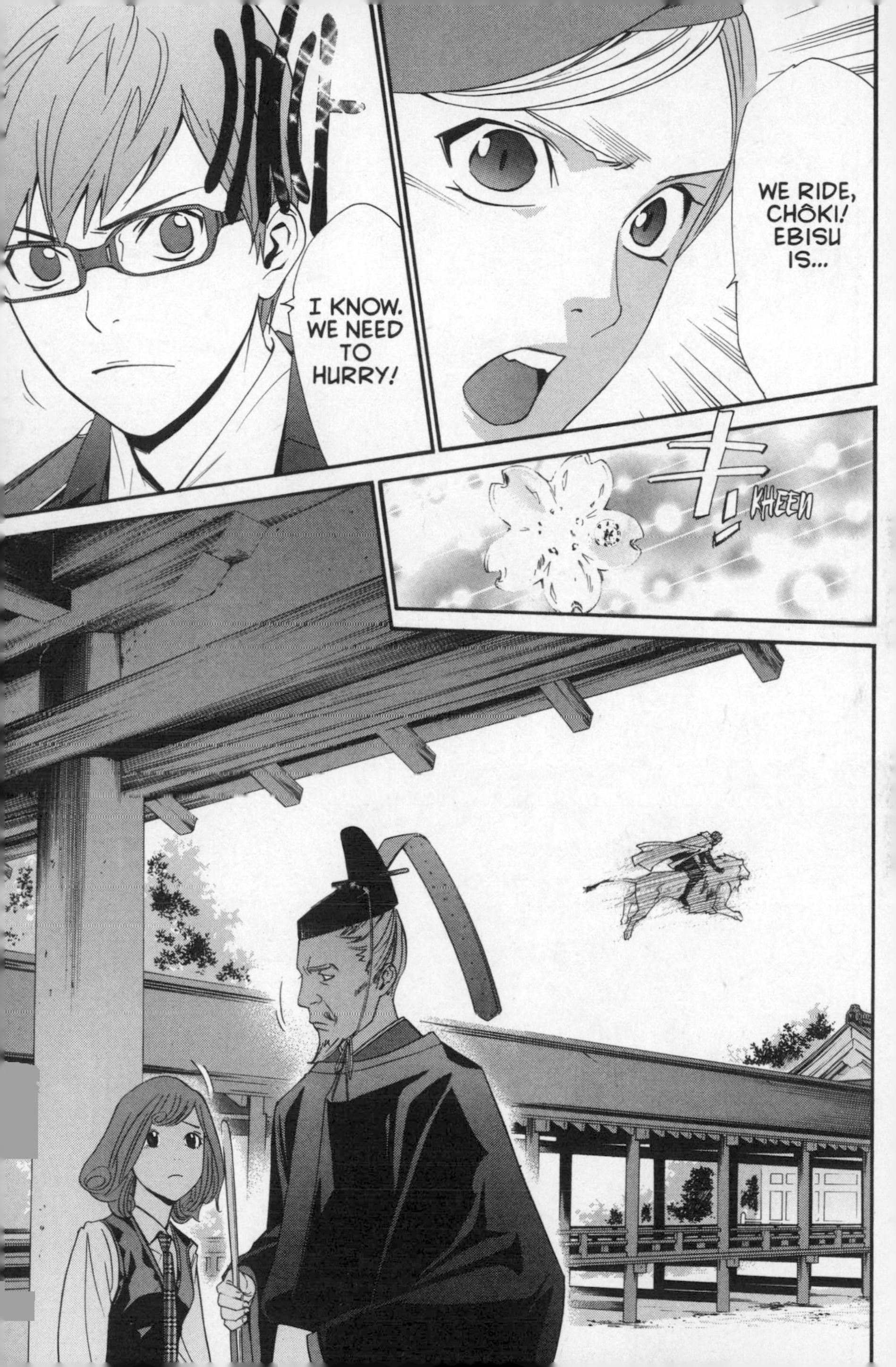
WE RIDE, CHÔKI! EBISU IS...
I KNOW. WE NEED TO HURRY!
KHEEN

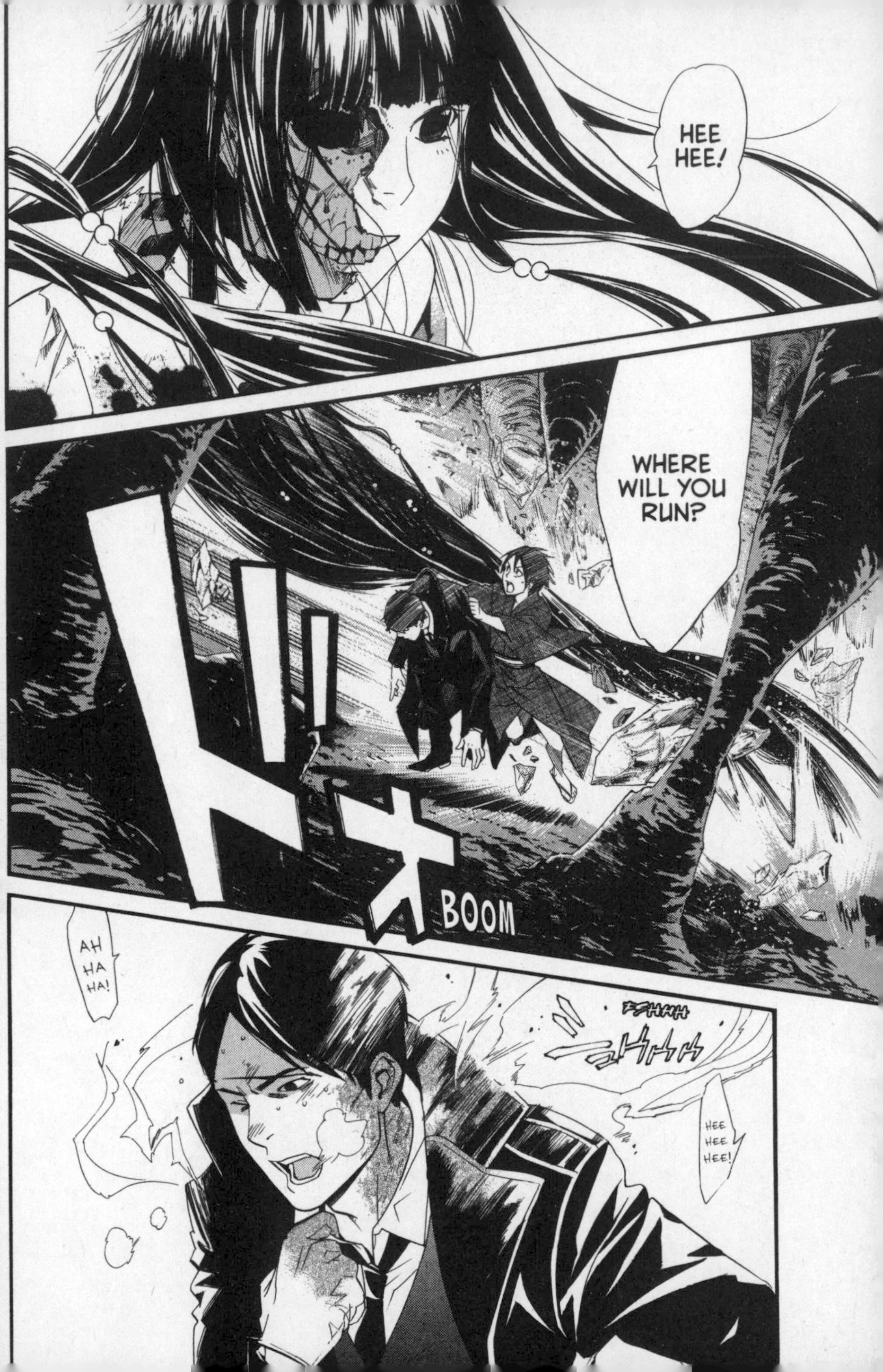
HEE HEE!
WHERE WILL YOU RUN?
BOOM
FSHHH
HEE HEE HEE!
AH HA HA!

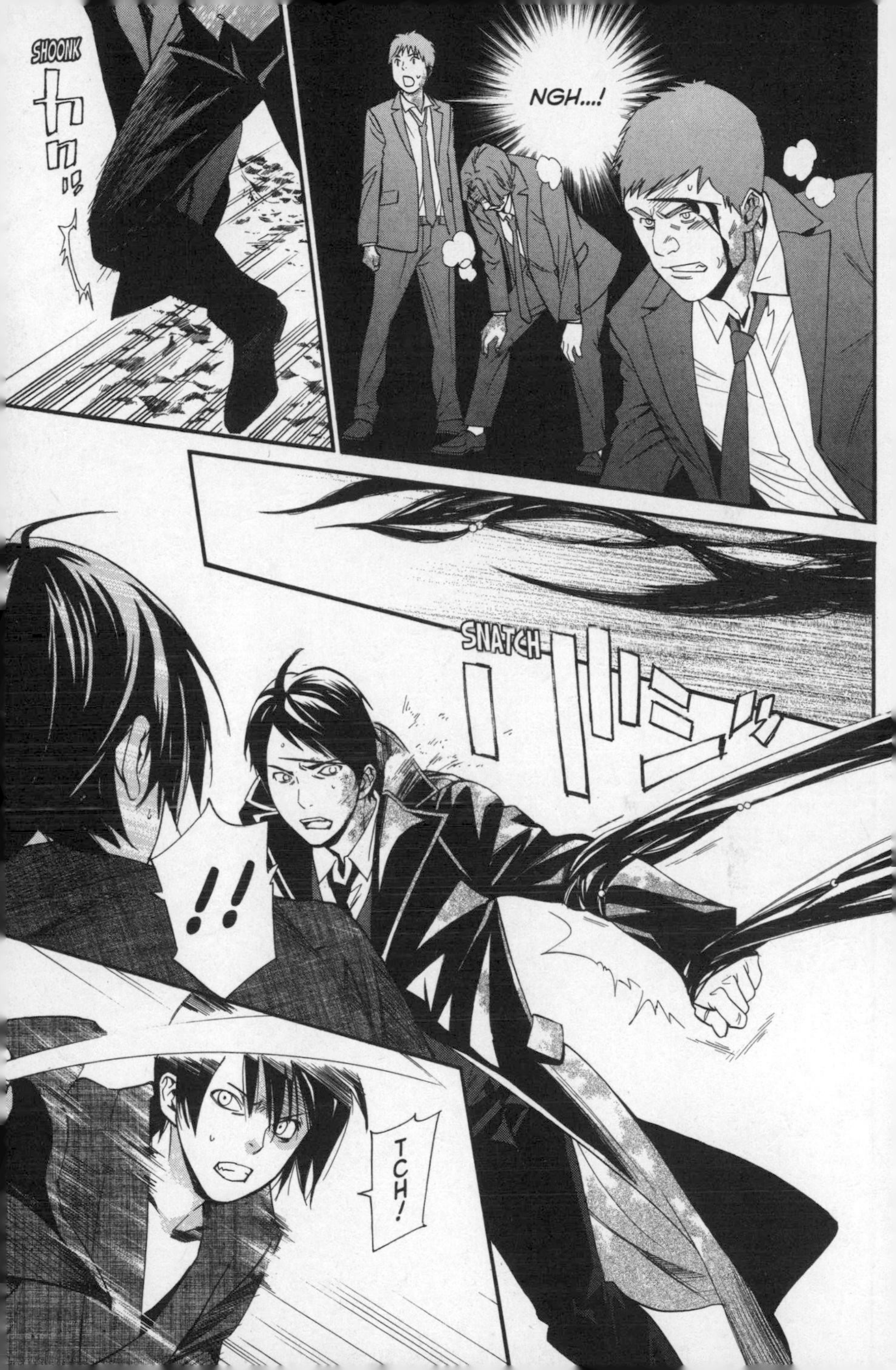
NGH...!
SHOONK
SNATCH
!!
TCH!

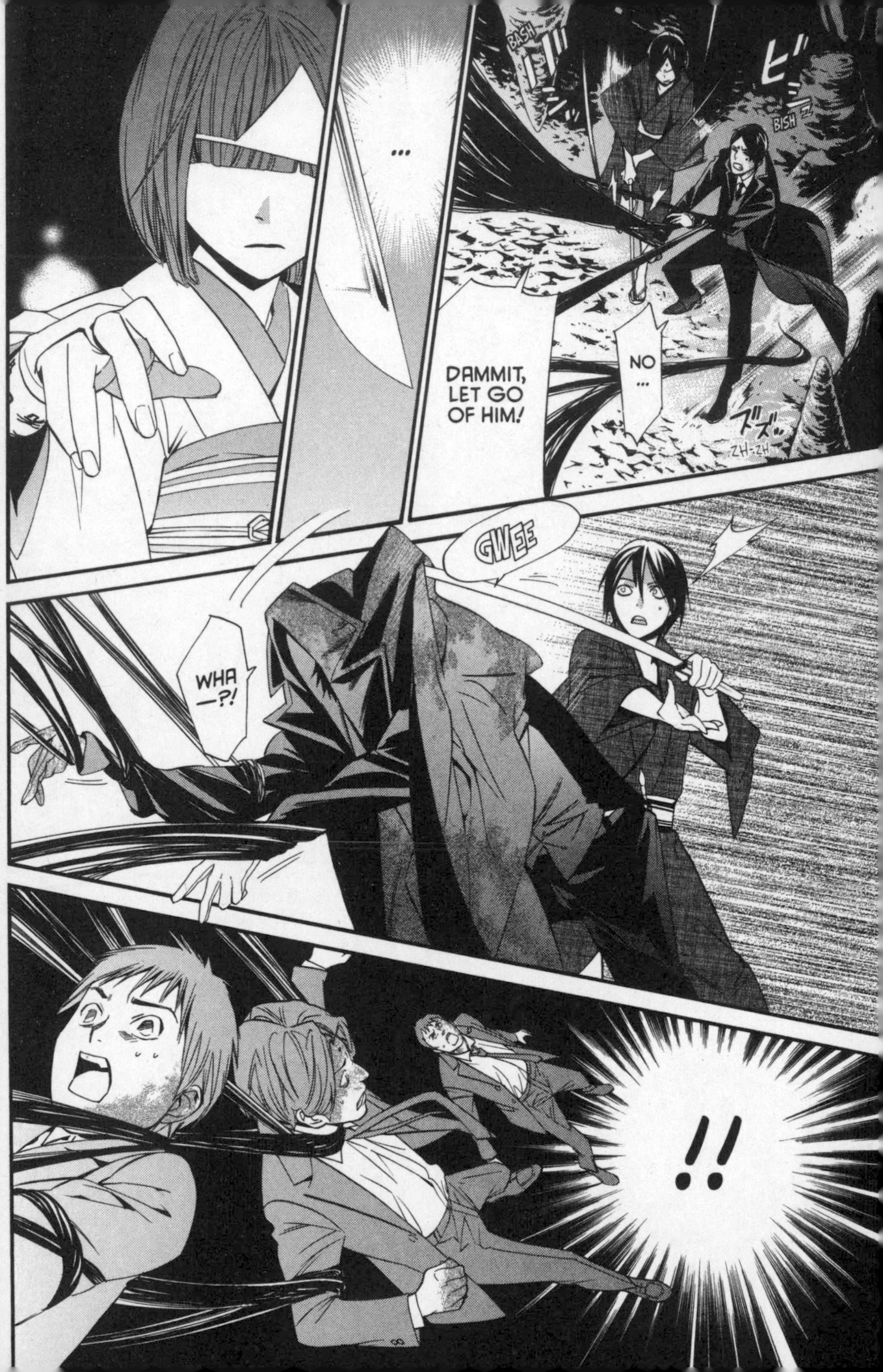
BASH
ビ
BISH
NO ...
ズズッ
ZH-ZH
...
DAMMIT, LET GO OF HIM!
GWEE
WHA—?!
!!

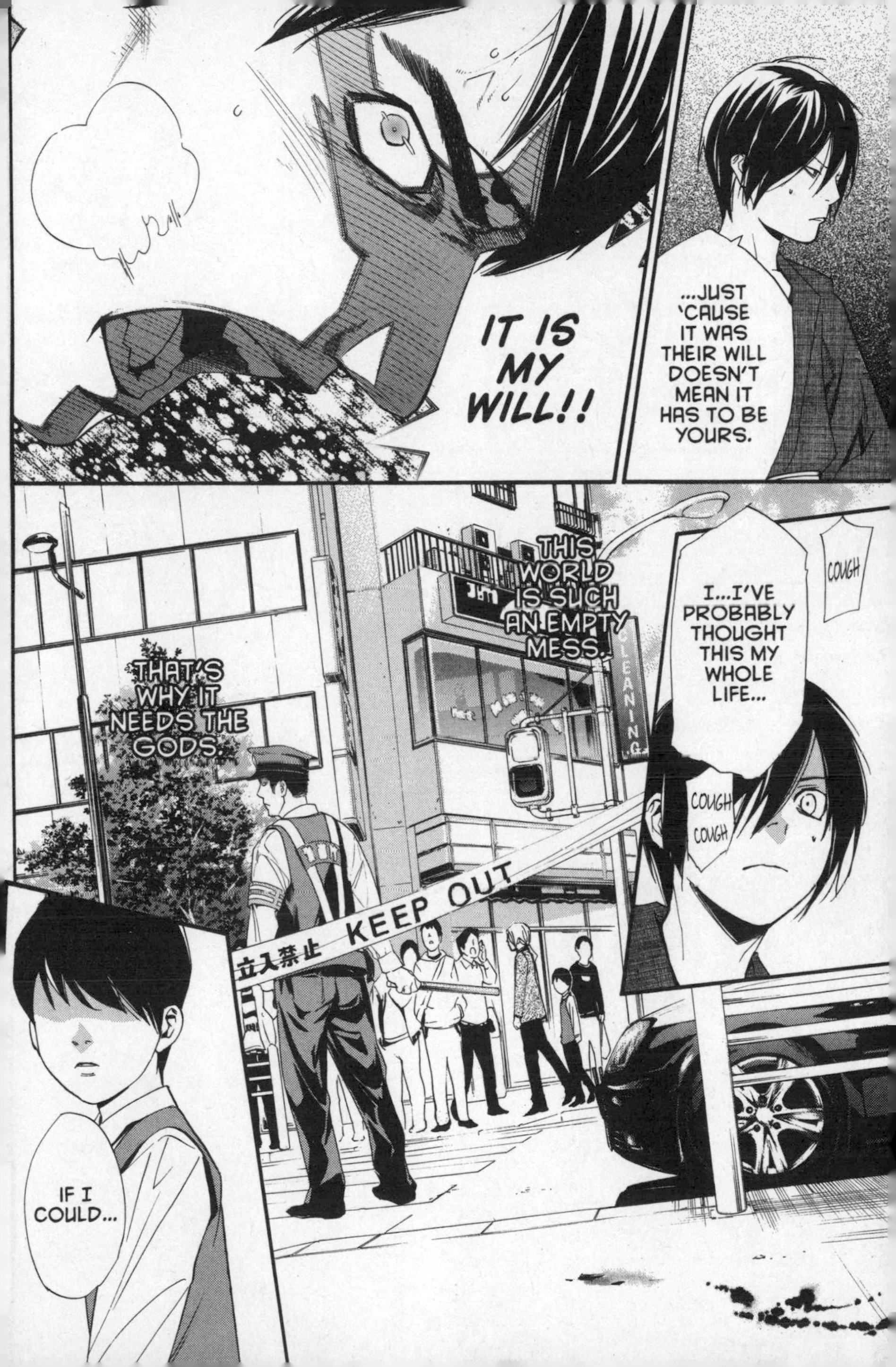
...JUST 'CAUSE IT WAS THEIR WILL DOESN'T MEAN IT HAS TO BE YOURS.
IT IS MY WILL!!
COUGH
I...I'VE PROBABLY THOUGHT THIS MY WHOLE LIFE...
COUGH
COUGH
CLEANING
THIS WORLD IS SUCH AN EMPTY MESS.
THAT'S WHY IT NEEDS THE GODS.
KEEP OUT
立入禁止
IF I COULD...

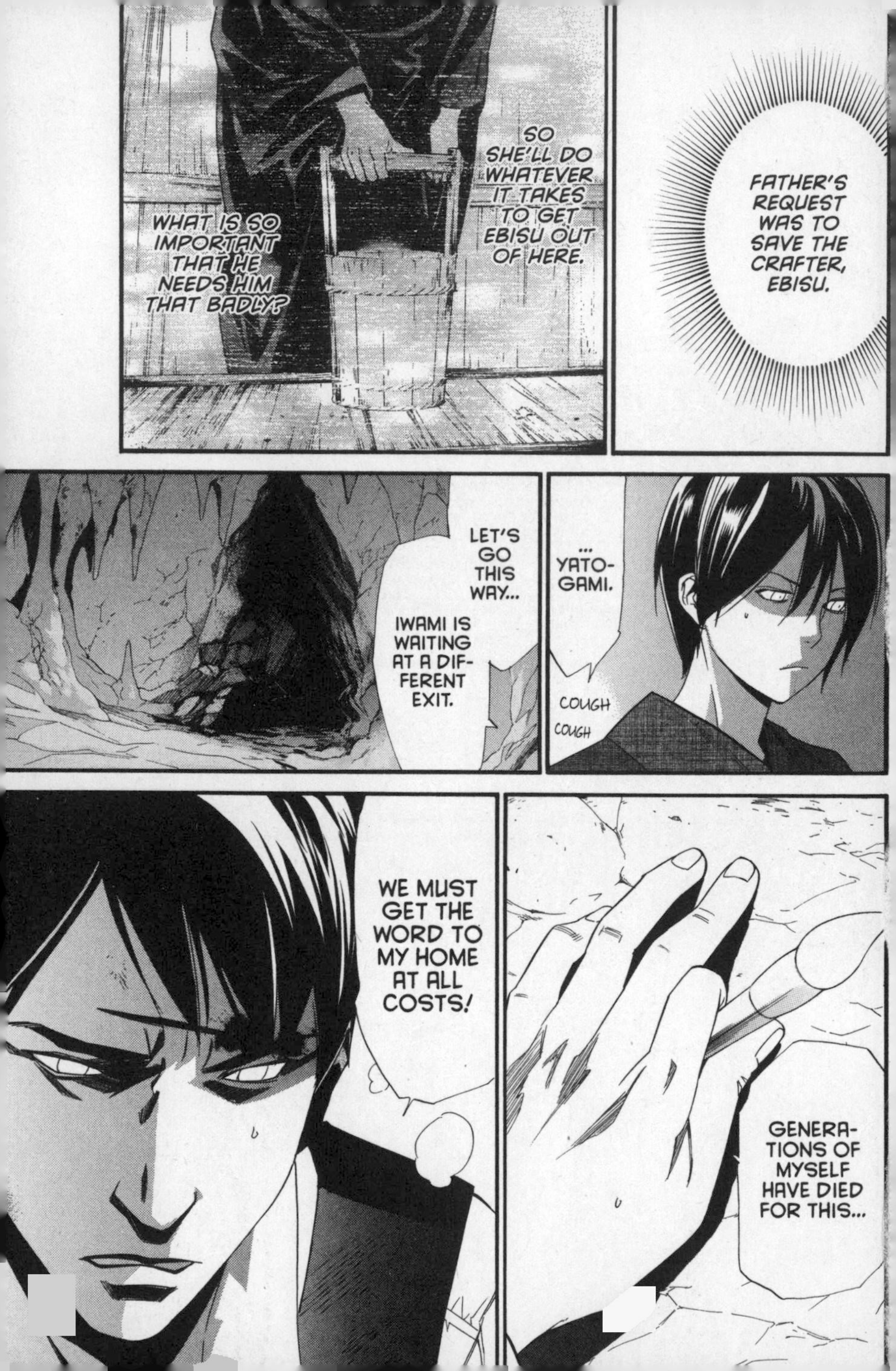
FATHER'S REQUEST WAS TO SAVE THE CRAFTER, EBISU.
SO SHE'LL DO WHATEVER IT TAKES TO GET EBISU OUT OF HERE.
WHAT IS SO IMPORTANT THAT HE NEEDS HIM THAT BADLY?
... YATO-GAMI.
COUGH
COUGH
LET'S GO THIS WAY...
IWAMI IS WAITING AT A DIF-FERENT EXIT.
GENERA-TIONS OF MYSELF HAVE DIED FOR THIS...
WE MUST GET THE WORD TO MY HOME AT ALL COSTS!

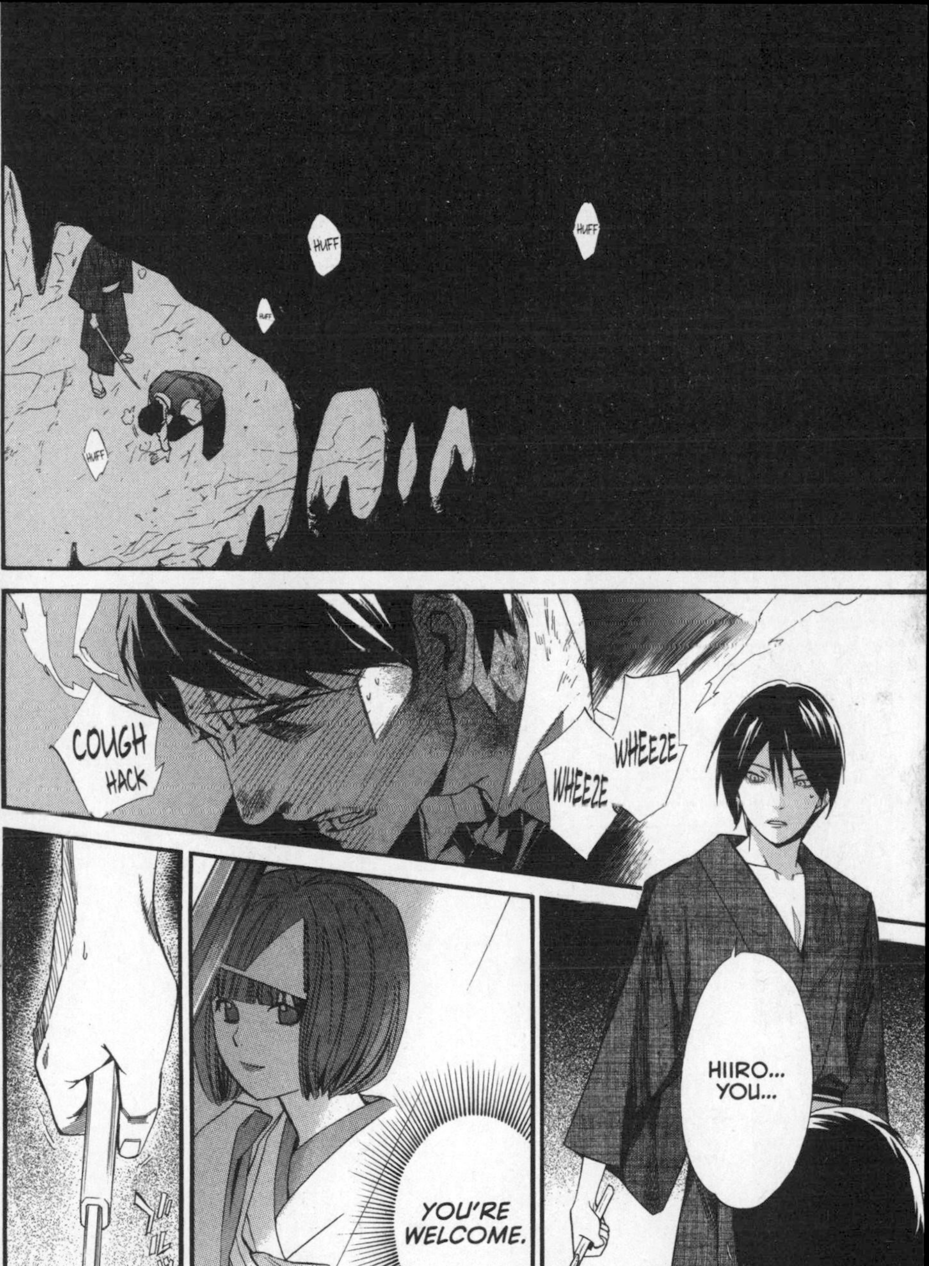
HUFF
HUFF
HUFF
HUFF
WHEEZE
WHEEZE
COUGH
HACK
HIIRO... YOU...
COUGH
COUGH
YOU'RE WELCOME.
TREMBLE

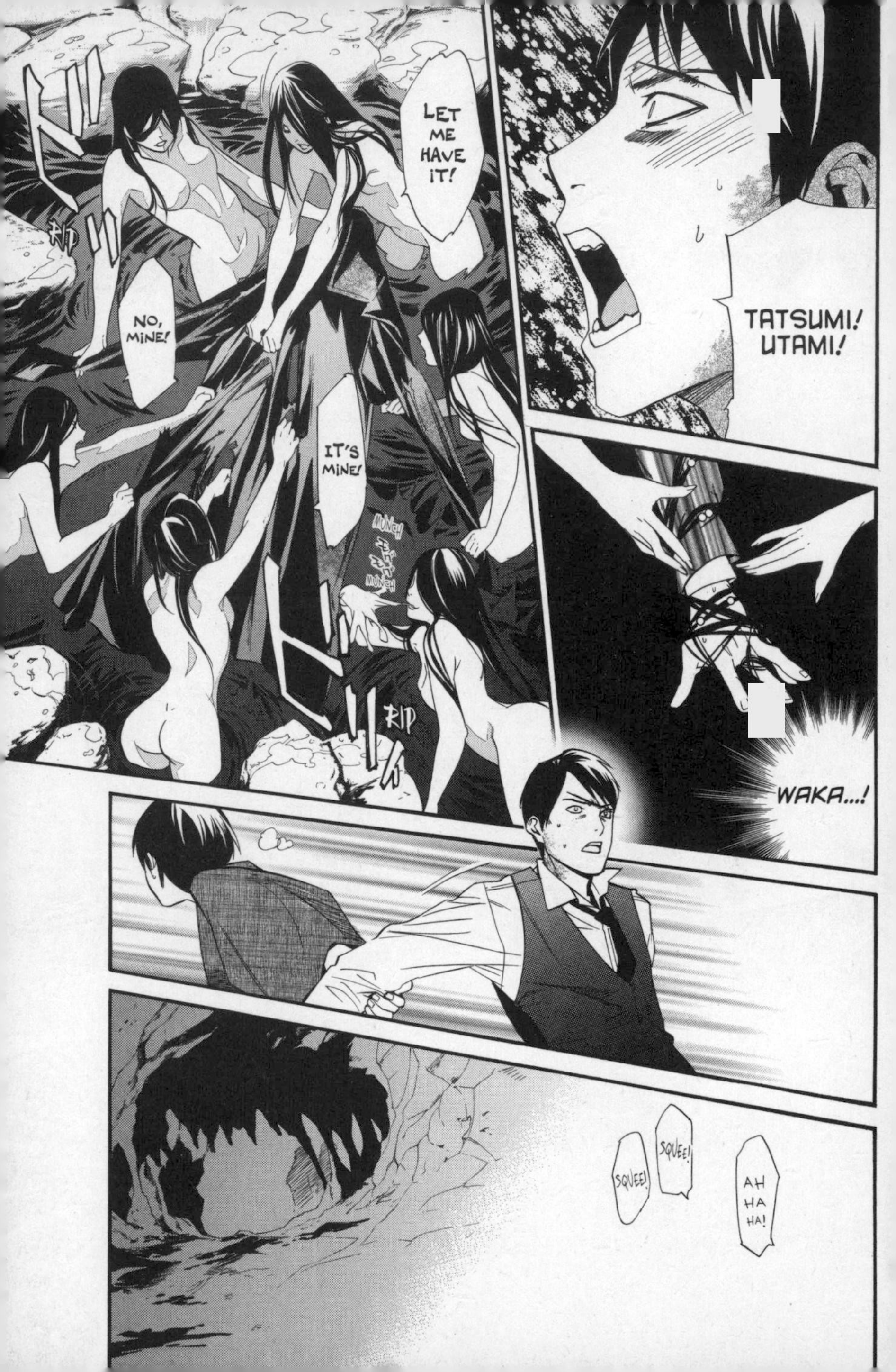
TATSUMI! UTAMI!
WAKA...!
LET ME HAVE IT!
RIP
NO, MINE!
IT'S MINE!
MUNCH MUNCH
RIP
AH HA HA!
SQUEE!
SQUEE!

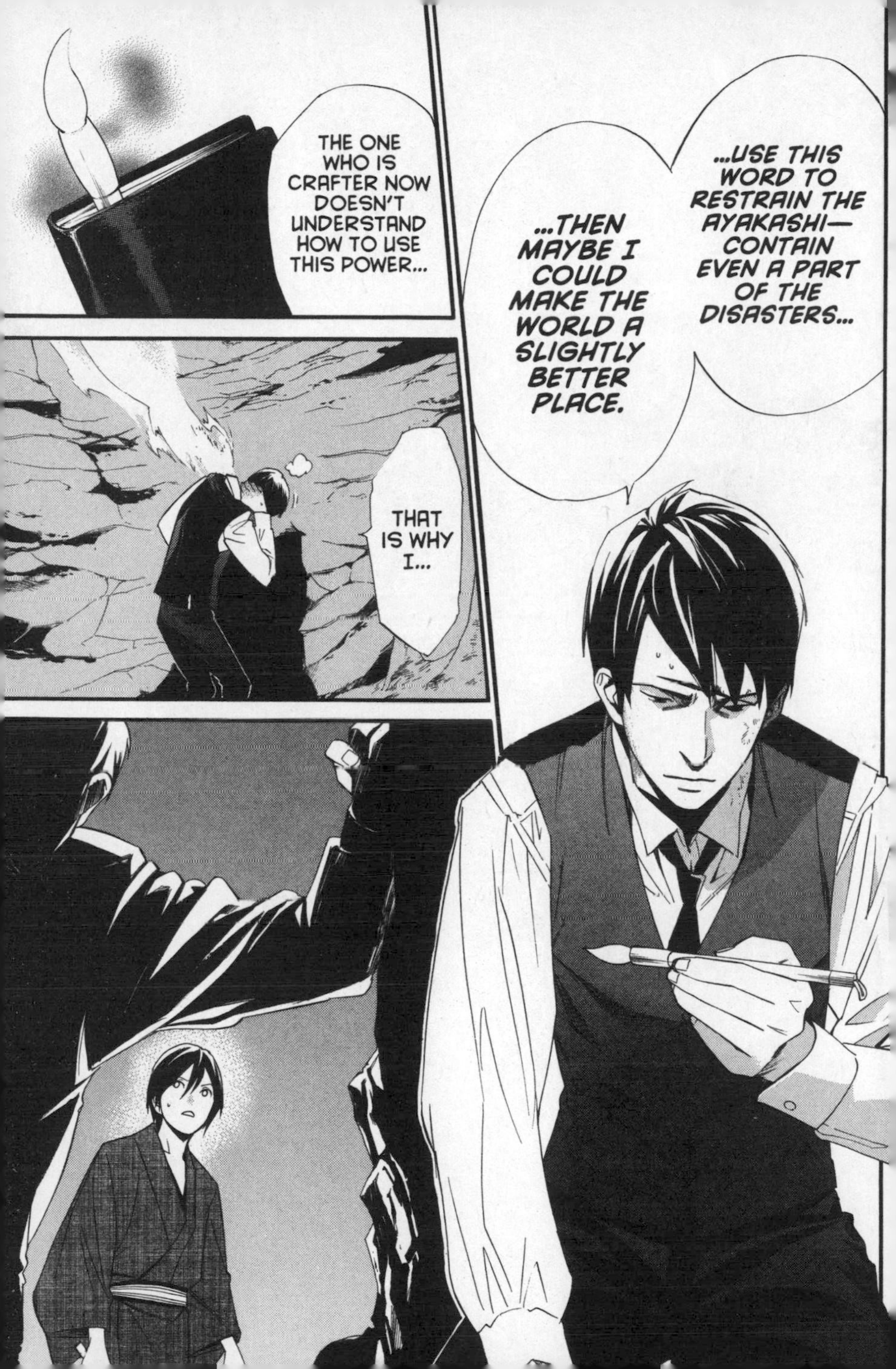
THE ONE WHO IS CRAFTER NOW DOESN'T UNDERSTAND HOW TO USE THIS POWER...
THAT IS WHY I...
...USE THIS WORD TO RESTRAIN THE AYAKASHI—CONTAIN EVEN A PART OF THE DISASTERS...
...THEN MAYBE I COULD MAKE THE WORLD A SLIGHTLY BETTER PLACE.

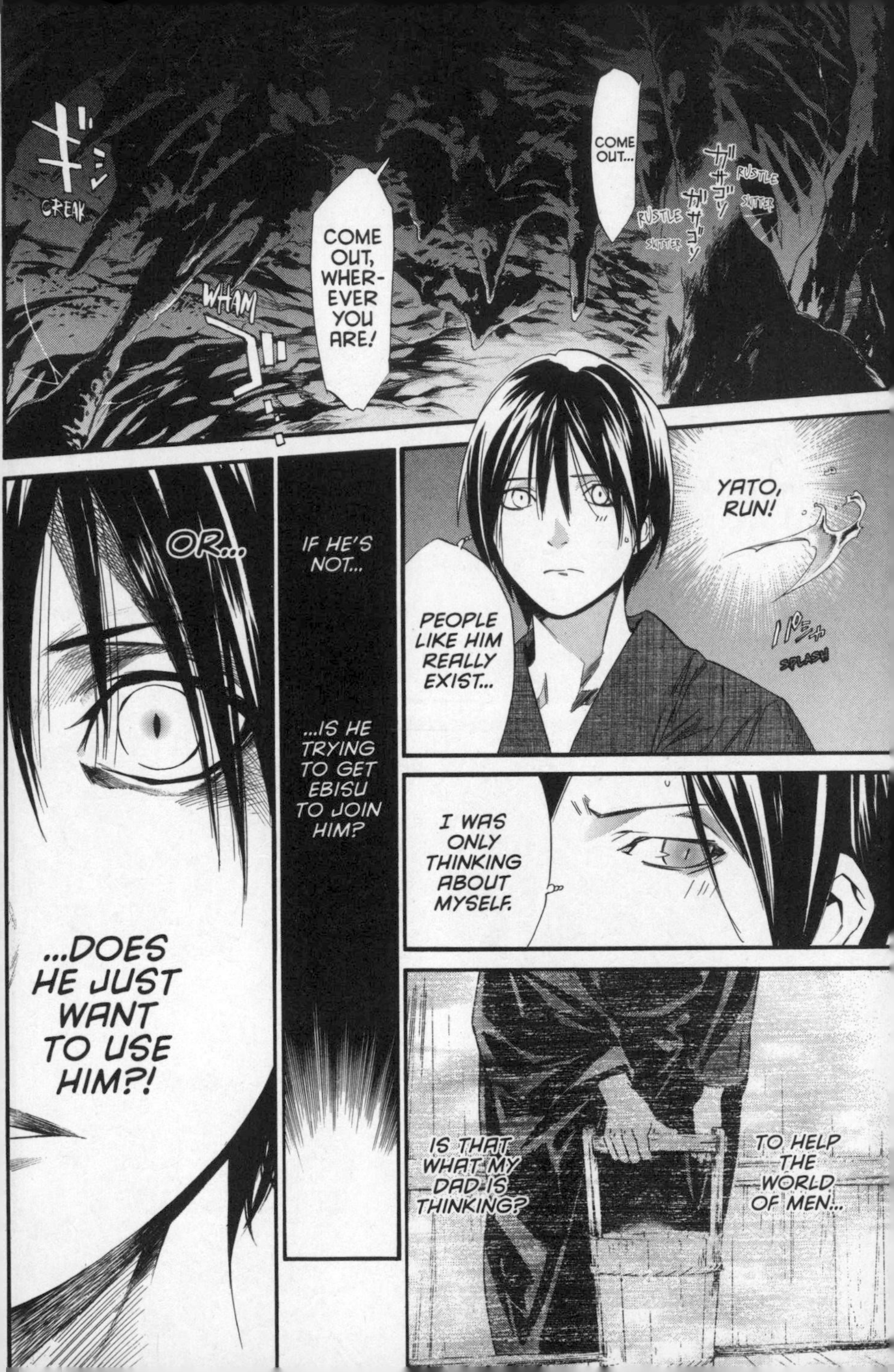
COME OUT...
RUSTLE
SKITTER
RUSTLE
SKITTER
CREAK
COME OUT, WHEREVER YOU ARE!
WHAM
YATO, RUN!
SPLASH
PEOPLE LIKE HIM REALLY EXIST...
I WAS ONLY THINKING ABOUT MYSELF.
TO HELP THE WORLD OF MEN...
IS THAT WHAT MY DAD IS THINKING?
IF HE'S NOT...
...IS HE TRYING TO GET EBISU TO JOIN HIM?
OR...
...DOES HE JUST WANT TO USE HIM?!

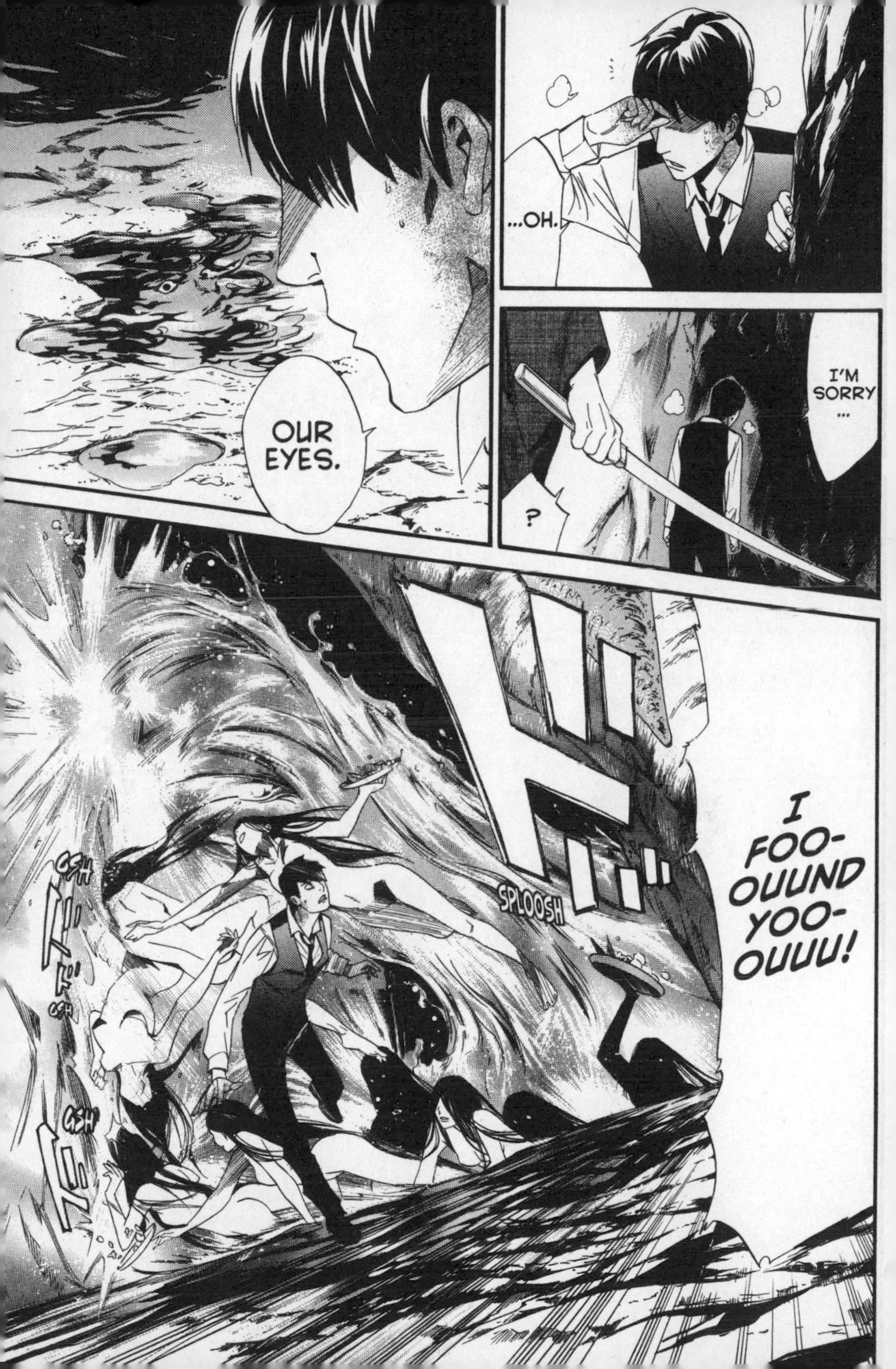
...OH.
I'M SORRY ...
?
OUR EYES.
I FOO-OUUND YOO-OUUU!
SPLOOSH
GSH
GSH
GSH

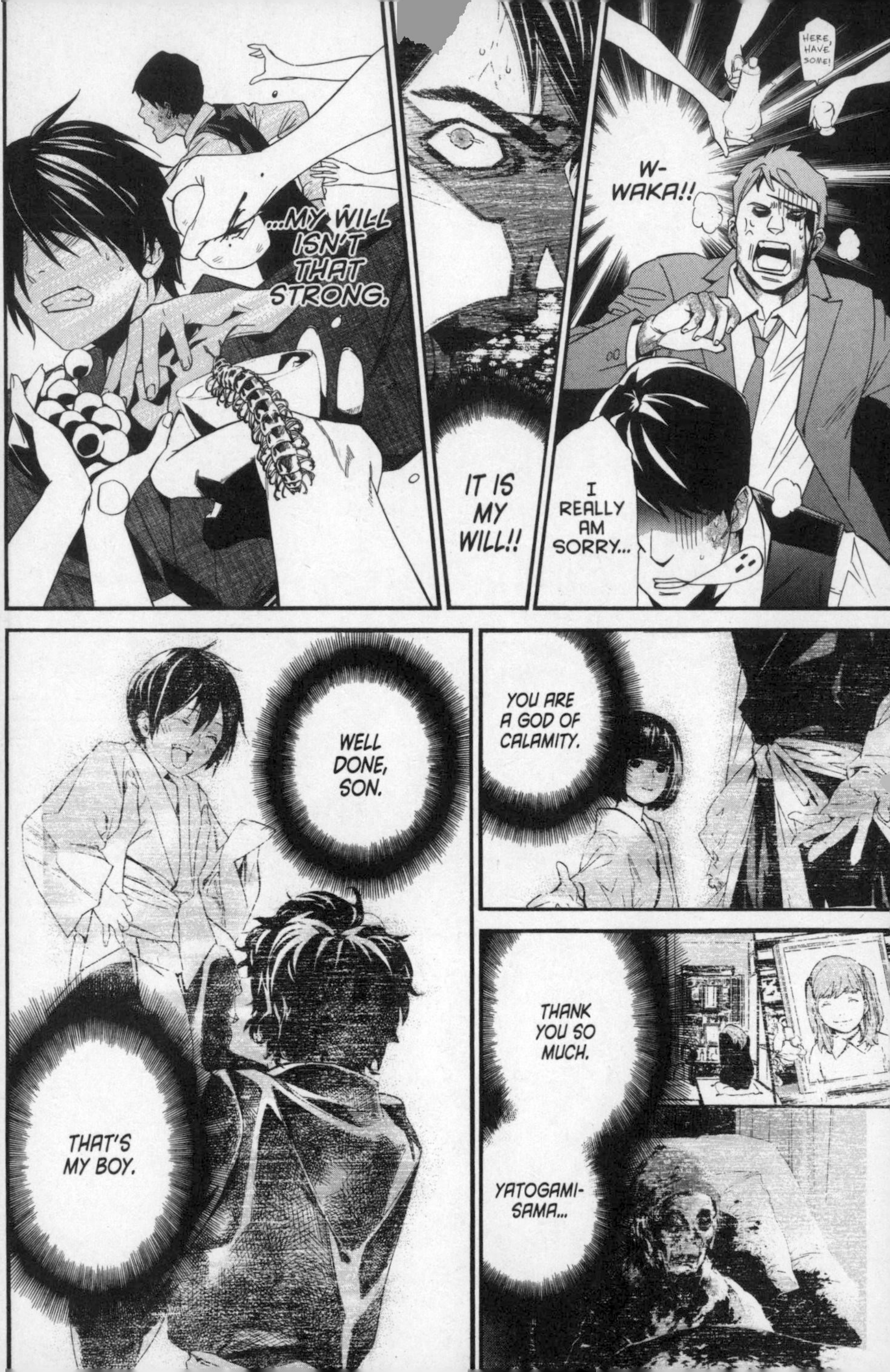
HERE, HAVE SOME!
W-WAKA!!
I REALLY AM SORRY...
IT IS MY WILL!!
...MY WILL ISN'T THAT STRONG.
YOU ARE A GOD OF CALAMITY.
THANK YOU SO MUCH.
YATOGAMI-SAMA...
WELL DONE, SON.
THAT'S MY BOY.

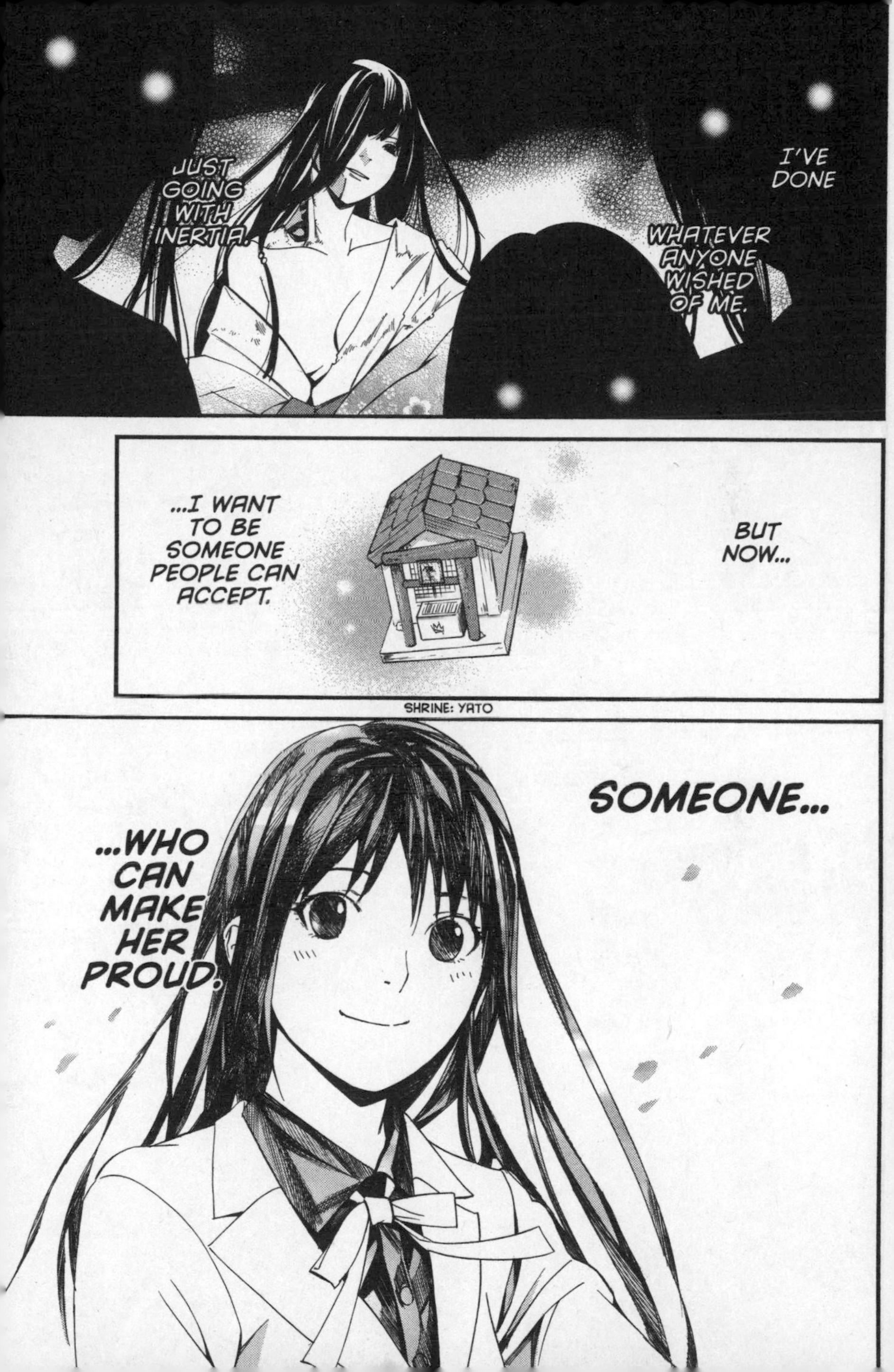
I'VE DONE
WHATEVER ANYONE WISHED OF ME.
JUST GOING WITH INERTIA.
BUT NOW...
...I WANT TO BE SOMEONE PEOPLE CAN ACCEPT.
SHRINE: YATO
SOMEONE...
...WHO CAN MAKE HER PROUD.

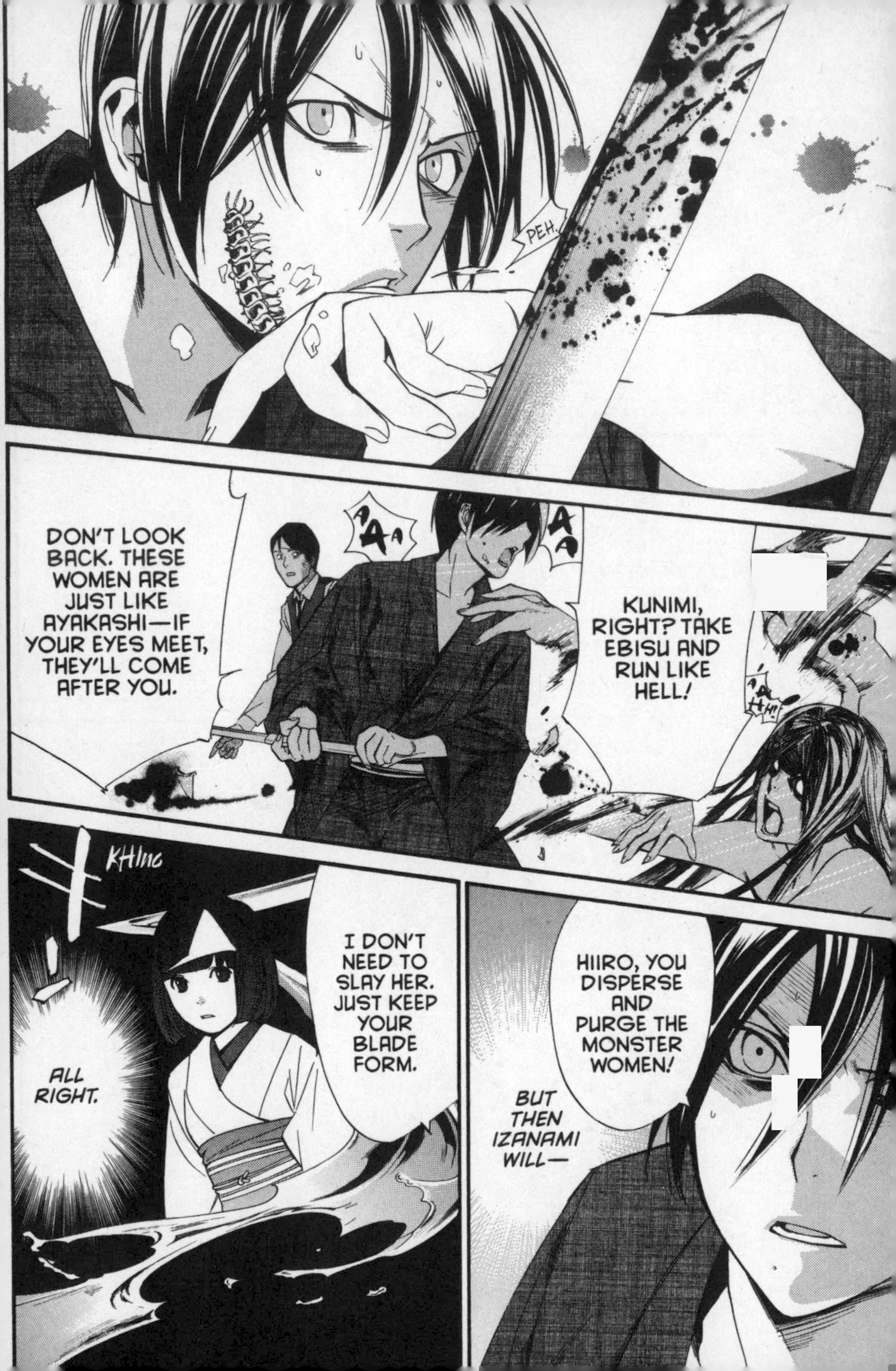
PEH.
KUNIMI, RIGHT? TAKE EBISU AND RUN LIKE HELL!
DON'T LOOK BACK. THESE WOMEN ARE JUST LIKE AYAKASHI—IF YOUR EYES MEET, THEY'LL COME AFTER YOU.
HIIRO, YOU DISPERSE AND PURGE THE MONSTER WOMEN!
BUT THEN IZANAMI WILL—
KHING
I DON'T NEED TO SLAY HER. JUST KEEP YOUR BLADE FORM.
ALL RIGHT.

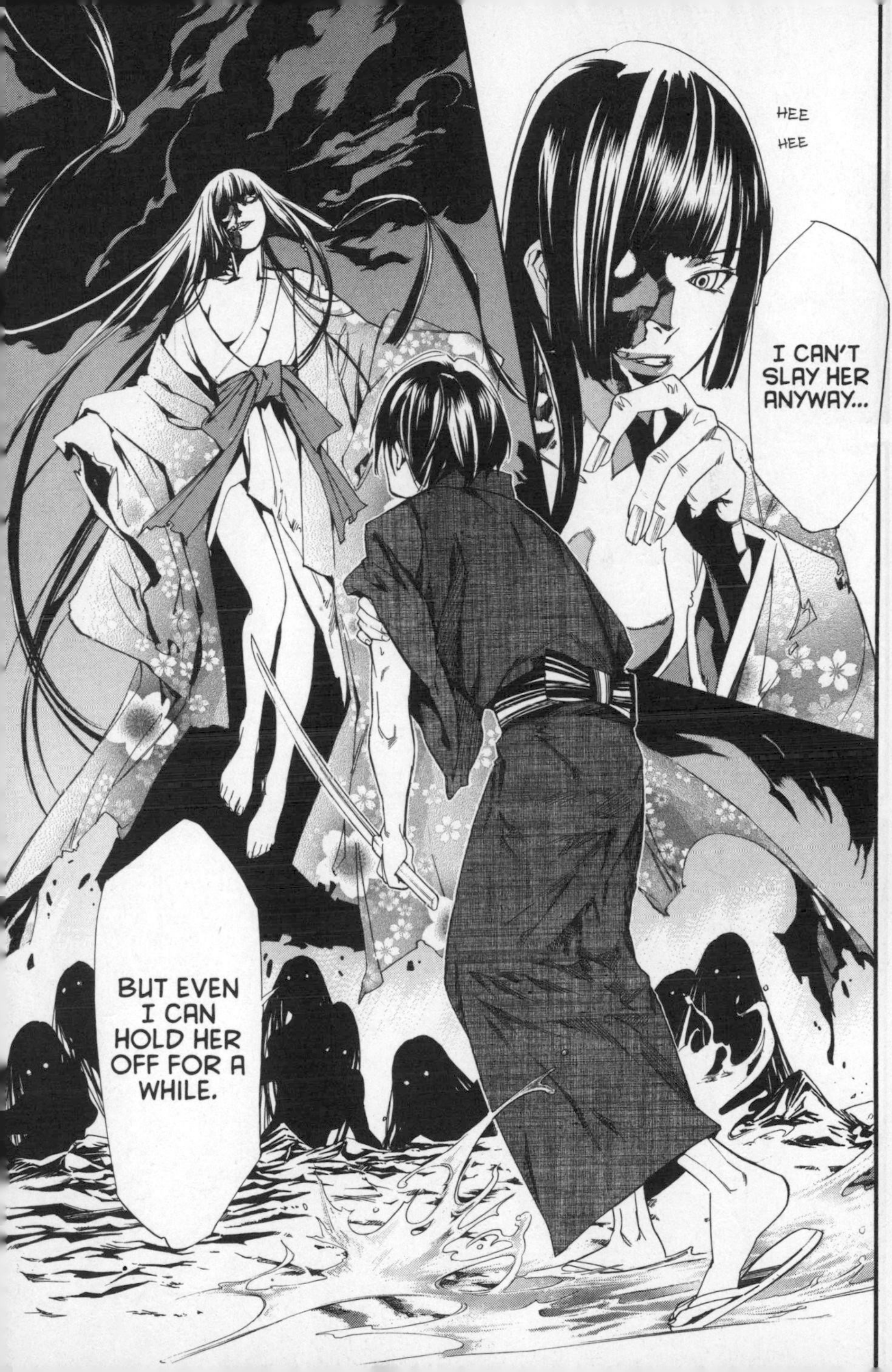
HEE
HEE
I CAN'T SLAY HER ANYWAY...
BUT EVEN I CAN HOLD HER OFF FOR A WHILE.

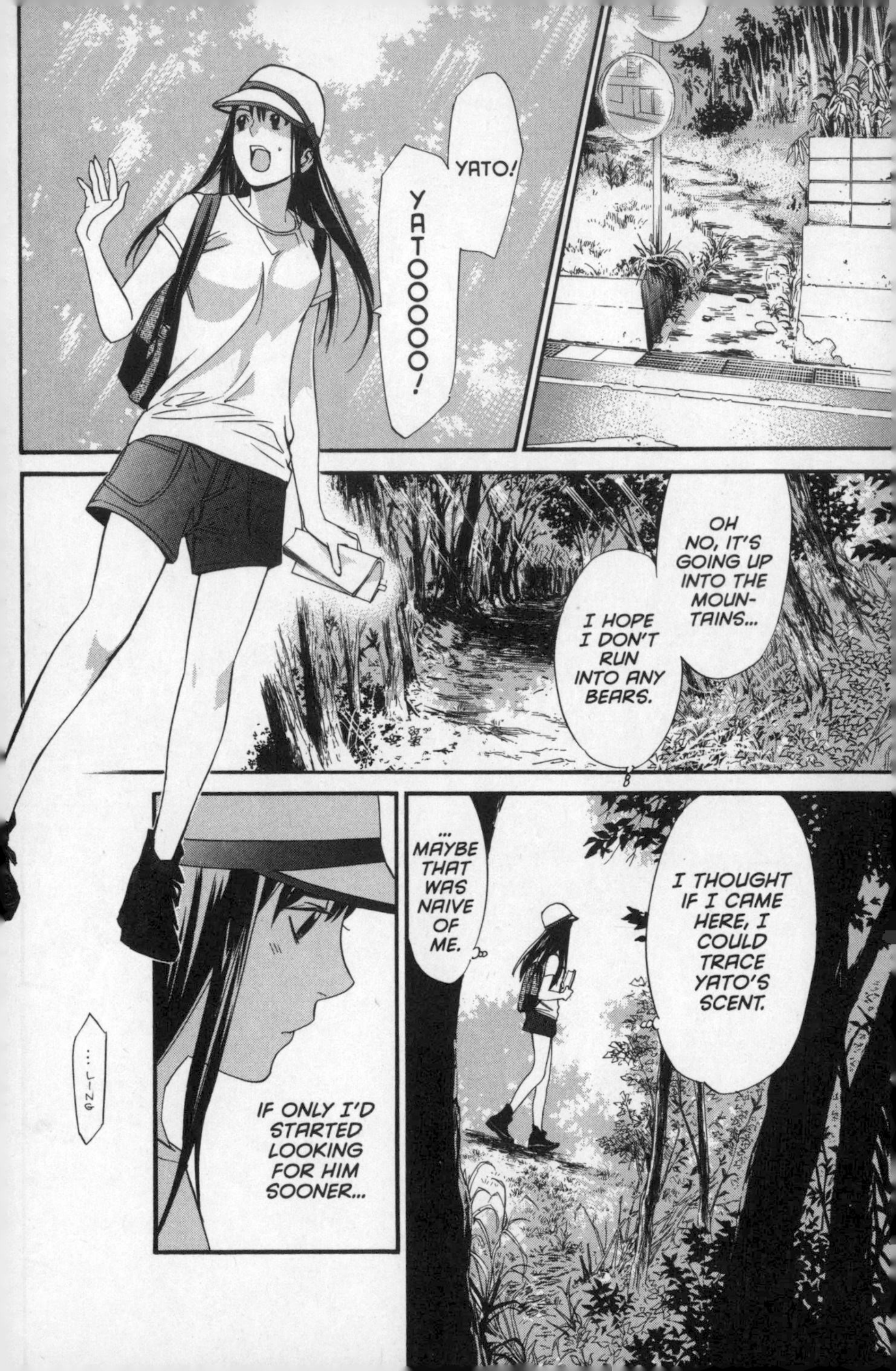
YATO!
YATOOOOO!
OH NO, IT'S GOING UP INTO THE MOUNTAINS...
I HOPE I DON'T RUN INTO ANY BEARS.
I THOUGHT IF I CAME HERE, I COULD TRACE YATO'S SCENT.
...MAYBE THAT WAS NAIVE OF ME.
...LING
IF ONLY I'D STARTED LOOKING FOR HIM SOONER...

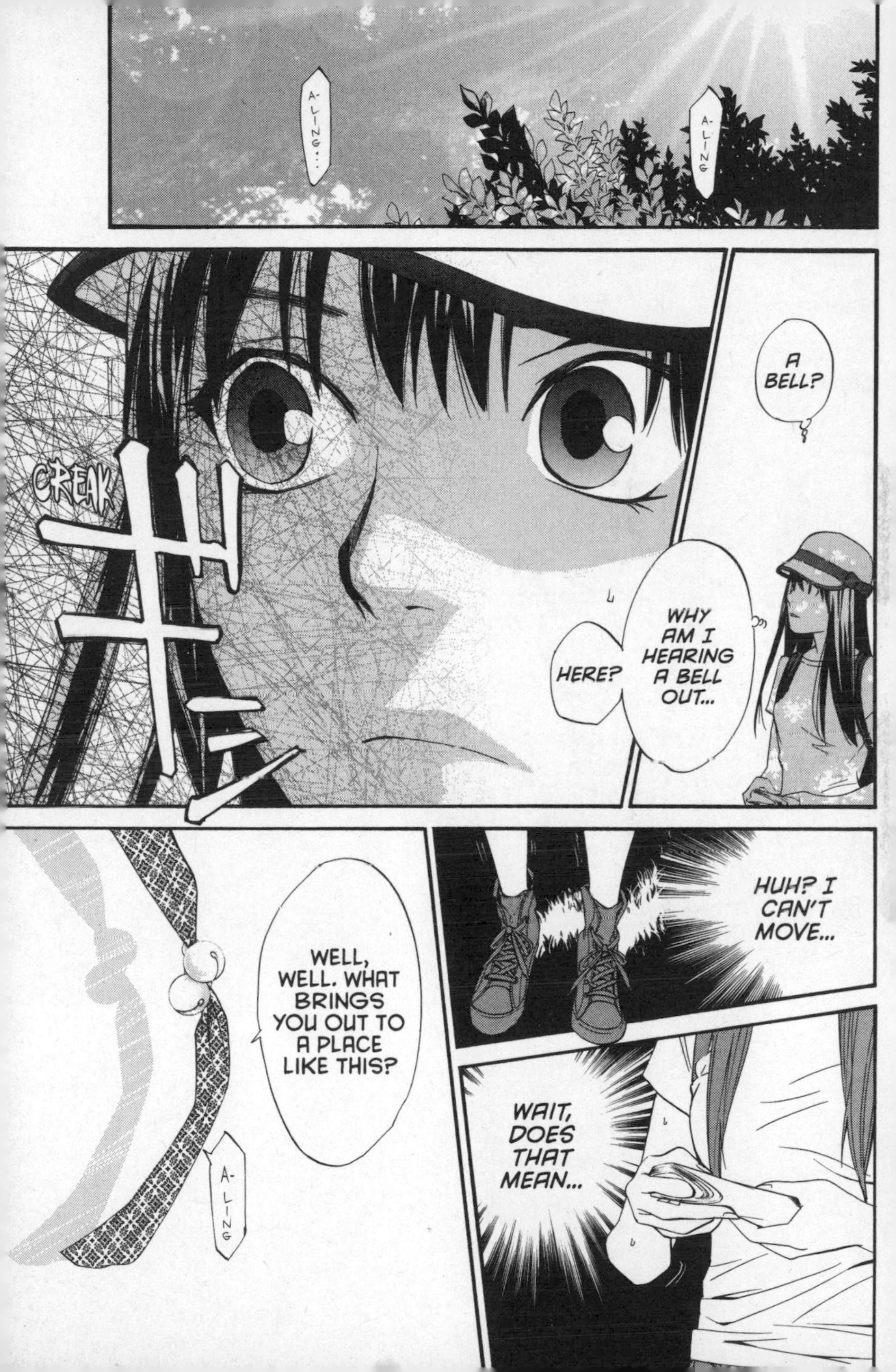
A-LING
A-LING...
A BELL?
WHY AM I HEARING A BELL OUT...
HERE?
CREAK
HUH? I CAN'T MOVE...
WELL, WELL. WHAT BRINGS YOU OUT TO A PLACE LIKE THIS?
A-LING
WAIT, DOES THAT MEAN...

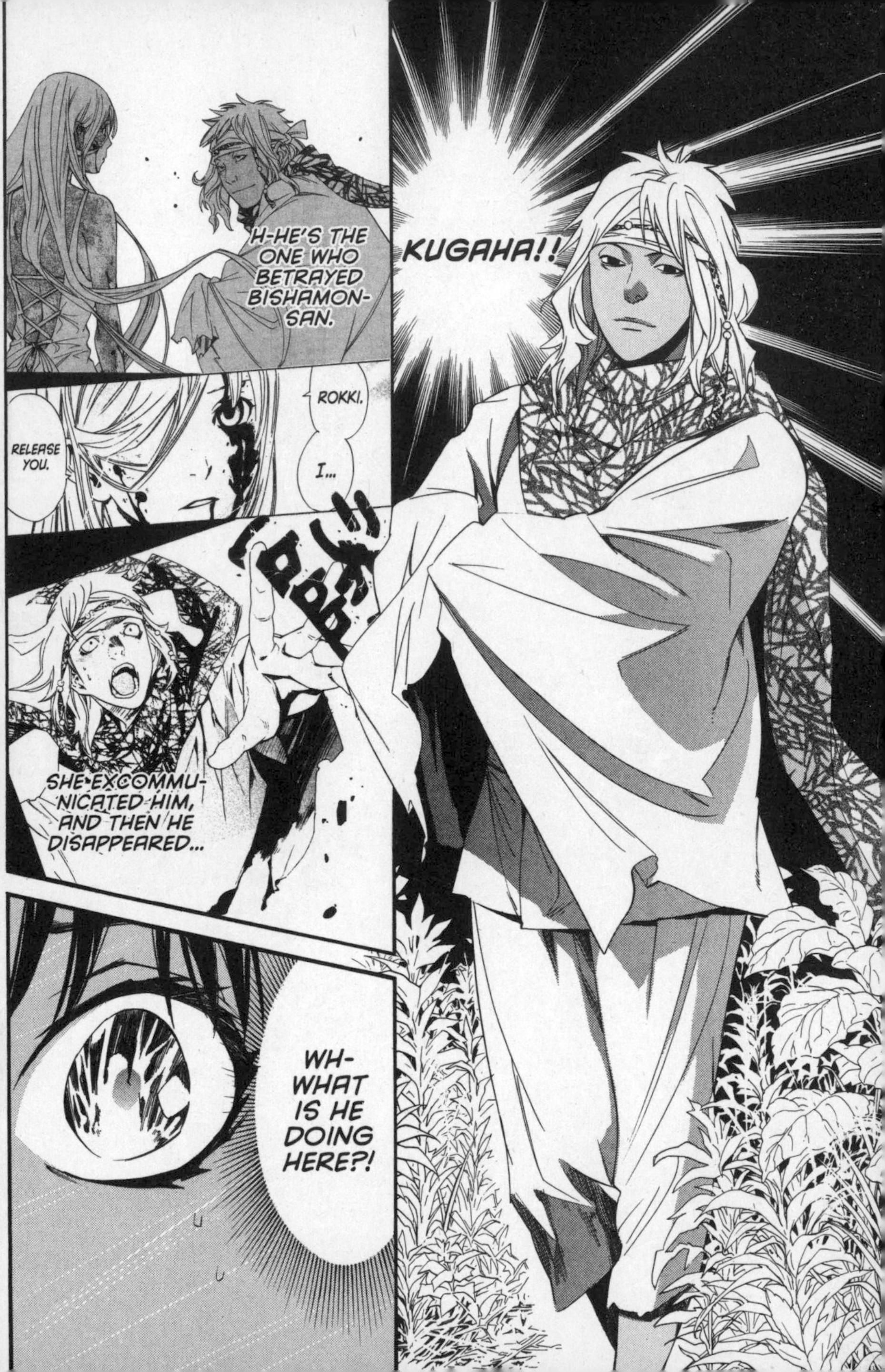
KUGAHA!!
H-HE'S THE ONE WHO BETRAYED BISHAMON-SAN.
ROKKI.
I...
RELEASE YOU.
SHE EXCOMMUNICATED HIM, AND THEN HE DISAPPEARED...
WH-WHAT IS HE DOING HERE?!

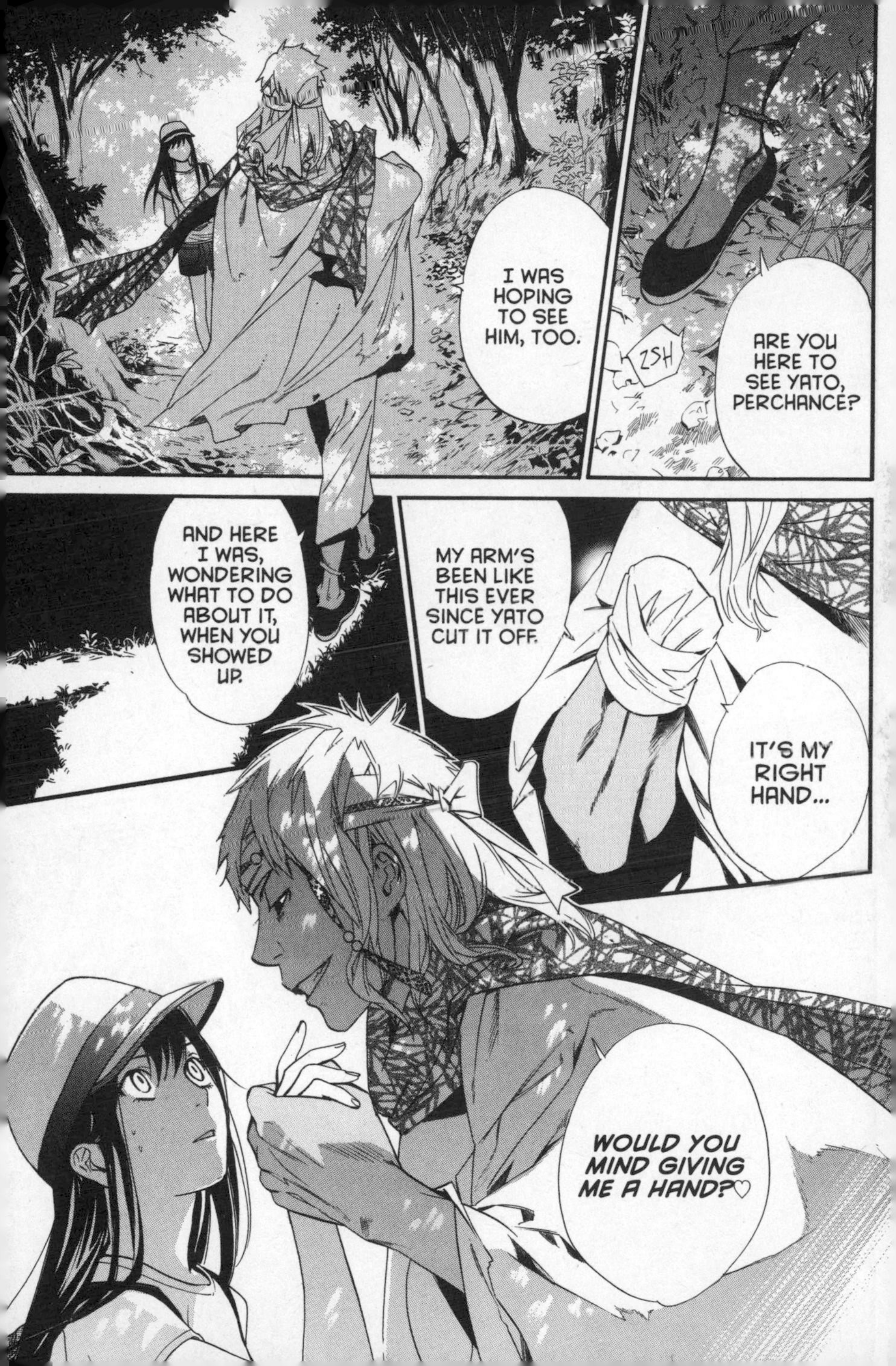
ZSH
ARE YOU HERE TO SEE YATO, PERCHANCE?
I WAS HOPING TO SEE HIM, TOO.
MY ARM'S BEEN LIKE THIS EVER SINCE YATO CUT IT OFF.
IT'S MY RIGHT HAND...
AND HERE I WAS, WONDERING WHAT TO DO ABOUT IT, WHEN YOU SHOWED UP.
WOULD YOU MIND GIVING ME A HAND?♡

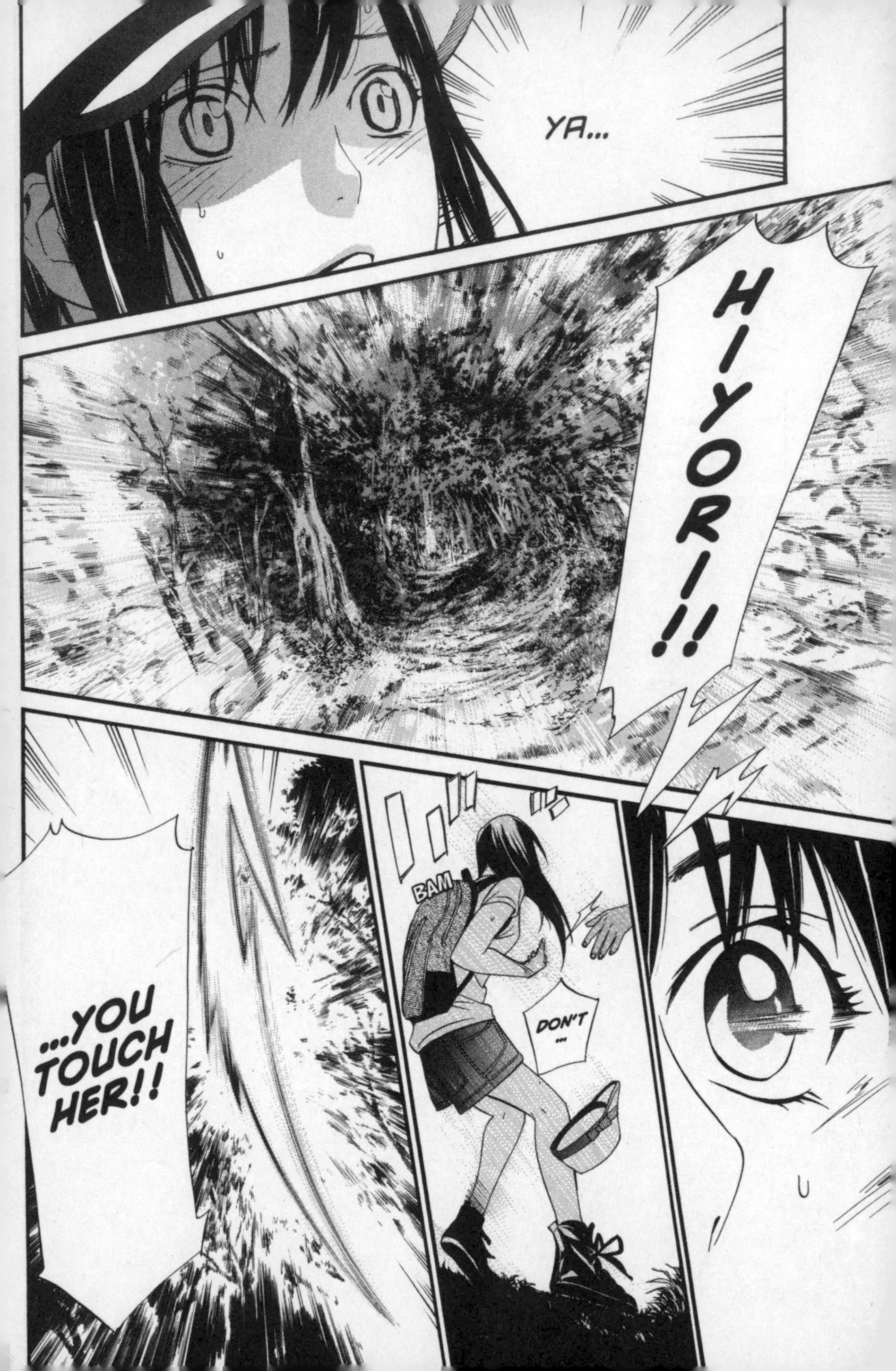
YA...
HIYORI!!
BAM
DON'T ...
...YOU TOUCH HER!!

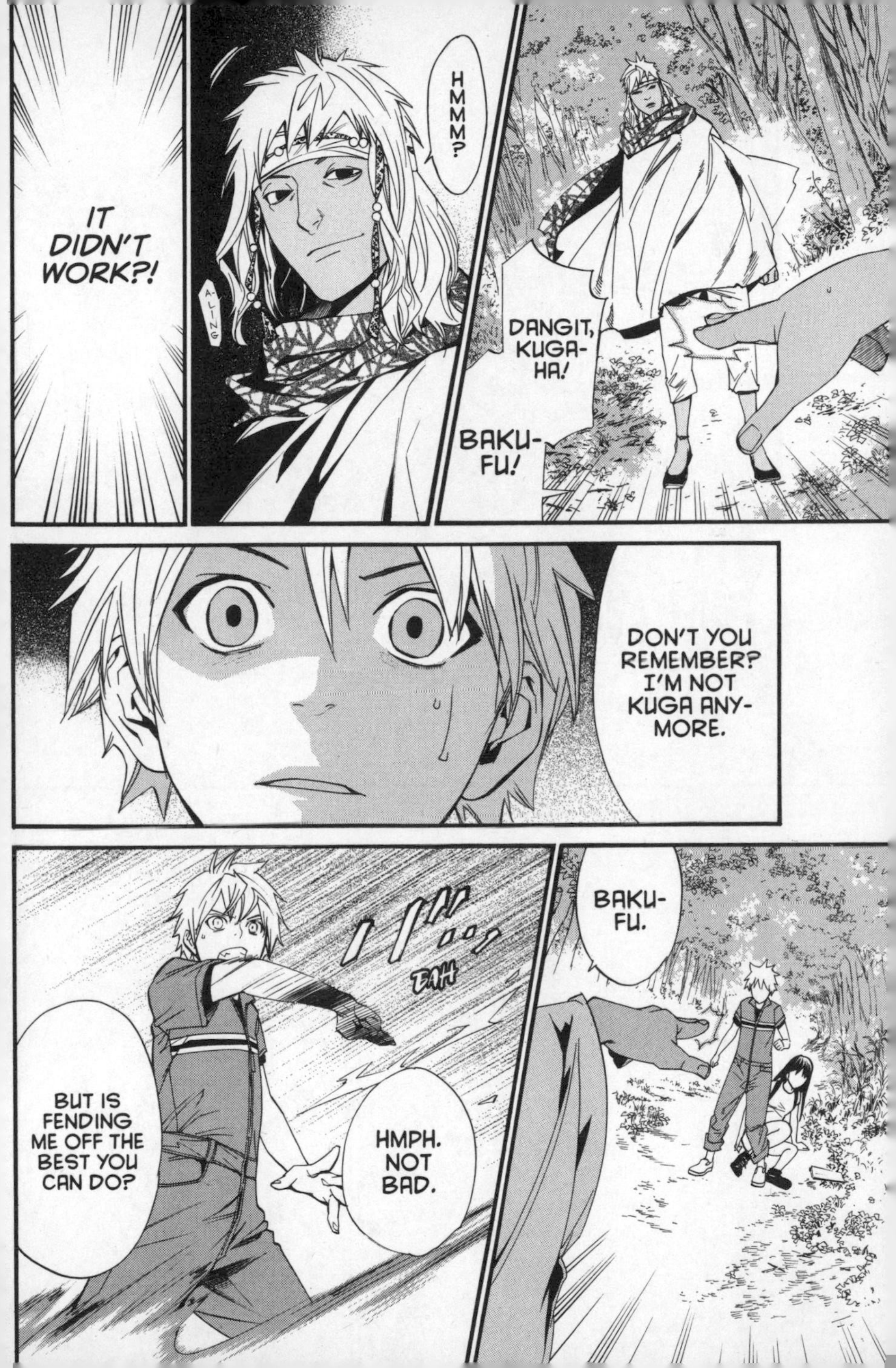
DANGIT, KUGA-HA!
BAKU-FU!
HMMM?
A-LING
IT DIDN'T WORK?!
DON'T YOU REMEMBER? I'M NOT KUGA ANYMORE.
BAKU-FU.
TAH
HMPH. NOT BAD.
BUT IS FENDING ME OFF THE BEST YOU CAN DO?

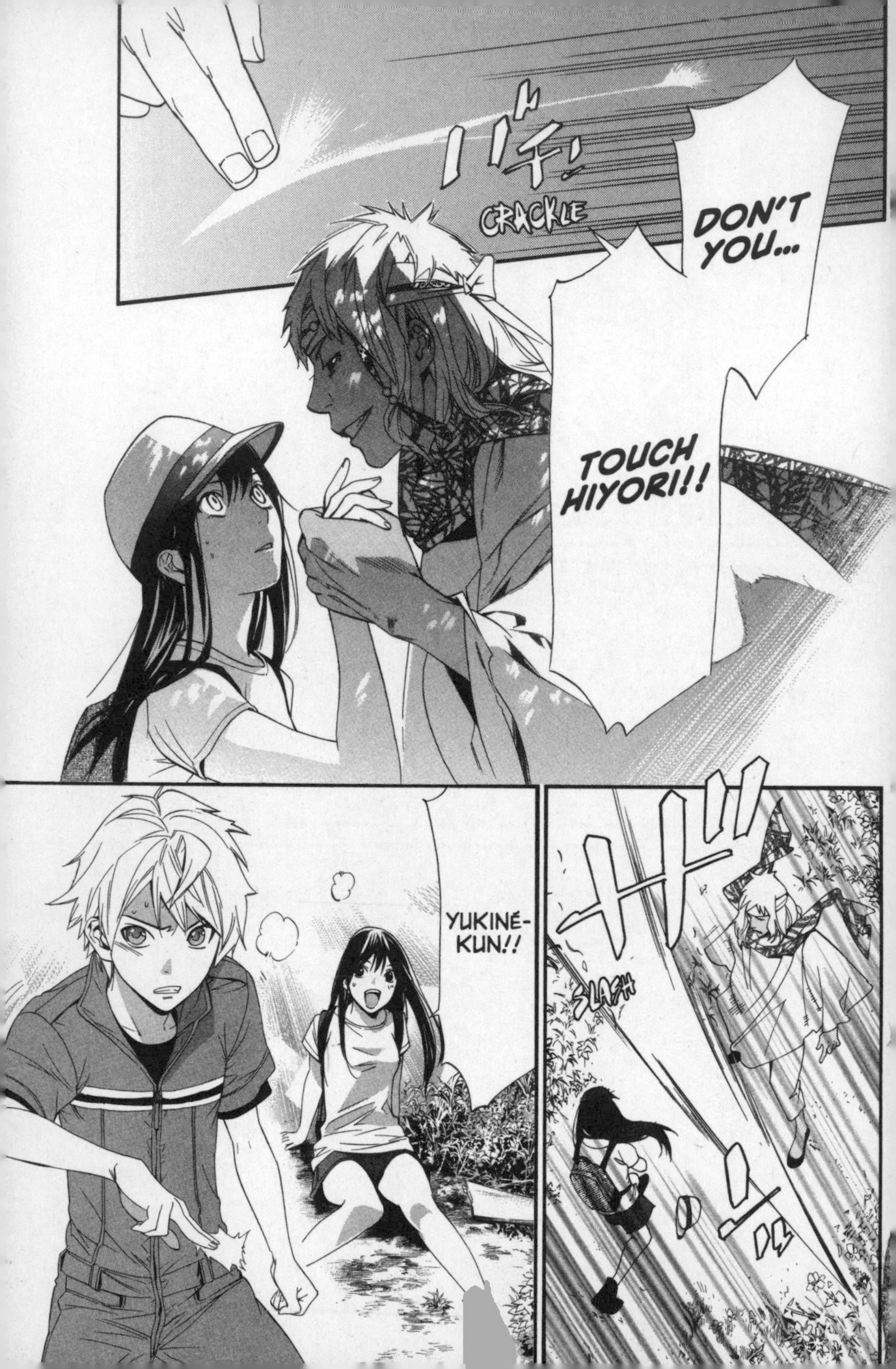
CRACKLE
DON'T YOU...
TOUCH HIYORI!!
SLASH
YUKINÉ-KUN!!

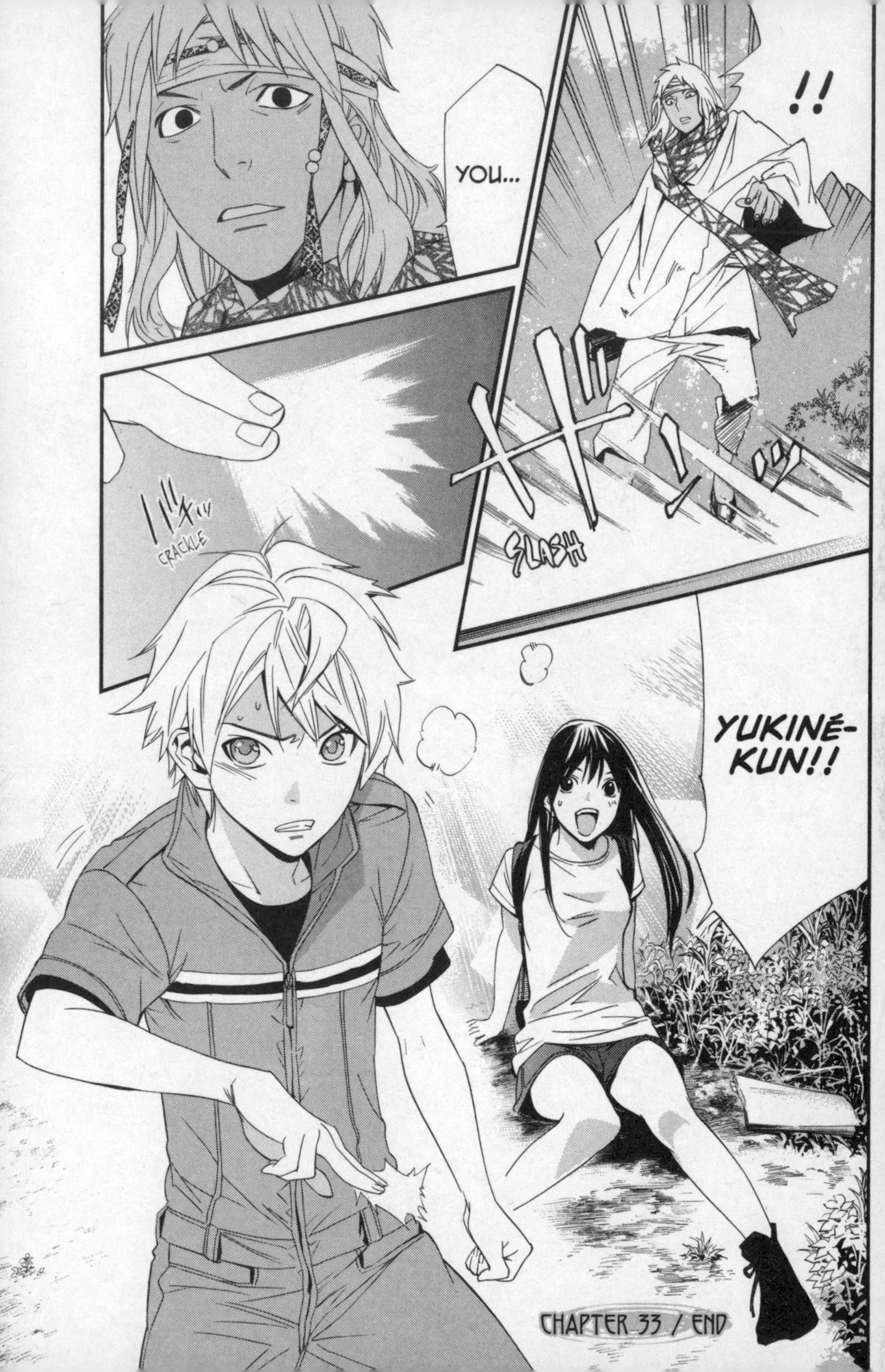
!!
SLASH
YOU...
CRACKLE
YUKINÉ-KUN!!
CHAPTER 33 / END

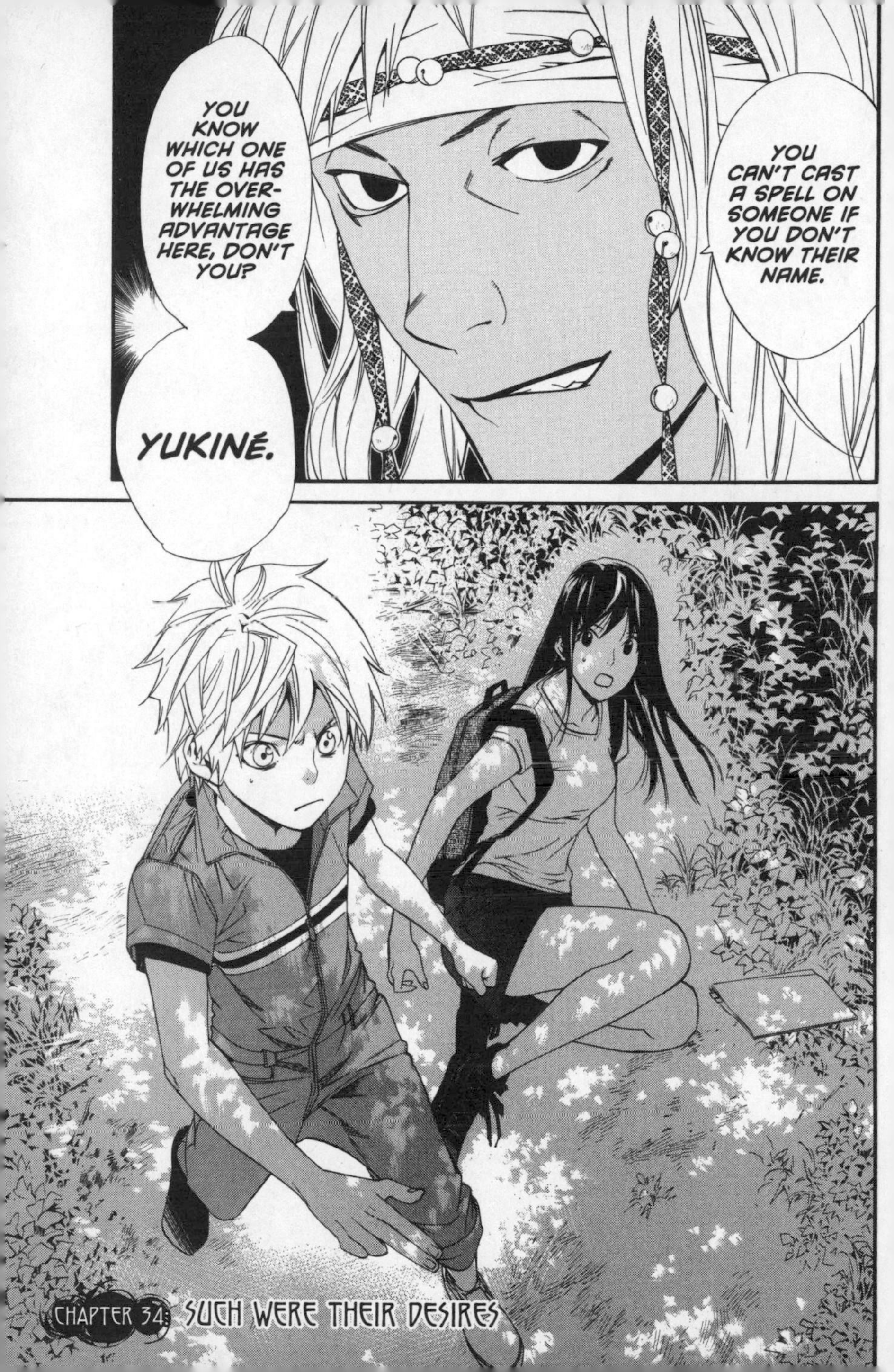
YOU CAN'T CAST A SPELL ON SOMEONE IF YOU DON'T KNOW THEIR NAME.
YOU KNOW WHICH ONE OF US HAS THE OVER-WHELMING ADVANTAGE HERE, DON'T YOU?
YUKINÉ.
CHAPTER 34: SUCH WERE THEIR DESIRES

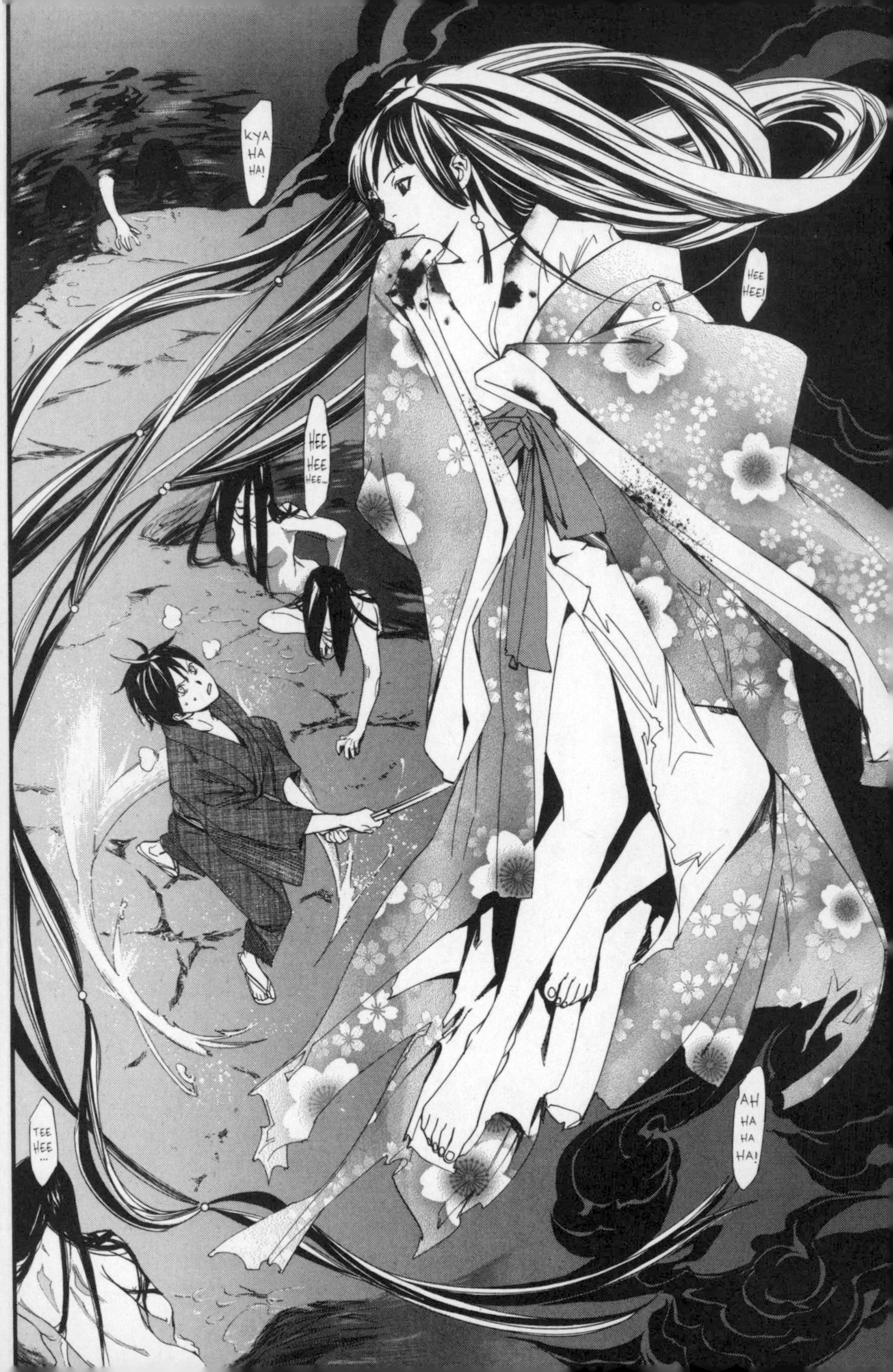
KYA HA HA!
HEE HEE!
HEE HEE HEE...
AH HA HA HA!
TEE HEE...

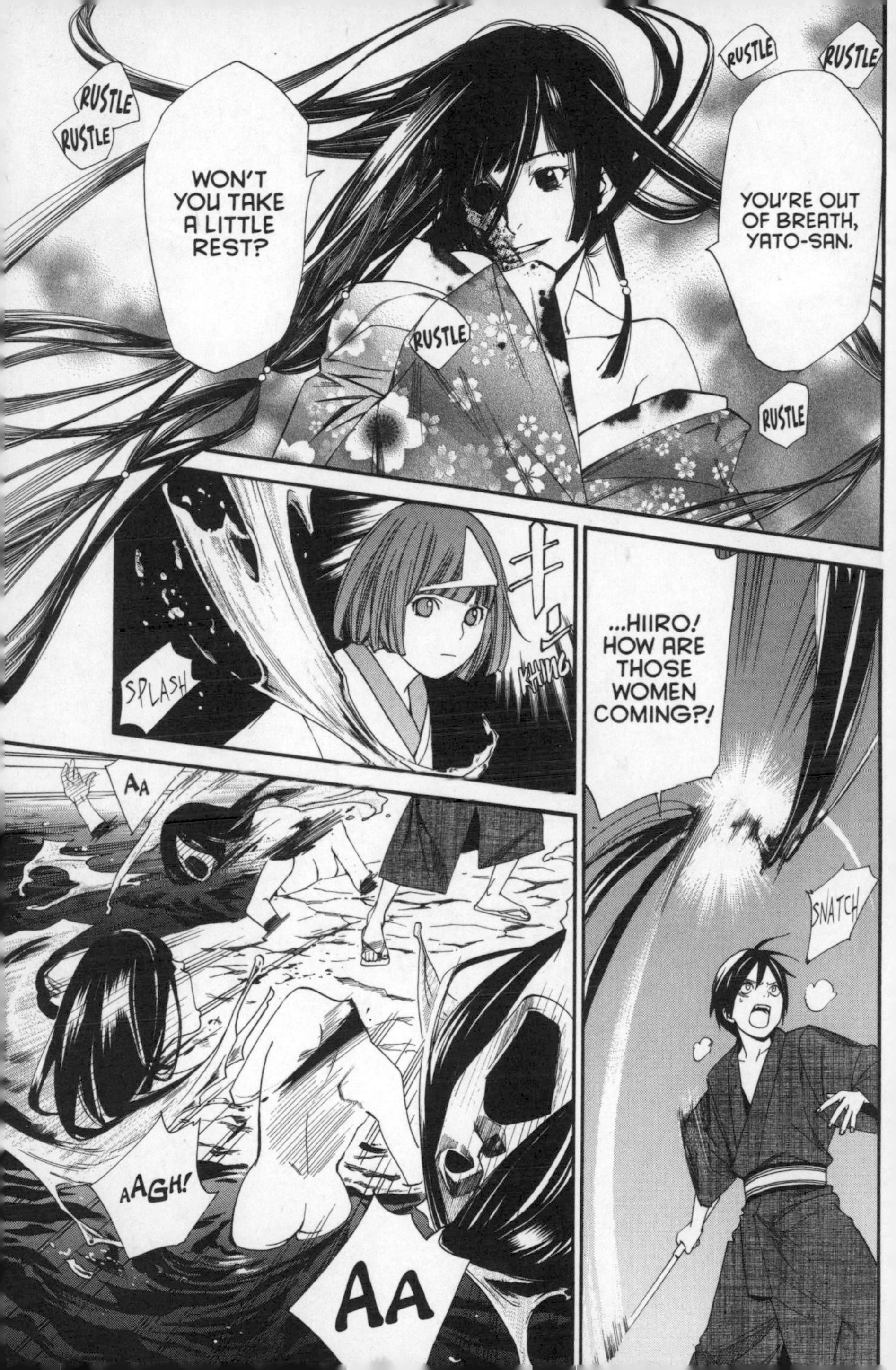
RUSTLE
RUSTLE
YOU'RE OUT OF BREATH, YATO-SAN.
WON'T YOU TAKE A LITTLE REST?
RUSTLE
RUSTLE
RUSTLE
RUSTLE
...HIIRO! HOW ARE THOSE WOMEN COMING?!
SNATCH
KHING
SPLASH
AA
AAGH!
AA

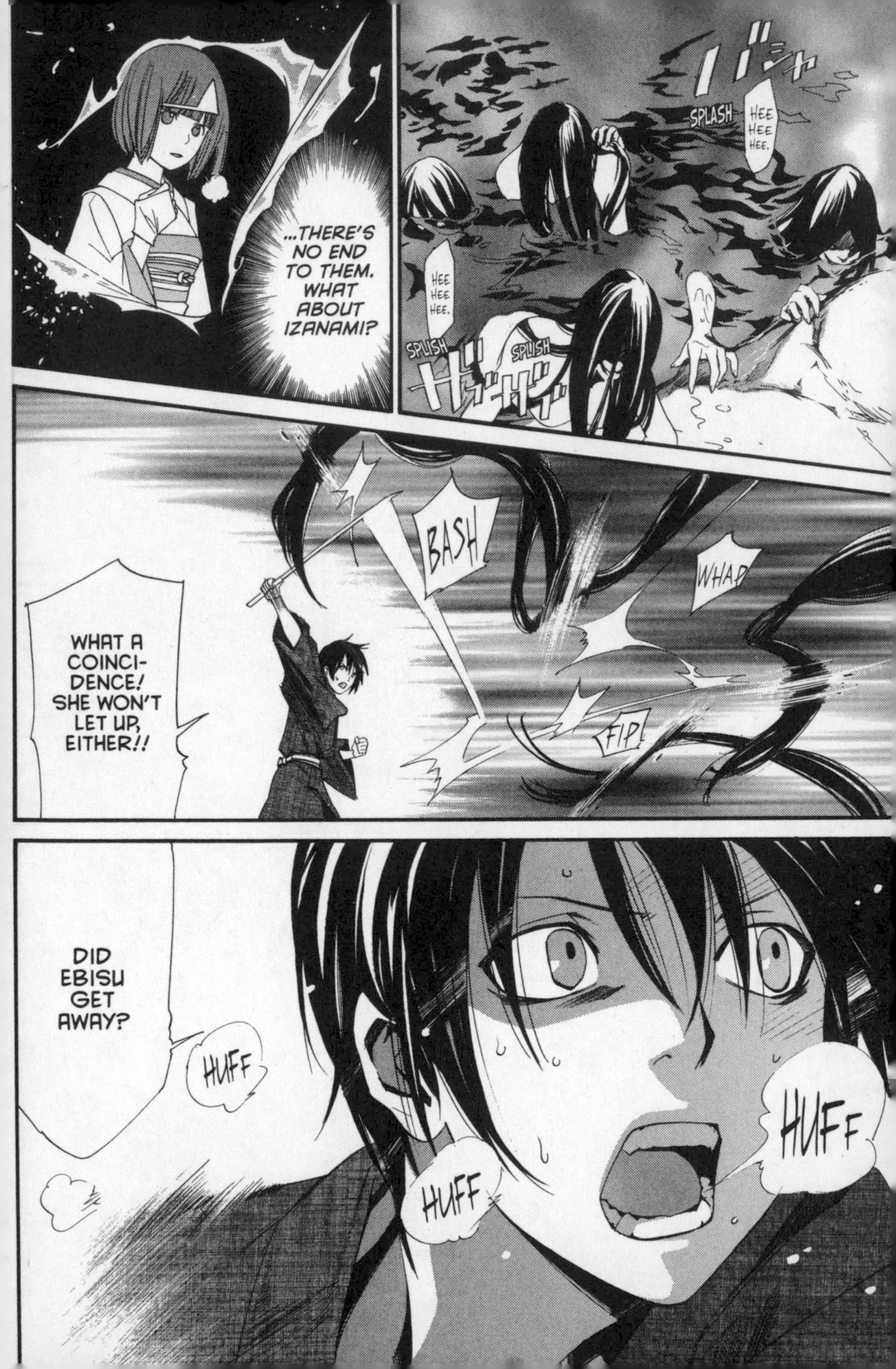
SPLASH
HEE HEE HEE.
HEE HEE HEE.
SPLISH
SPLISH
...THERE'S NO END TO THEM. WHAT ABOUT IZANAMI?
BASH
WHAP
FIP
WHAT A COINCI-DENCE! SHE WON'T LET UP, EITHER!!
DID EBISU GET AWAY?
HUFF
HUFF
HUFF
HUFF

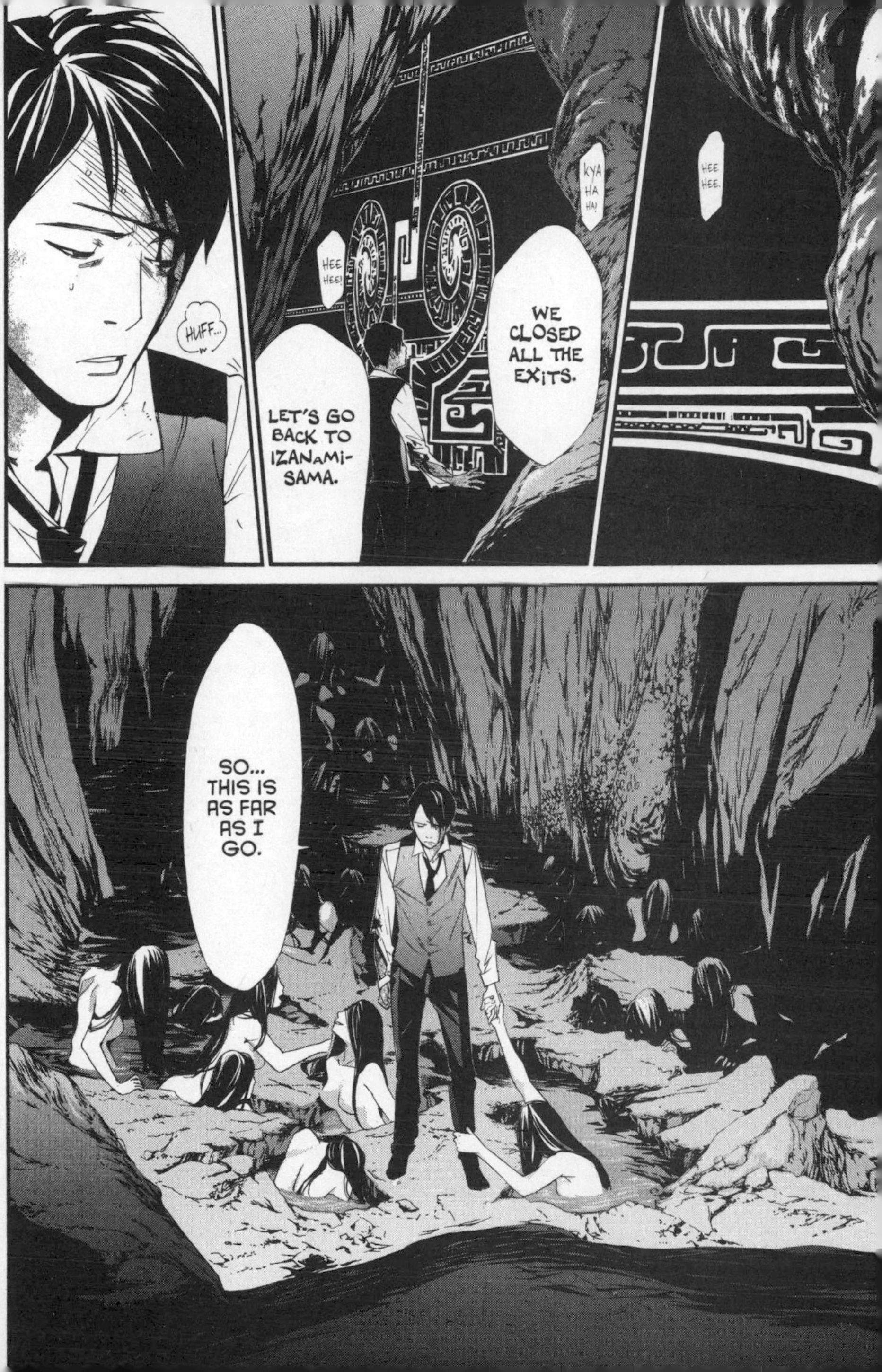
HEE HEE.
KYA HA HA!
WE CLOSED ALL THE EXITS.
HEE HEE!
LET'S GO BACK TO IZANAMI-SAMA.
HUFF...
SO... THIS IS AS FAR AS I GO.

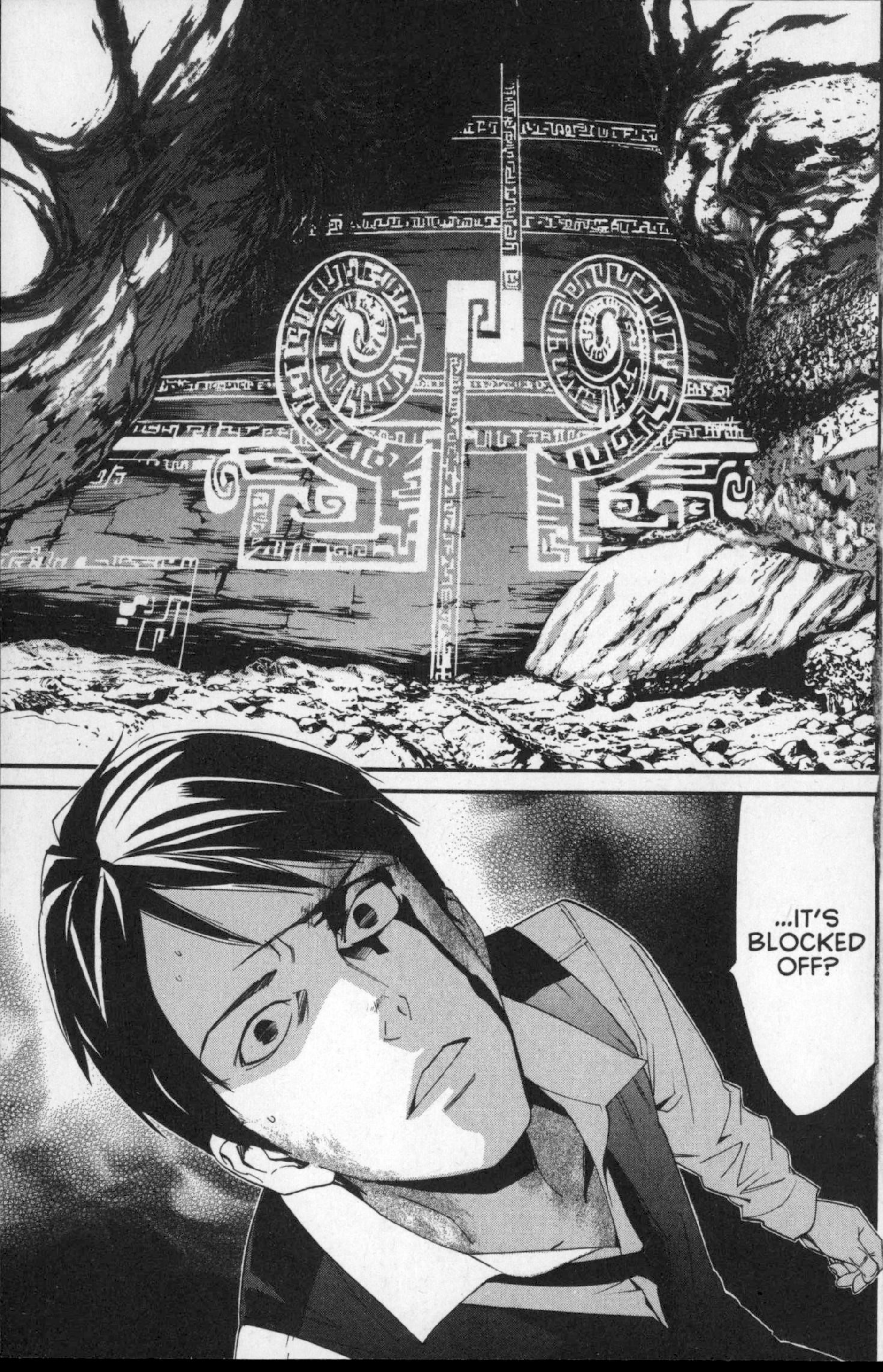
...IT'S BLOCKED OFF?

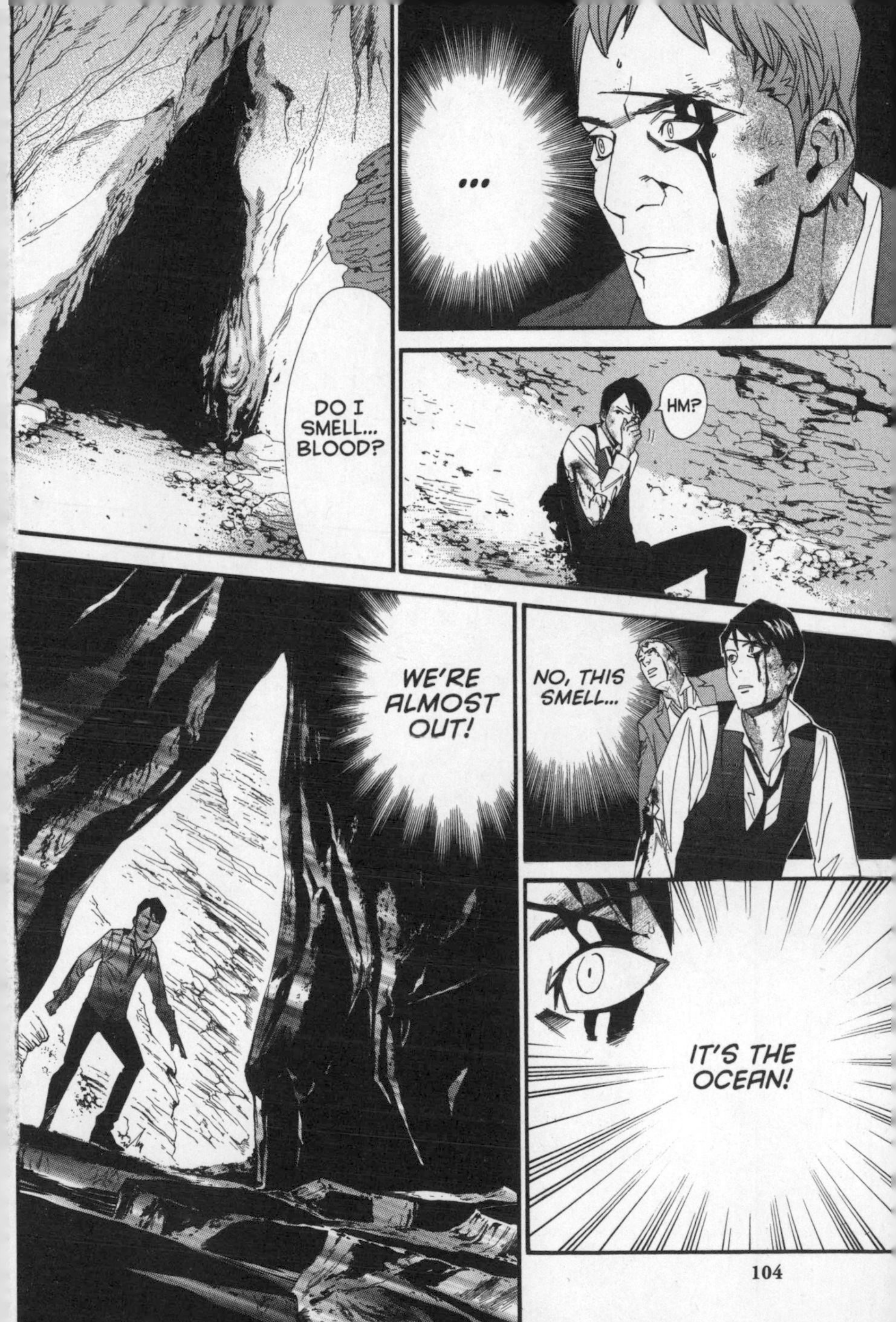

...
HM?
DO I SMELL... BLOOD?
NO, THIS SMELL...
IT'S THE OCEAN!
WE'RE ALMOST OUT!

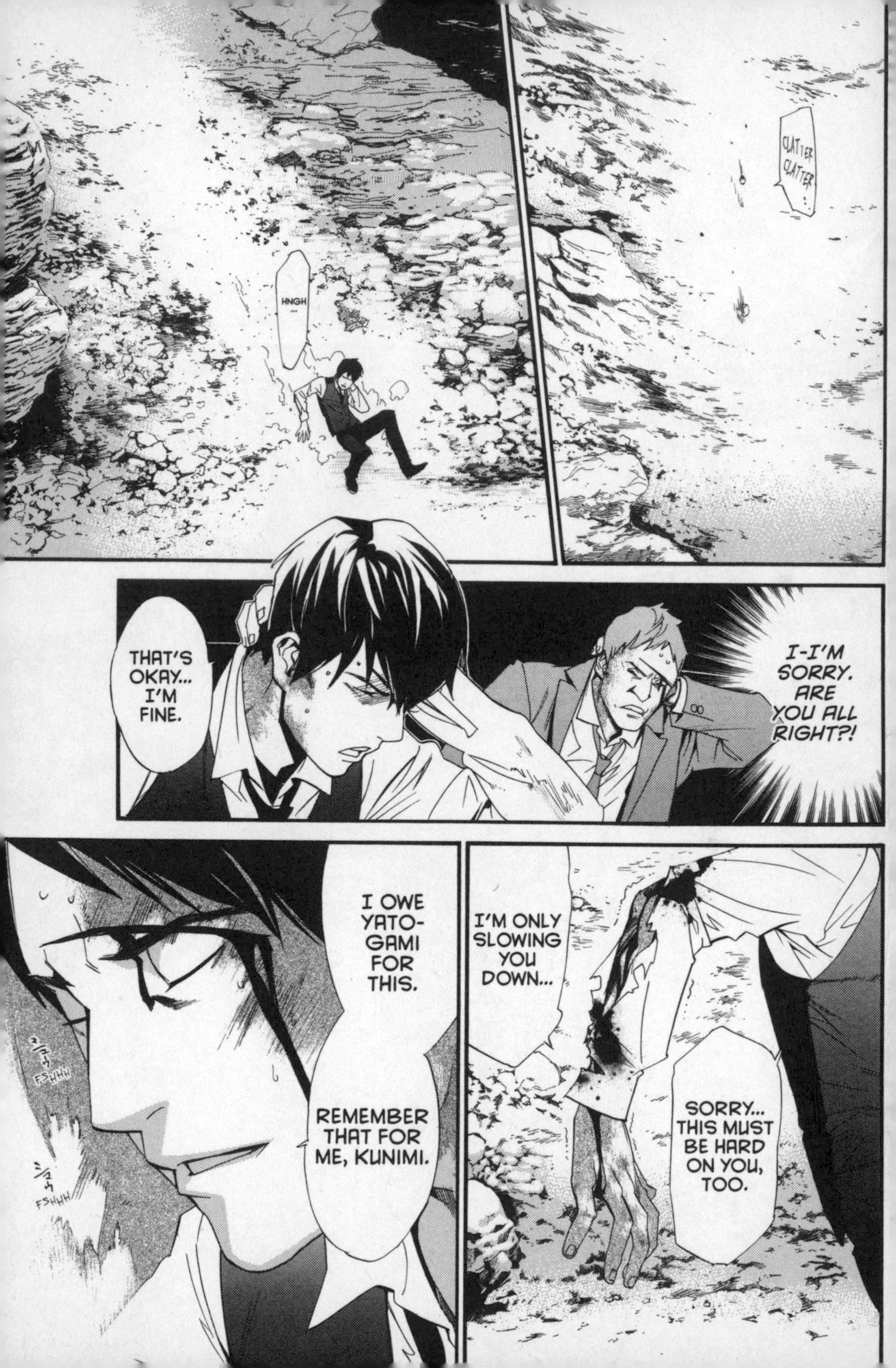
CLATTER CLATTER
HNGH...
I-I'M SORRY. ARE YOU ALL RIGHT?!
THAT'S OKAY... I'M FINE.
I'M ONLY SLOWING YOU DOWN...
SORRY... THIS MUST BE HARD ON YOU, TOO.
I OWE YATO-GAMI FOR THIS.
REMEMBER THAT FOR ME, KUNIMI.
FSHHH
FSHHH

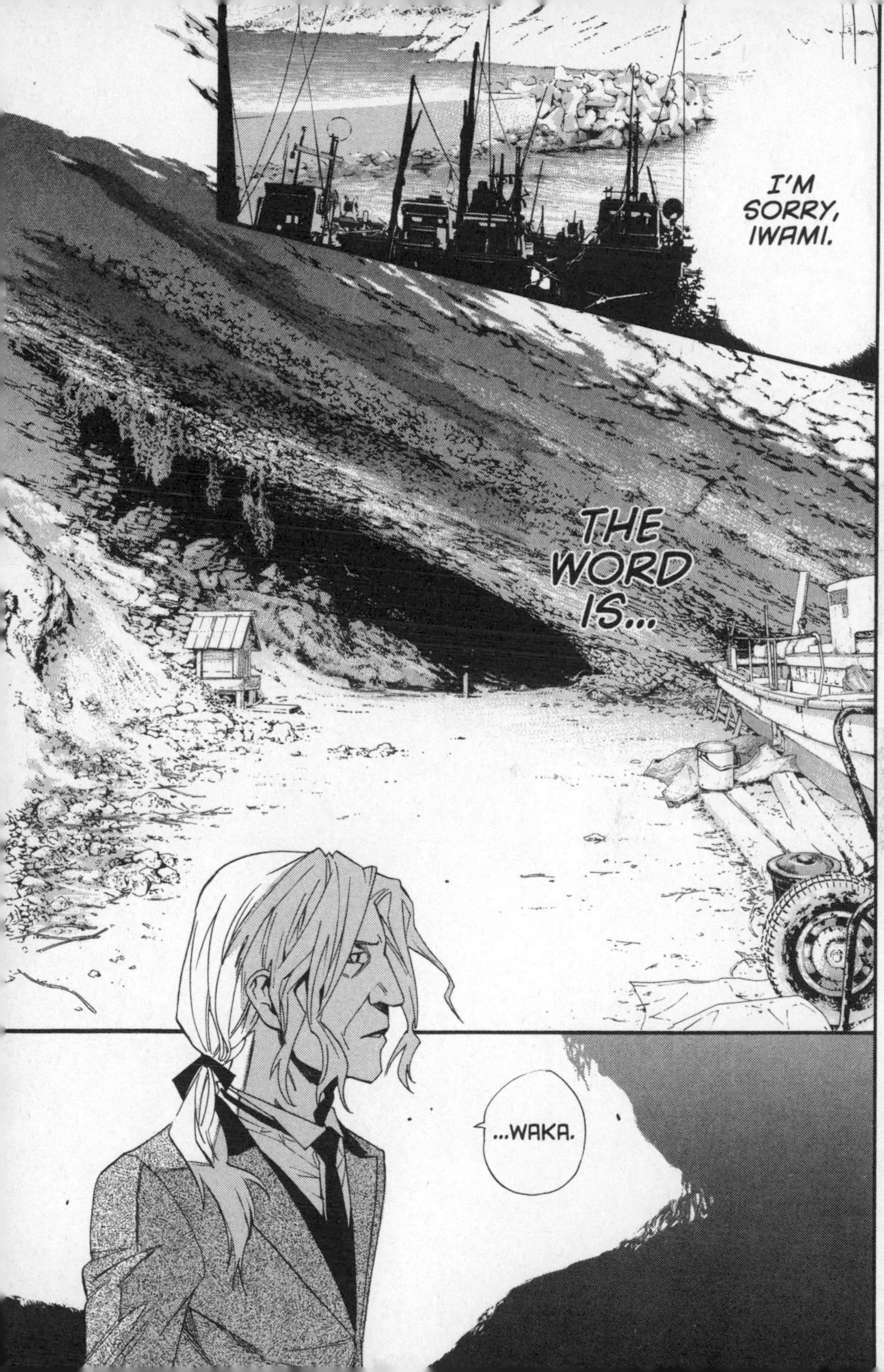
I'M SORRY, IWAMI.
THE WORD IS...
...WAKA.

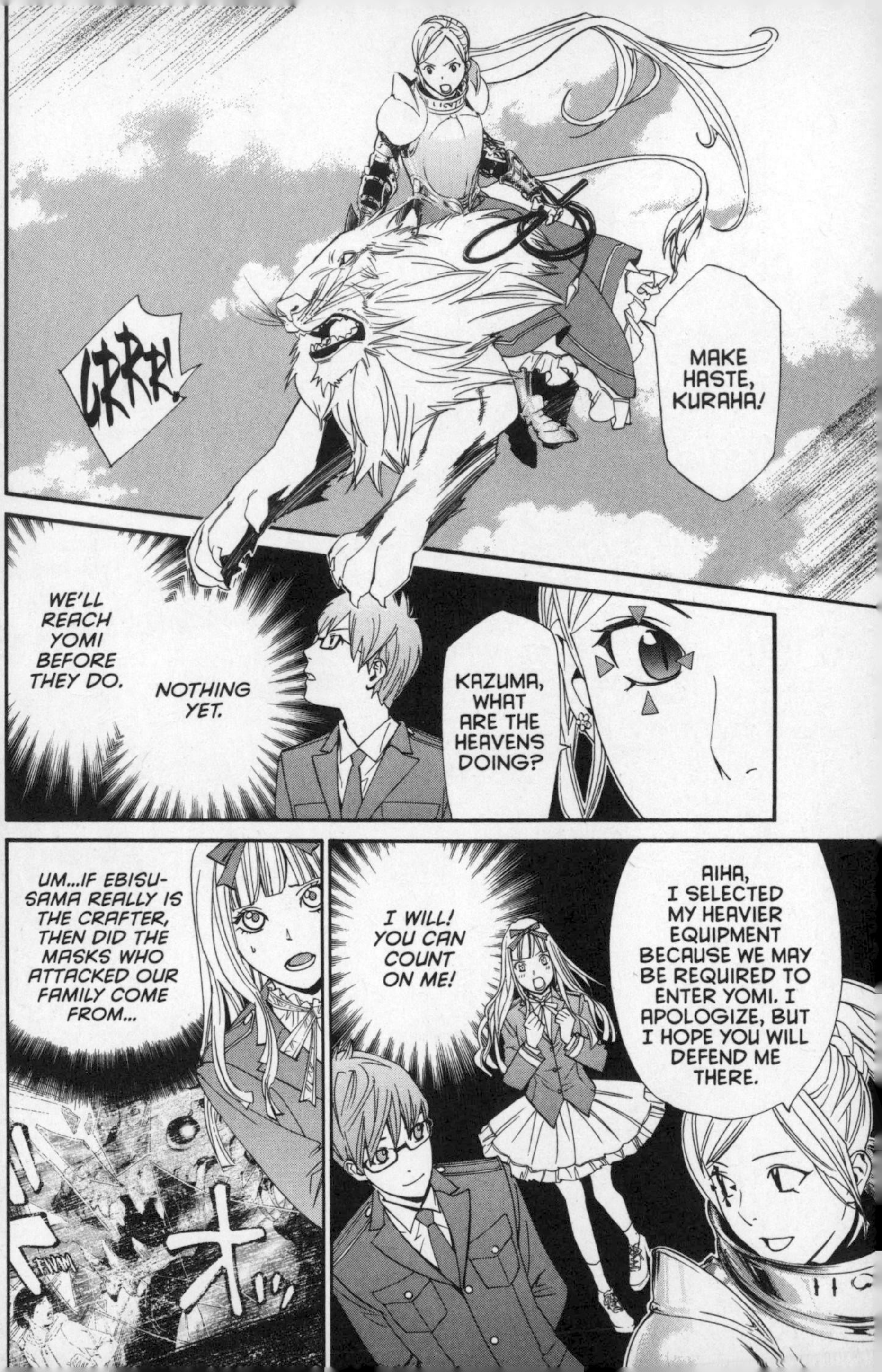
MAKE HASTE, KURAHA!
GRRR!
KAZUMA, WHAT ARE THE HEAVENS DOING?
NOTHING YET.
WE'LL REACH YOMI BEFORE THEY DO.
AIHA, I SELECTED MY HEAVIER EQUIPMENT BECAUSE WE MAY BE REQUIRED TO ENTER YOMI. I APOLOGIZE, BUT I HOPE YOU WILL DEFEND ME THERE.
I WILL! YOU CAN COUNT ON ME!
UM...IF EBISU-SAMA REALLY IS THE CRAFTER, THEN DID THE MASKS WHO ATTACKED OUR FAMILY COME FROM...

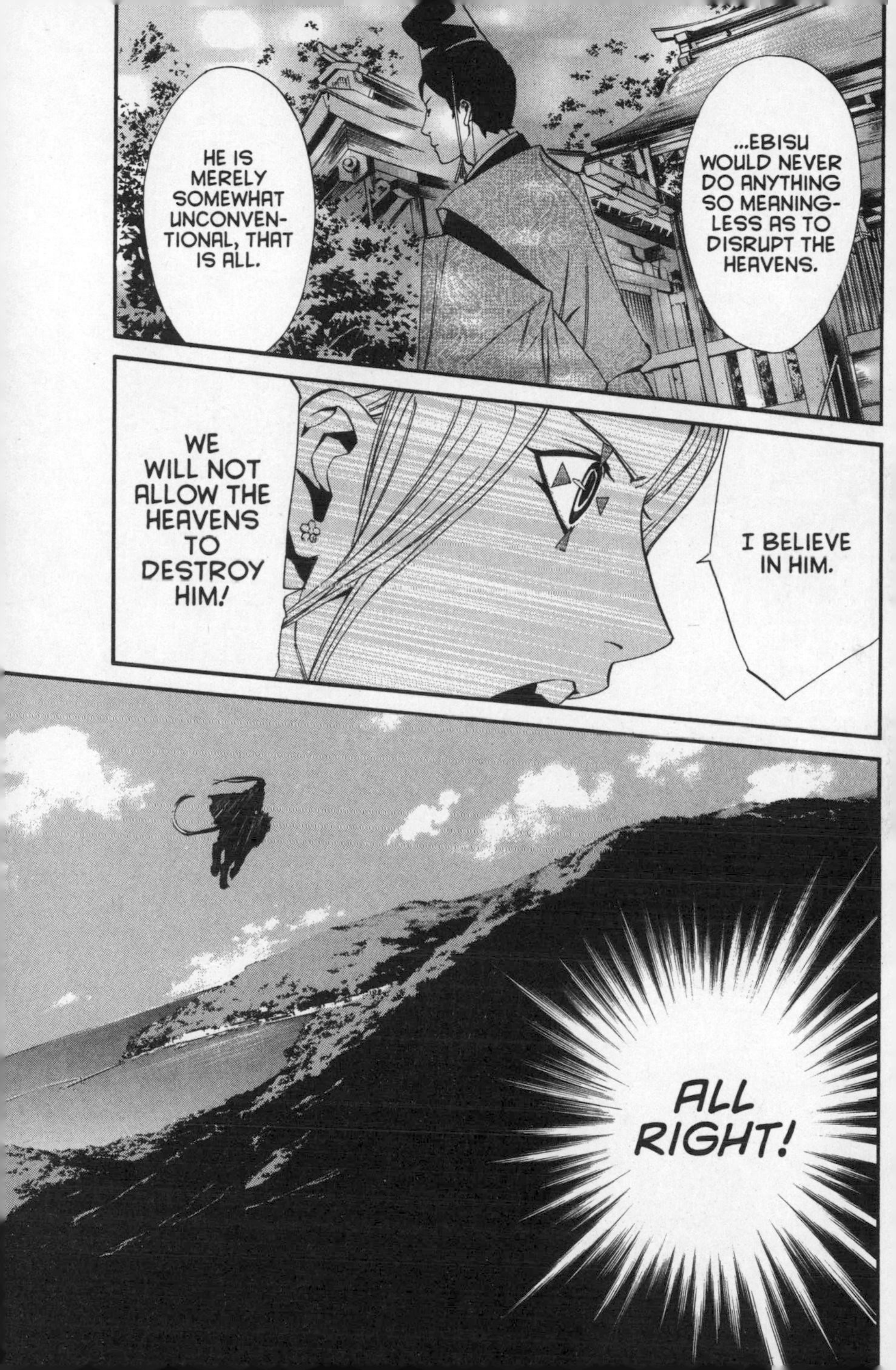
...EBISU WOULD NEVER DO ANYTHING SO MEANINGLESS AS TO DISRUPT THE HEAVENS.
HE IS MERELY SOMEWHAT UNCONVENTIONAL, THAT IS ALL.
I BELIEVE IN HIM.
WE WILL NOT ALLOW THE HEAVENS TO DESTROY HIM!
ALL RIGHT!

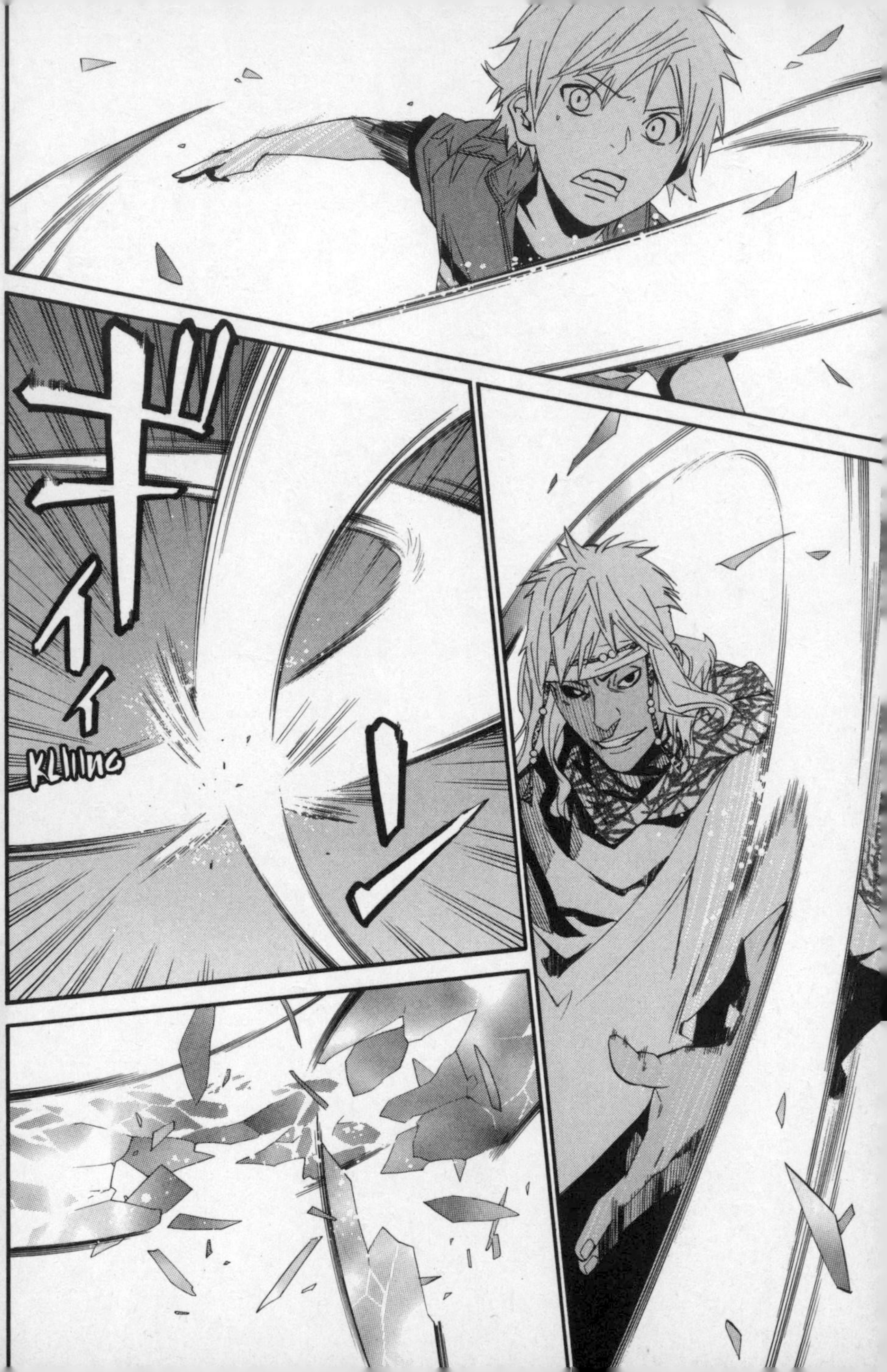
ギィイ
KLIIING

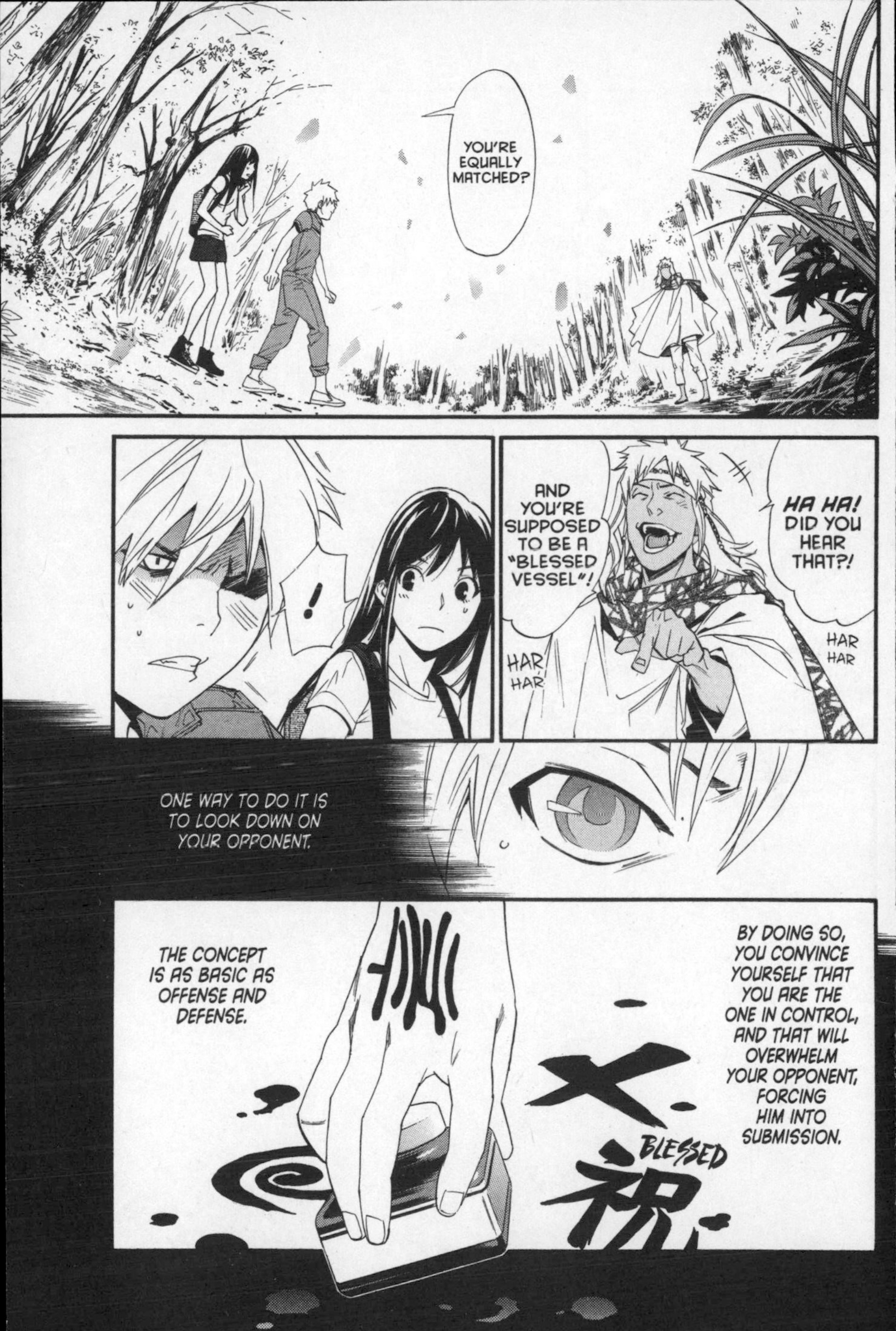

YOU'RE EQUALLY MATCHED?
HA HA! DID YOU HEAR THAT?!
HAR HAR
AND YOU'RE SUPPOSED TO BE A "BLESSED VESSEL"!
HAR HAR
!
ONE WAY TO DO IT IS TO LOOK DOWN ON YOUR OPPONENT.
BY DOING SO, YOU CONVINCE YOURSELF THAT YOU ARE THE ONE IN CONTROL, AND THAT WILL OVERWHELM YOUR OPPONENT, FORCING HIM INTO SUBMISSION.
BLESSED
THE CONCEPT IS AS BASIC AS OFFENSE AND DEFENSE.

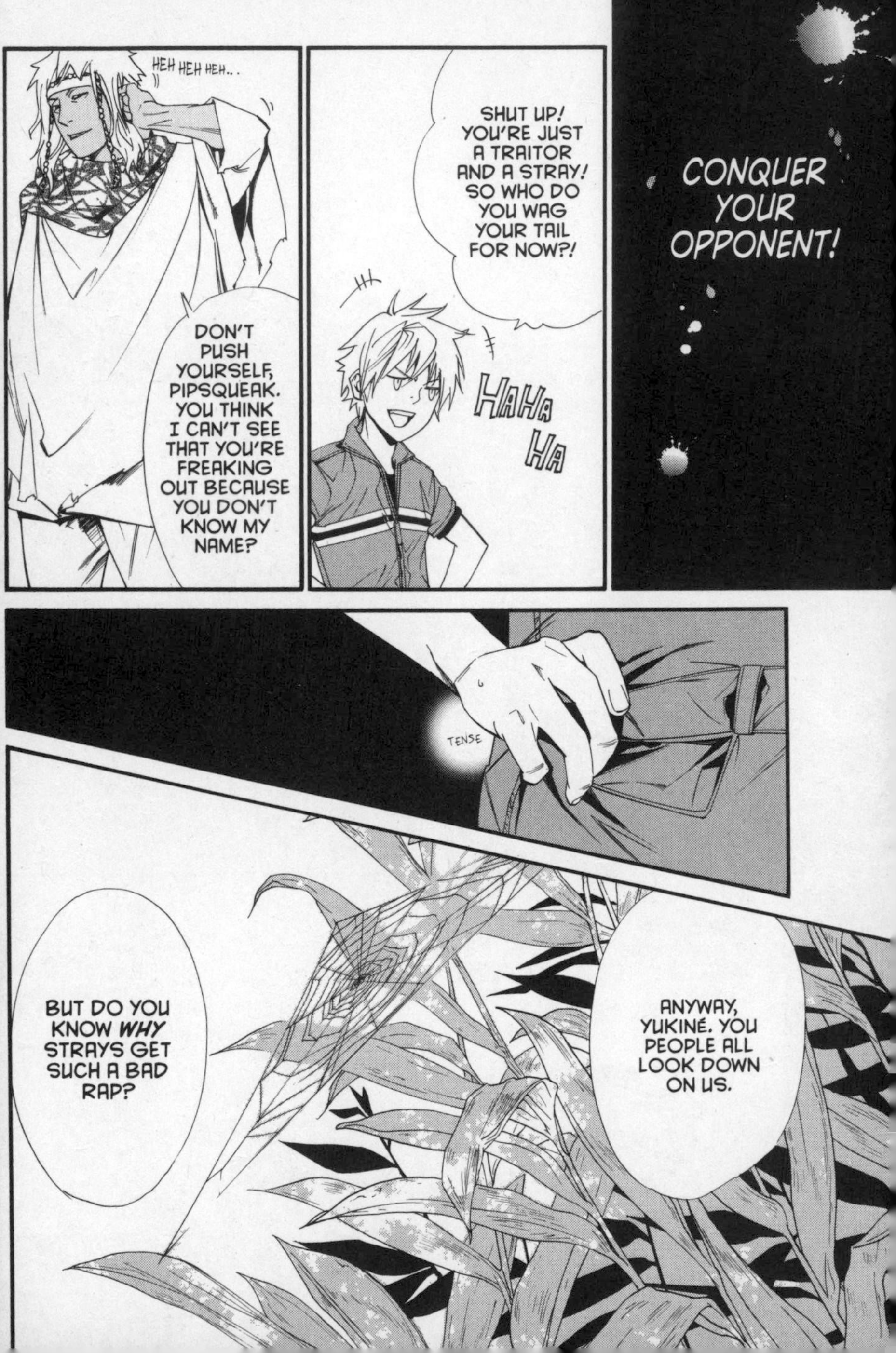
CONQUER YOUR OPPONENT!
SHUT UP! YOU'RE JUST A TRAITOR AND A STRAY! SO WHO DO YOU WAG YOUR TAIL FOR NOW?!
HAHA HA
HEH HEH HEH...
DON'T PUSH YOURSELF, PIPSQUEAK. YOU THINK I CAN'T SEE THAT YOU'RE FREAKING OUT BECAUSE YOU DON'T KNOW MY NAME?
TENSE
ANYWAY, YUKINÉ. YOU PEOPLE ALL LOOK DOWN ON US.
BUT DO YOU KNOW *WHY* STRAYS GET SUCH A BAD RAP?

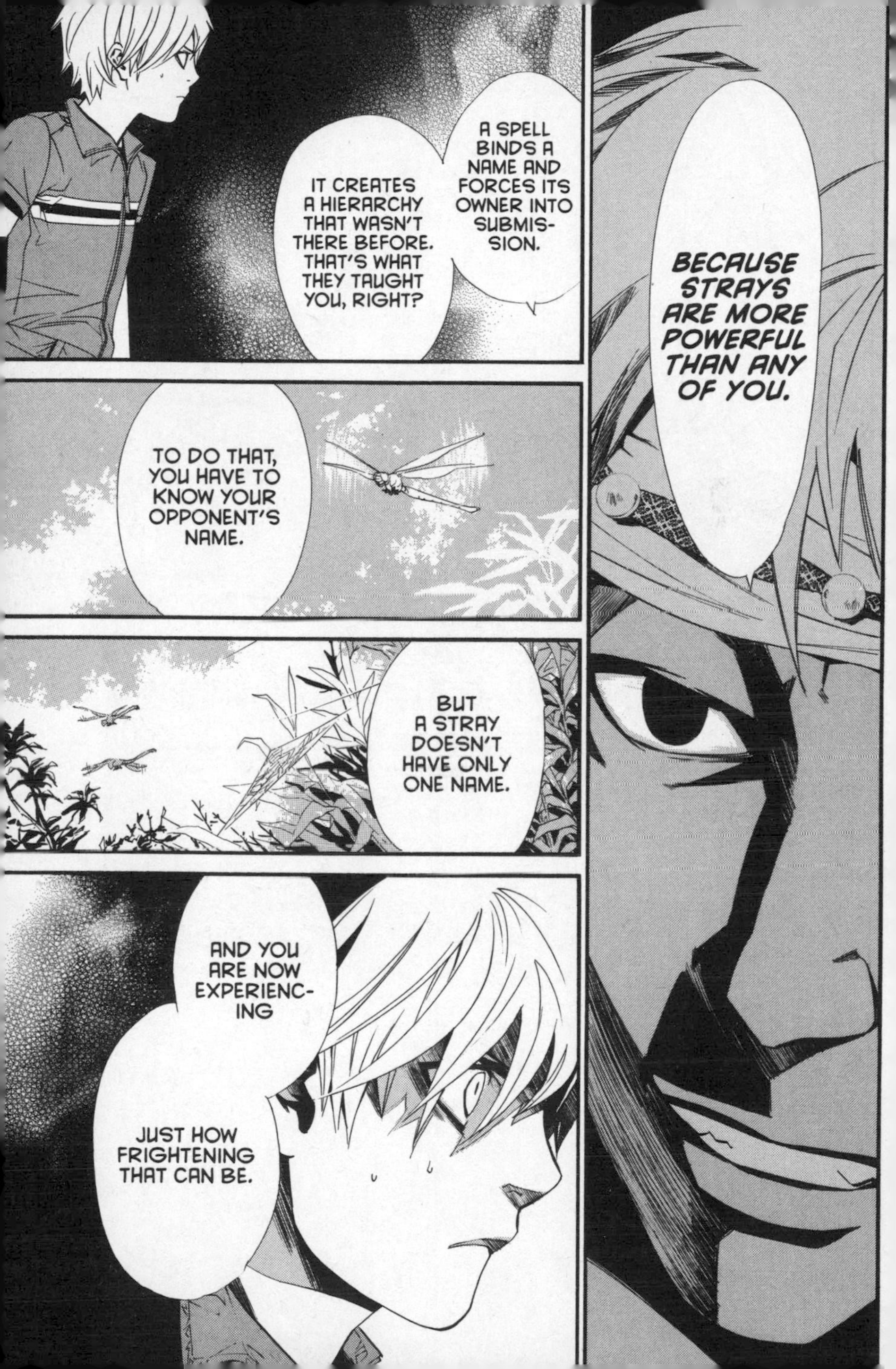
BECAUSE STRAYS ARE MORE POWERFUL THAN ANY OF YOU.
A SPELL BINDS A NAME AND FORCES ITS OWNER INTO SUBMISSION.
IT CREATES A HIERARCHY THAT WASN'T THERE BEFORE. THAT'S WHAT THEY TAUGHT YOU, RIGHT?
TO DO THAT, YOU HAVE TO KNOW YOUR OPPONENT'S NAME.
BUT A STRAY DOESN'T HAVE ONLY ONE NAME.
AND YOU ARE NOW EXPERIENCING
JUST HOW FRIGHTENING THAT CAN BE.

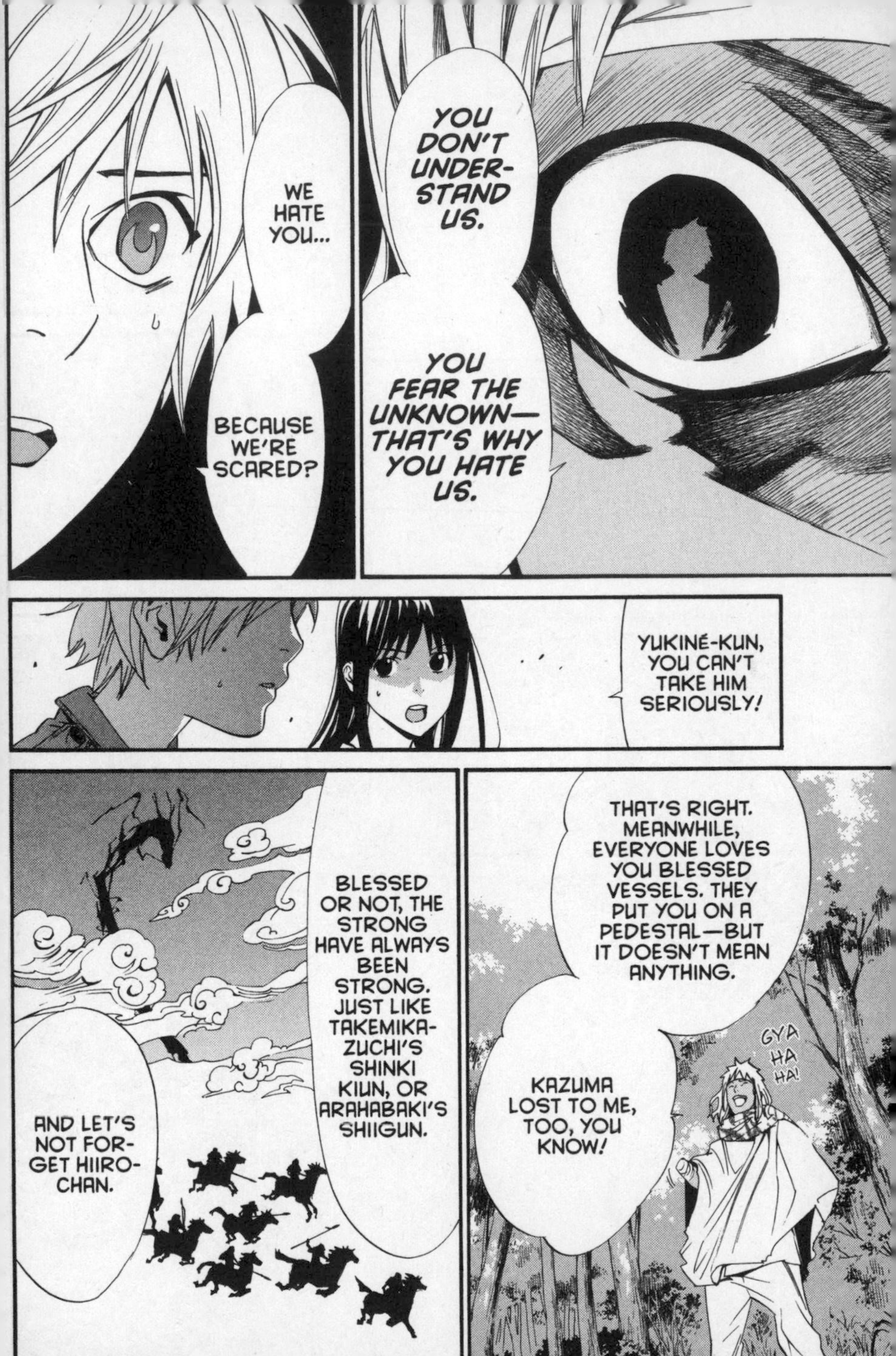
YOU DON'T UNDER-STAND US.
YOU FEAR THE UNKNOWN—THAT'S WHY YOU HATE US.
WE HATE YOU...
BECAUSE WE'RE SCARED?
YUKINÉ-KUN, YOU CAN'T TAKE HIM SERIOUSLY!
THAT'S RIGHT. MEANWHILE, EVERYONE LOVES YOU BLESSED VESSELS. THEY PUT YOU ON A PEDESTAL—BUT IT DOESN'T MEAN ANYTHING.
KAZUMA LOST TO ME, TOO, YOU KNOW!
GYA HA HA!
BLESSED OR NOT, THE STRONG HAVE ALWAYS BEEN STRONG. JUST LIKE TAKEMIKA-ZUCHI'S SHINKI KIUN, OR ARAHABAKI'S SHIIGUN.
AND LET'S NOT FOR-GET HIIRO-CHAN.

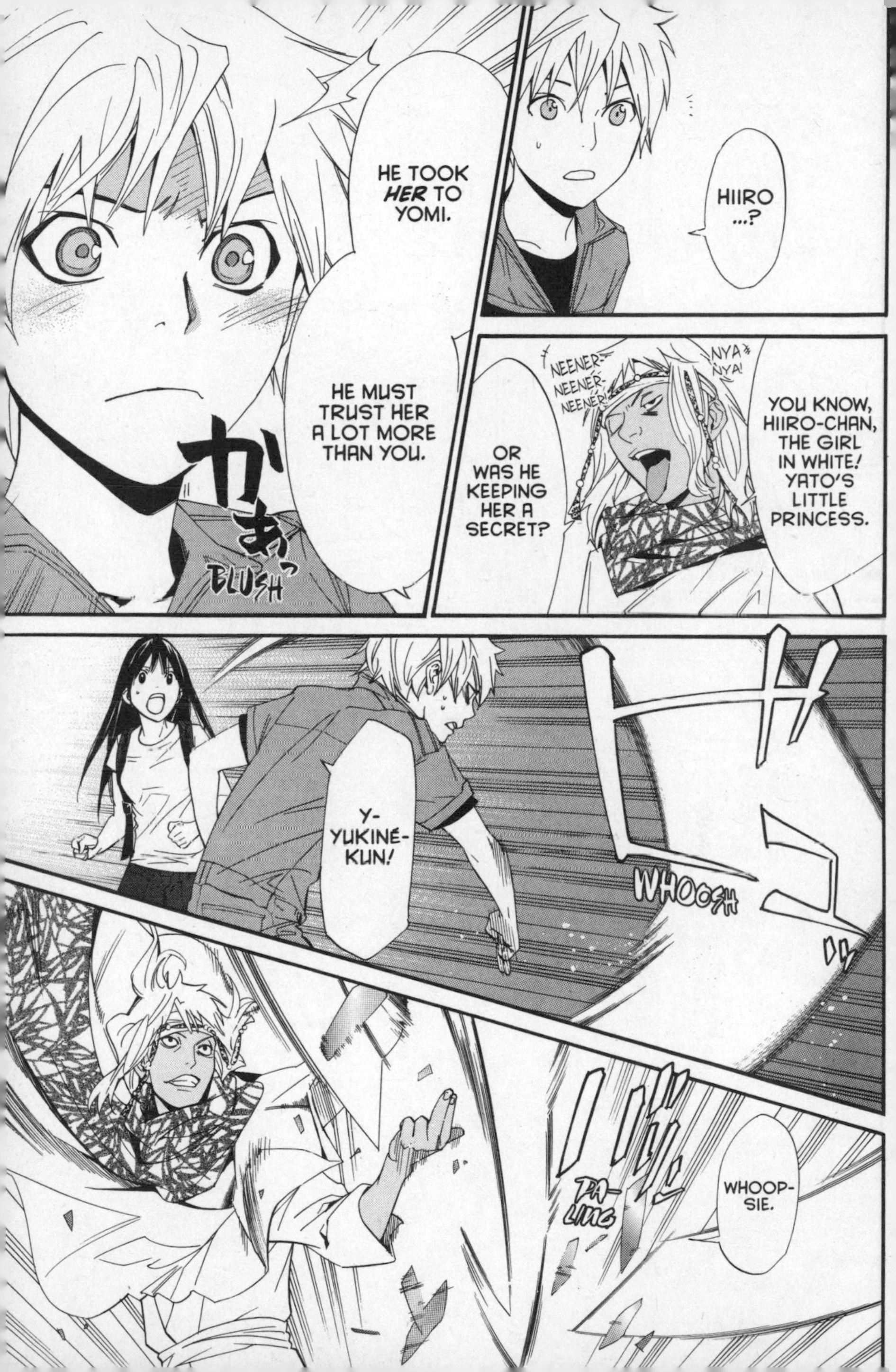

HIIRO ...?
YOU KNOW, HIIRO-CHAN, THE GIRL IN WHITE! YATO'S LITTLE PRINCESS.
NYA NYA!
NEENER-NEENER-NEENER!
OR WAS HE KEEPING HER A SECRET?
HE TOOK *HER* TO YOMI.
HE MUST TRUST HER A LOT MORE THAN YOU.
BLUSH
WHOOSH
Y-YUKINÉ-KUN!
WHOOP-SIE.
DA-LING

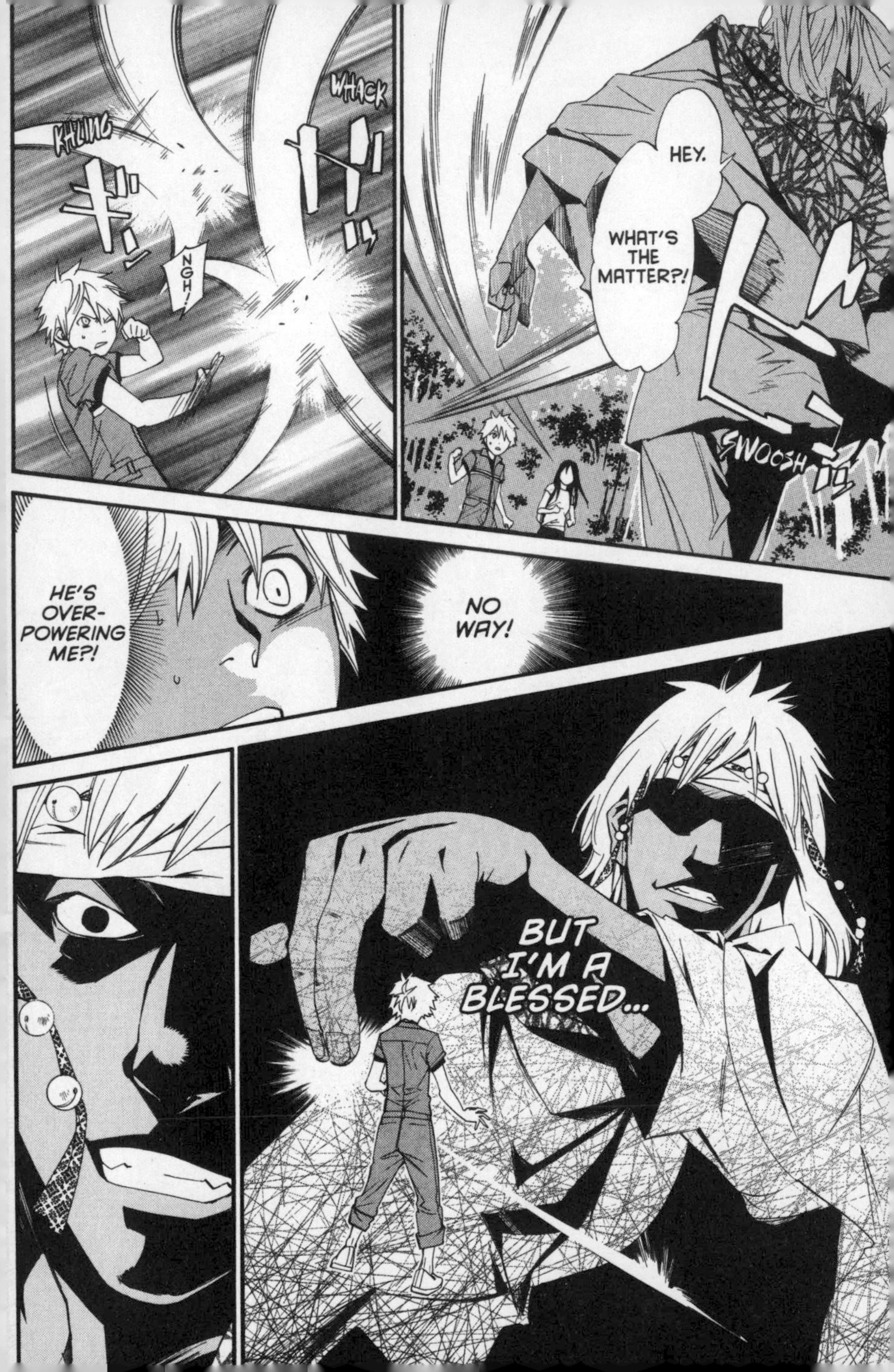
HEY.
WHAT'S THE MATTER?!
SWOOSH
WHACK
KHLING
NGH!
NO WAY!
HE'S OVER-POWERING ME?!
BUT I'M A BLESSED...

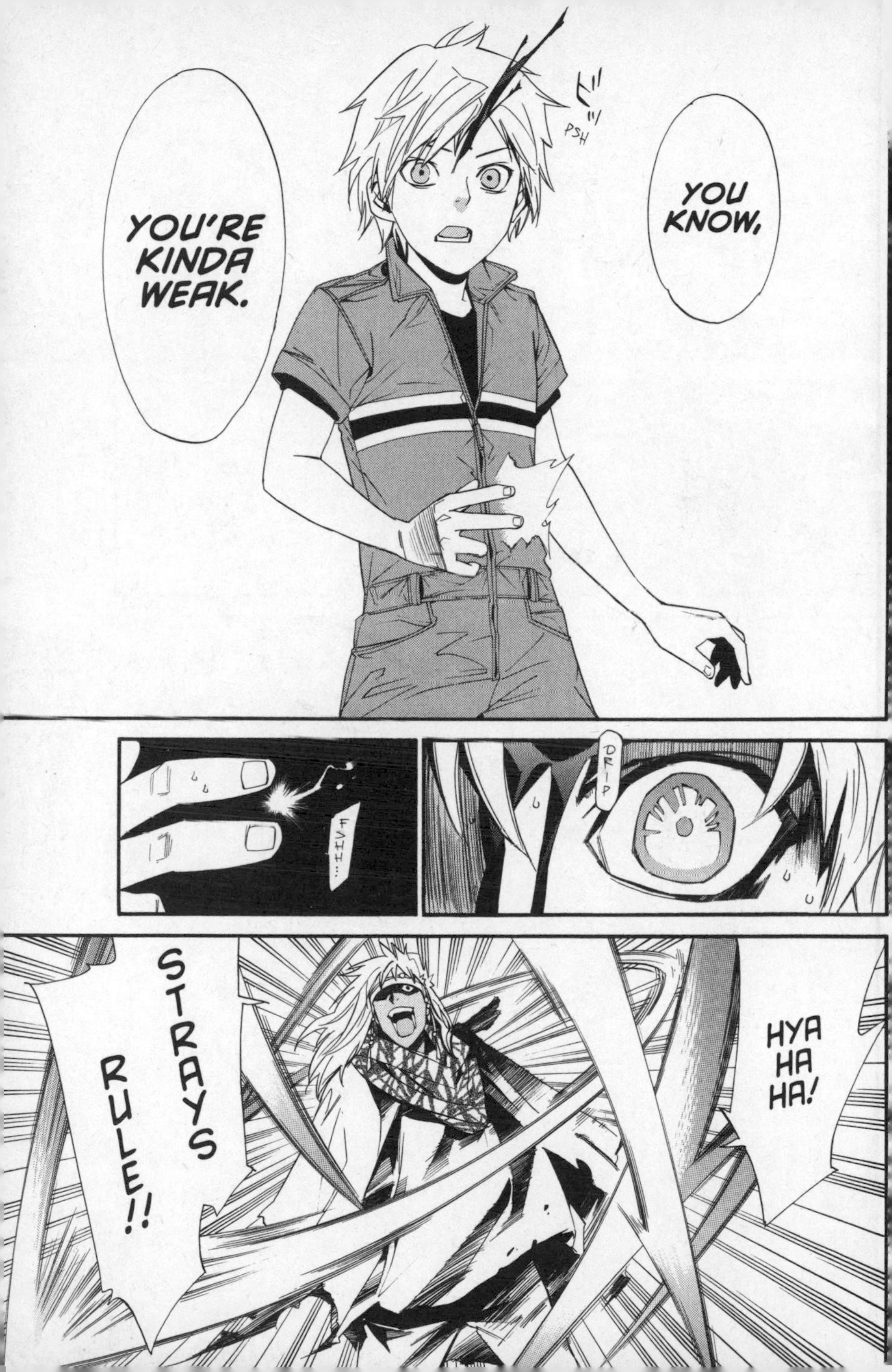
PSH
YOU KNOW,
YOU'RE KINDA WEAK.
DRIP
FSHH...
HYA HA HA!
STRAYS RULE!!

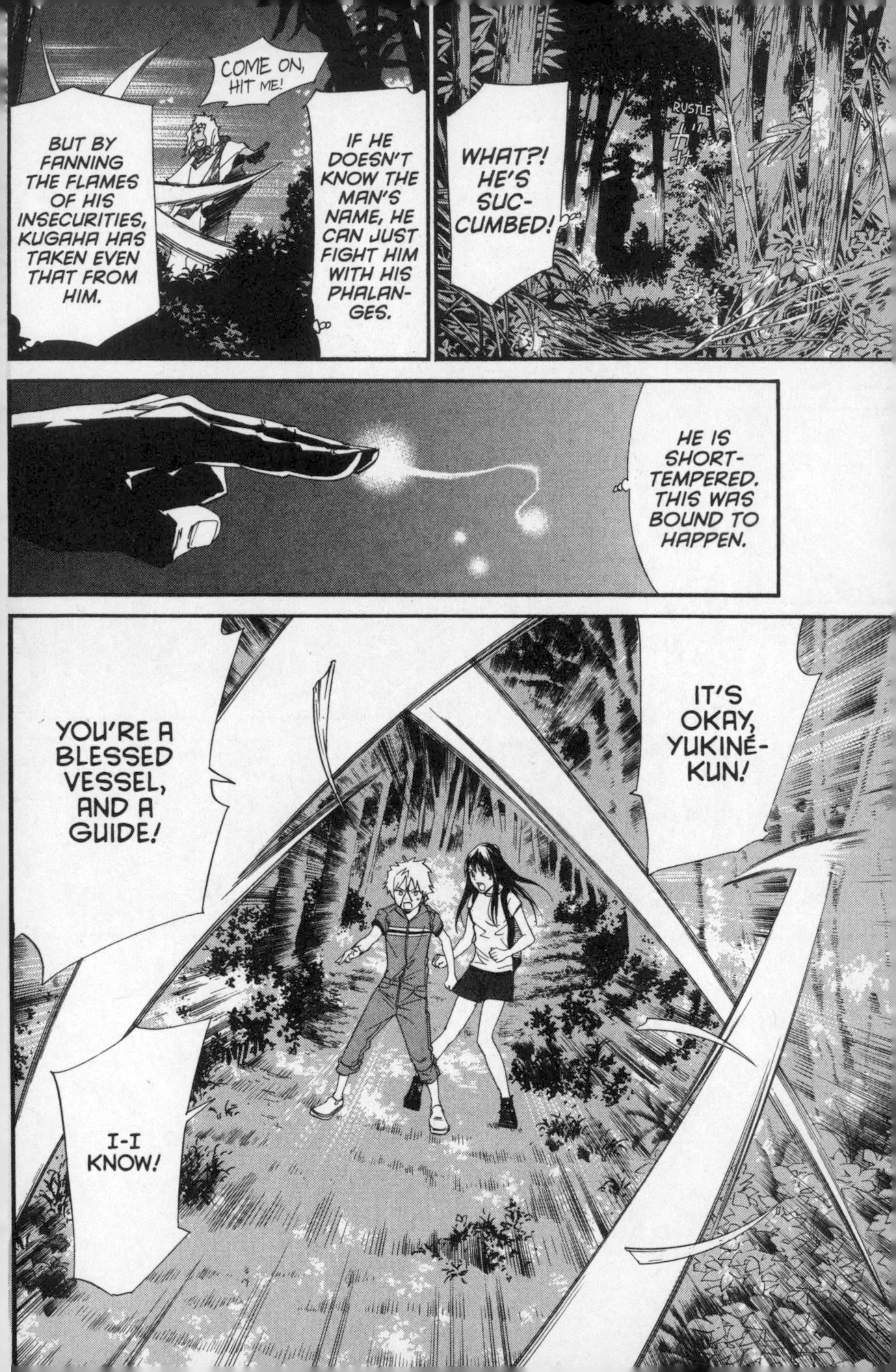
RUSTLE
WHAT?! HE'S SUCCUMBED!
COME ON, HIT ME!
IF HE DOESN'T KNOW THE MAN'S NAME, HE CAN JUST FIGHT HIM WITH HIS PHALANGES.
BUT BY FANNING THE FLAMES OF HIS INSECURITIES, KUGAHA HAS TAKEN EVEN THAT FROM HIM.
HE IS SHORT-TEMPERED. THIS WAS BOUND TO HAPPEN.
IT'S OKAY, YUKINÉ-KUN!
YOU'RE A BLESSED VESSEL, AND A GUIDE!
I-I KNOW!

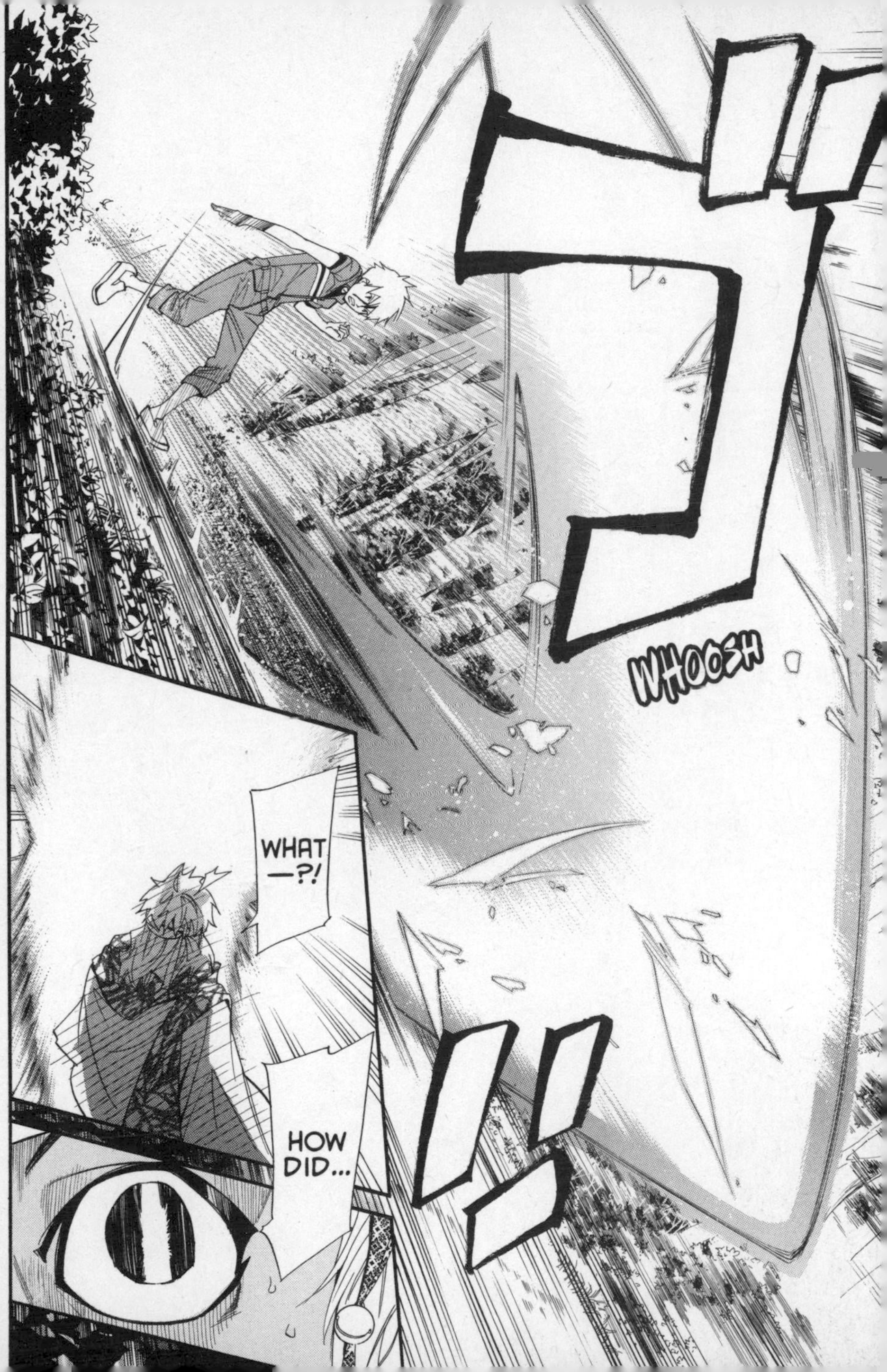
WHOOSH
WHAT —?!
HOW DID...

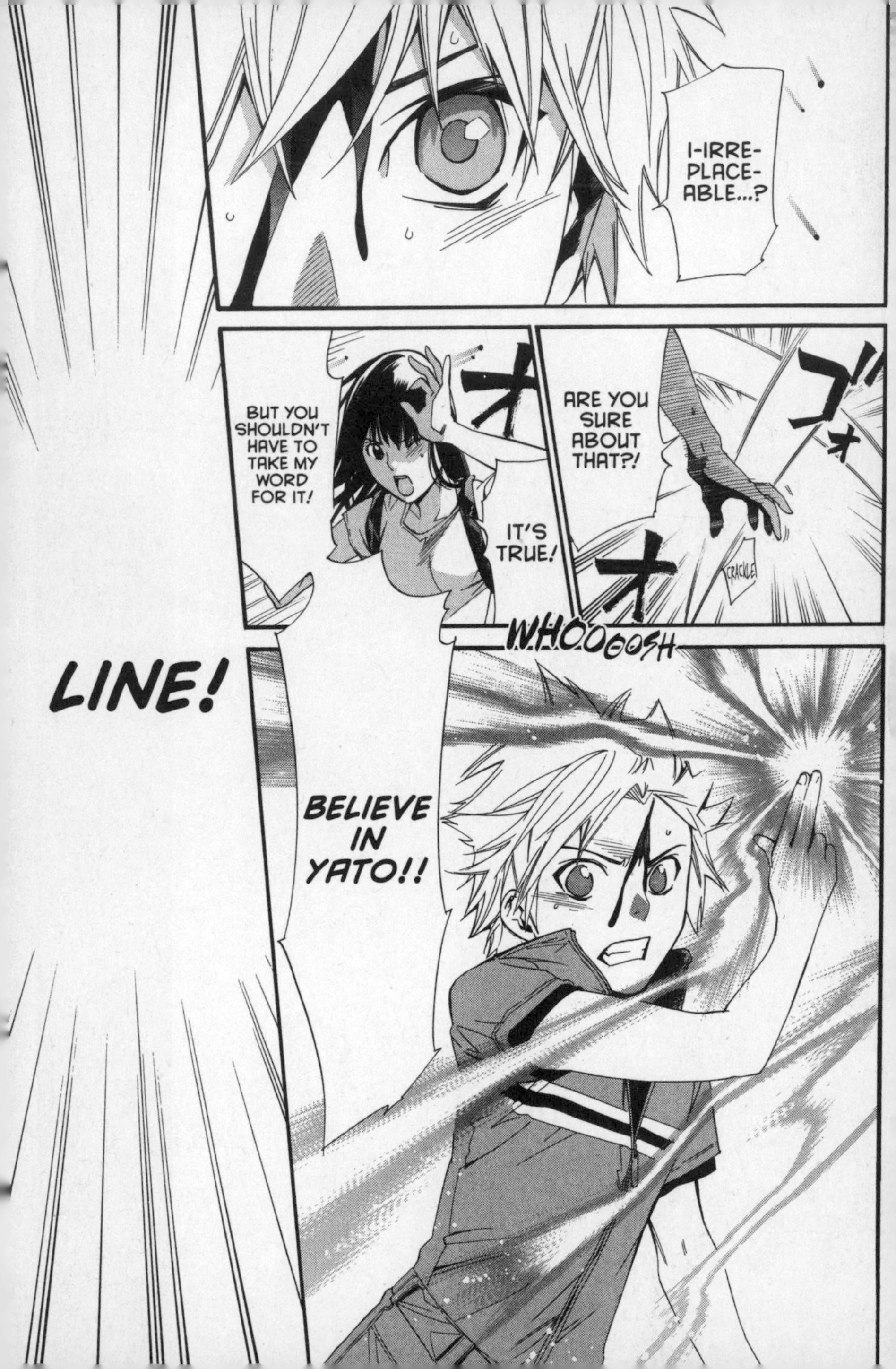
I-IRRE-PLACE-ABLE...?
ARE YOU SURE ABOUT THAT?!
ゴォ
CRACKLE
オ
IT'S TRUE!
BUT YOU SHOULDN'T HAVE TO TAKE MY WORD FOR IT!
オ
WHOOOOOSH
BELIEVE IN YATO!!
LINE!

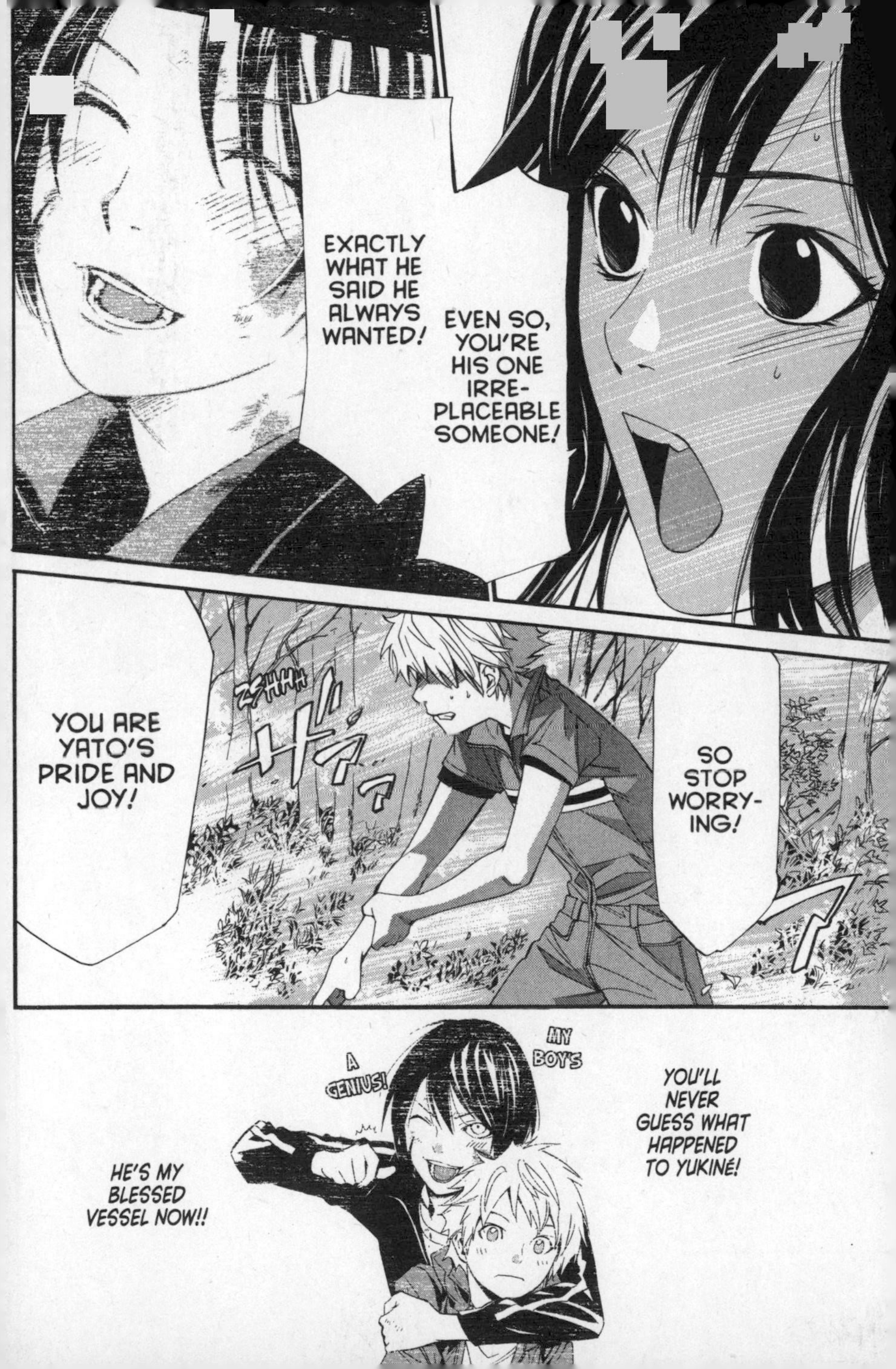
EVEN SO, YOU'RE HIS ONE IRRE-PLACEABLE SOMEONE!
EXACTLY WHAT HE SAID HE ALWAYS WANTED!
SO STOP WORRY-ING!
ZSHHH
YOU ARE YATO'S PRIDE AND JOY!
YOU'LL NEVER GUESS WHAT HAPPENED TO YUKINÉ!
MY BOY'S
A GENIUS!
HE'S MY BLESSED VESSEL NOW!!

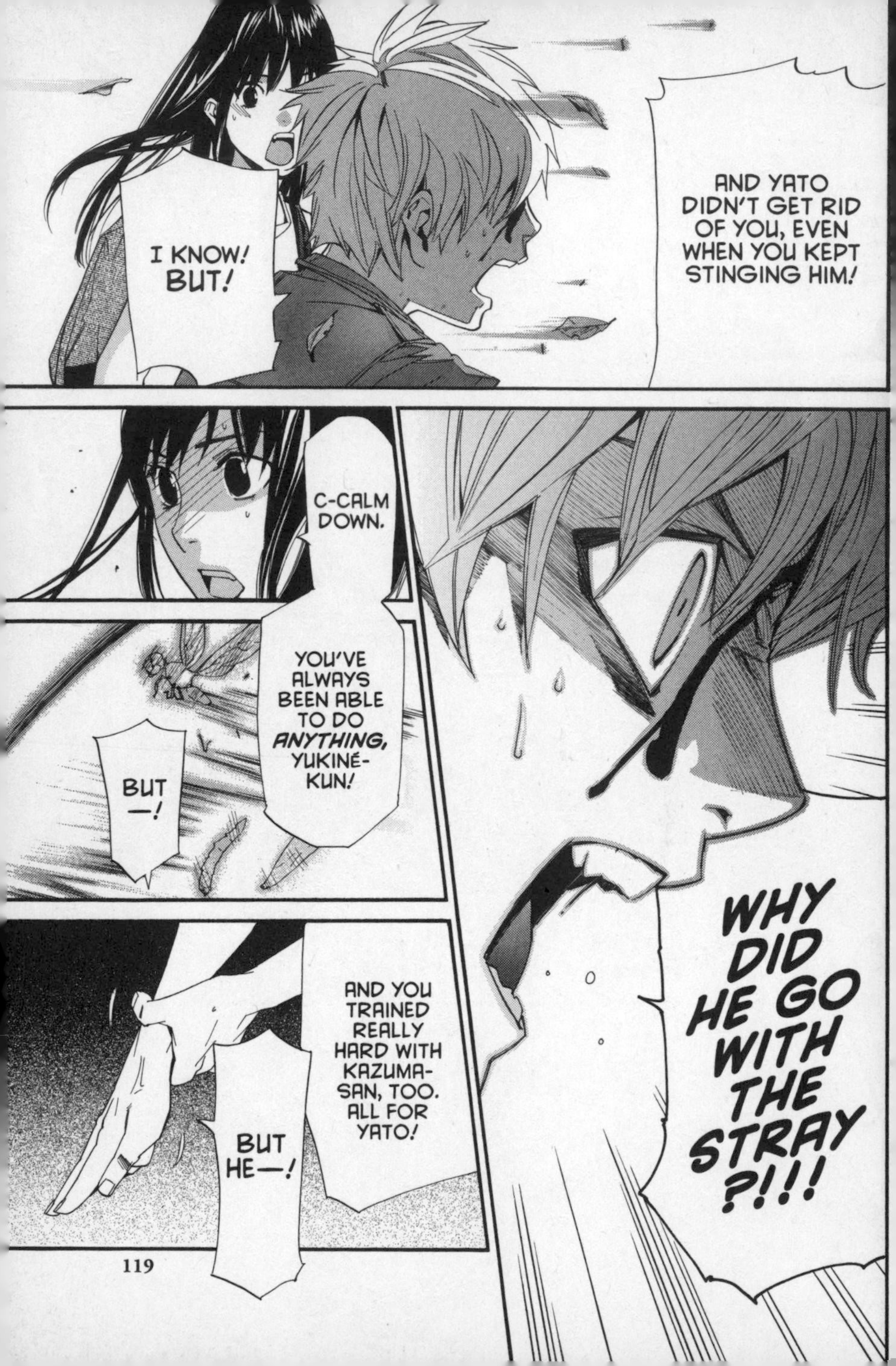
AND YATO DIDN'T GET RID OF YOU, EVEN WHEN YOU KEPT STINGING HIM!
I KNOW! BUT!
WHY DID HE GO WITH THE STRAY?!!!
C-CALM DOWN.
YOU'VE ALWAYS BEEN ABLE TO DO *ANYTHING*, YUKINÉ-KUN!
BUT—!
AND YOU TRAINED REALLY HARD WITH KAZUMA-SAN, TOO. ALL FOR YATO!
BUT HE—!

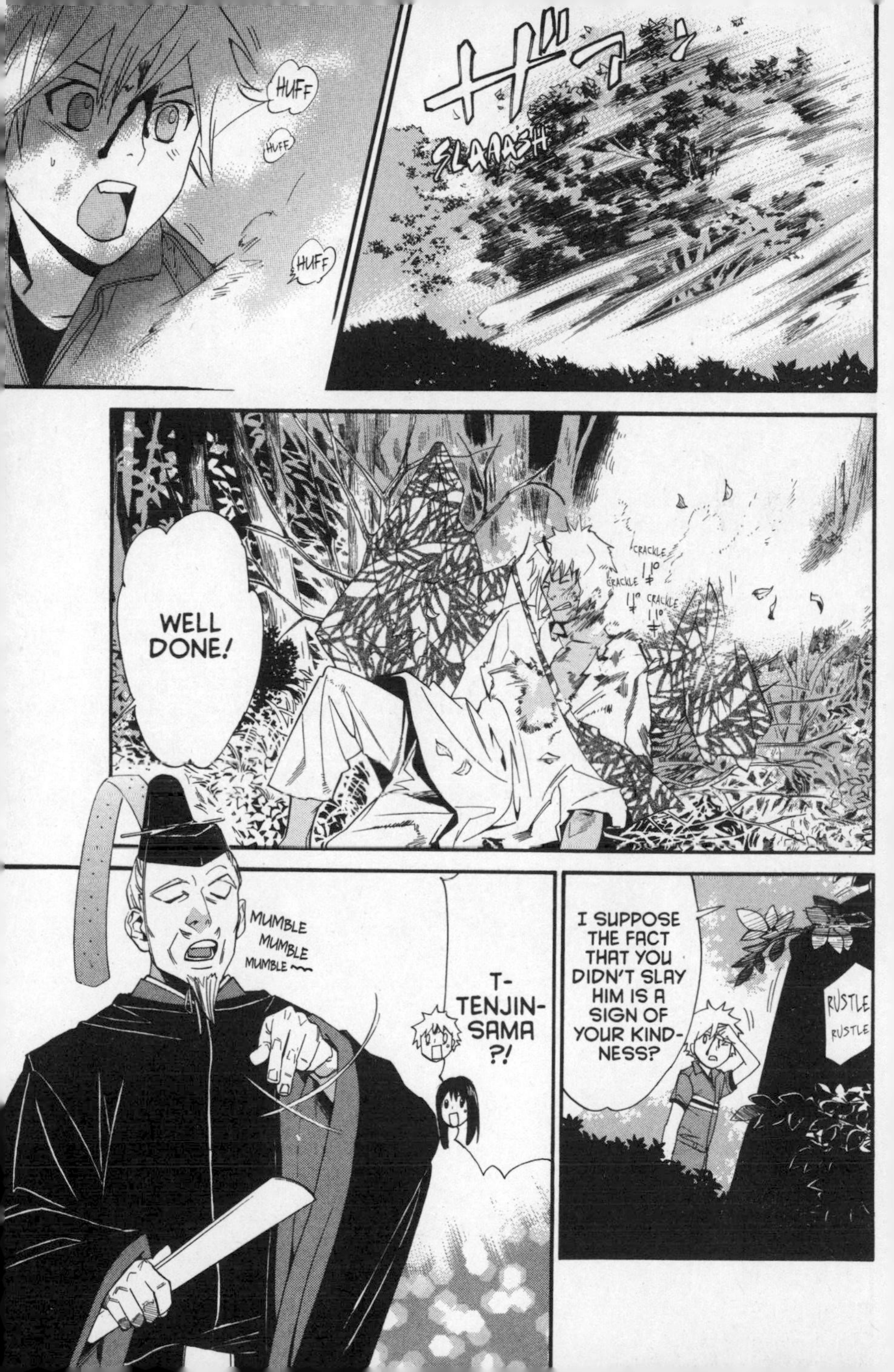
SLAAASH
HUFF
HUFF
HUFF
CRACKLE
CRACKLE
CRACKLE
WELL DONE!
I SUPPOSE THE FACT THAT YOU DIDN'T SLAY HIM IS A SIGN OF YOUR KINDNESS?
RUSTLE
RUSTLE
T-TENJIN-SAMA?!
MUMBLE
MUMBLE
MUMBLE ~~

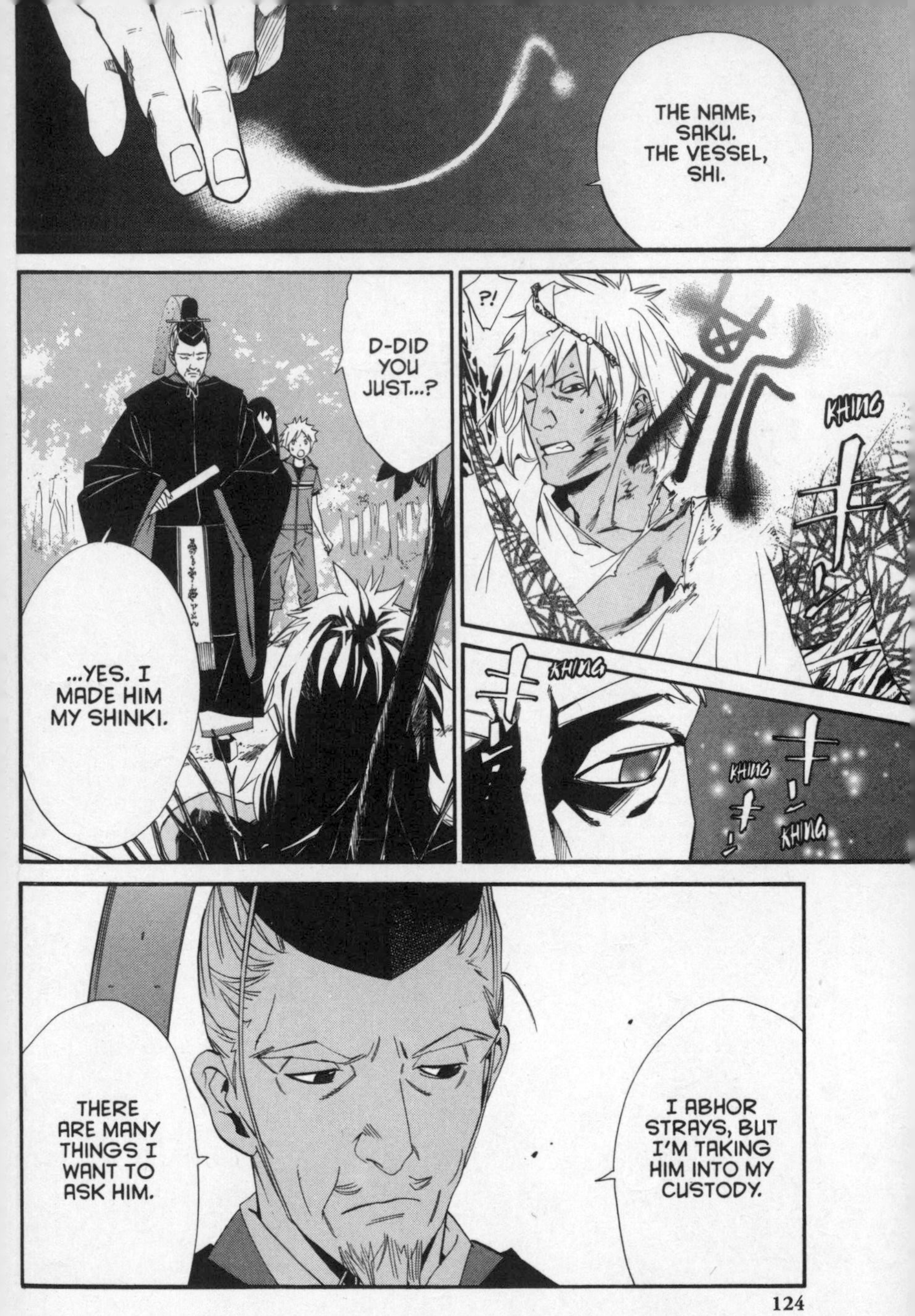
THE NAME, SAKU. THE VESSEL, SHI.
?!
KHING
KHING
KHING
KHING
D-DID YOU JUST...?
...YES. I MADE HIM MY SHINKI.
I ABHOR STRAYS, BUT I'M TAKING HIM INTO MY CUSTODY.
THERE ARE MANY THINGS I WANT TO ASK HIM.

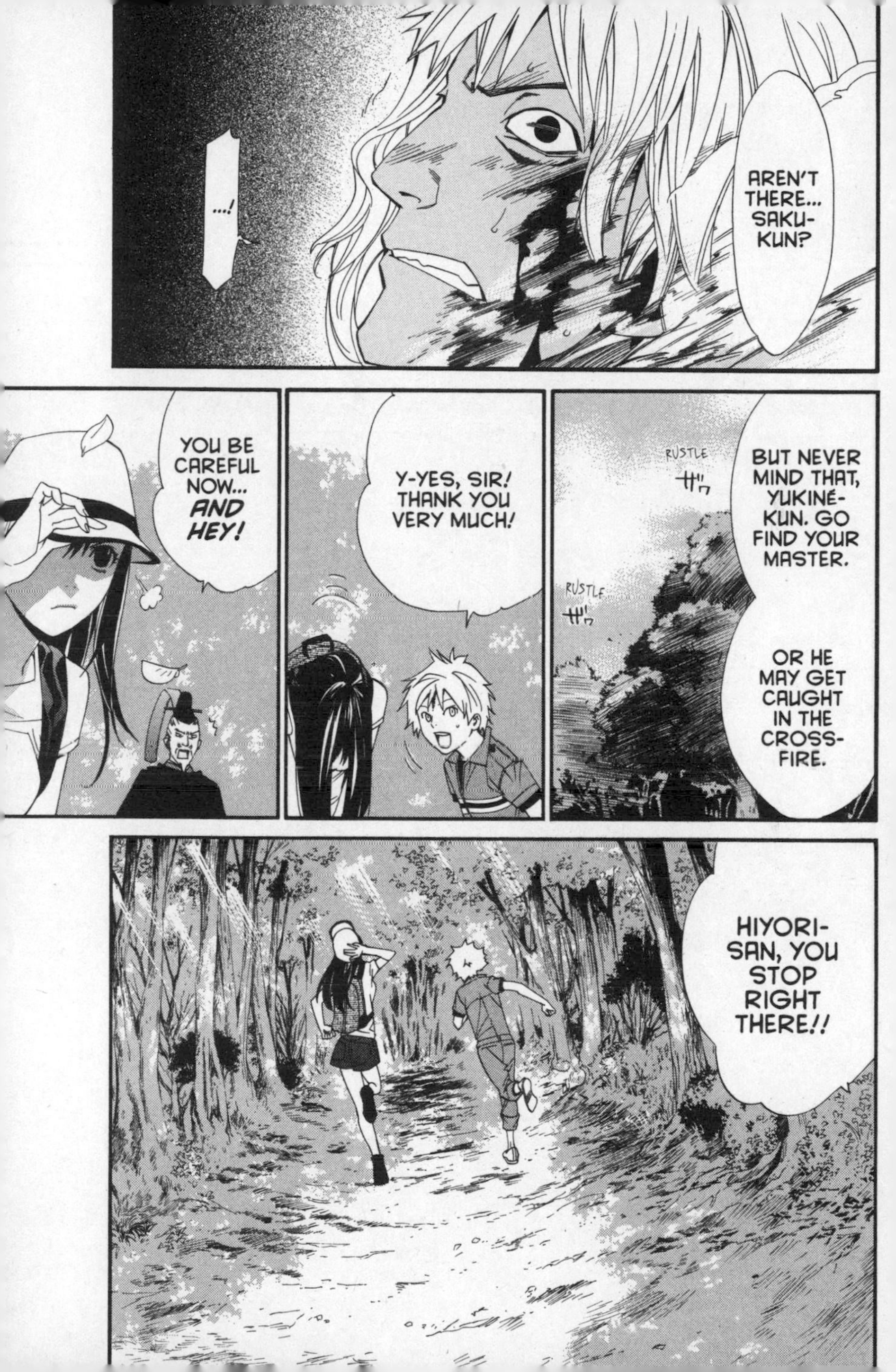
AREN'T THERE... SAKU-KUN?
...!
RUSTLE
RUSTLE
BUT NEVER MIND THAT, YUKINÉ-KUN. GO FIND YOUR MASTER.
OR HE MAY GET CAUGHT IN THE CROSS-FIRE.
Y-YES, SIR! THANK YOU VERY MUCH!
YOU BE CAREFUL NOW... *AND HEY!*
HIYORI-SAN, YOU STOP RIGHT THERE!!

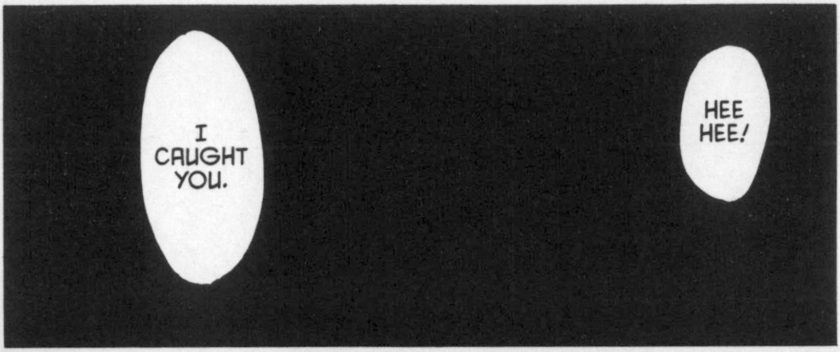
HEE HEE!
I CAUGHT YOU.

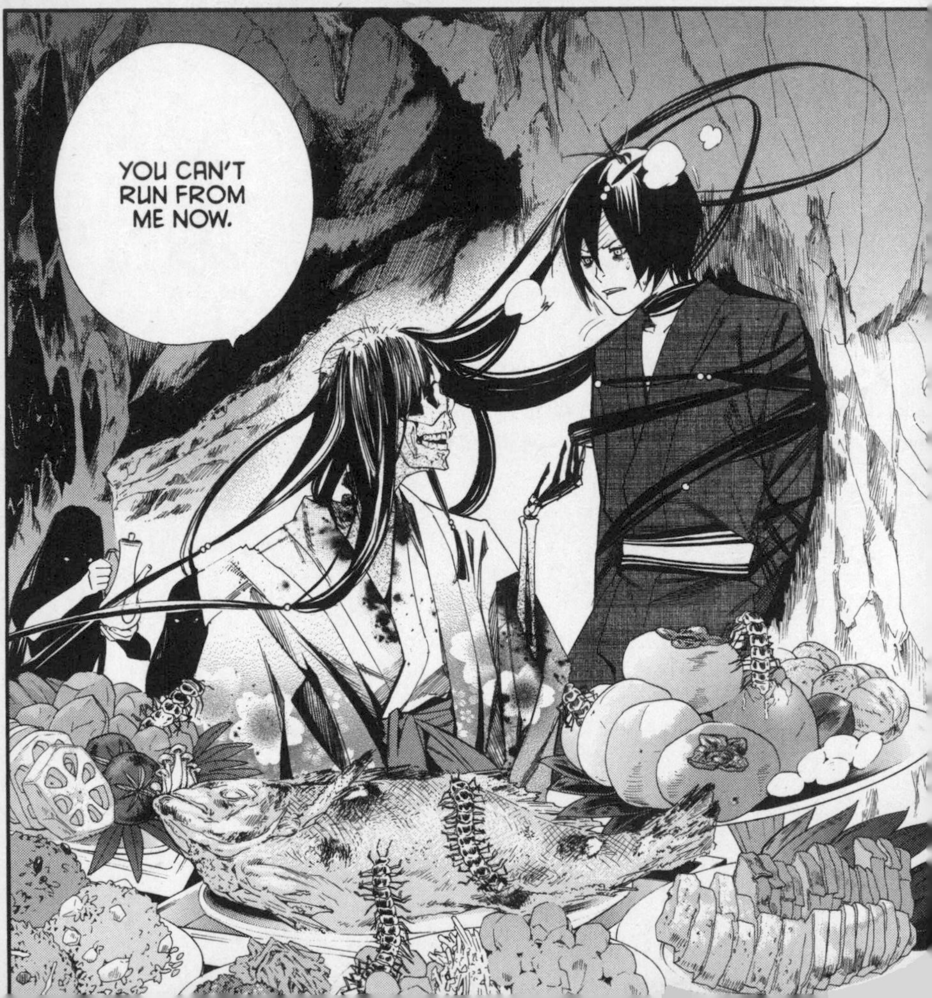
YOU CAN'T RUN FROM ME NOW.

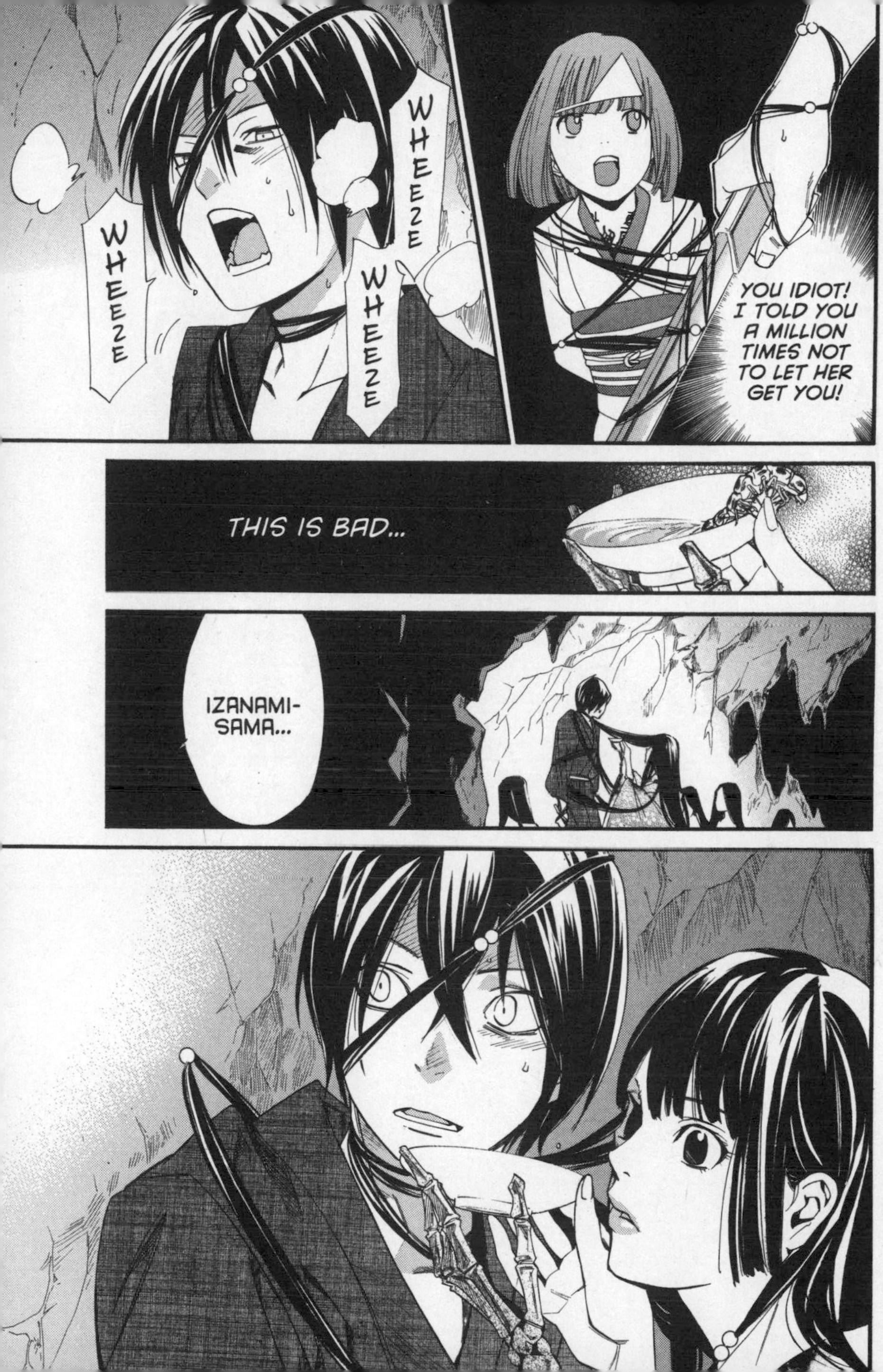
YOU IDIOT! I TOLD YOU A MILLION TIMES NOT TO LET HER GET YOU!
WHEEZE
WHEEZE
WHEEZE
THIS IS BAD...
IZANAMI-SAMA...

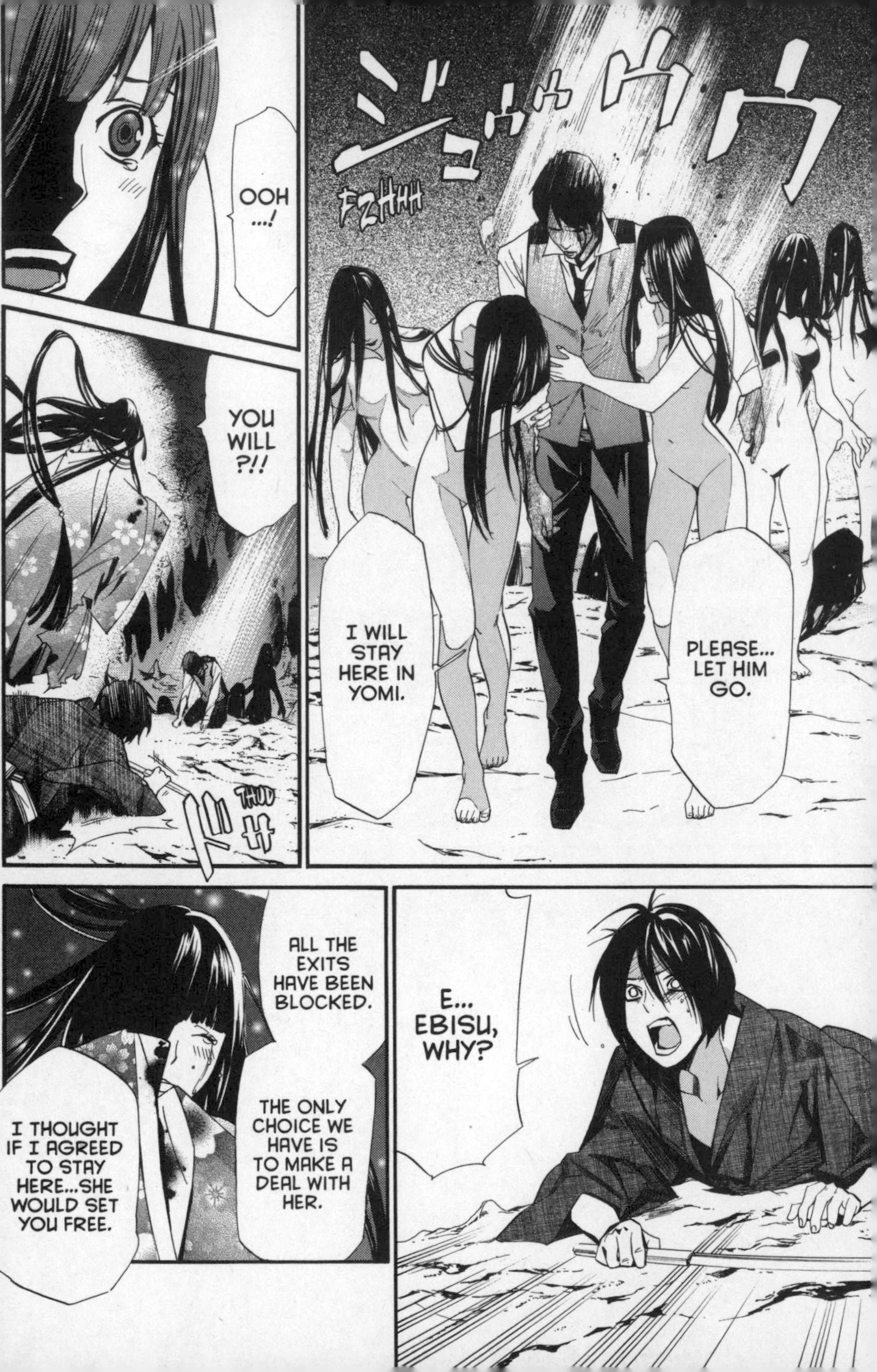
FZHHH
PLEASE... LET HIM GO.
I WILL STAY HERE IN YOMI.
OOH ...!
YOU WILL ?!!
THUD
E... EBISU, WHY?
ALL THE EXITS HAVE BEEN BLOCKED.
THE ONLY CHOICE WE HAVE IS TO MAKE A DEAL WITH HER.
I THOUGHT IF I AGREED TO STAY HERE...SHE WOULD SET YOU FREE.

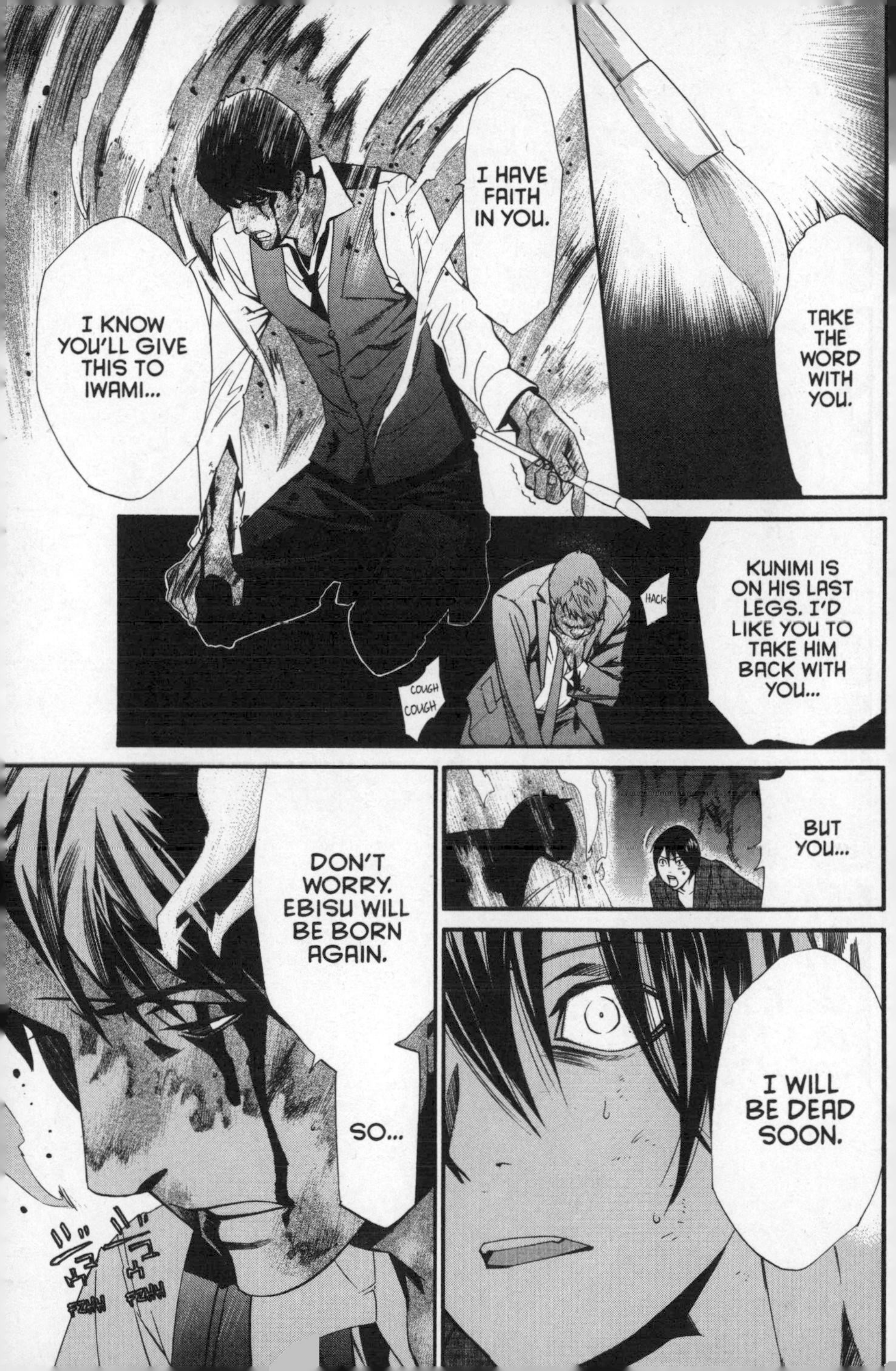
TAKE THE WORD WITH YOU.
I HAVE FAITH IN YOU.
I KNOW YOU'LL GIVE THIS TO IWAMI...
KUNIMI IS ON HIS LAST LEGS. I'D LIKE YOU TO TAKE HIM BACK WITH YOU...
HACK
COUGH COUGH
BUT YOU...
I WILL BE DEAD SOON.
DON'T WORRY. EBISU WILL BE BORN AGAIN.
SO...

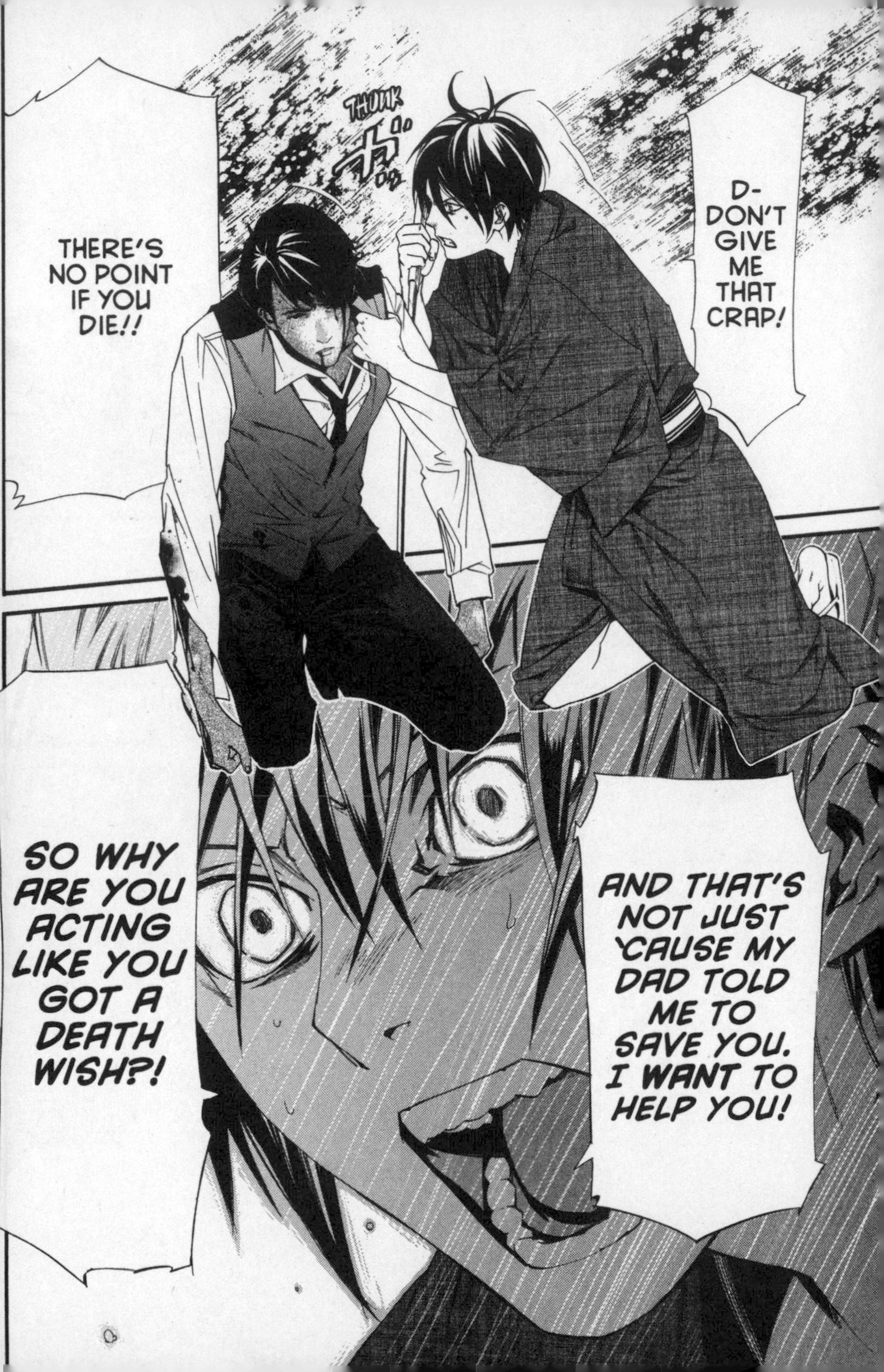
D-DON'T GIVE ME THAT CRAP!
THUNK
THERE'S NO POINT IF YOU DIE!!
AND THAT'S NOT JUST 'CAUSE MY DAD TOLD ME TO SAVE YOU. I WANT TO HELP YOU!
SO WHY ARE YOU ACTING LIKE YOU GOT A DEATH WISH?!

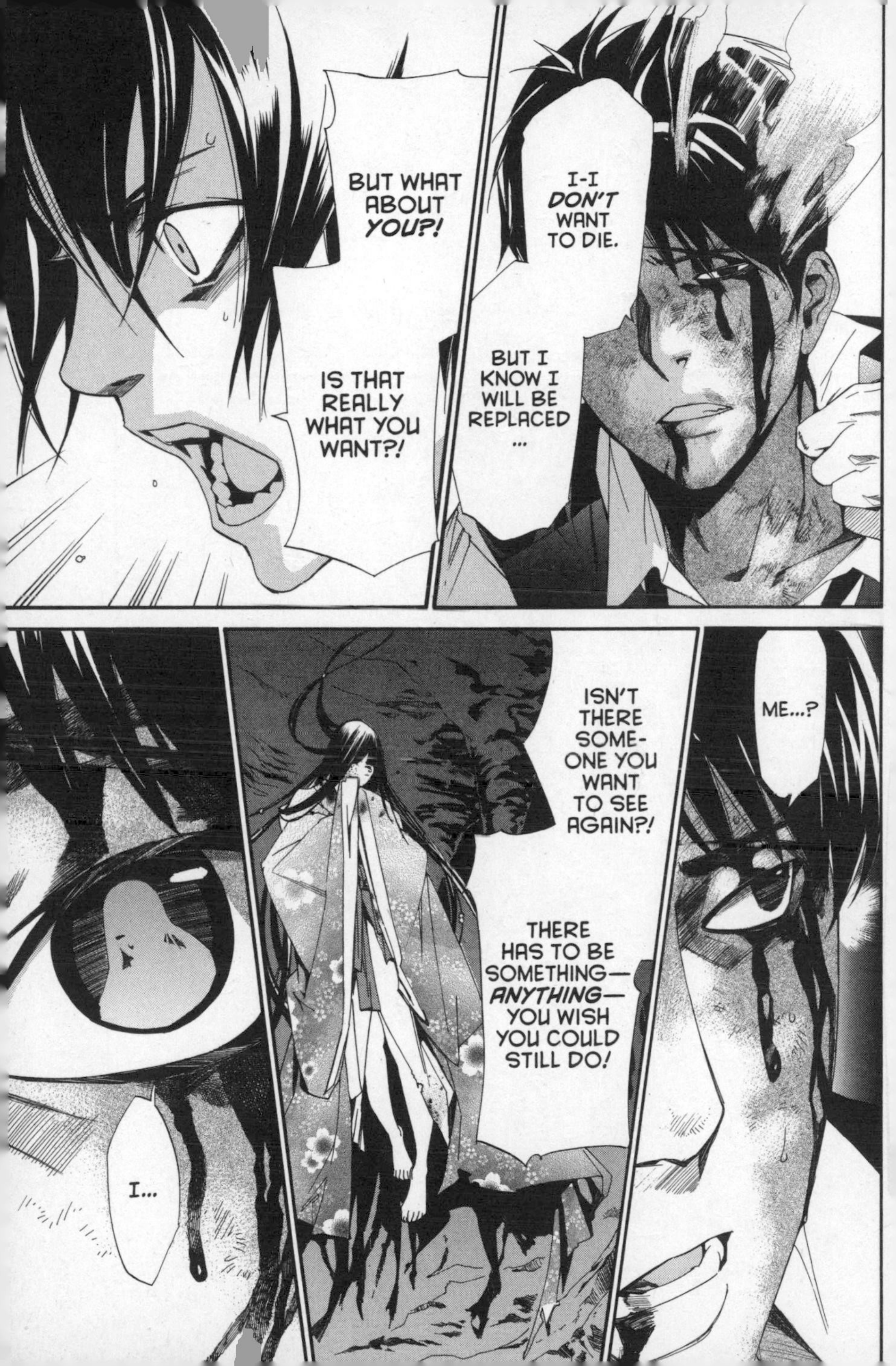
I-I *DON'T* WANT TO DIE.
BUT I KNOW I WILL BE REPLACED ...
BUT WHAT ABOUT *YOU?!*
IS THAT REALLY WHAT YOU WANT?!
ME...?
ISN'T THERE SOME-ONE YOU WANT TO SEE AGAIN?!
THERE HAS TO BE SOMETHING—*ANYTHING*—YOU WISH YOU COULD STILL DO!
I...

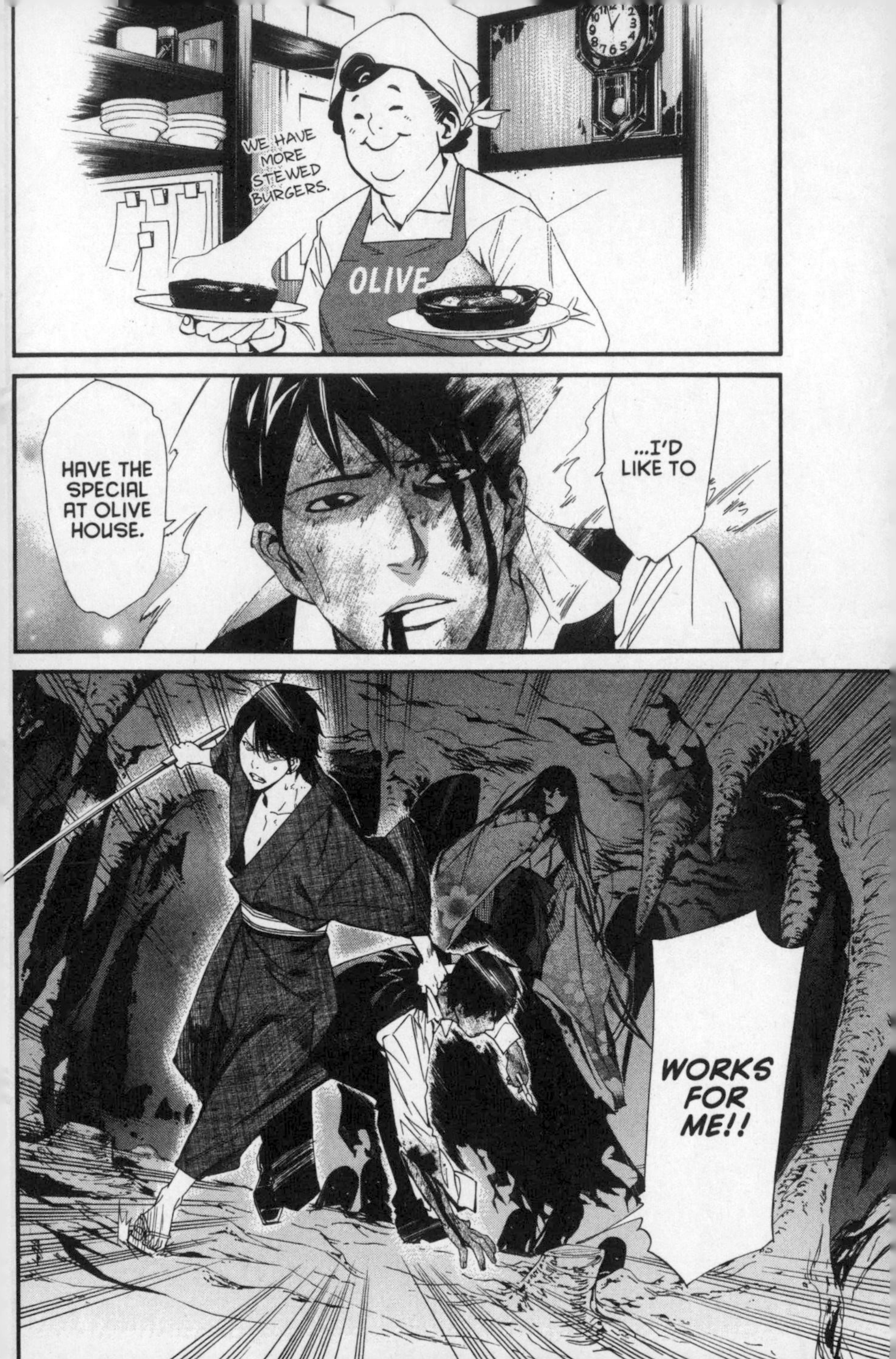
WE HAVE MORE STEWED BURGERS.
OLIVE
...I'D LIKE TO
HAVE THE SPECIAL AT OLIVE HOUSE.
WORKS FOR ME!!

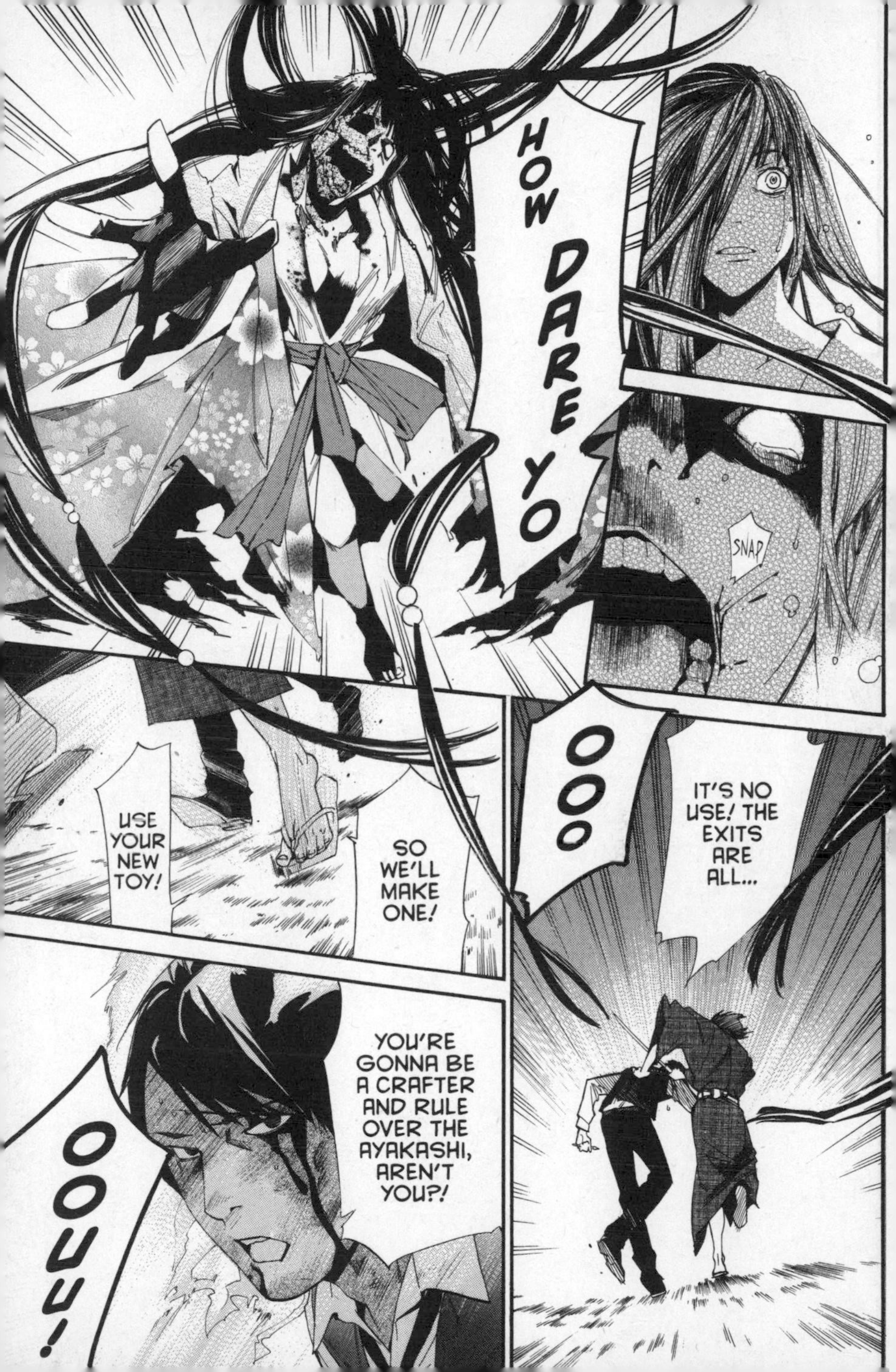
SNAP
HOW DARE YO
OOO
IT'S NO USE! THE EXITS ARE ALL...
SO WE'LL MAKE ONE!
USE YOUR NEW TOY!
YOU'RE GONNA BE A CRAFTER AND RULE OVER THE AYAKASHI, AREN'T YOU?!
OOUUU!

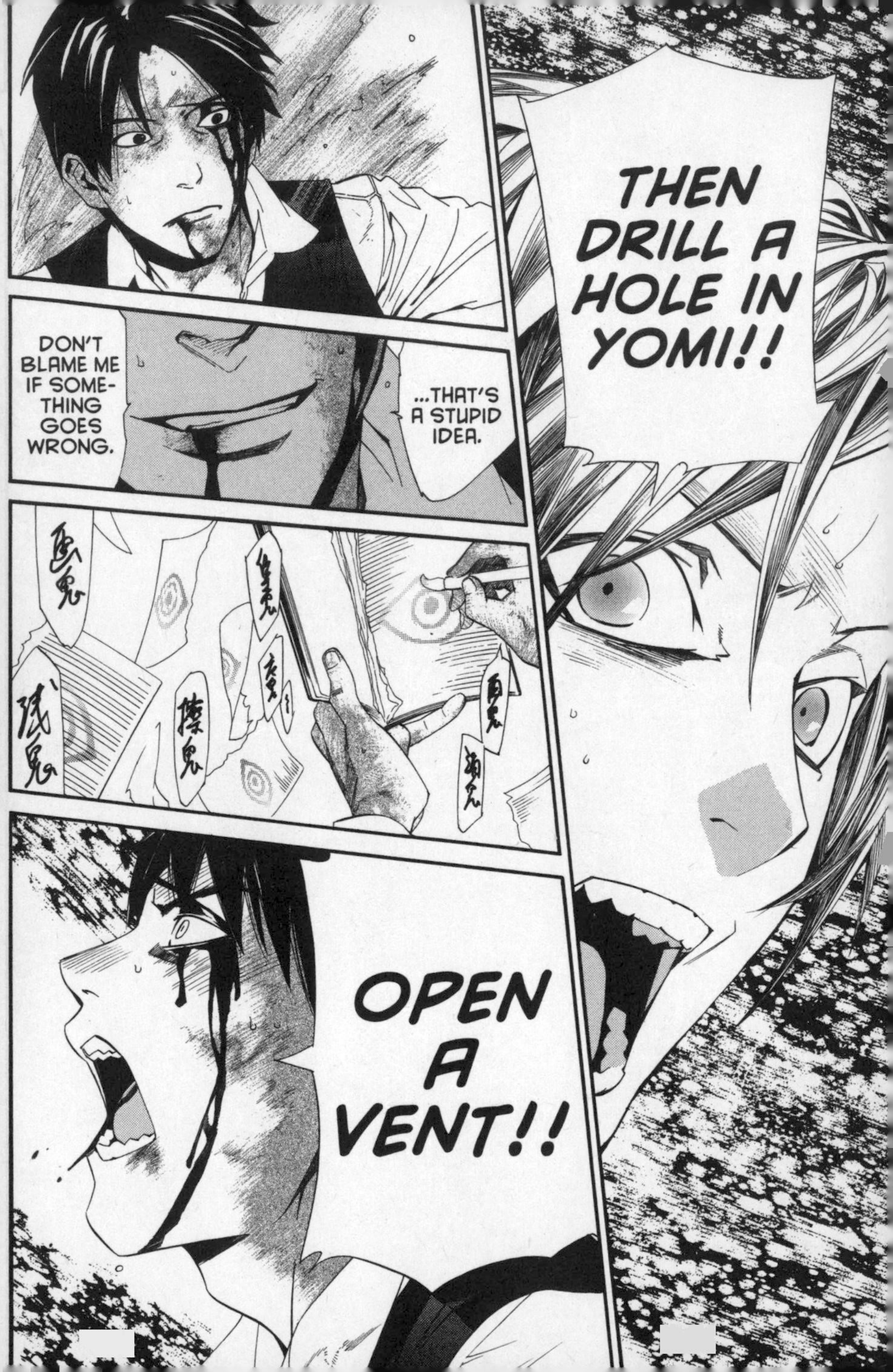
THEN DRILL A HOLE IN YOMI!!
...THAT'S A STUPID IDEA.
DON'T BLAME ME IF SOME-THING GOES WRONG.
OPEN A VENT!!

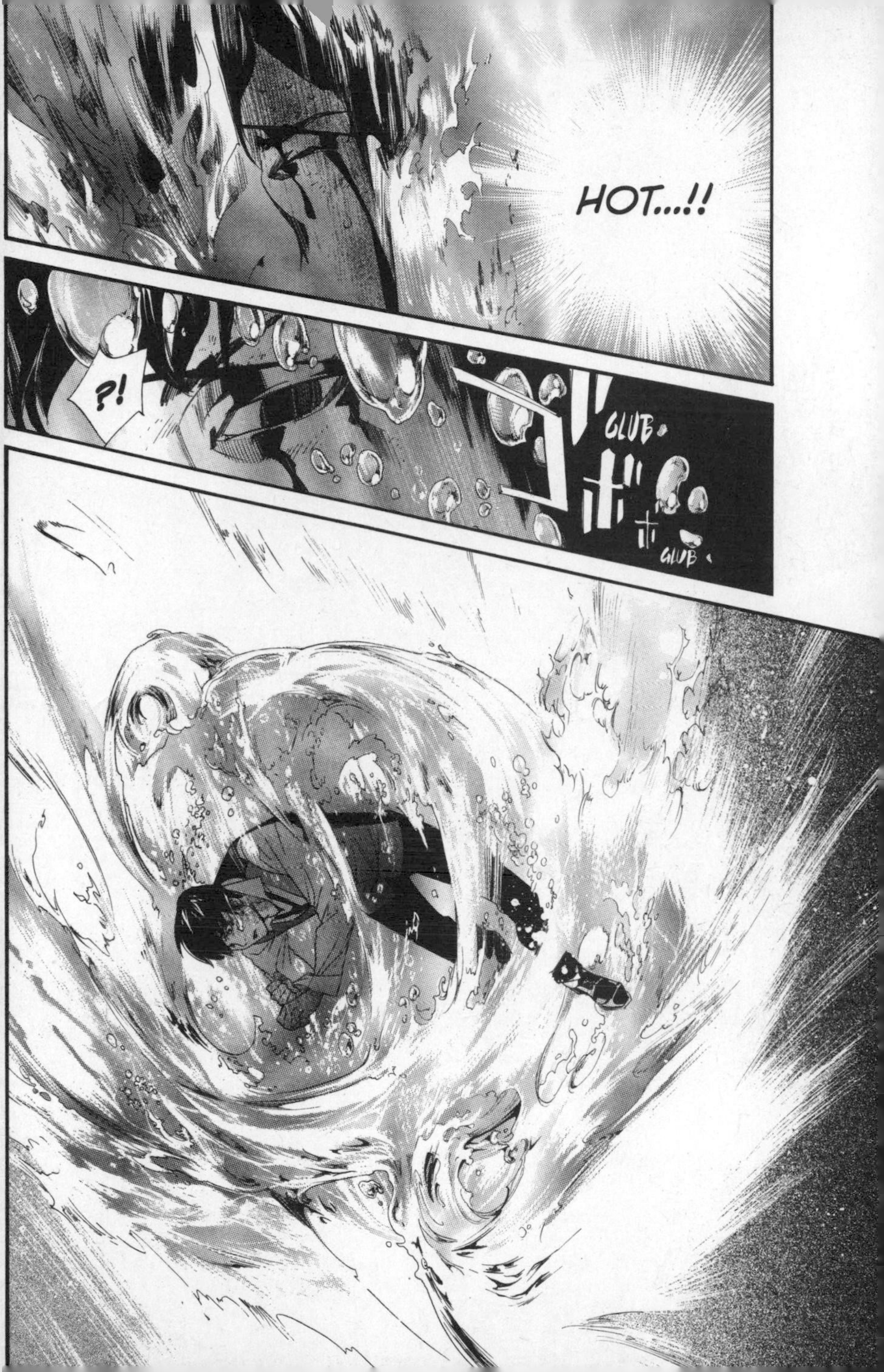
HOT...!!
GLUB
GLUB
?!

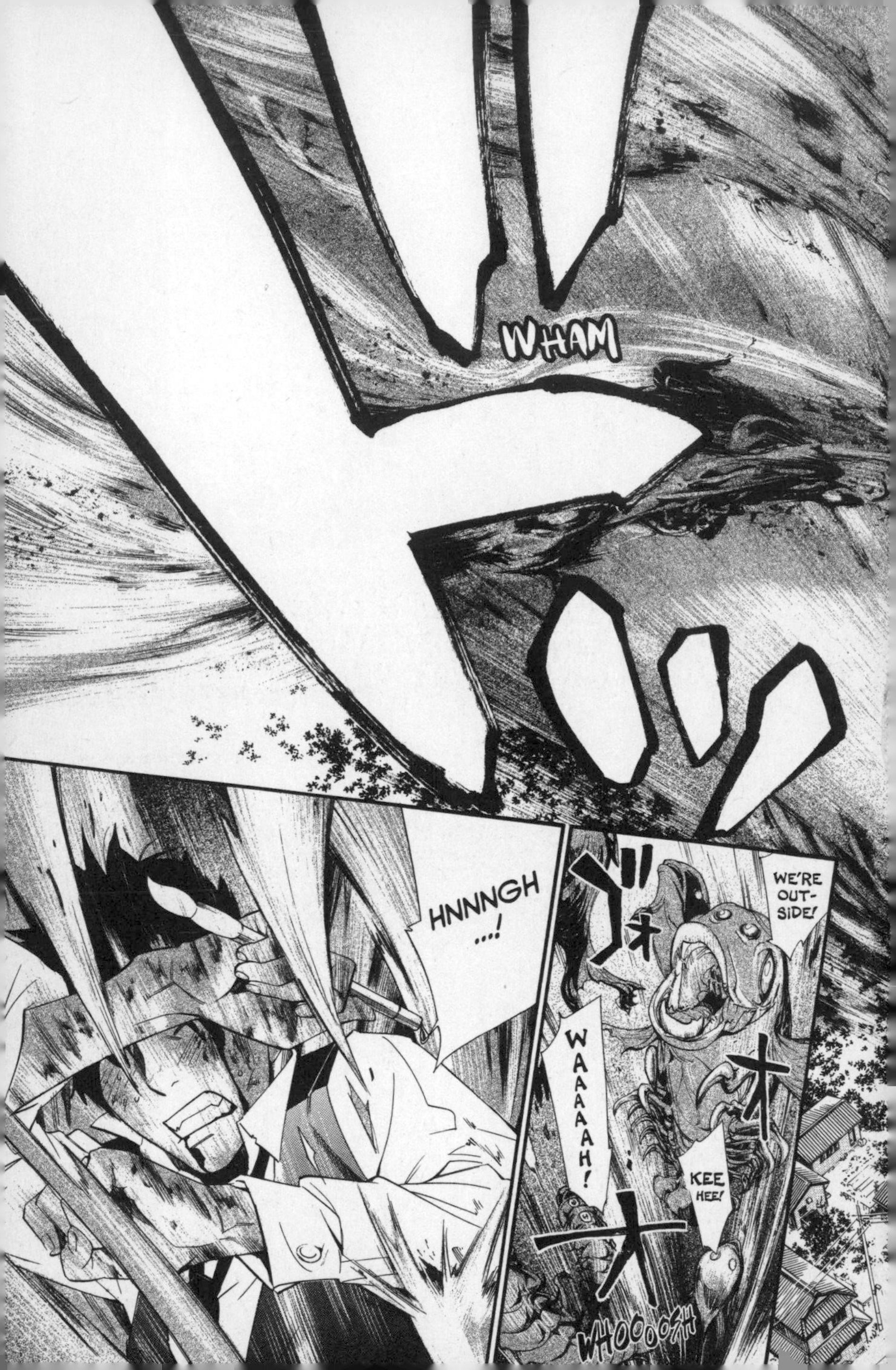
WHAM
WE'RE OUT-SIDE!
WAAAAAH!
KEE HEE!
WHOOOOSH
HNNNGH ...!

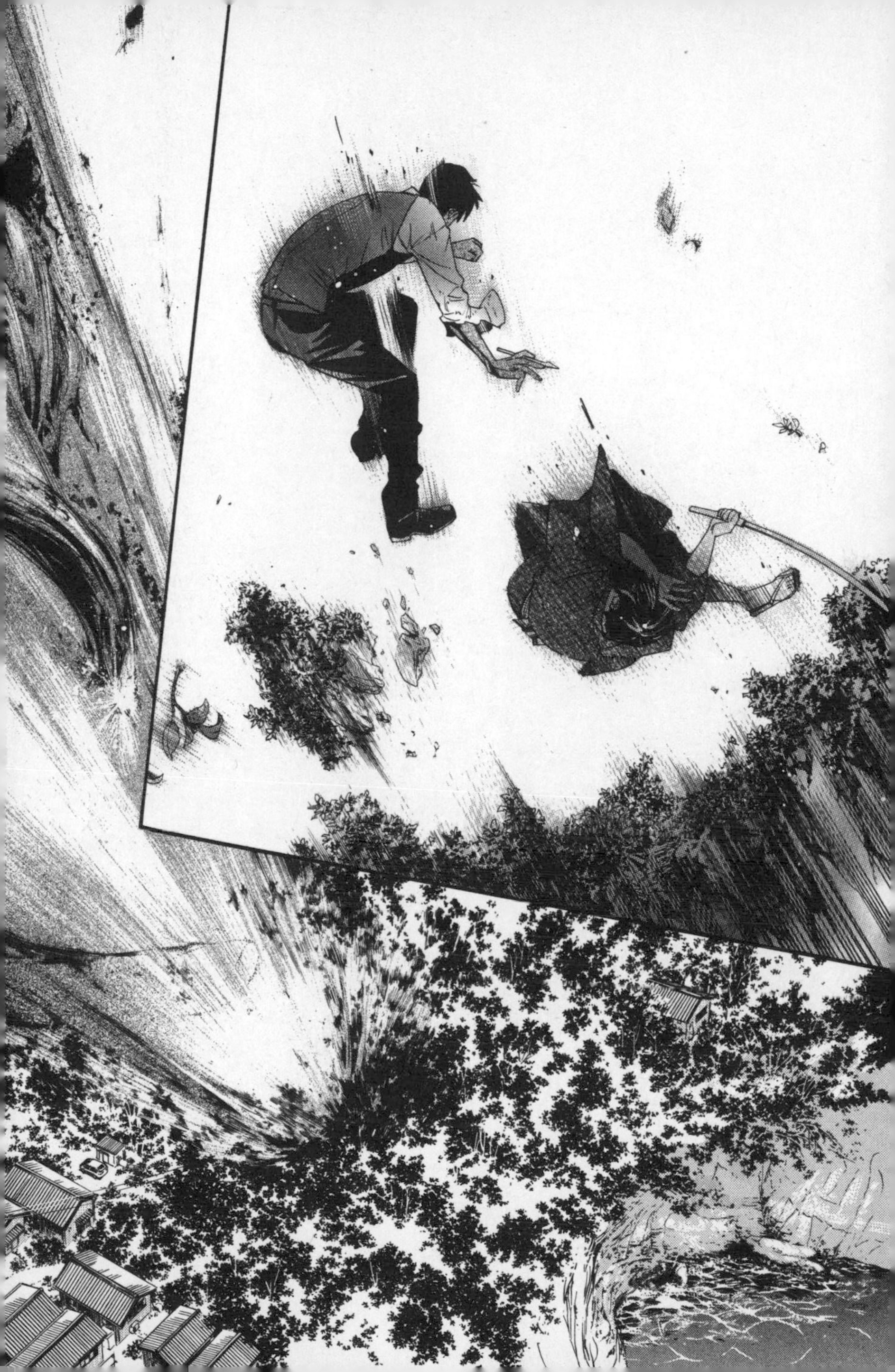

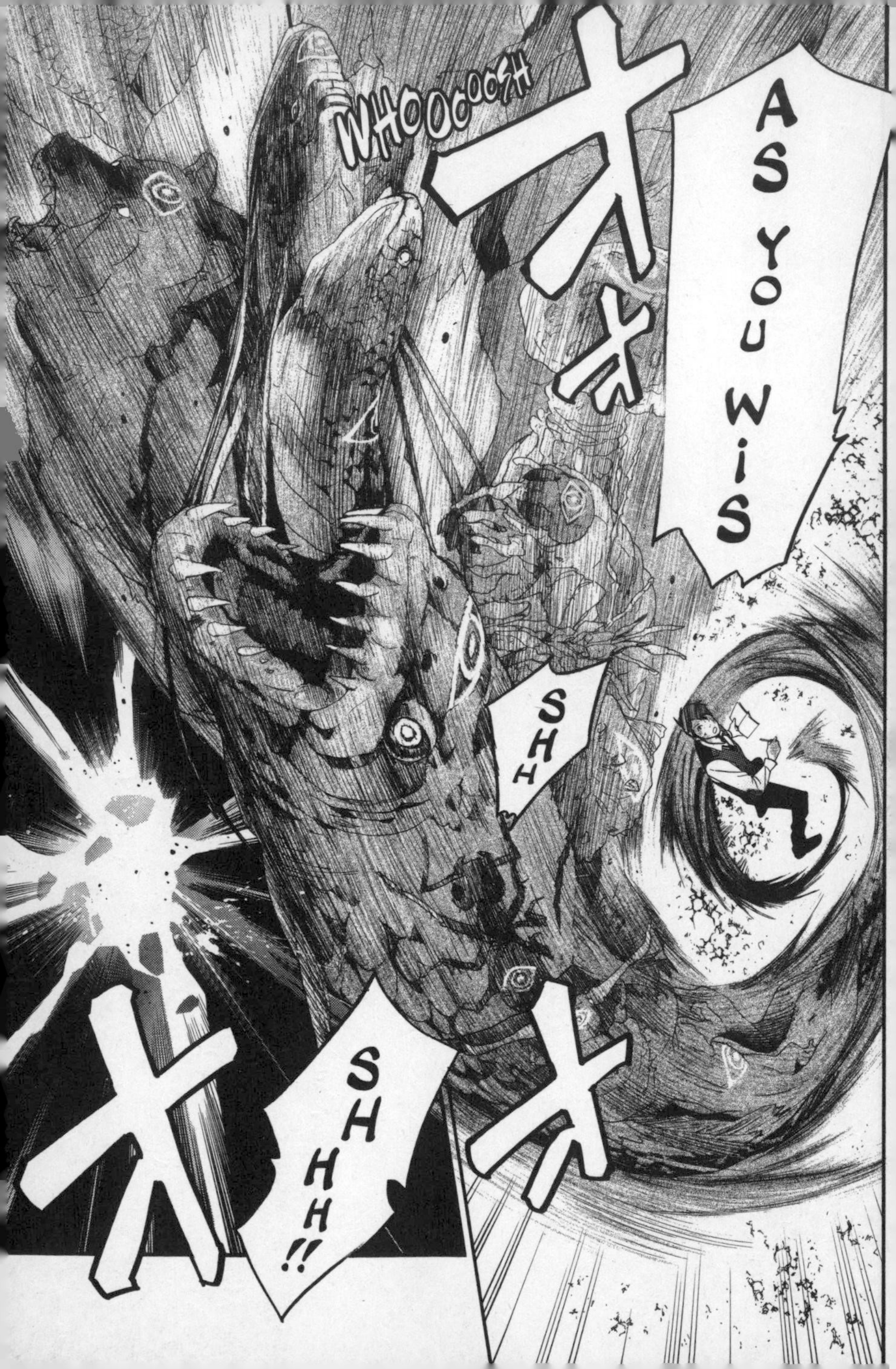
AS YOU WiS
WHOOoooSH
SHH
SHHHH!!

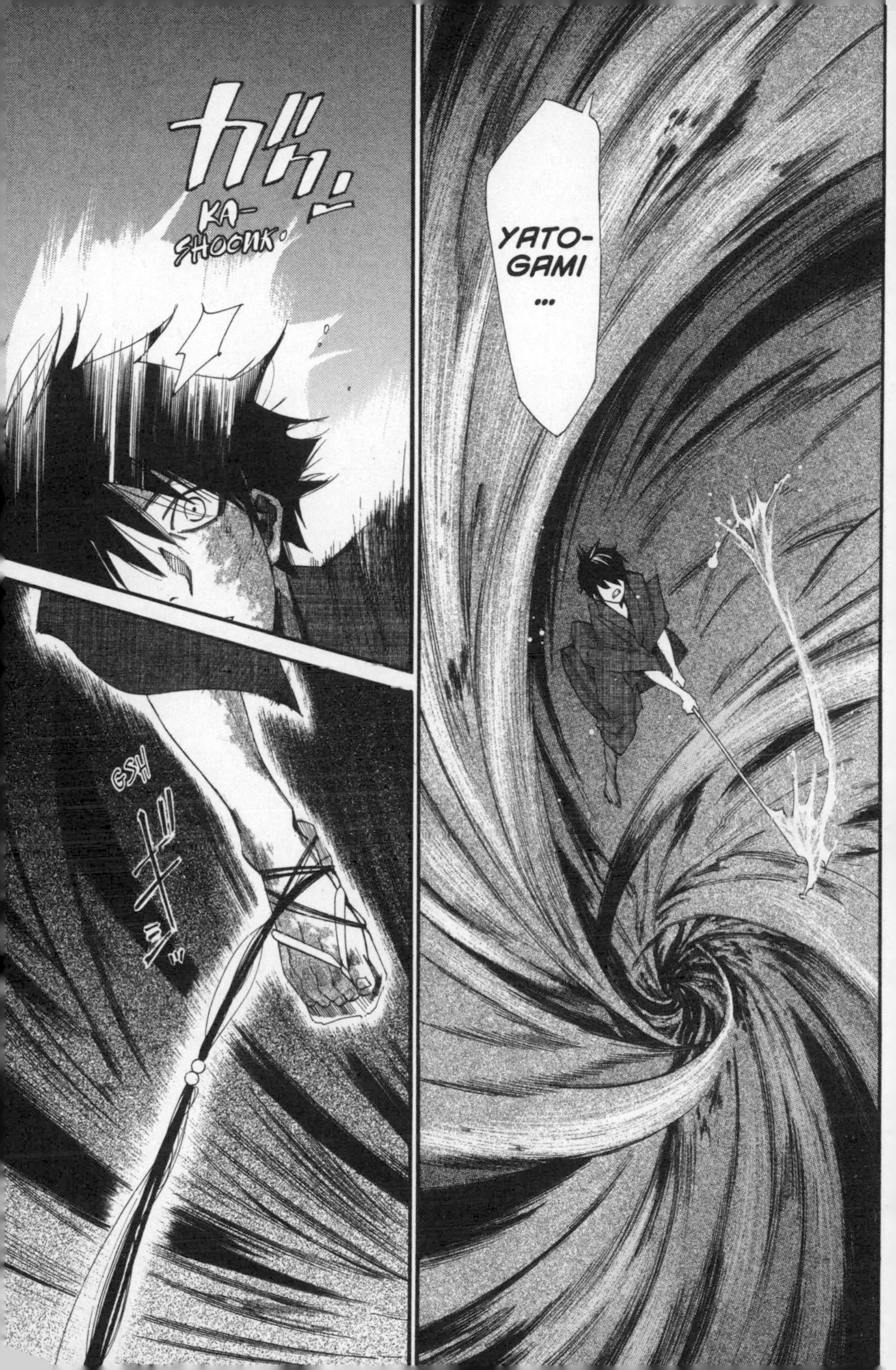
YATO-GAMI ...
KA-SHOONK
GSH

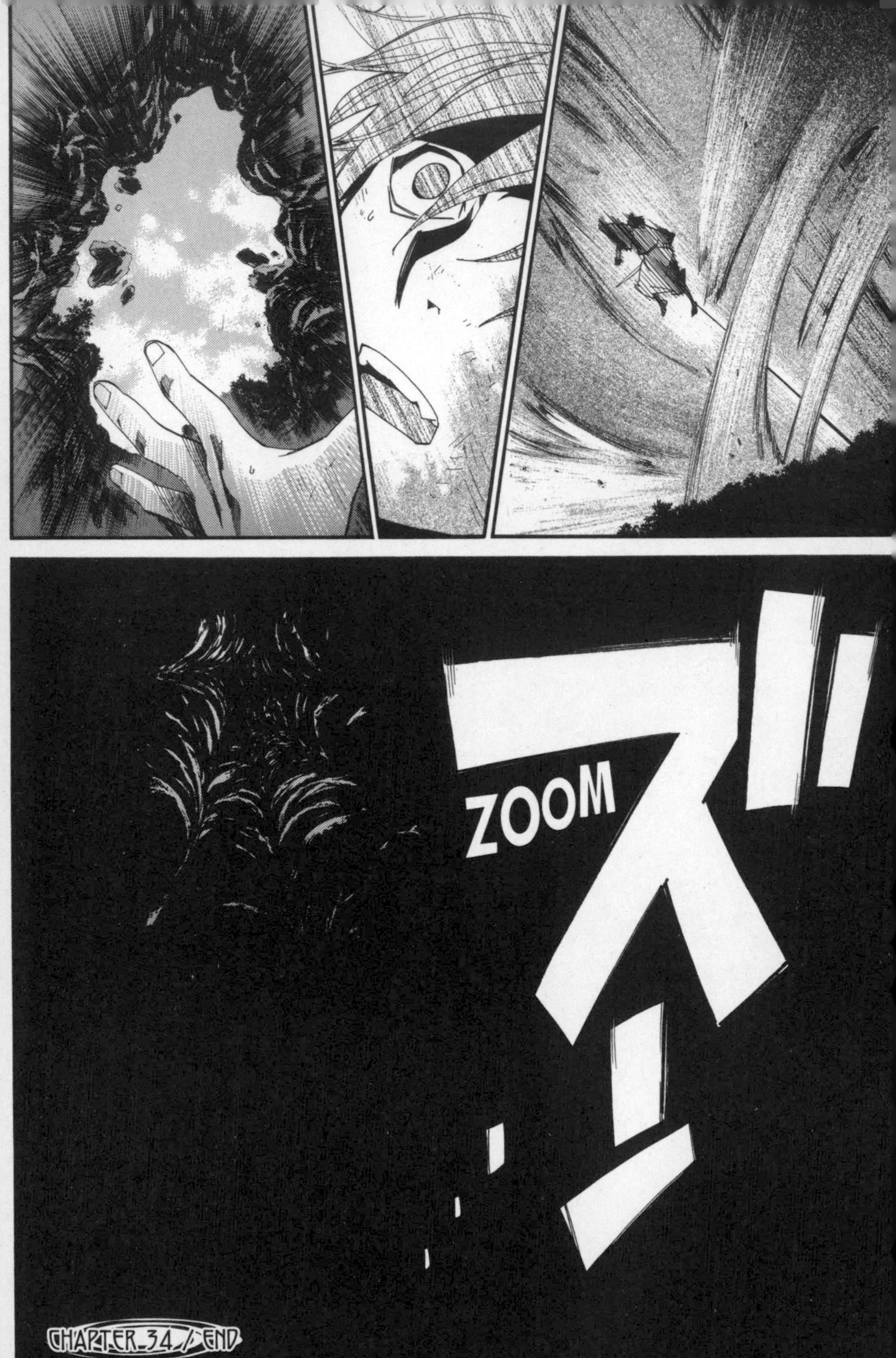
ZOOM
CHAPTER 34 / END

野

邑

神

[illegible]

曼

師

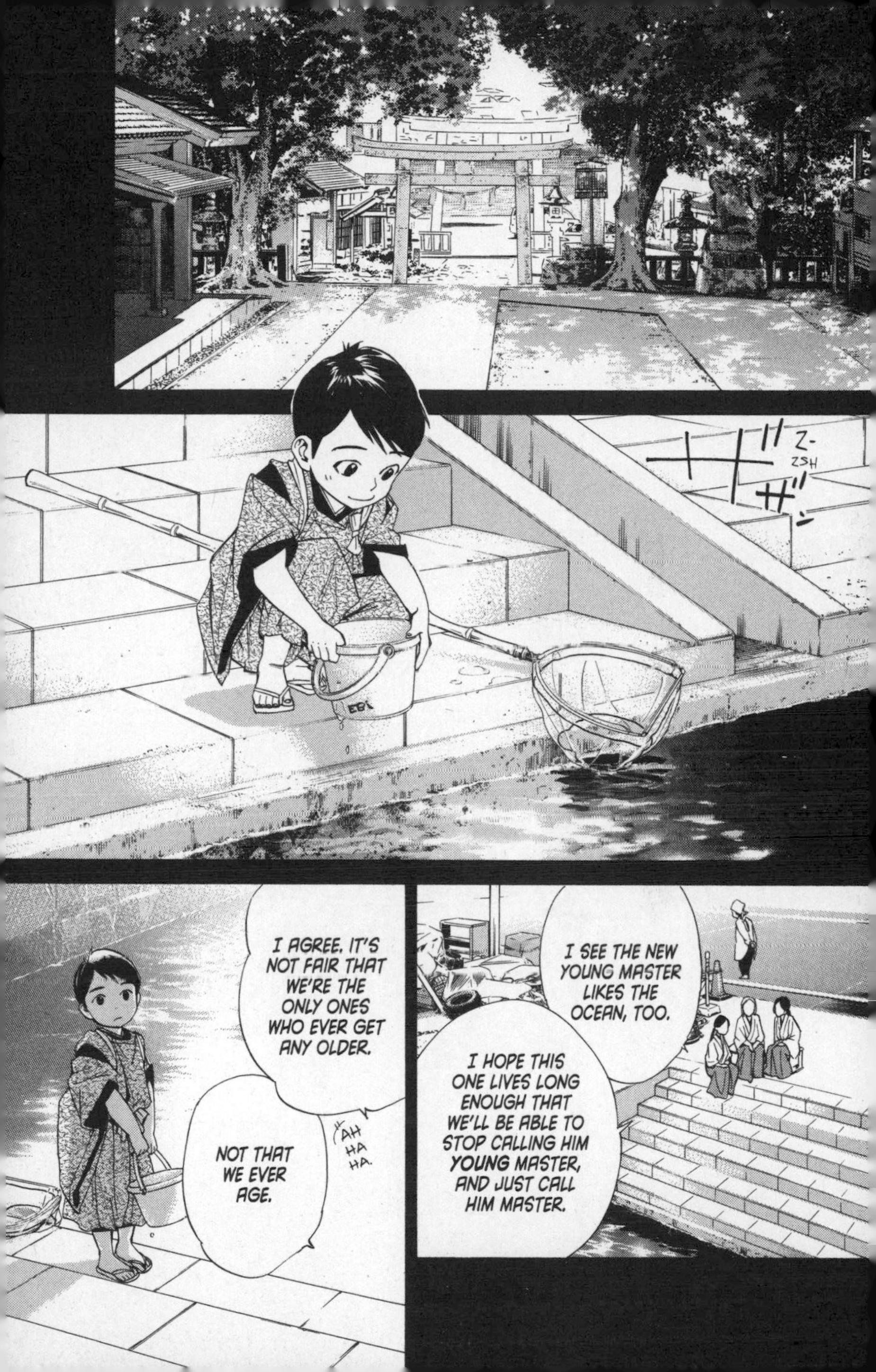
Z-ZSH
I SEE THE NEW YOUNG MASTER LIKES THE OCEAN, TOO.
I HOPE THIS ONE LIVES LONG ENOUGH THAT WE'LL BE ABLE TO STOP CALLING HIM **YOUNG** MASTER, AND JUST CALL HIM MASTER.
I AGREE. IT'S NOT FAIR THAT WE'RE THE ONLY ONES WHO EVER GET ANY OLDER.
NOT THAT WE EVER AGE.
AH HA HA.

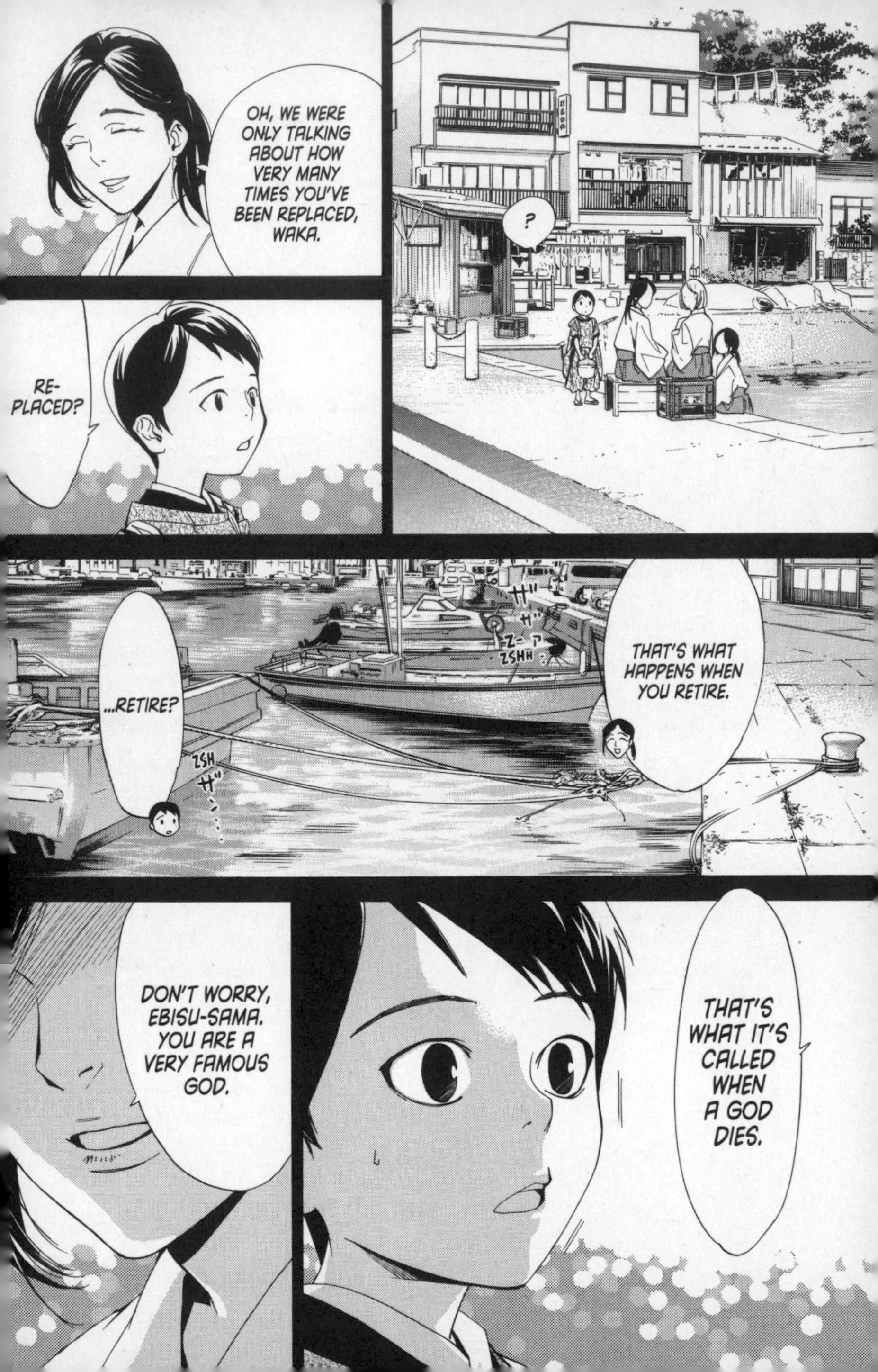
?
OH, WE WERE ONLY TALKING ABOUT HOW VERY MANY TIMES YOU'VE BEEN REPLACED, WAKA.
RE-PLACED?
THAT'S WHAT HAPPENS WHEN YOU RETIRE.
ZSHH
...RETIRE?
ZSH
THAT'S WHAT IT'S CALLED WHEN A GOD DIES.
DON'T WORRY, EBISU-SAMA. YOU ARE A VERY FAMOUS GOD.

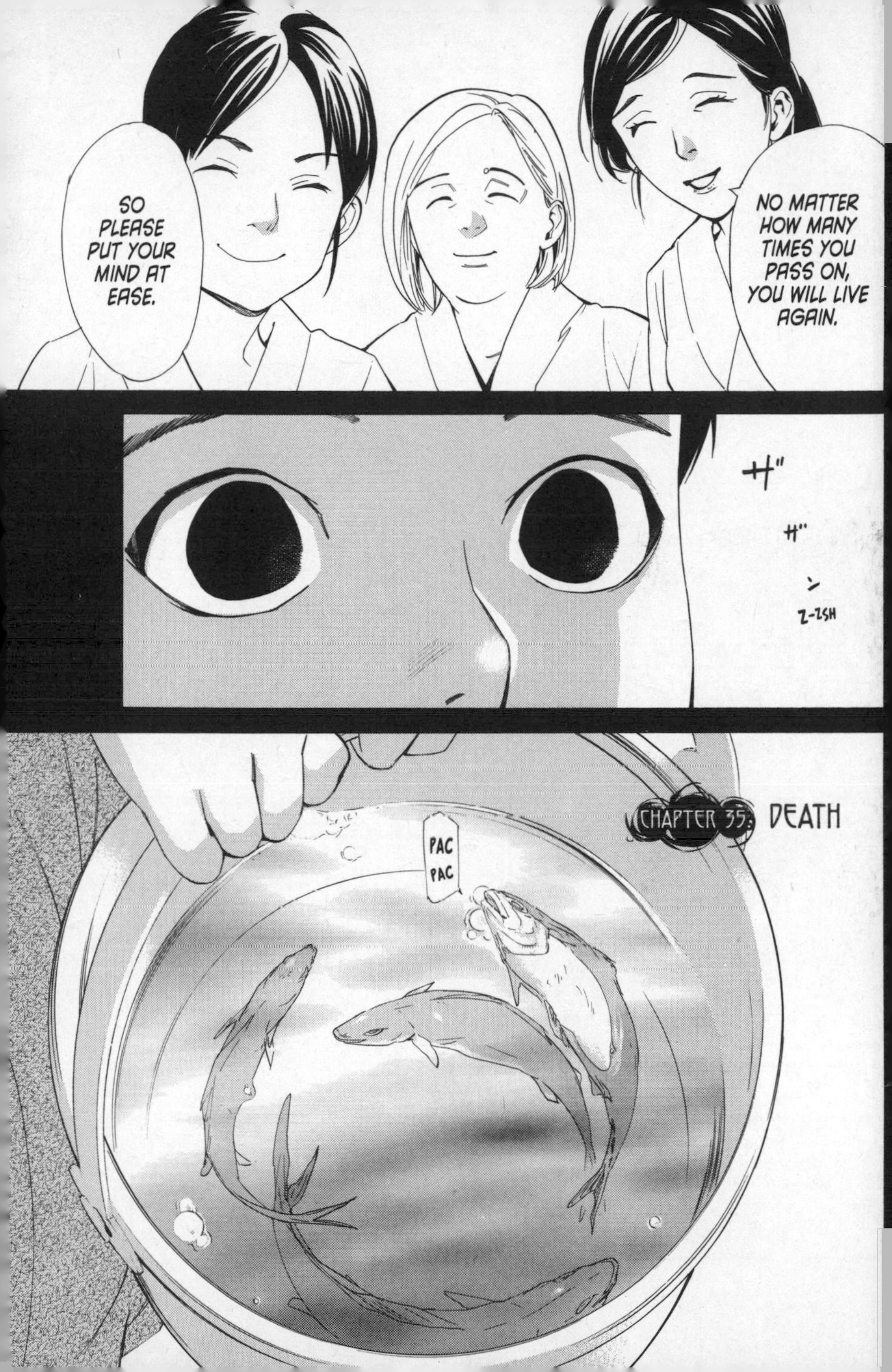
NO MATTER HOW MANY TIMES YOU PASS ON, YOU WILL LIVE AGAIN.
SO PLEASE PUT YOUR MIND AT EASE.
ザザン
Z-ZSH
CHAPTER 35: DEATH
PAC PAC

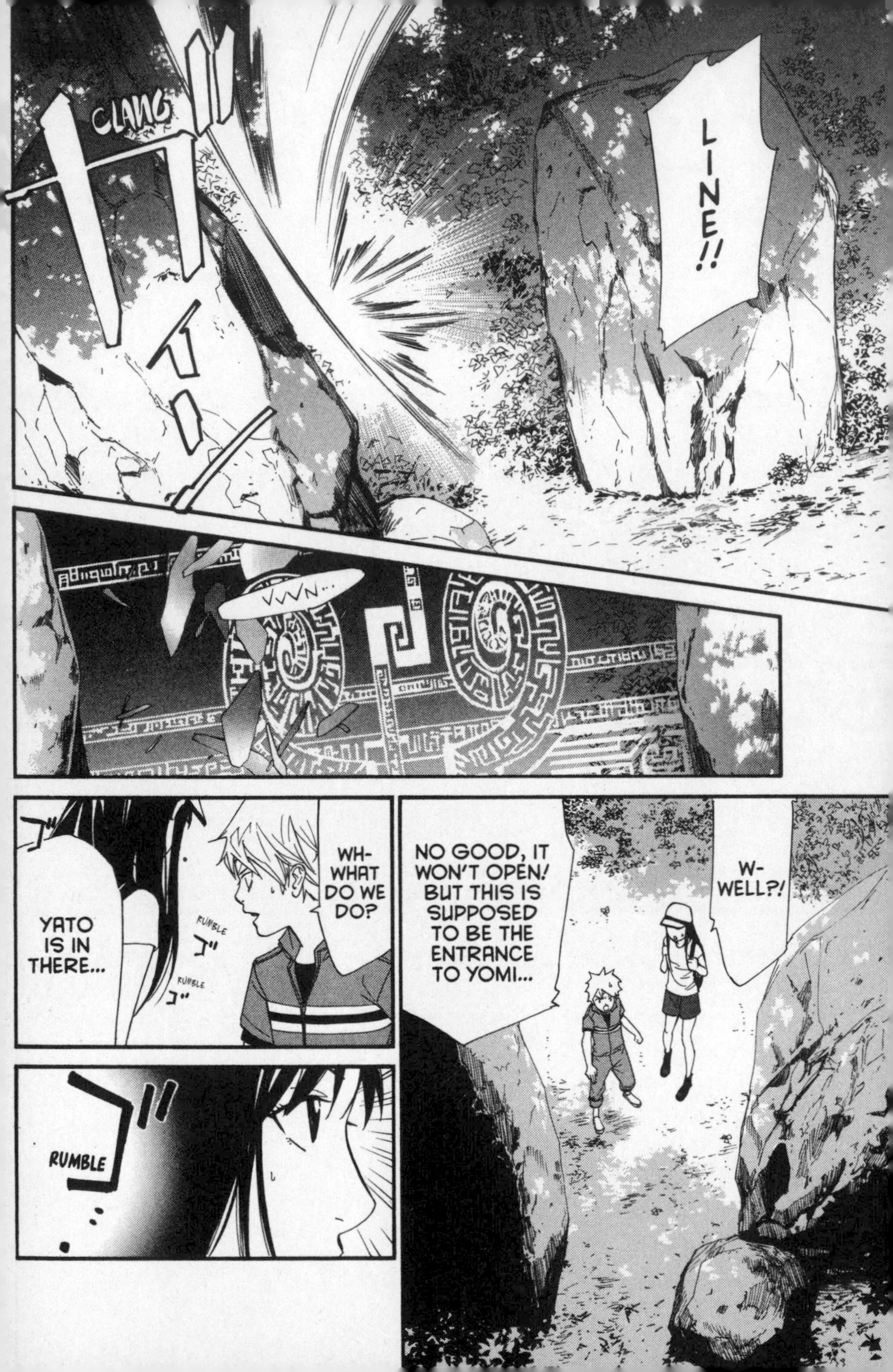
LINE!!
CLANG
VVVN...
W-WELL?!
NO GOOD, IT WON'T OPEN! BUT THIS IS SUPPOSED TO BE THE ENTRANCE TO YOMI...
WH-WHAT DO WE DO?
RUMBLE
RUMBLE
YATO IS IN THERE...
RUMBLE

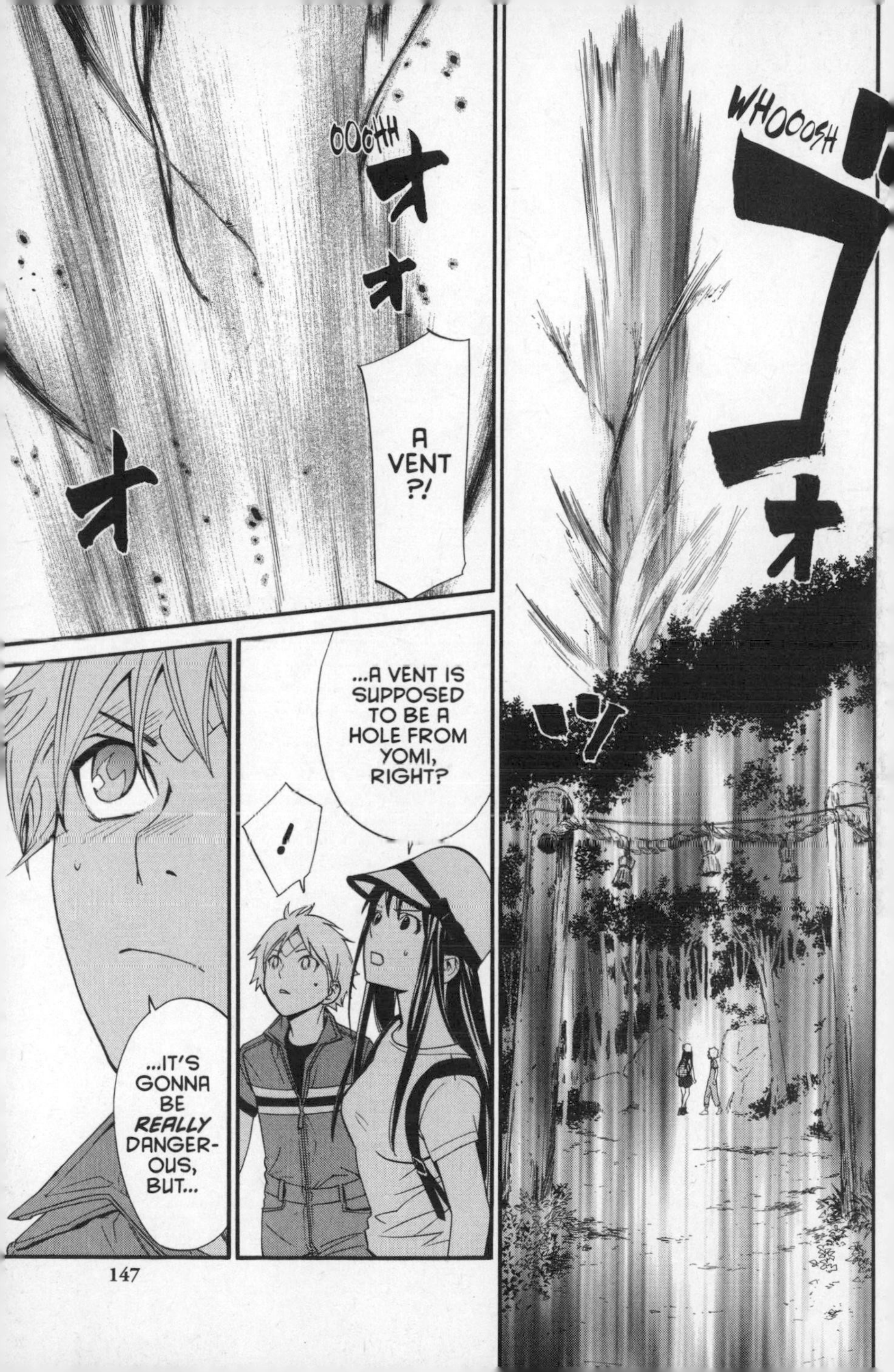
WHOOOSH
OOOHH
A VENT ?!
...A VENT IS SUPPOSED TO BE A HOLE FROM YOMI, RIGHT?
!
...IT'S GONNA BE *REALLY* DANGEROUS, BUT...

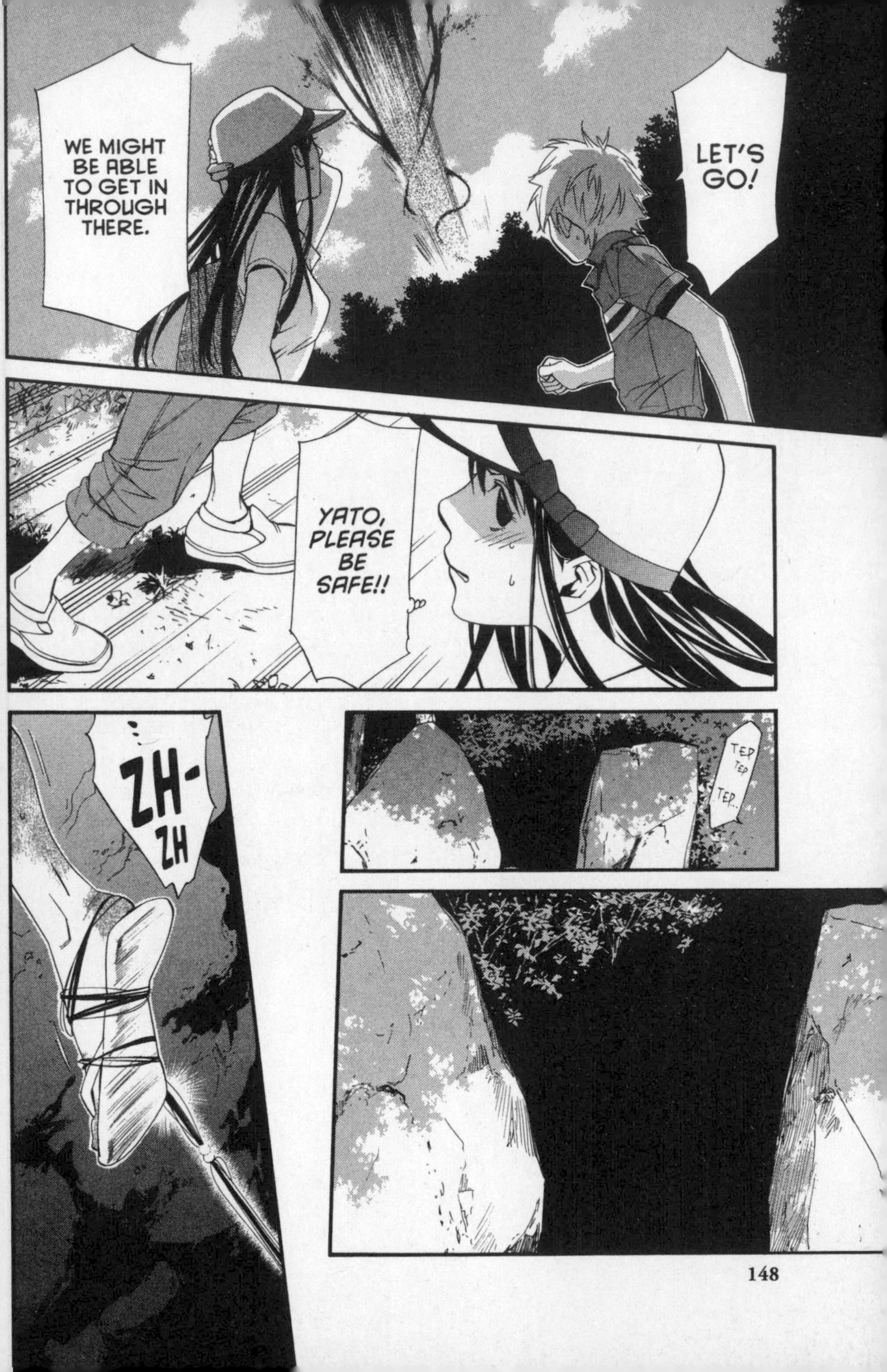
LET'S GO!
WE MIGHT BE ABLE TO GET IN THROUGH THERE.
YATO, PLEASE BE SAFE!!
TEP TEP TEP...
...
ZH- ZH

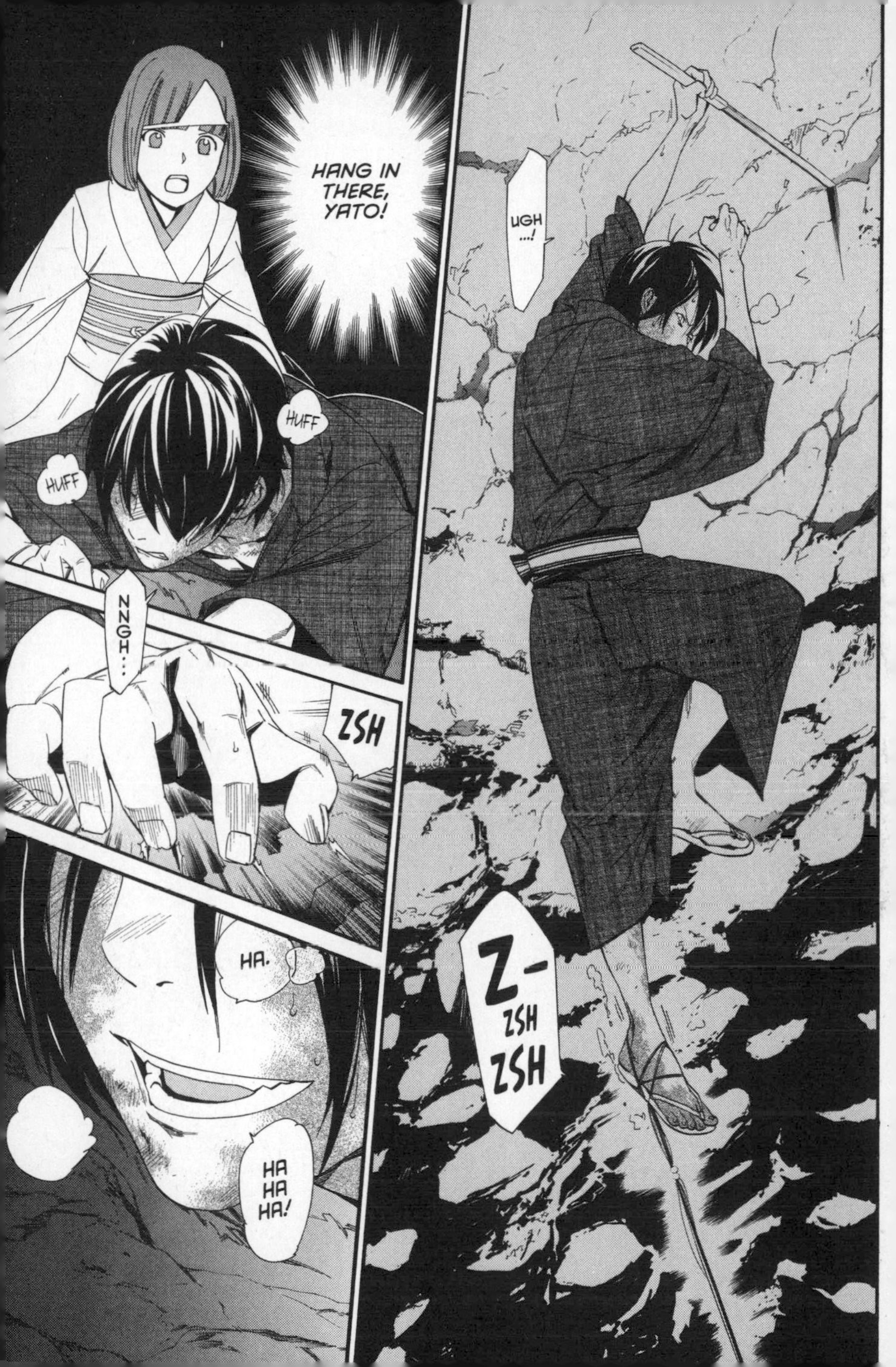
UGH ...!
Z-ZSH ZSH
HANG IN THERE, YATO!
HUFF
HUFF
NNGH...
ZSH
HA.
HA HA HA!

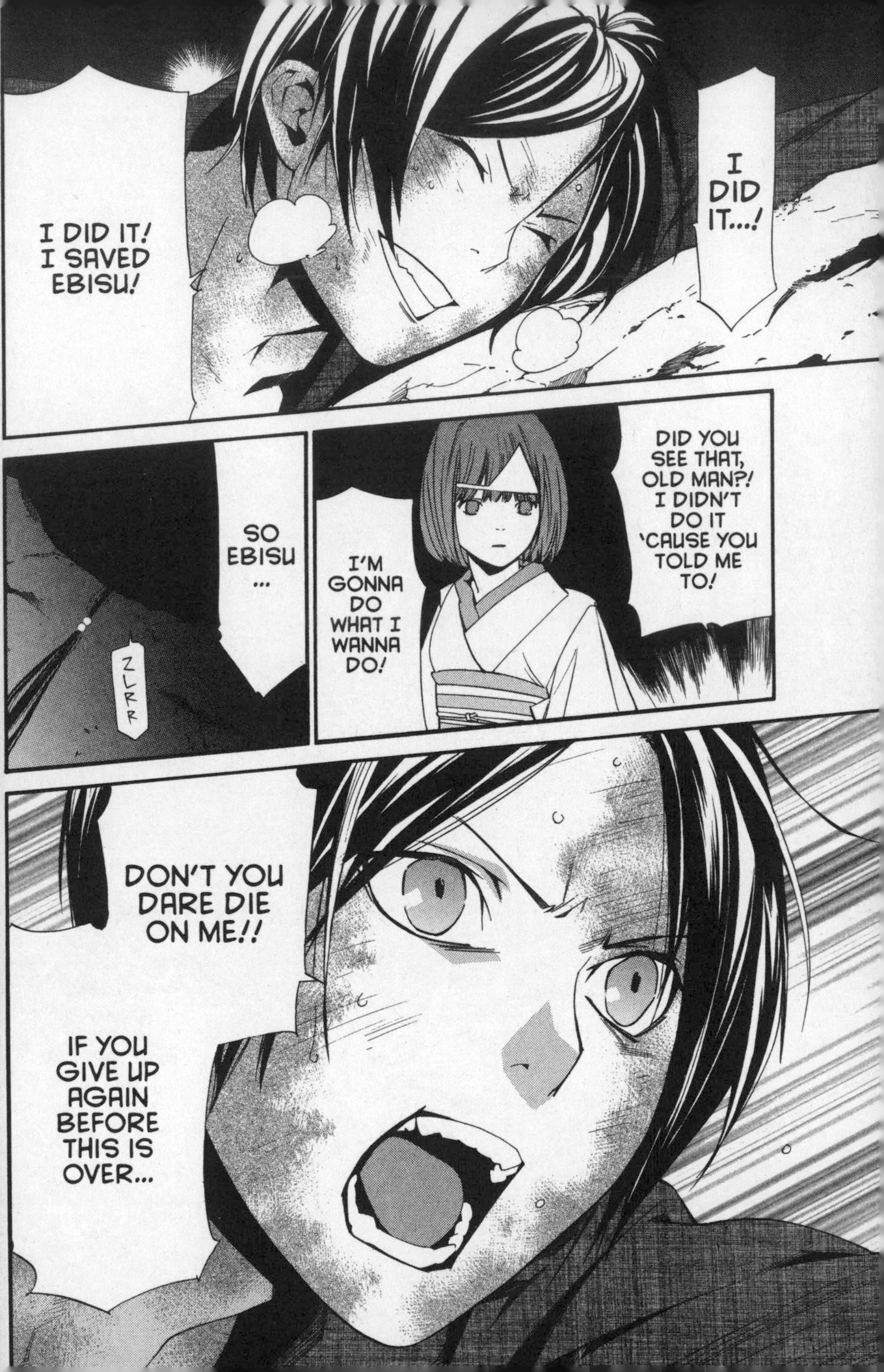
I DID IT...!
I DID IT! I SAVED EBISU!
DID YOU SEE THAT, OLD MAN?! I DIDN'T DO IT 'CAUSE YOU TOLD ME TO!
I'M GONNA DO WHAT I WANNA DO!
SO EBISU ...
ZLRR
DON'T YOU DARE DIE ON ME!!
IF YOU GIVE UP AGAIN BEFORE THIS IS OVER...

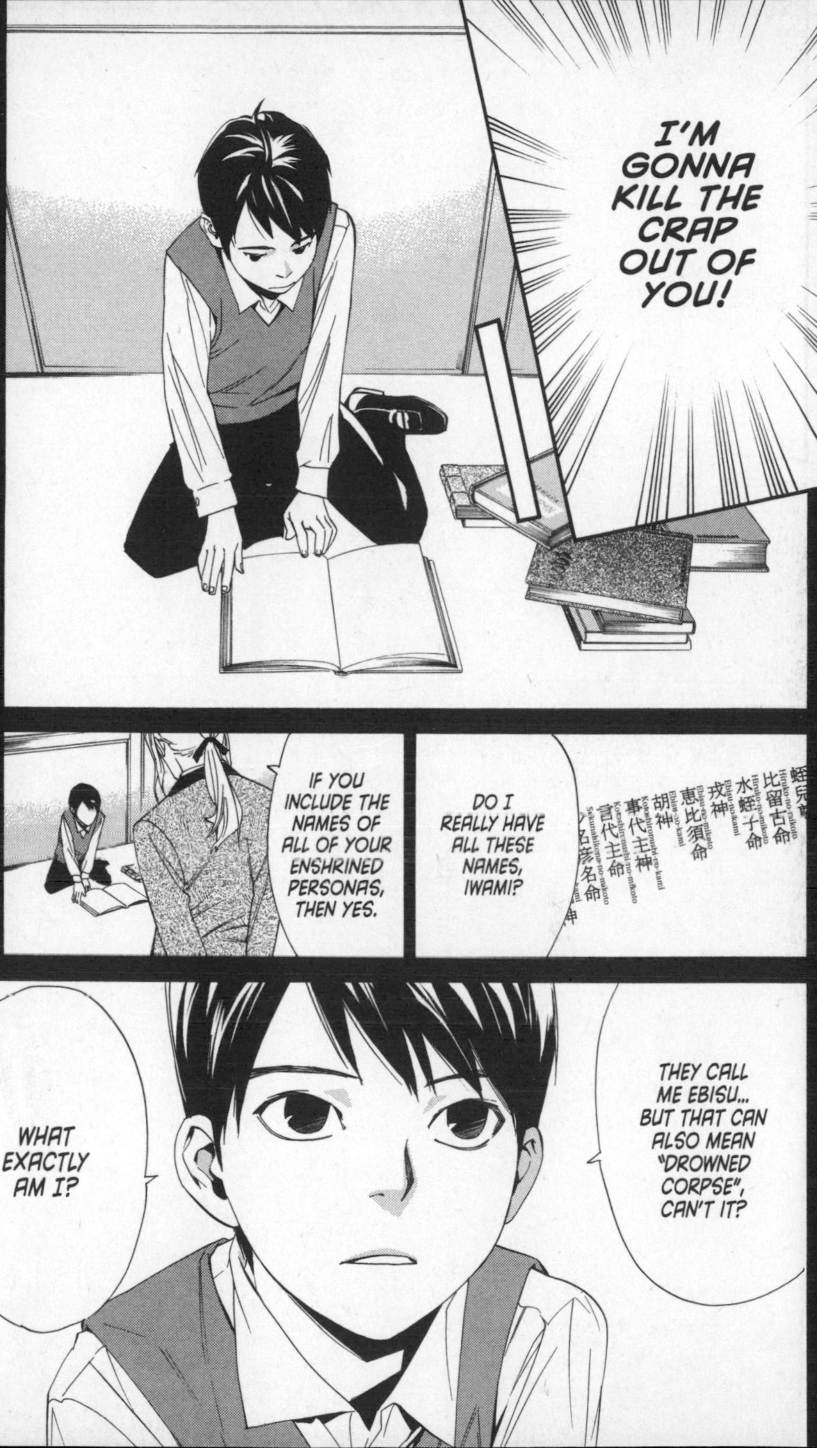
I'M GONNA KILL THE CRAP OUT OF YOU!
DO I REALLY HAVE ALL THESE NAMES, IWAMI?
比留古命
水蛭子命
戎神
恵比須命
胡神
事代主神
言代主命
IF YOU INCLUDE THE NAMES OF ALL OF YOUR ENSHRINED PERSONAS, THEN YES.
THEY CALL ME EBISU... BUT THAT CAN ALSO MEAN "DROWNED CORPSE", CAN'T IT?
WHAT EXACTLY AM I?

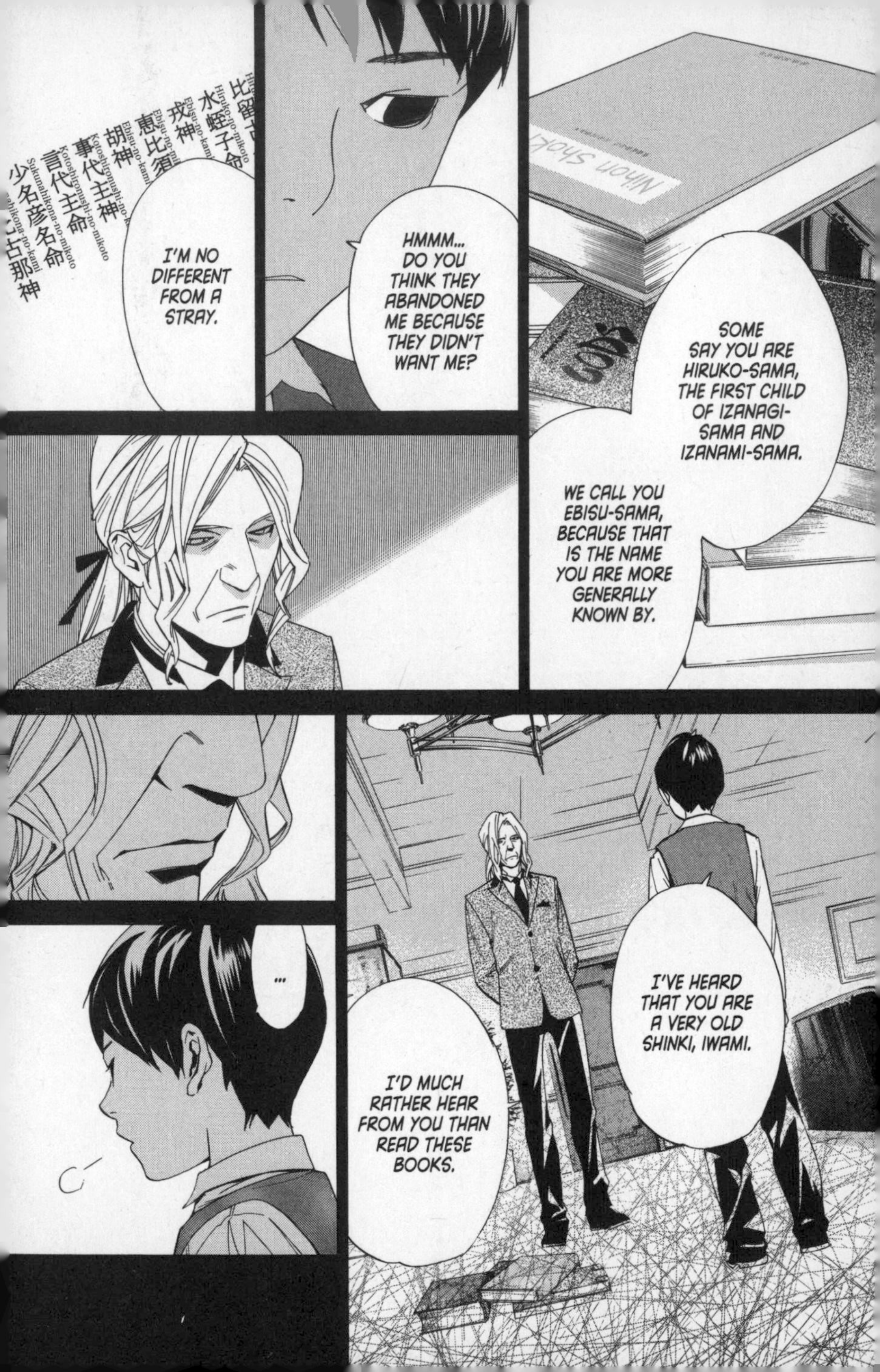
Nihon Shoki
SOME SAY YOU ARE HIRUKO-SAMA, THE FIRST CHILD OF IZANAGI-SAMA AND IZANAMI-SAMA.
HMMM... DO YOU THINK THEY ABANDONED ME BECAUSE THEY DIDN'T WANT ME?
水蛭子命
Hiruko-no-mikoto
戎神
Ebisu-no-kami
胡神
事代主神
言代主命
Kotoshironushi-no-mikoto
少名彦名命
Sukunahikona-no-mikoto
I'M NO DIFFERENT FROM A STRAY.
WE CALL YOU EBISU-SAMA, BECAUSE THAT IS THE NAME YOU ARE MORE GENERALLY KNOWN BY.
I'VE HEARD THAT YOU ARE A VERY OLD SHINKI, IWAMI.
I'D MUCH RATHER HEAR FROM YOU THAN READ THESE BOOKS.
...

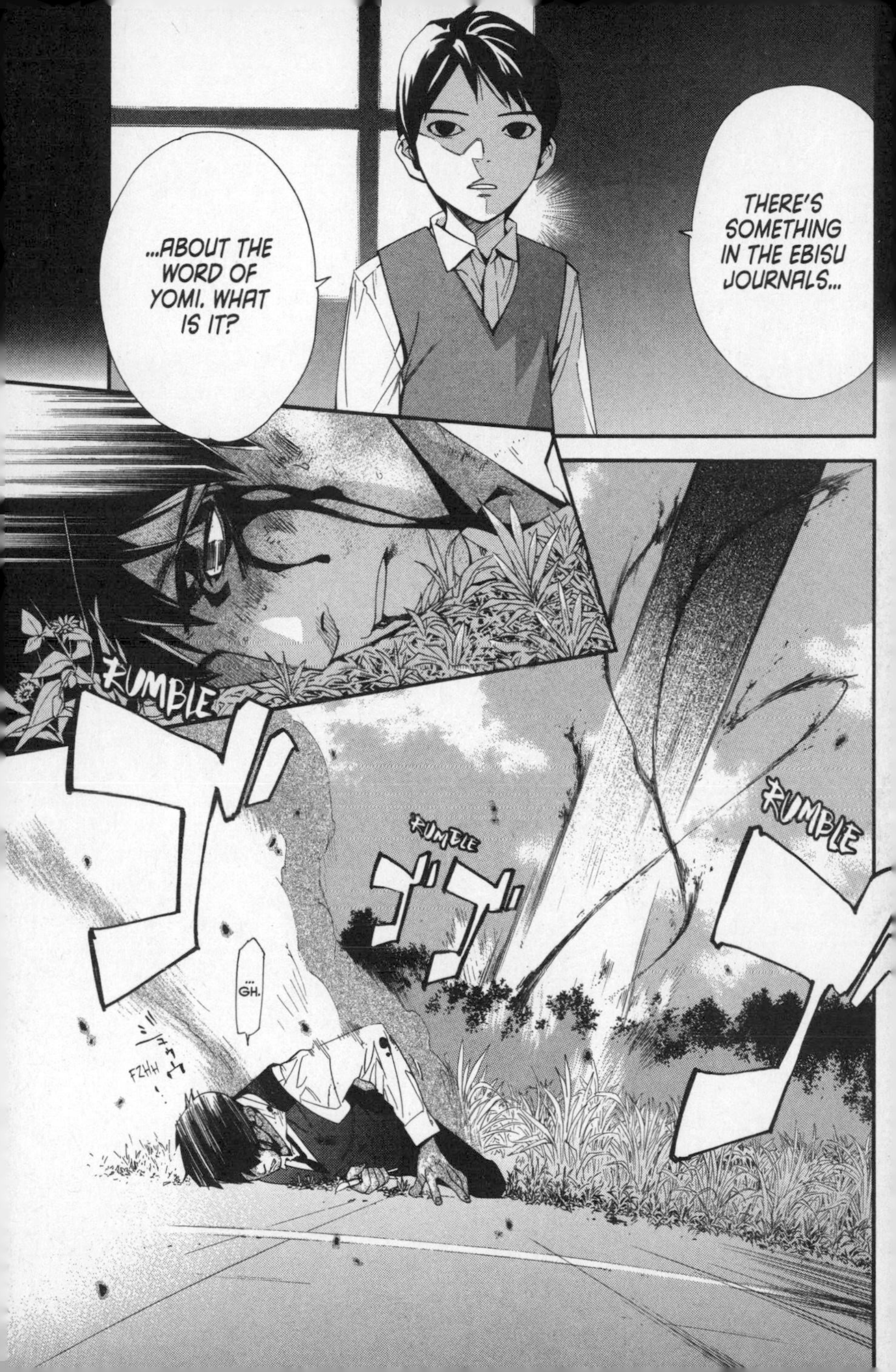
THERE'S SOMETHING IN THE EBISU JOURNALS...
...ABOUT THE WORD OF YOMI. WHAT IS IT?
RUMBLE
RUMBLE
RUMBLE
...GH.
FZHH

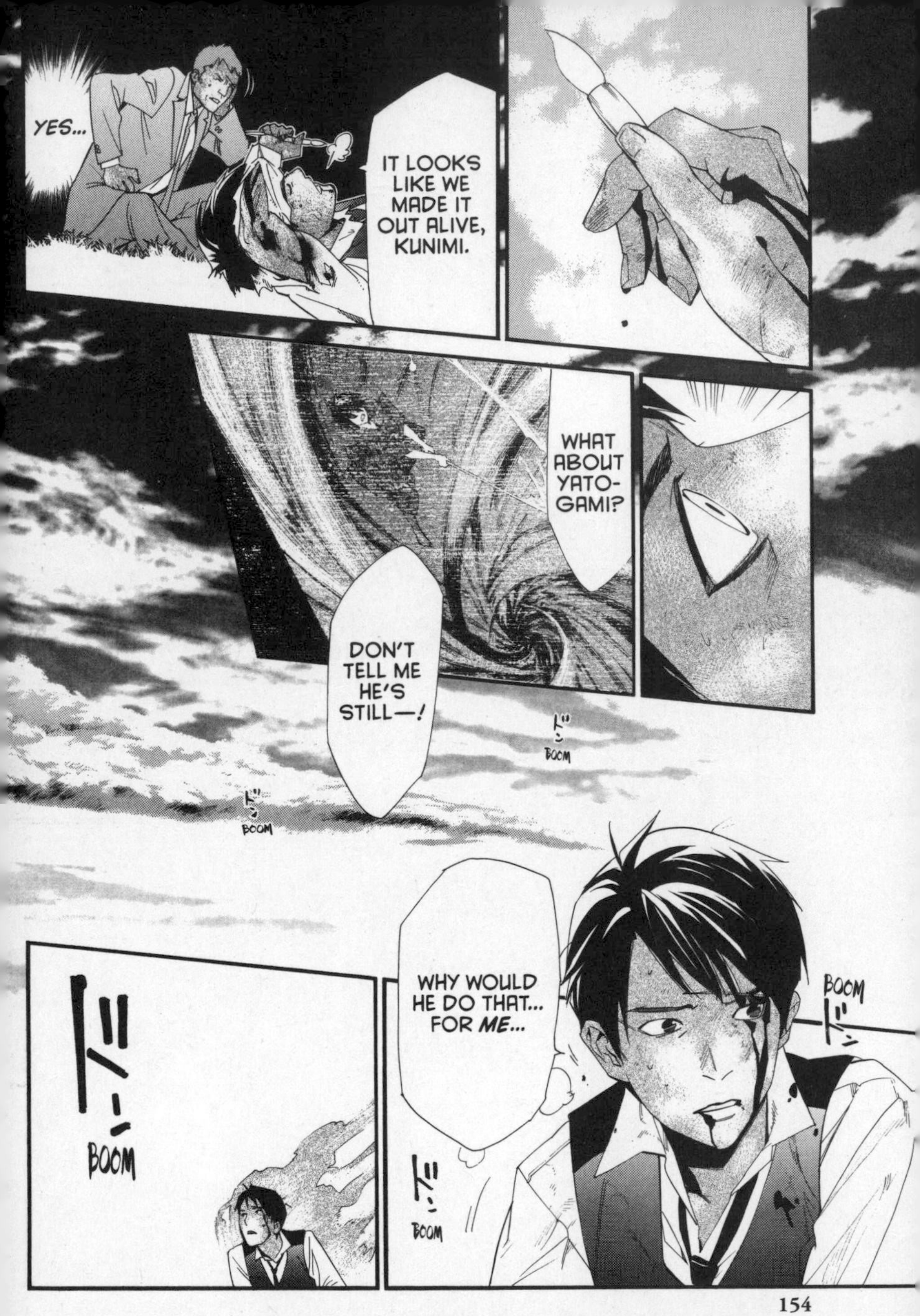
IT LOOKS LIKE WE MADE IT OUT ALIVE, KUNIMI.
YES...
WHAT ABOUT YATO-GAMI?
DON'T TELL ME HE'S STILL—!
ドン BOOM
ドン BOOM
BOOM ドン
WHY WOULD HE DO THAT... FOR *ME*...
ドン BOOM
ドーン BOOM

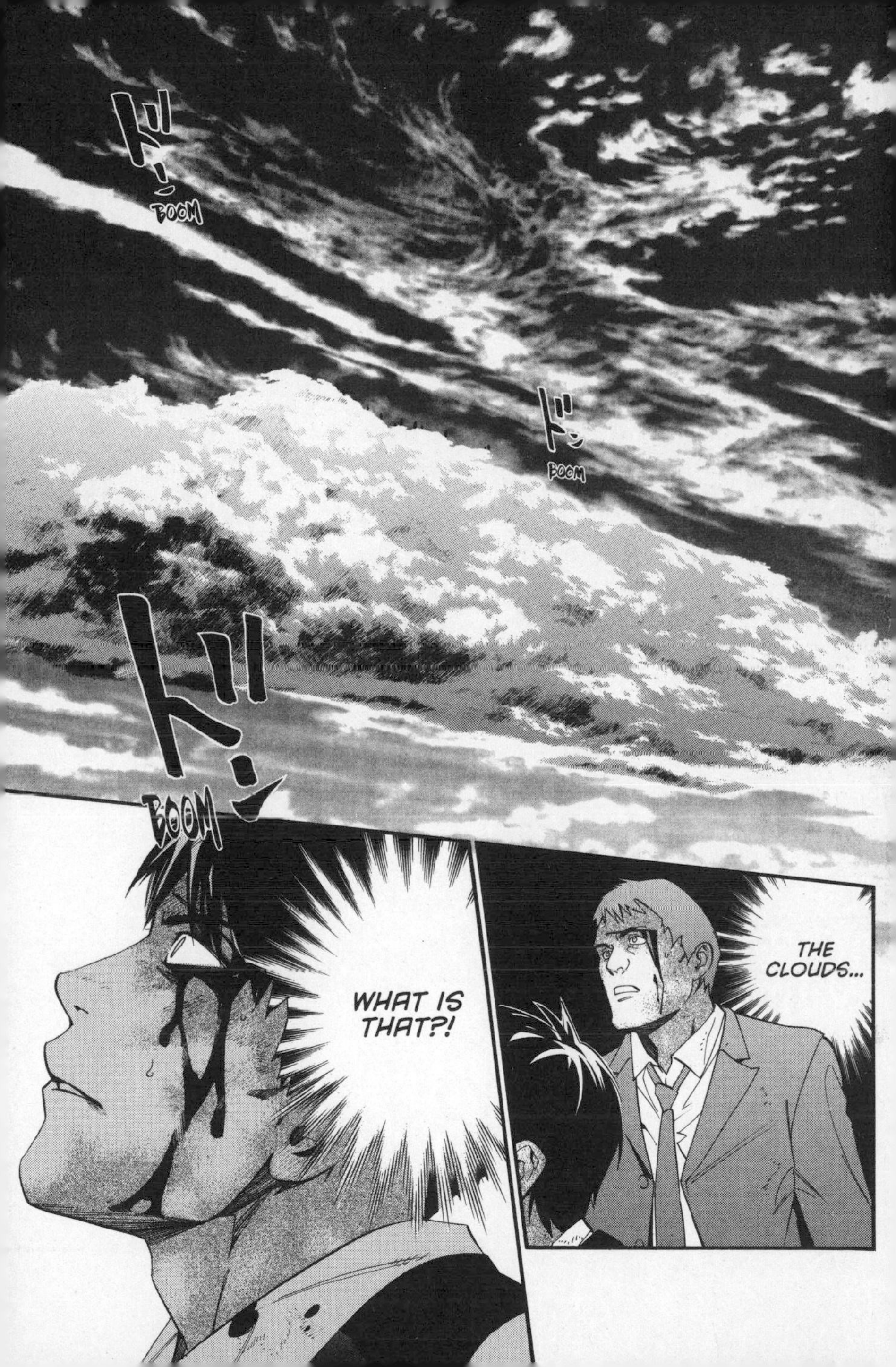
ドン
BOOM
ドン
BOOM
ドン
BOOM
THE CLOUDS...
WHAT IS THAT?!

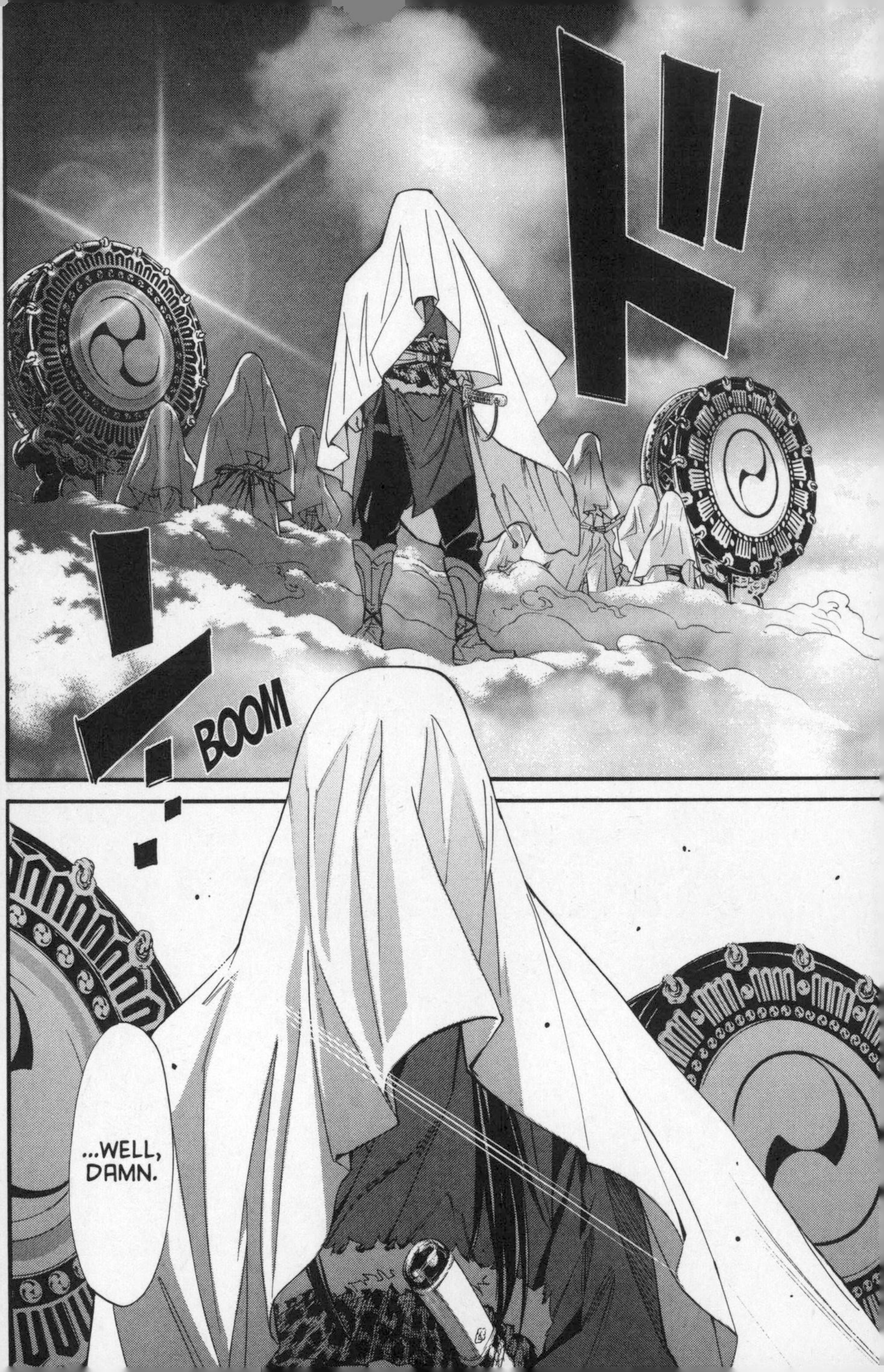
BOOM
...WELL, DAMN.

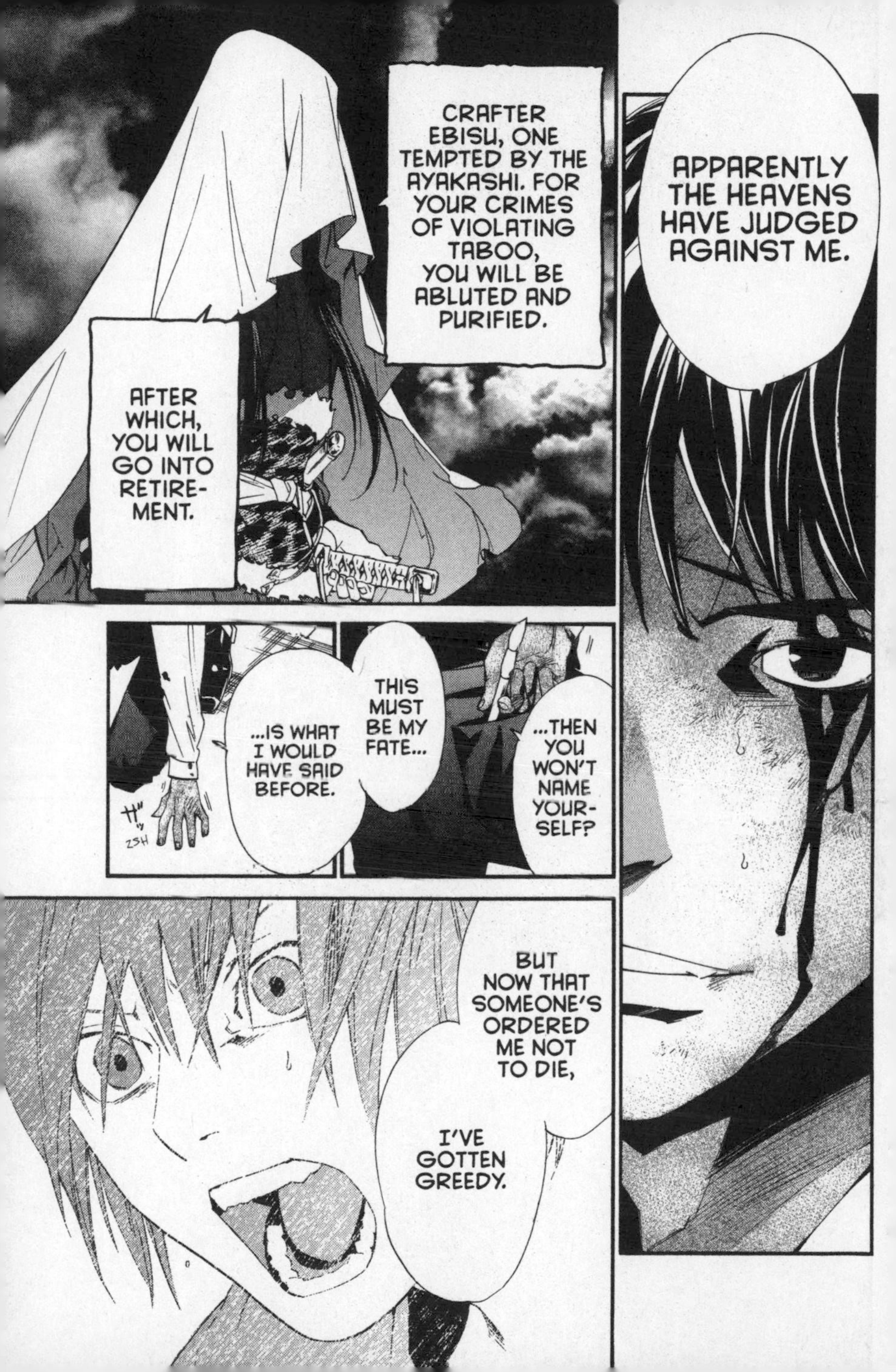
CRAFTER EBISU, ONE TEMPTED BY THE AYAKASHI. FOR YOUR CRIMES OF VIOLATING TABOO, YOU WILL BE ABLUTED AND PURIFIED.
AFTER WHICH, YOU WILL GO INTO RETIRE-MENT.
APPARENTLY THE HEAVENS HAVE JUDGED AGAINST ME.
...THEN YOU WON'T NAME YOUR-SELF?
THIS MUST BE MY FATE...
...IS WHAT I WOULD HAVE SAID BEFORE.
ZSH
BUT NOW THAT SOMEONE'S ORDERED ME NOT TO DIE,
I'VE GOTTEN GREEDY.

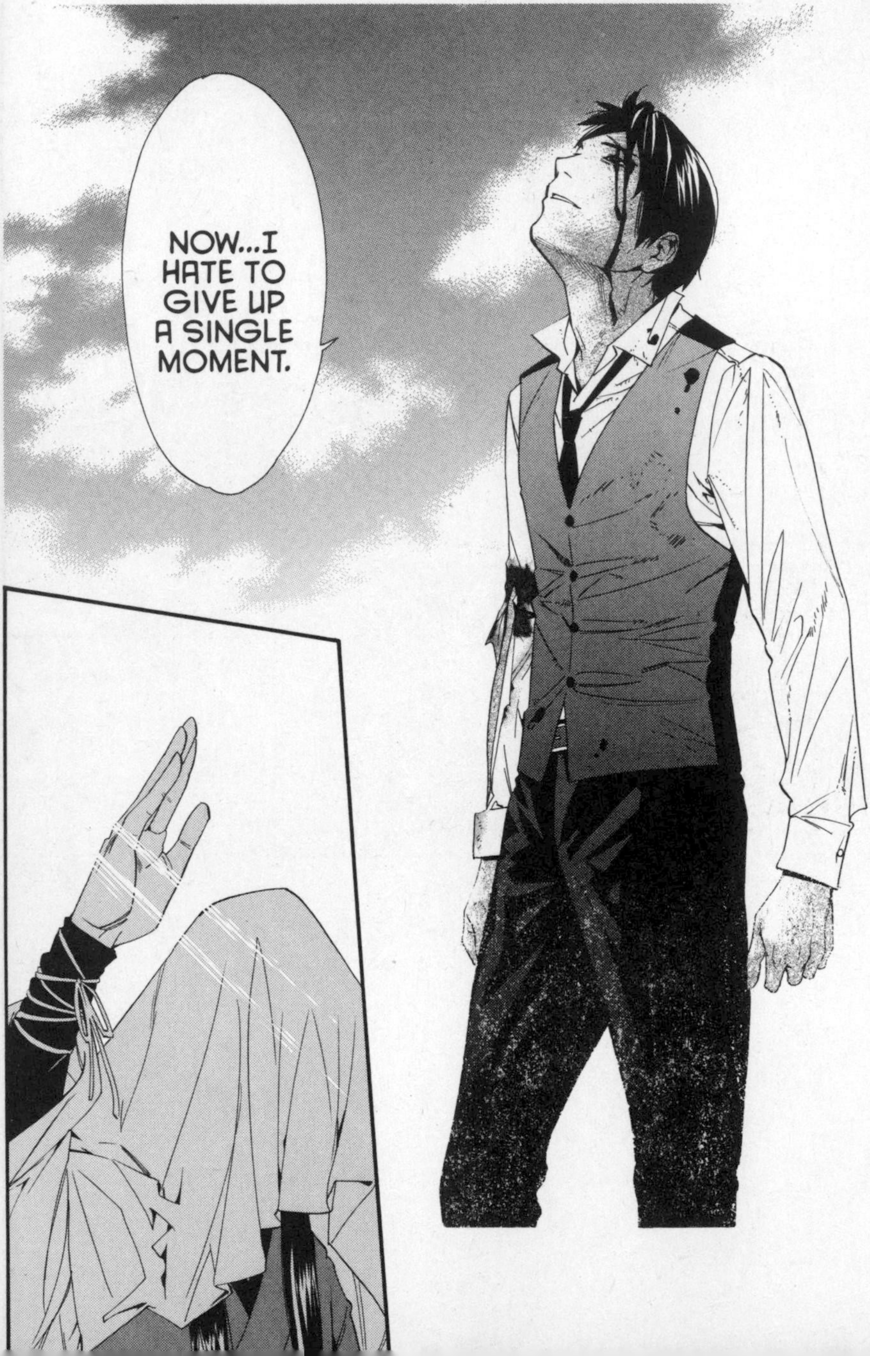
NOW...I HATE TO GIVE UP A SINGLE MOMENT.

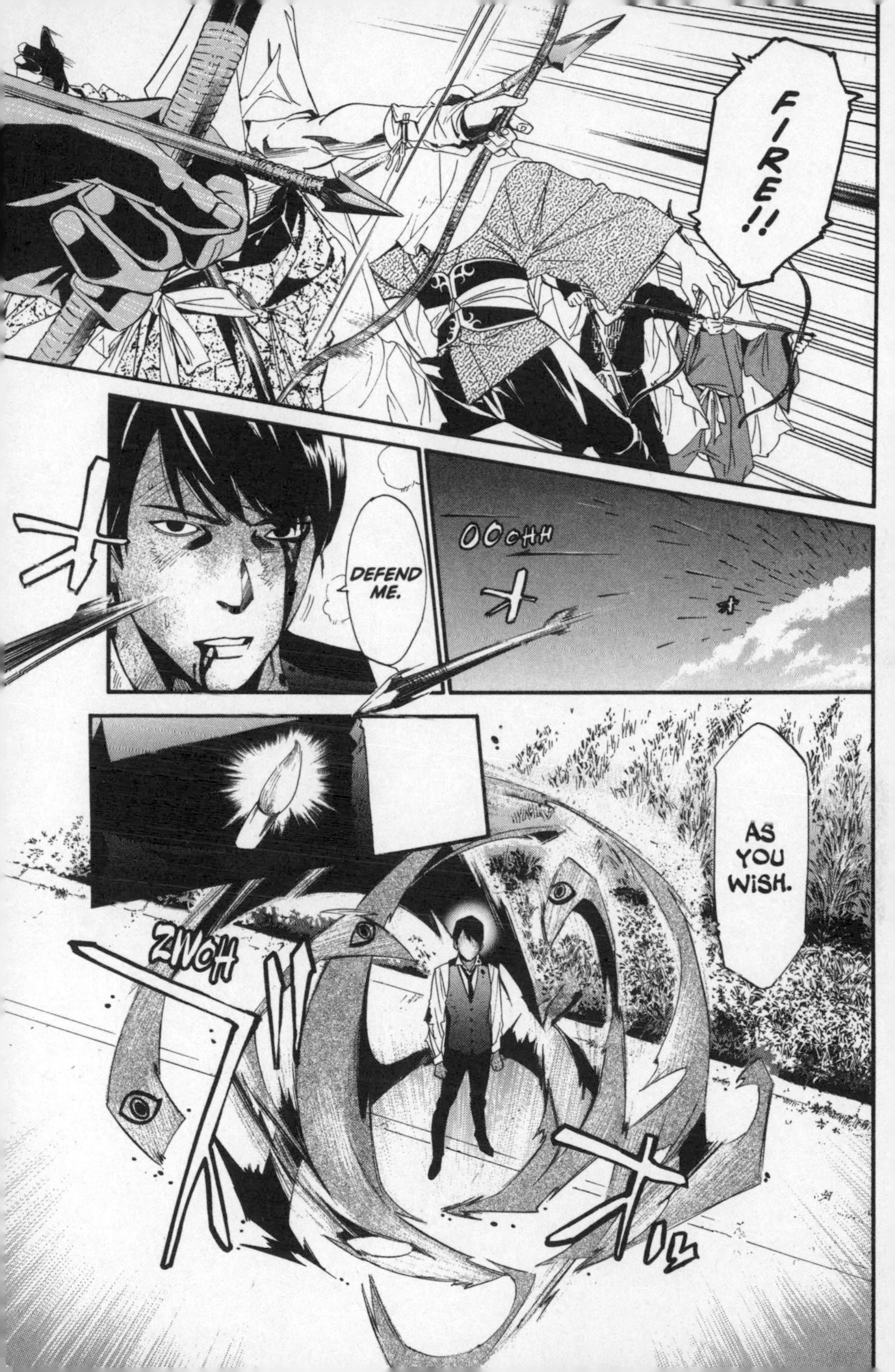
FIRE!!
OOOHH
DEFEND ME.
AS YOU WISH.
ZWOH

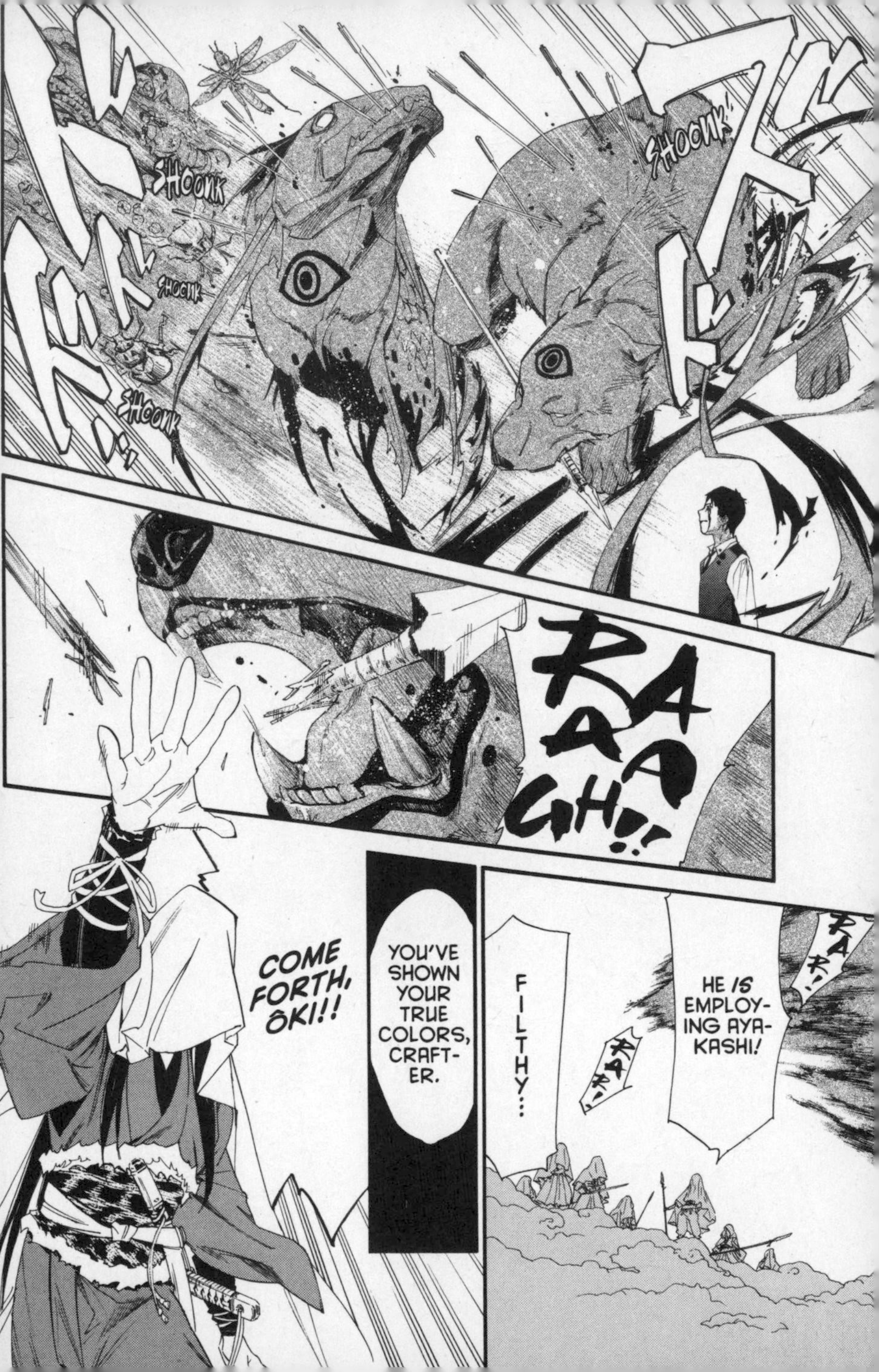
SHOONK!
SHOONK
SHOONK
SHOONK
RAAAGH!!
RAR!
HE IS EMPLOYING AYA-KASHI!
RAR!
FILTHY...
YOU'VE SHOWN YOUR TRUE COLORS, CRAFTER.
COME FORTH, ÔKI!!

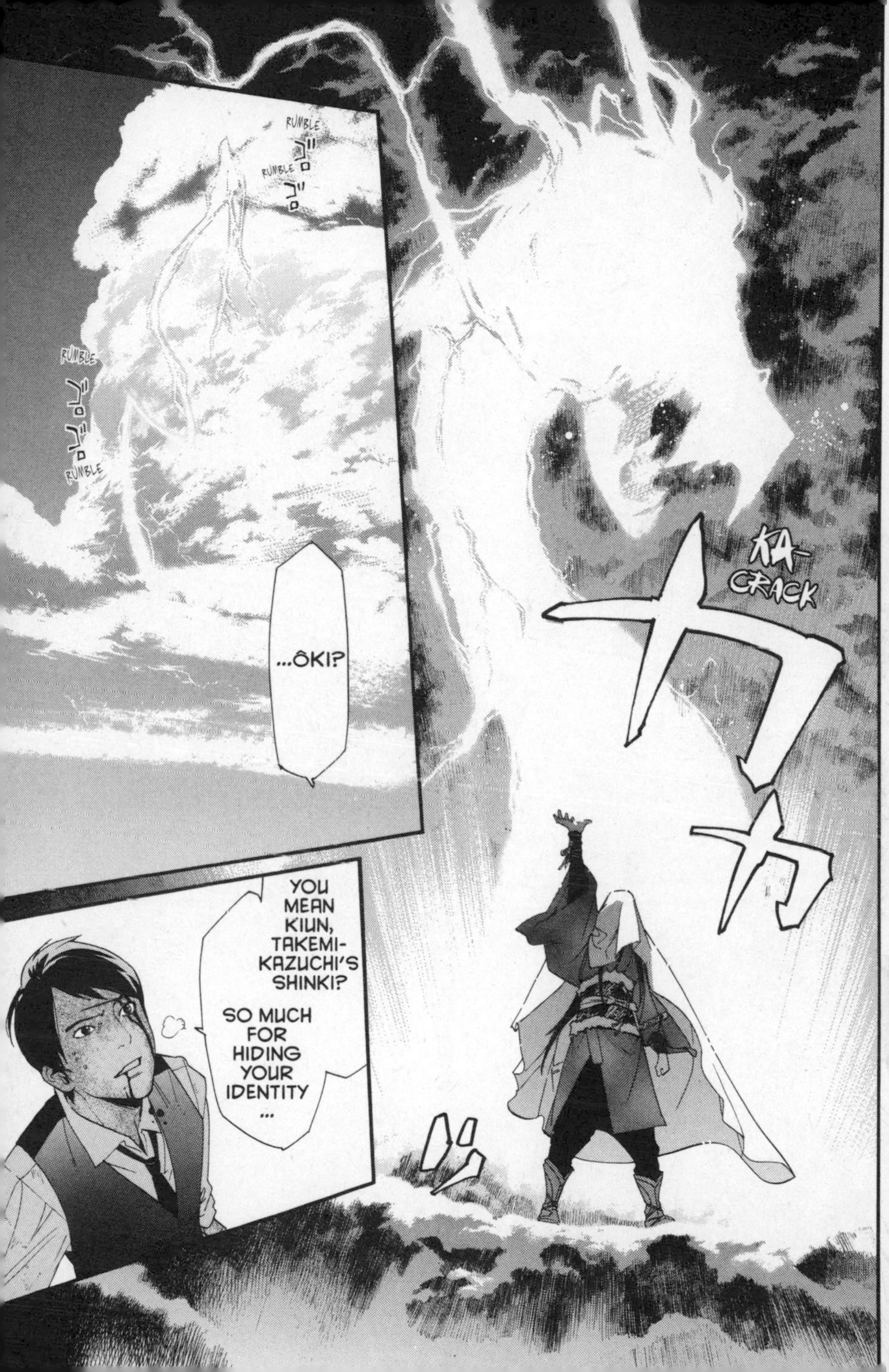
KA-CRACK
RUMBLE
RUMBLE
RUMBLE
RUMBLE
...ÔKI?
YOU MEAN KIUN, TAKEMI-KAZUCHI'S SHINKI?
SO MUCH FOR HIDING YOUR IDENTITY...

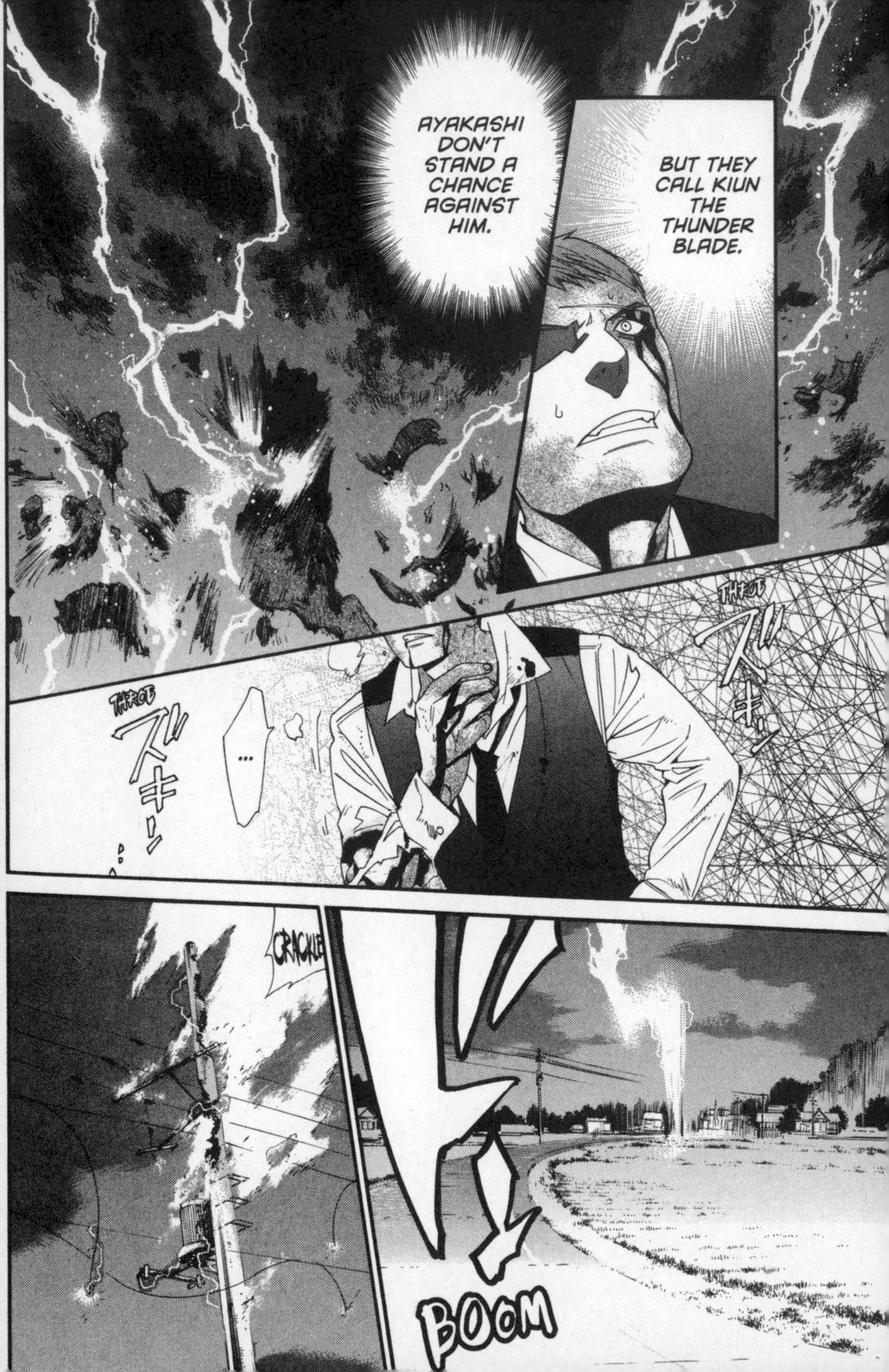
BUT THEY CALL KIUN THE THUNDER BLADE.
AYAKASHI DON'T STAND A CHANCE AGAINST HIM.
THROB
THROB
...
BOOM
CRACKLE

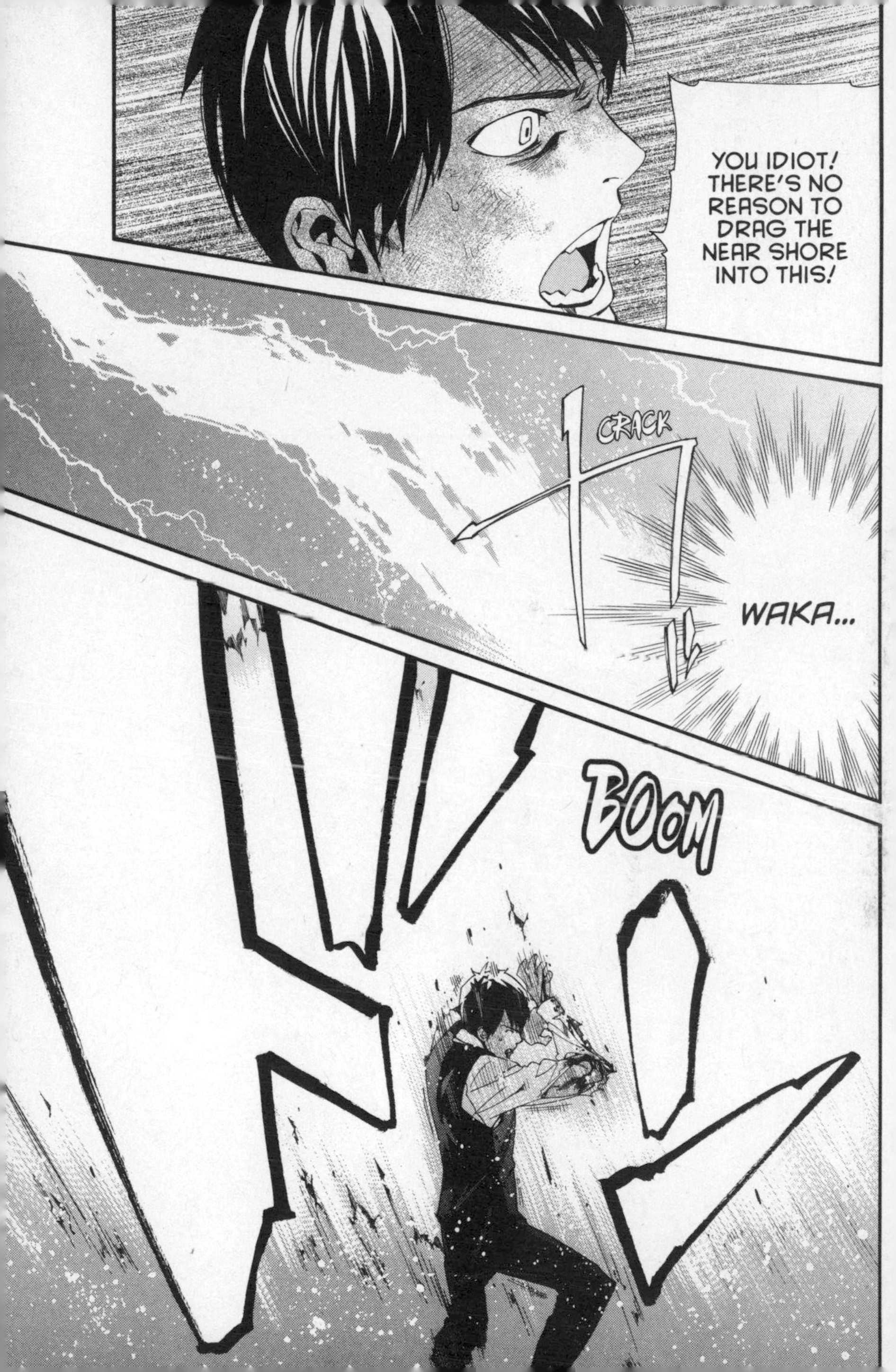
YOU IDIOT! THERE'S NO REASON TO DRAG THE NEAR SHORE INTO THIS!
CRACK
WAKA...
BOOM

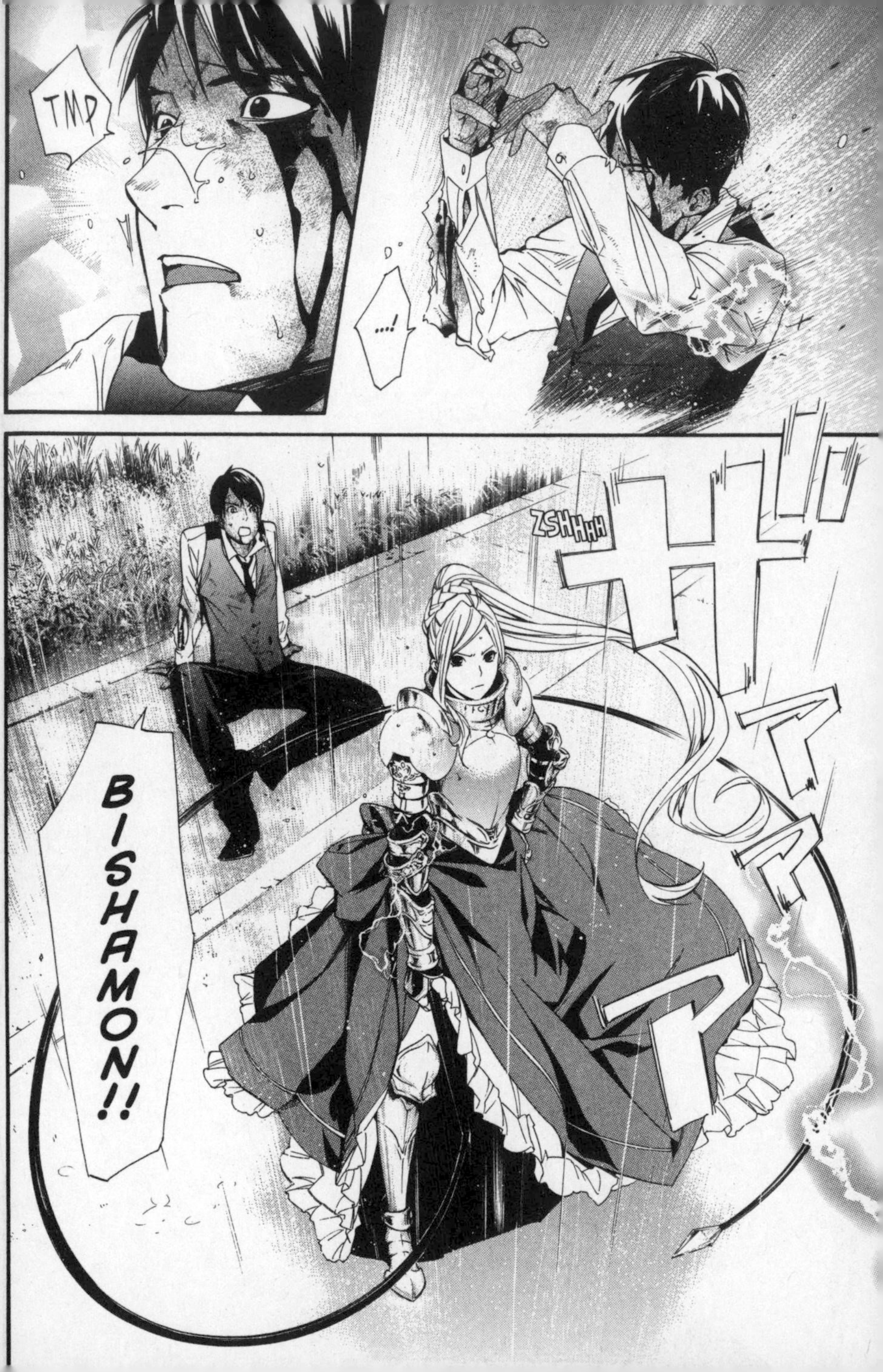
...!
TMP
ZSHHHH
BISHAMON!!

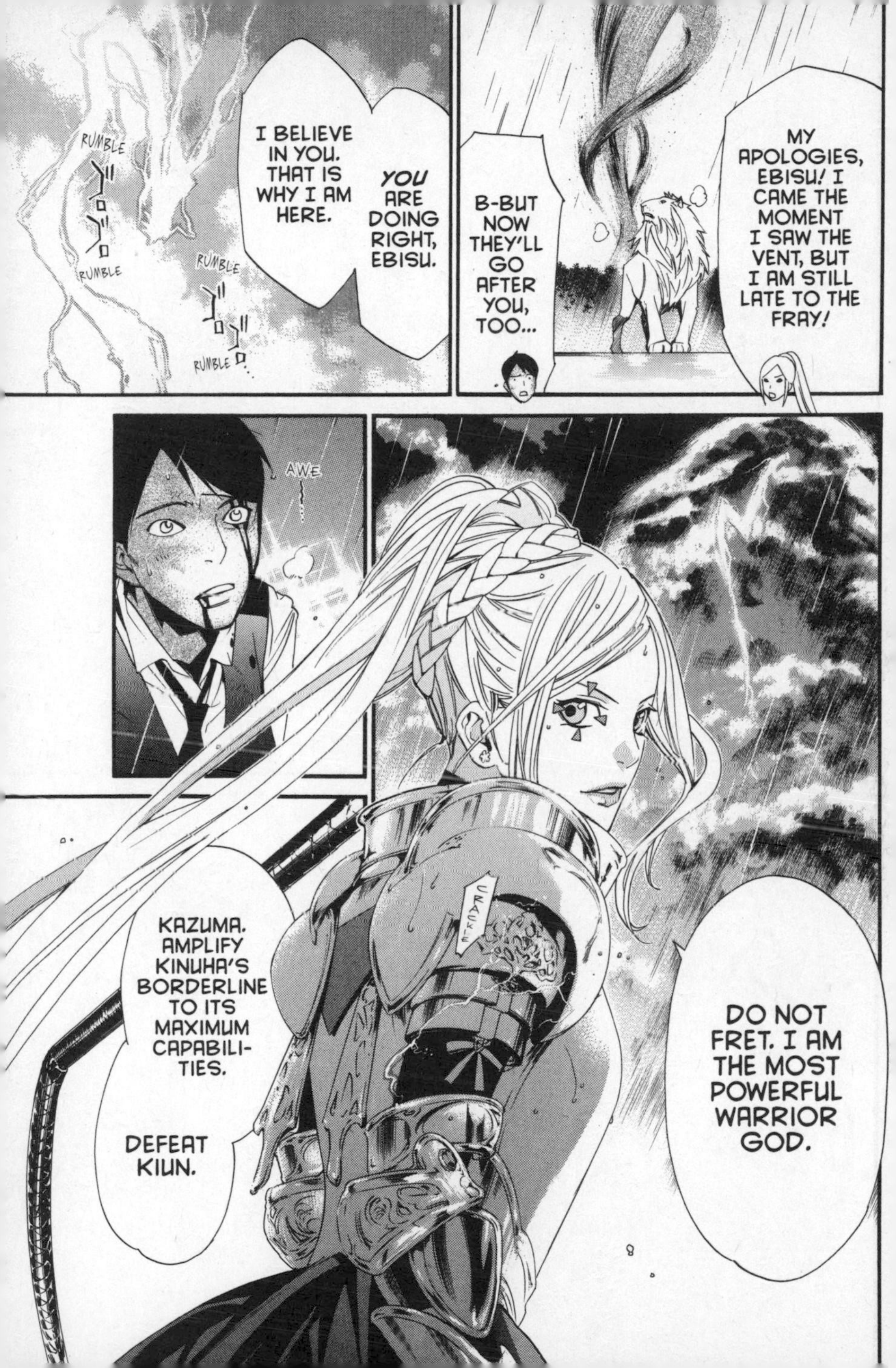
MY APOLOGIES, EBISU! I CAME THE MOMENT I SAW THE VENT, BUT I AM STILL LATE TO THE FRAY!
B-BUT NOW THEY'LL GO AFTER YOU, TOO...
YOU ARE DOING RIGHT, EBISU.
I BELIEVE IN YOU. THAT IS WHY I AM HERE.
RUMBLE
RUMBLE
RUMBLE
RUMBLE
DO NOT FRET. I AM THE MOST POWERFUL WARRIOR GOD.
CRACKLE
AWE
KAZUMA. AMPLIFY KINUHA'S BORDERLINE TO ITS MAXIMUM CAPABILITIES.
DEFEAT KIUN.

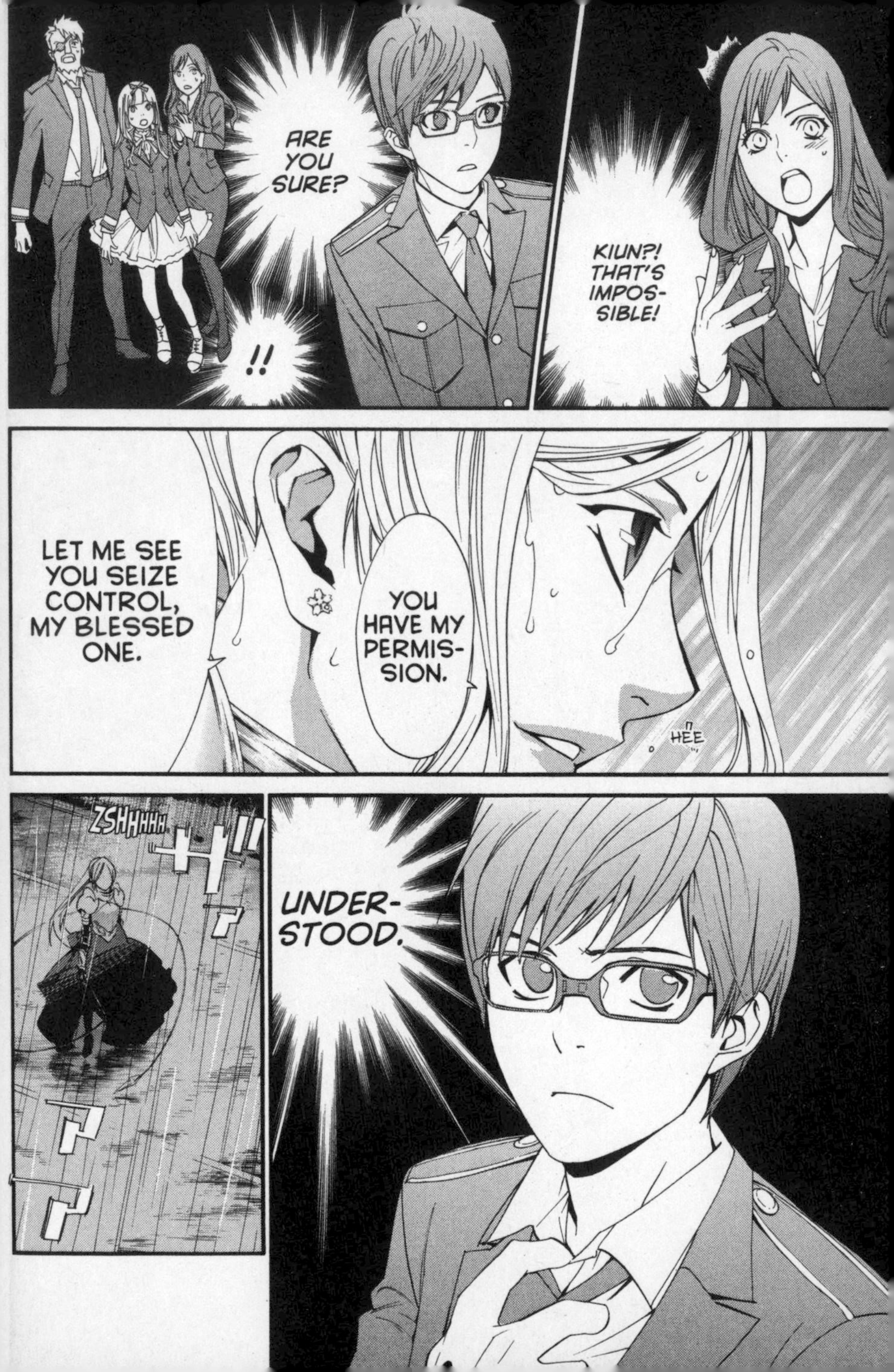
KIUN?! THAT'S IMPOS-SIBLE!
ARE YOU SURE?
!!
YOU HAVE MY PERMIS-SION.
LET ME SEE YOU SEIZE CONTROL, MY BLESSED ONE.
HEE
UNDER-STOOD.
ZSHHHHH

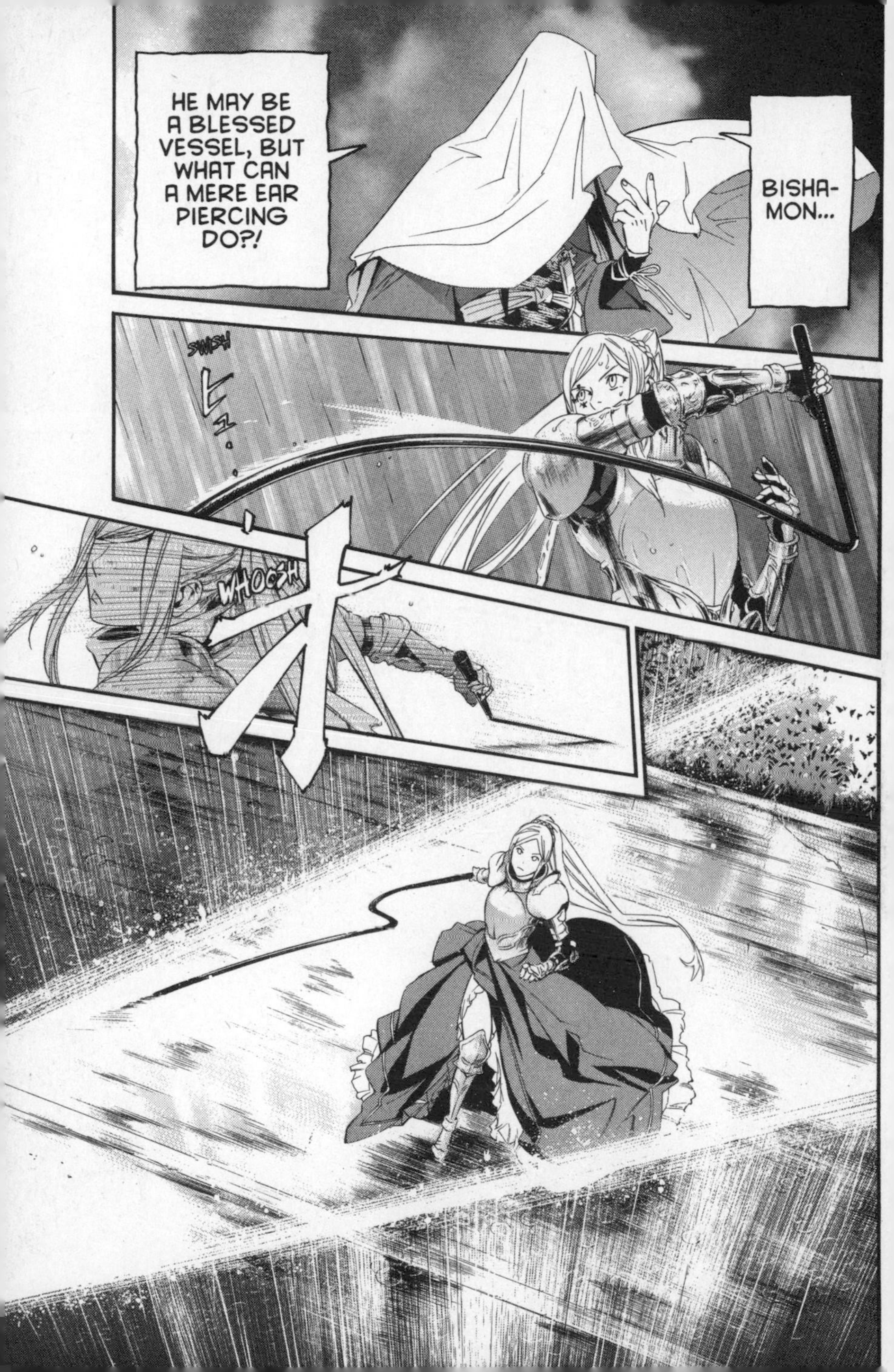
BISHA-MON...
HE MAY BE A BLESSED VESSEL, BUT WHAT CAN A MERE EAR PIERCING DO?!
SWISH
ヒュ
WHOOSH
オ

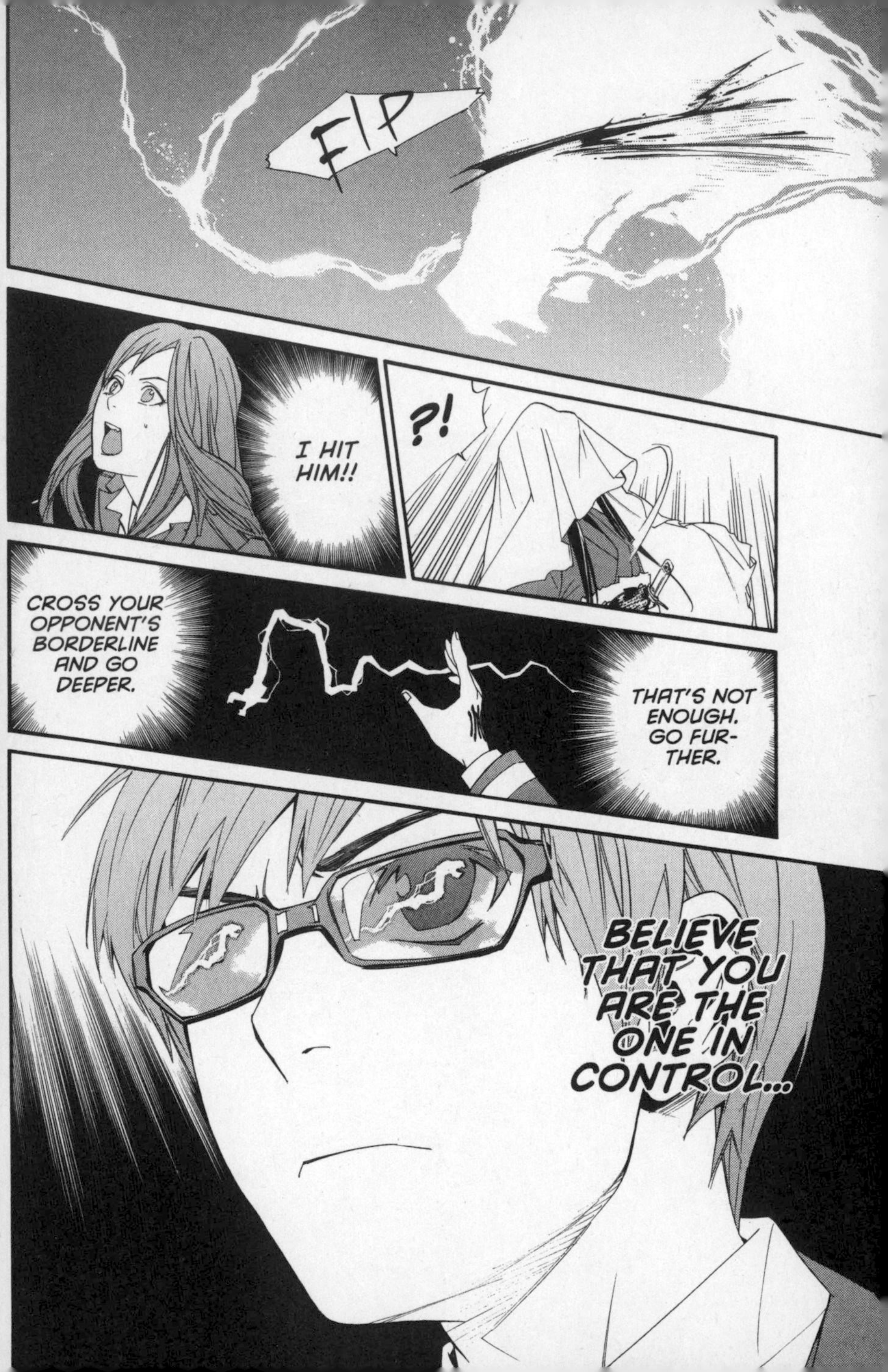
FIP
?!
I HIT HIM!!
THAT'S NOT ENOUGH. GO FUR-THER.
CROSS YOUR OPPONENT'S BORDERLINE AND GO DEEPER.
BELIEVE THAT YOU ARE THE ONE IN CONTROL...

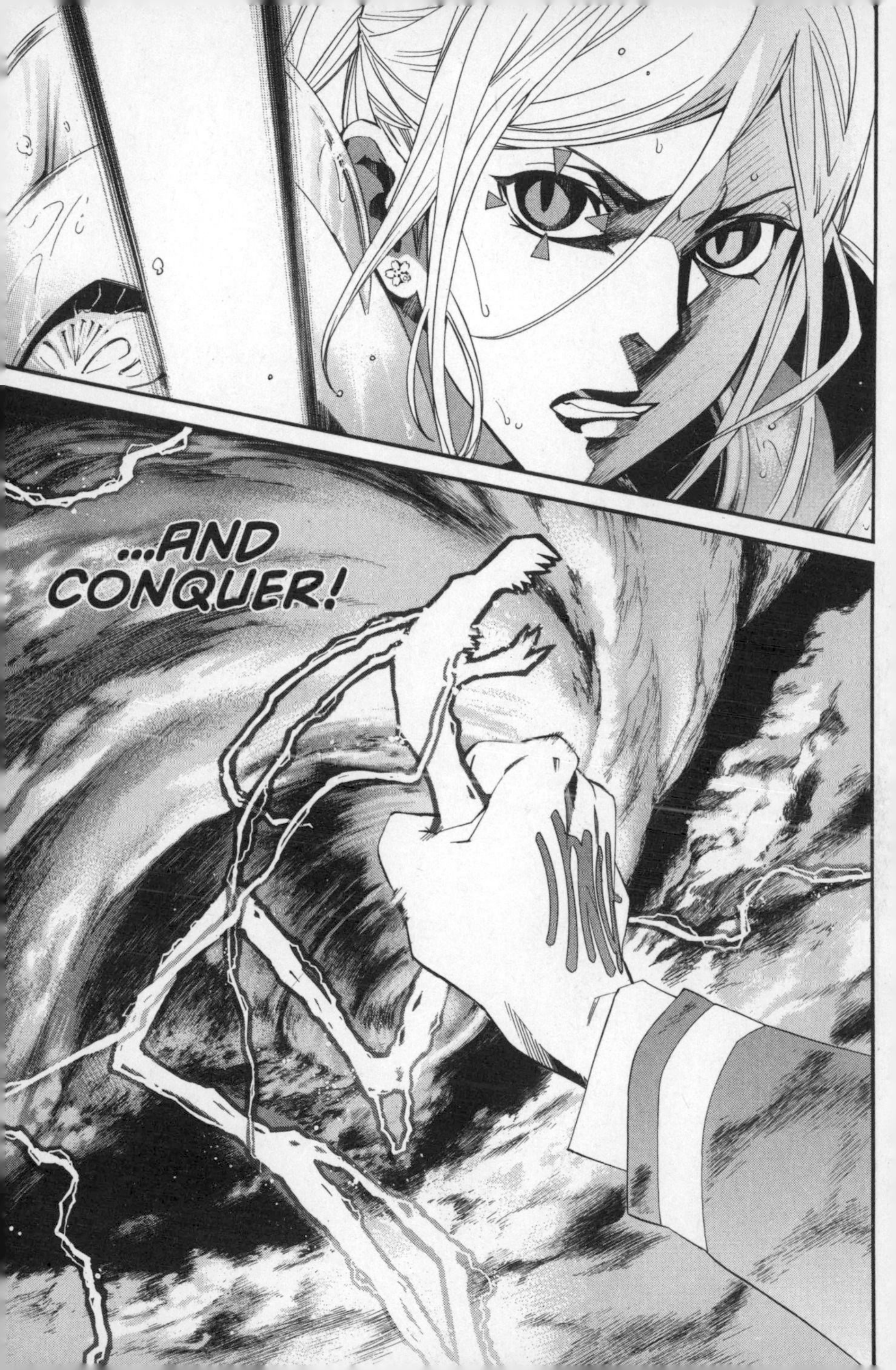
...AND CONQUER!

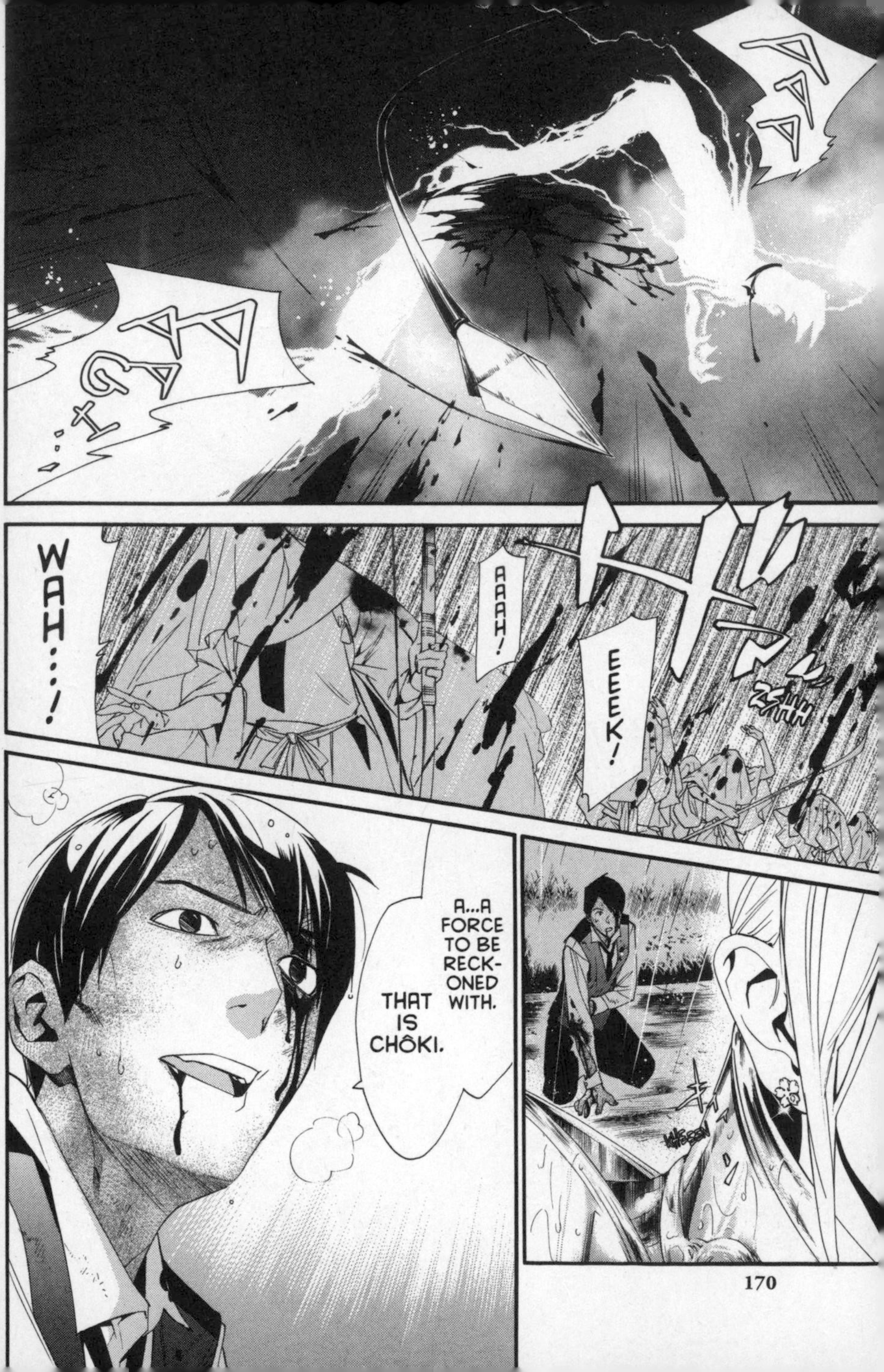

AAA
ZSHH
EEEK!
AAAAH!
WAH...!
A...A FORCE TO BE RECKONED WITH.
THAT IS CHÔKI.

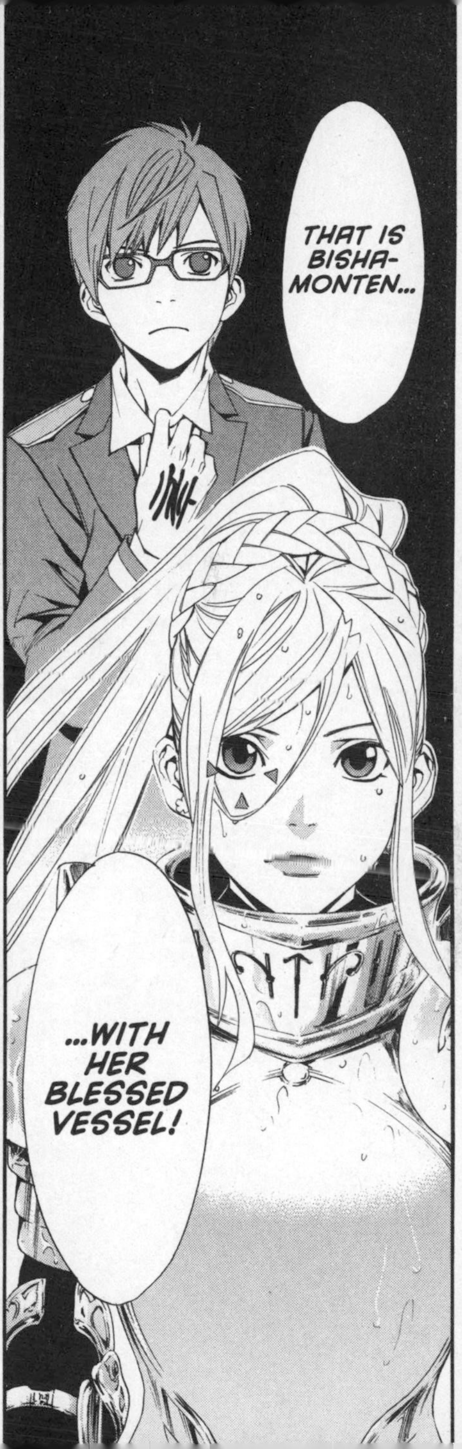
THAT IS BISHA-MONTEN...
...WITH HER BLESSED VESSEL!
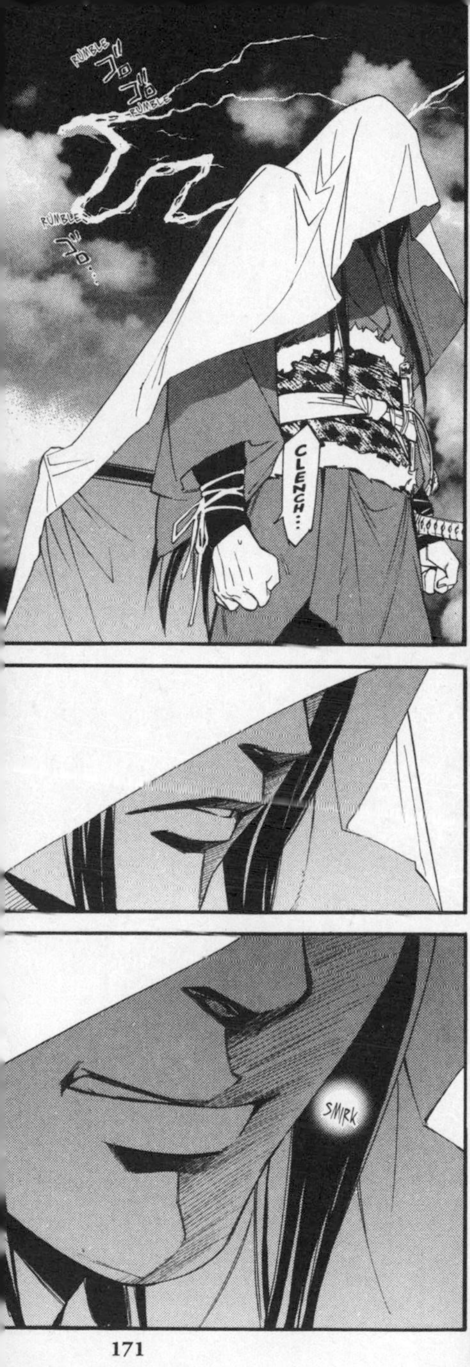
RUMBLE
RUMBLE
RUMBLE
CLENCH...
SMIRK

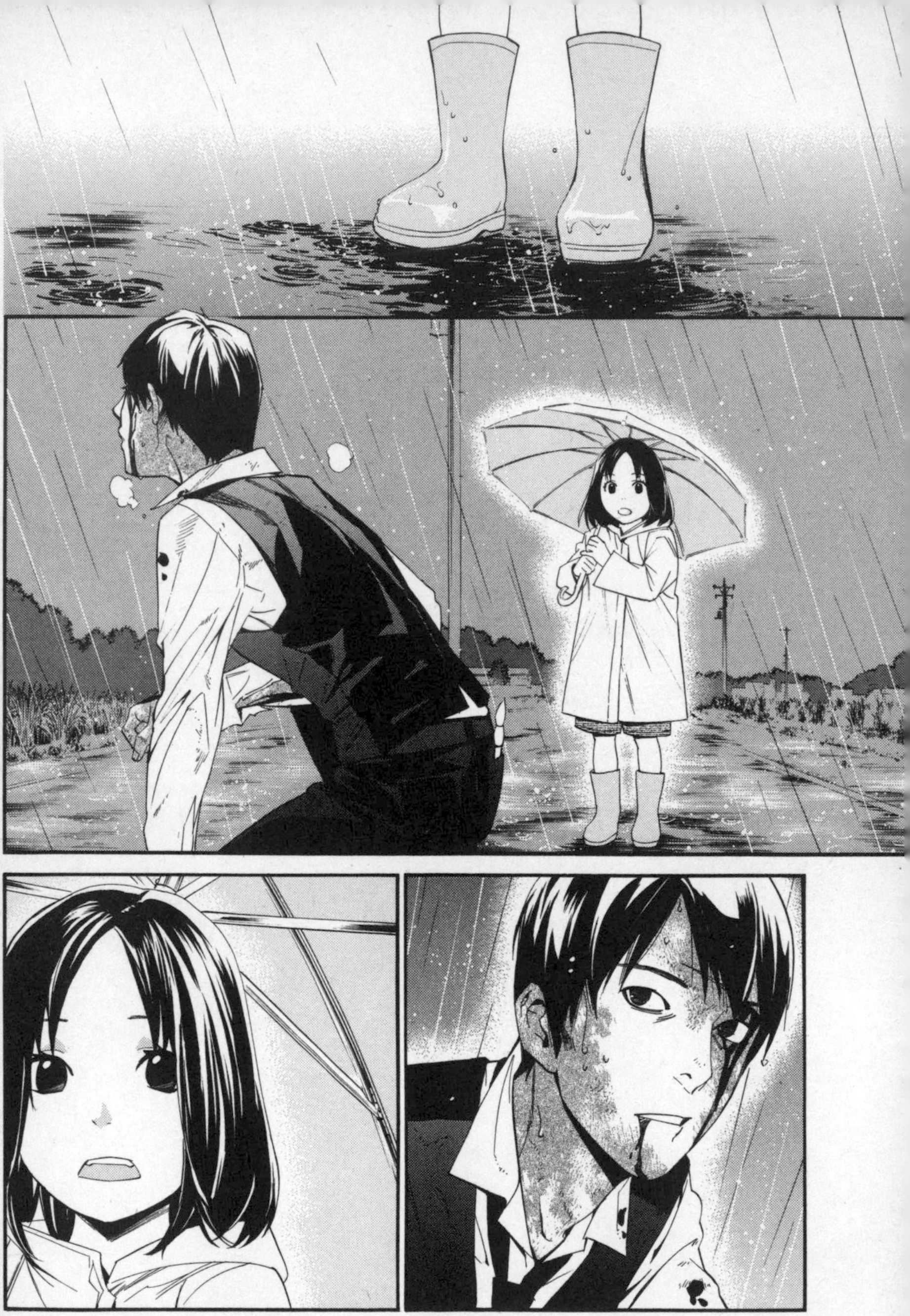

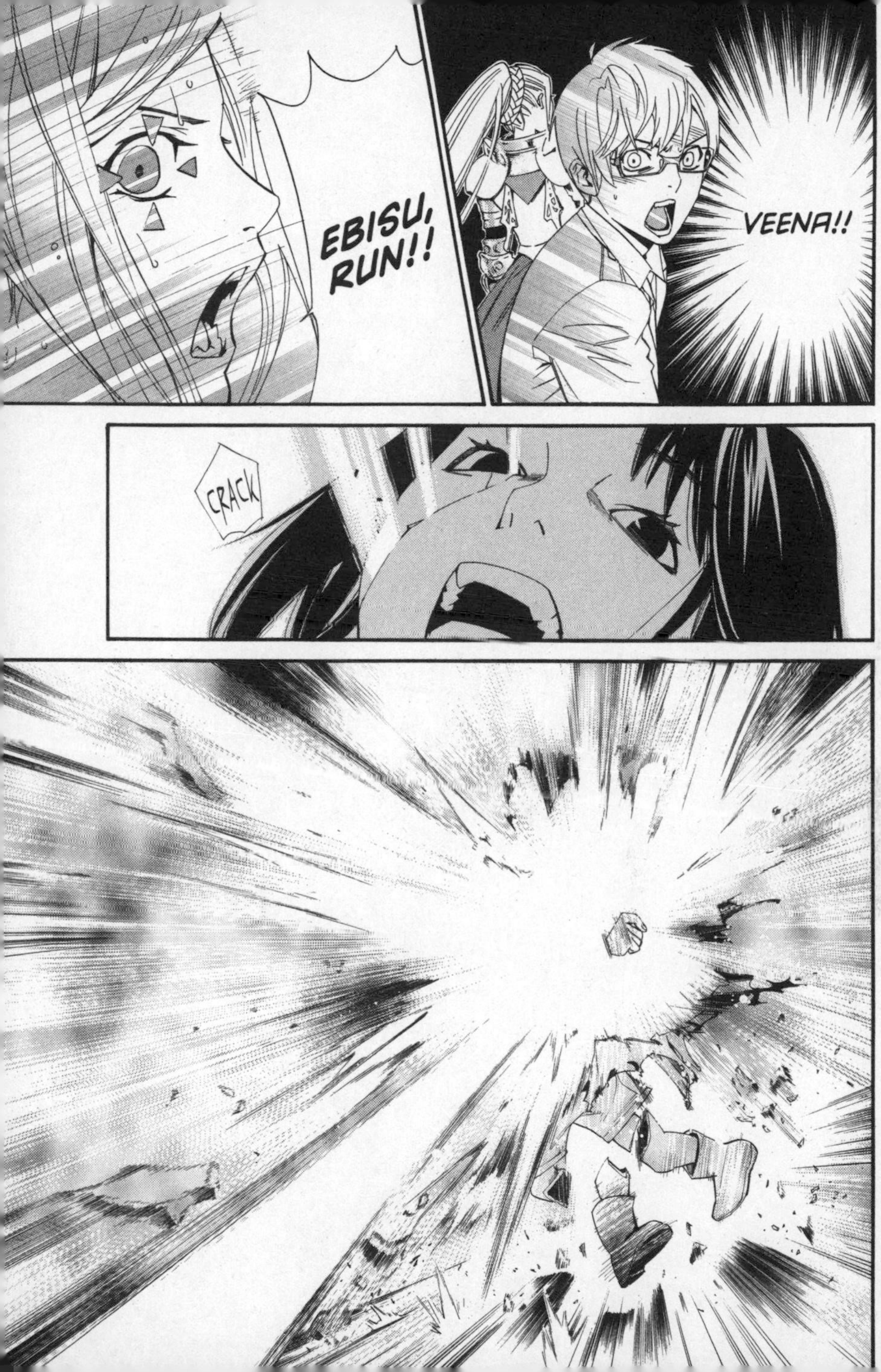
VEENA!!
EBISU, RUN!!
CRACK

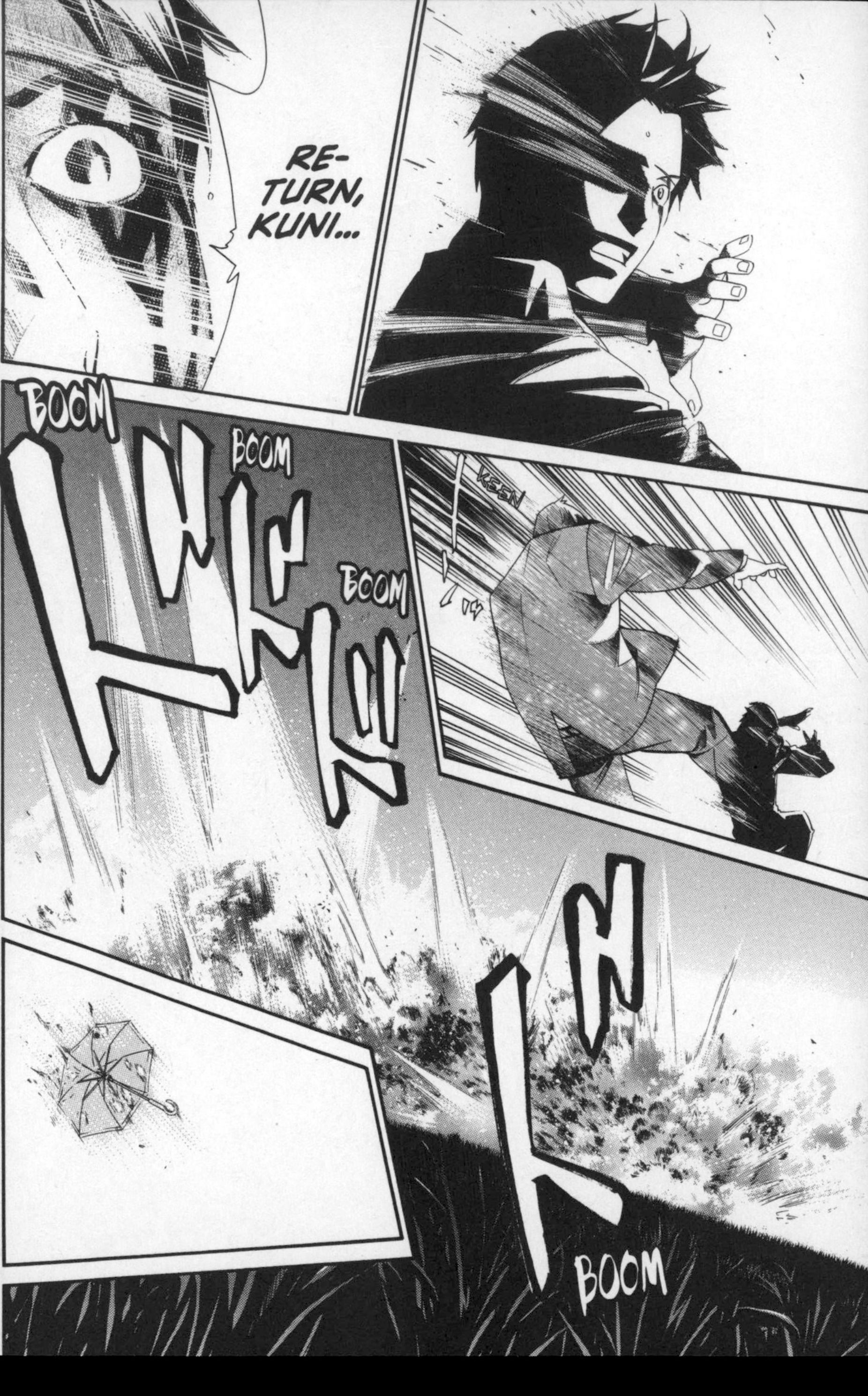
RE-TURN, KUNI...
KEEN
BOOM
BOOM
BOOM
BOOM

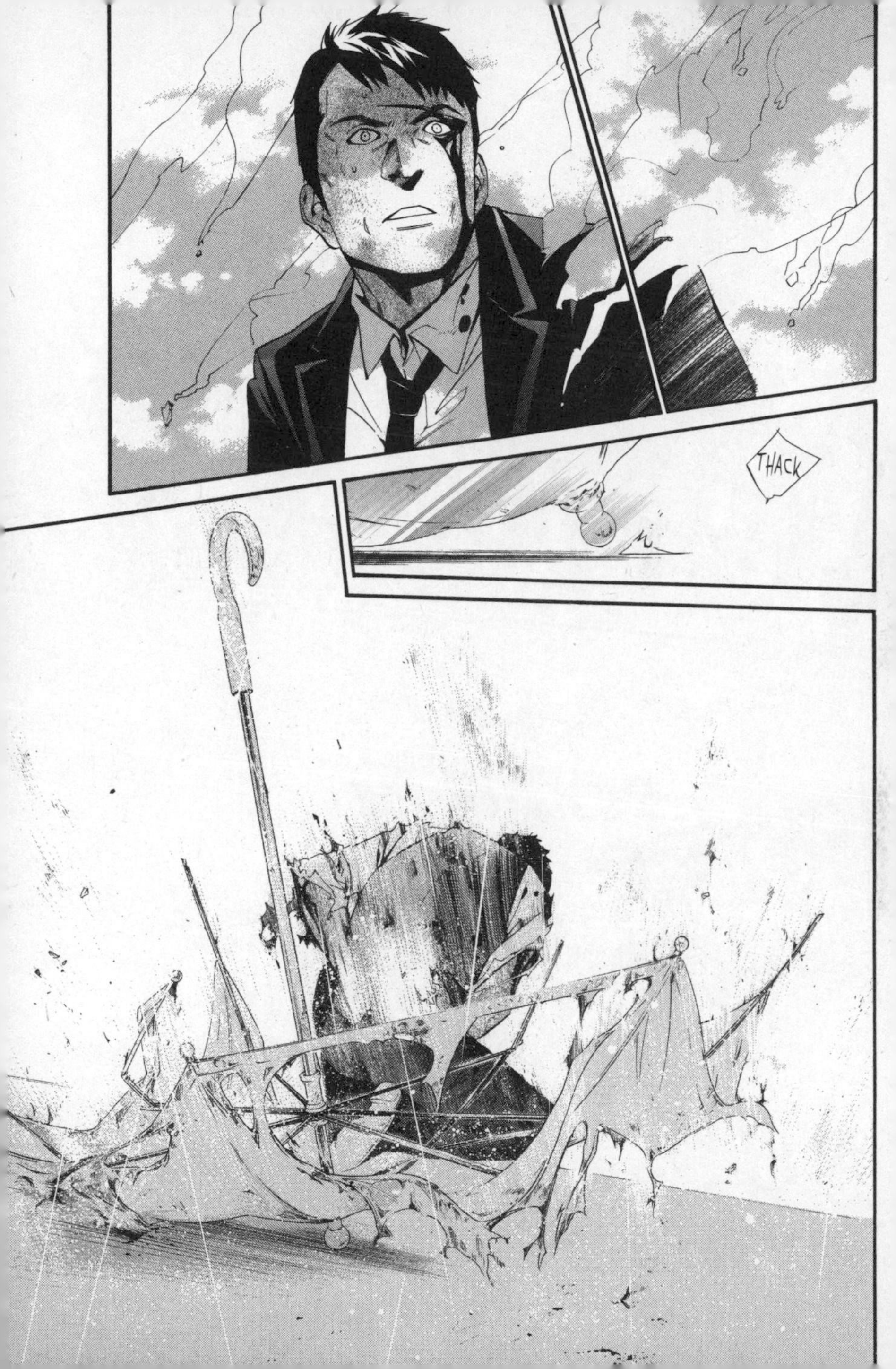
THACK

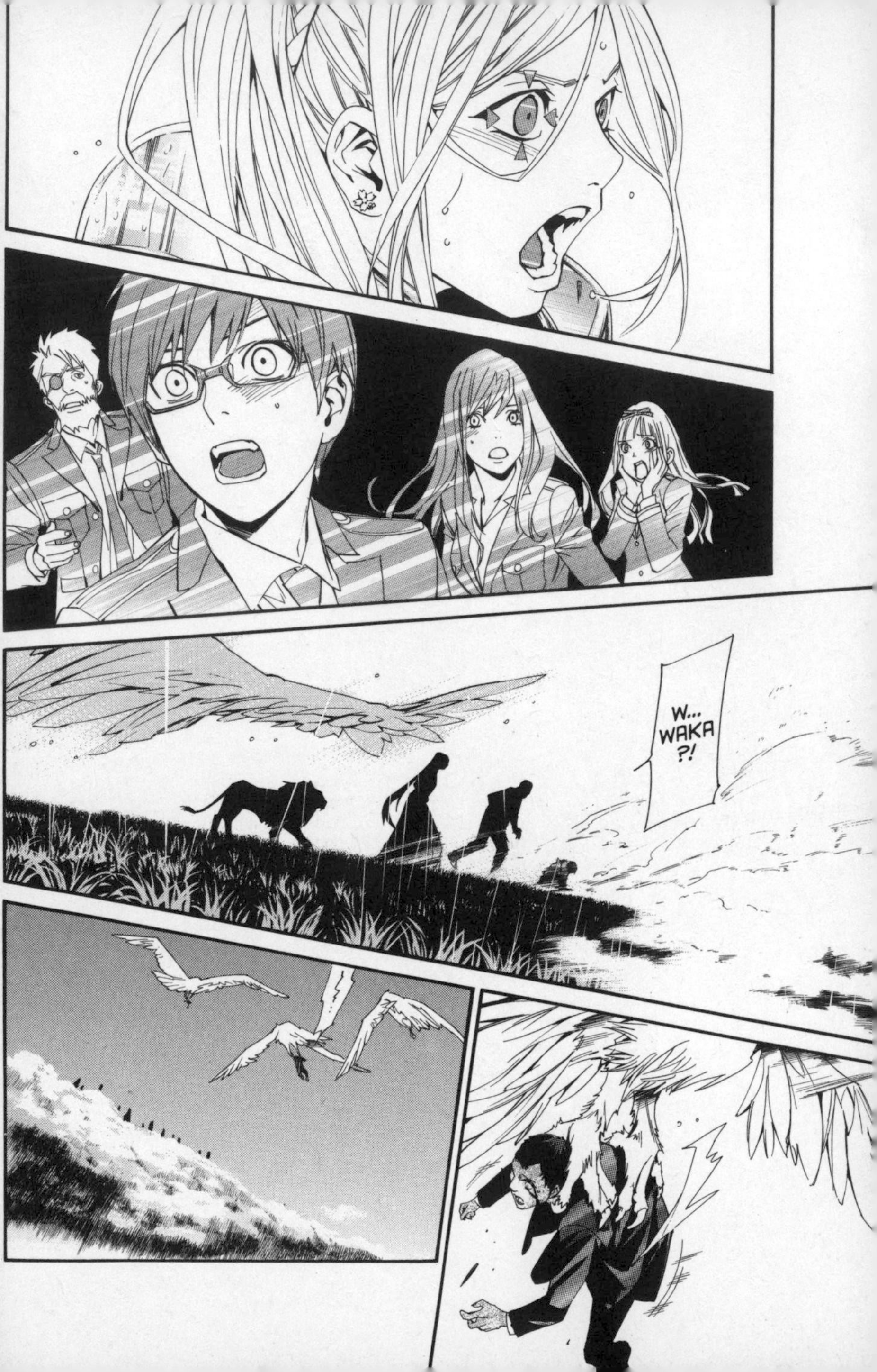
W... WAKA ?!

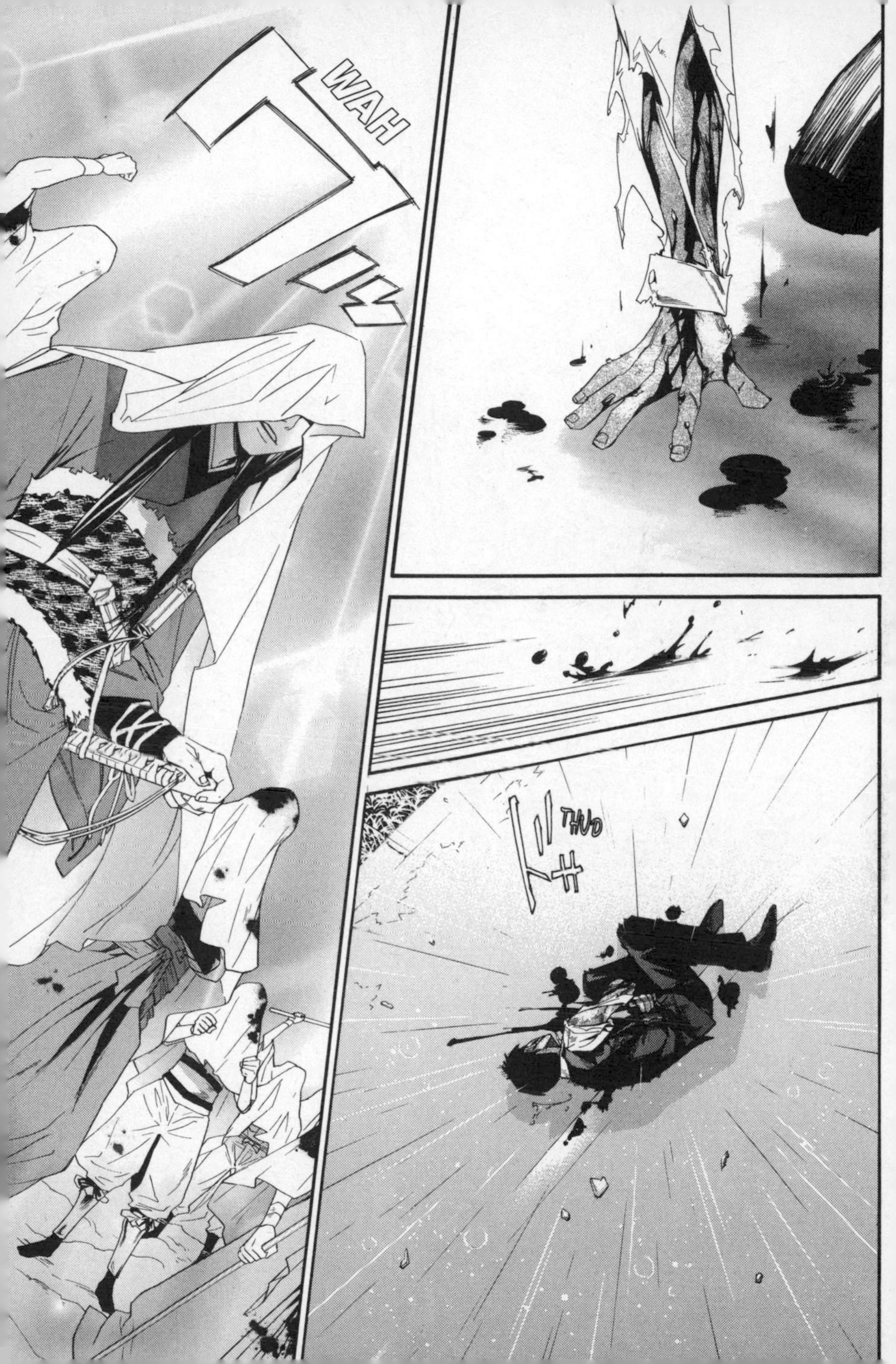
THUD
WAH

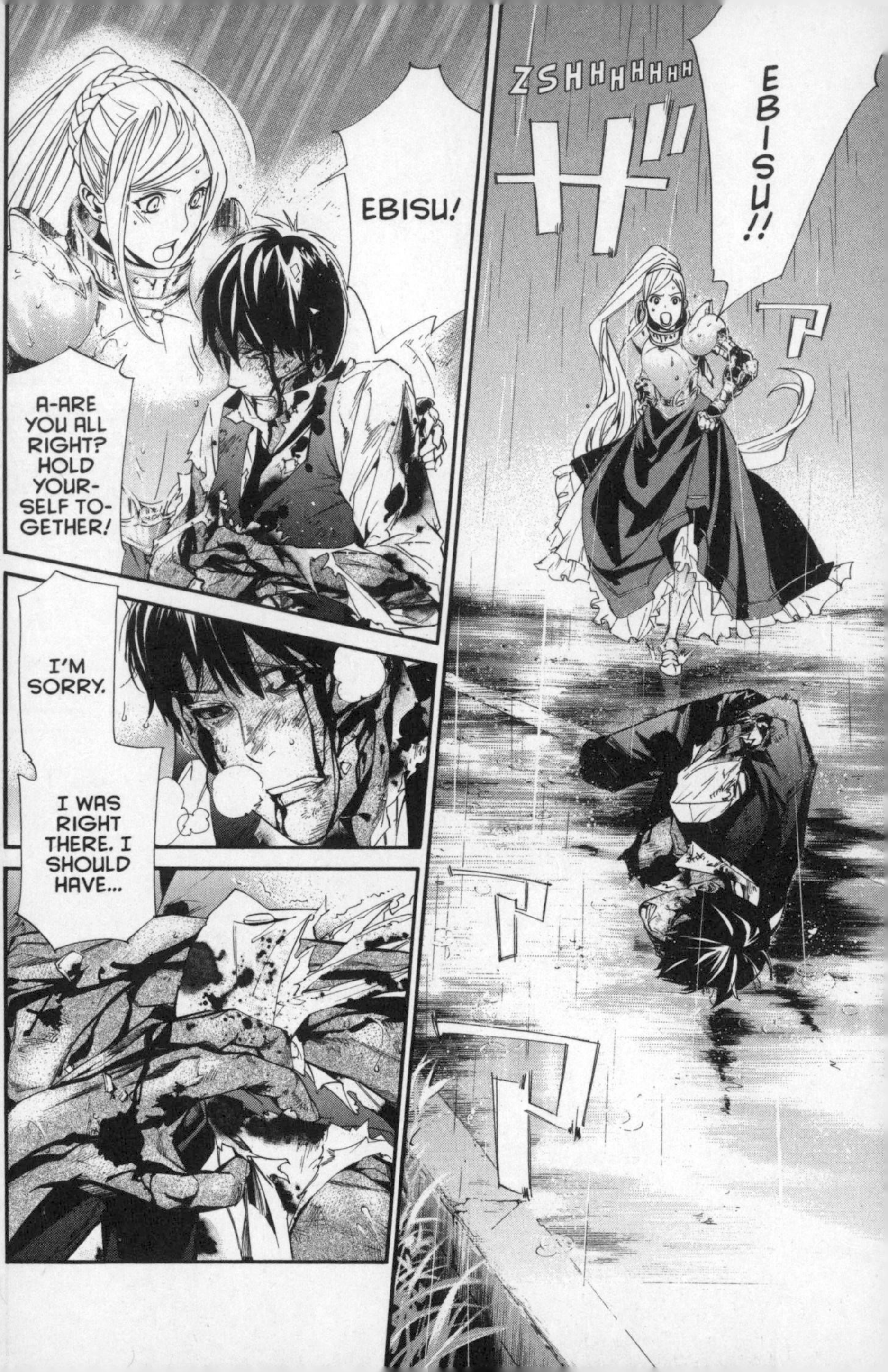
ZSHHHHHHHH
EBISU!!
EBISU!
A-ARE YOU ALL RIGHT? HOLD YOURSELF TOGETHER!
I'M SORRY.
I WAS RIGHT THERE. I SHOULD HAVE...

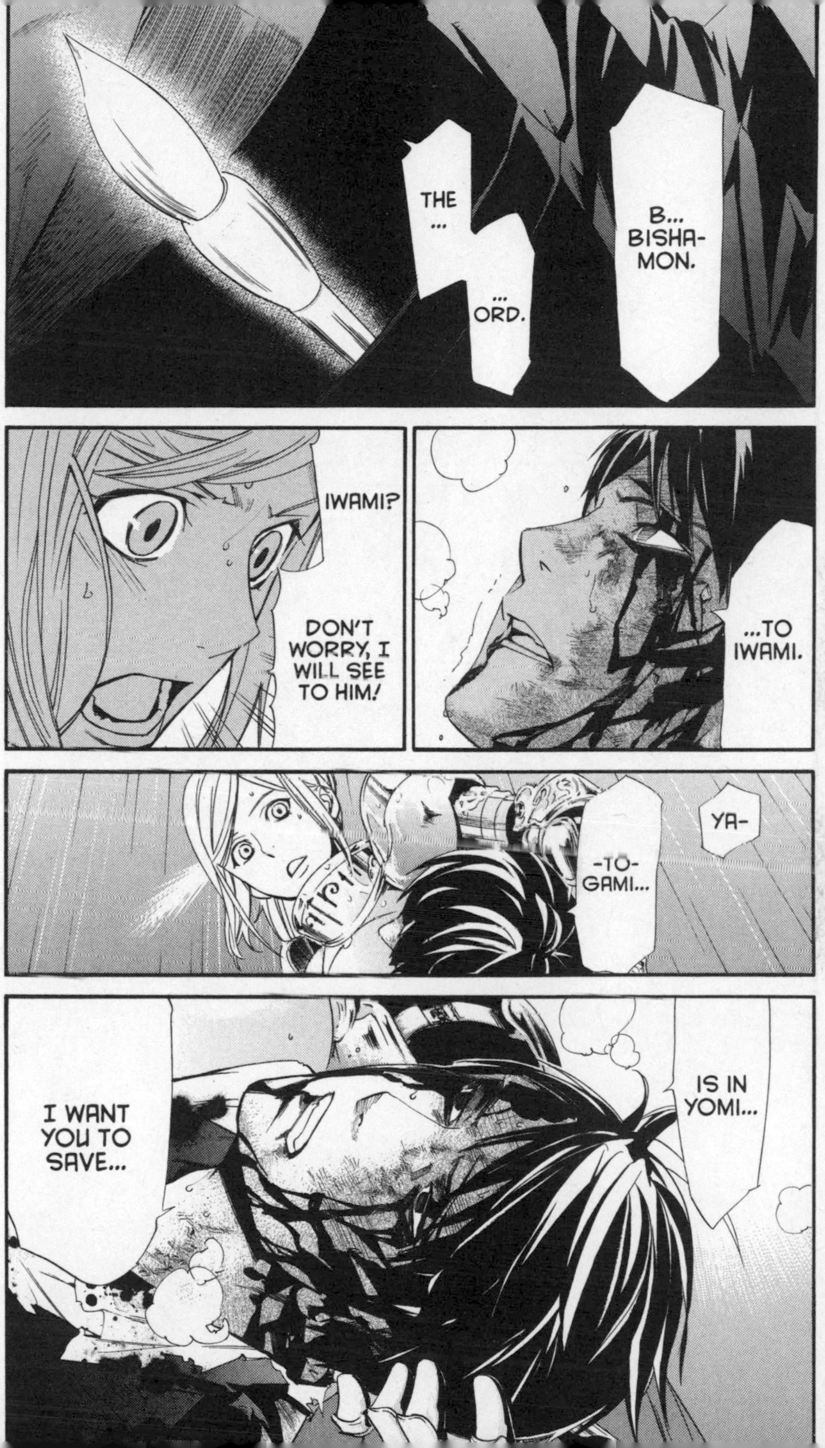
B...
BISHA-
MON.
THE
...
...
ORD.
...TO
IWAMI.
IWAMI?
DON'T
WORRY, I
WILL SEE
TO HIM!
YA-
-TO-
GAMI...
IS IN
YOMI...
I WANT
YOU TO
SAVE...

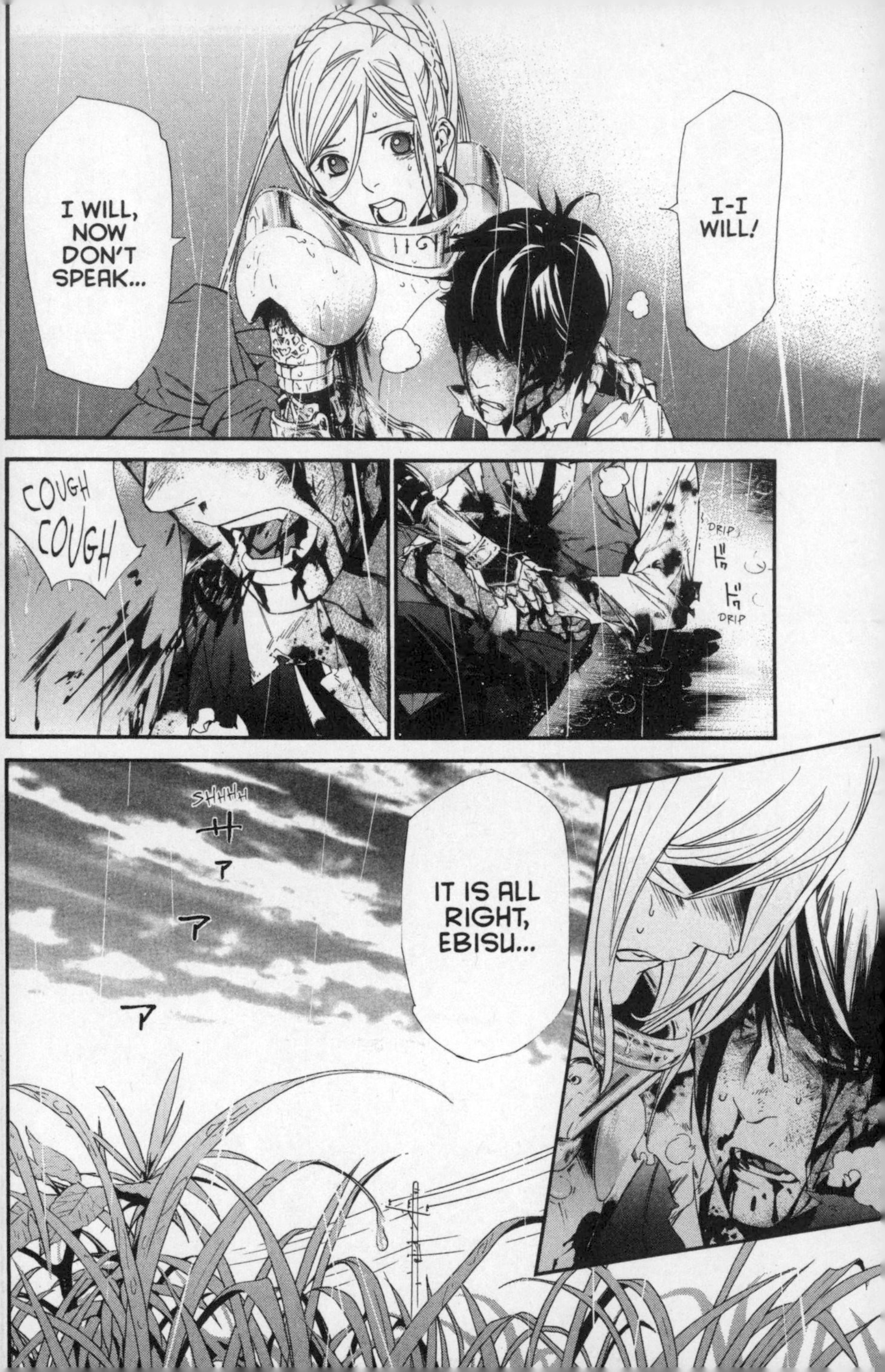
I-I WILL!
I WILL, NOW DON'T SPEAK...
DRIP
ド
ド
DRIP
COUGH COUGH
IT IS ALL RIGHT, EBISU...
SHHHH
サァァァ

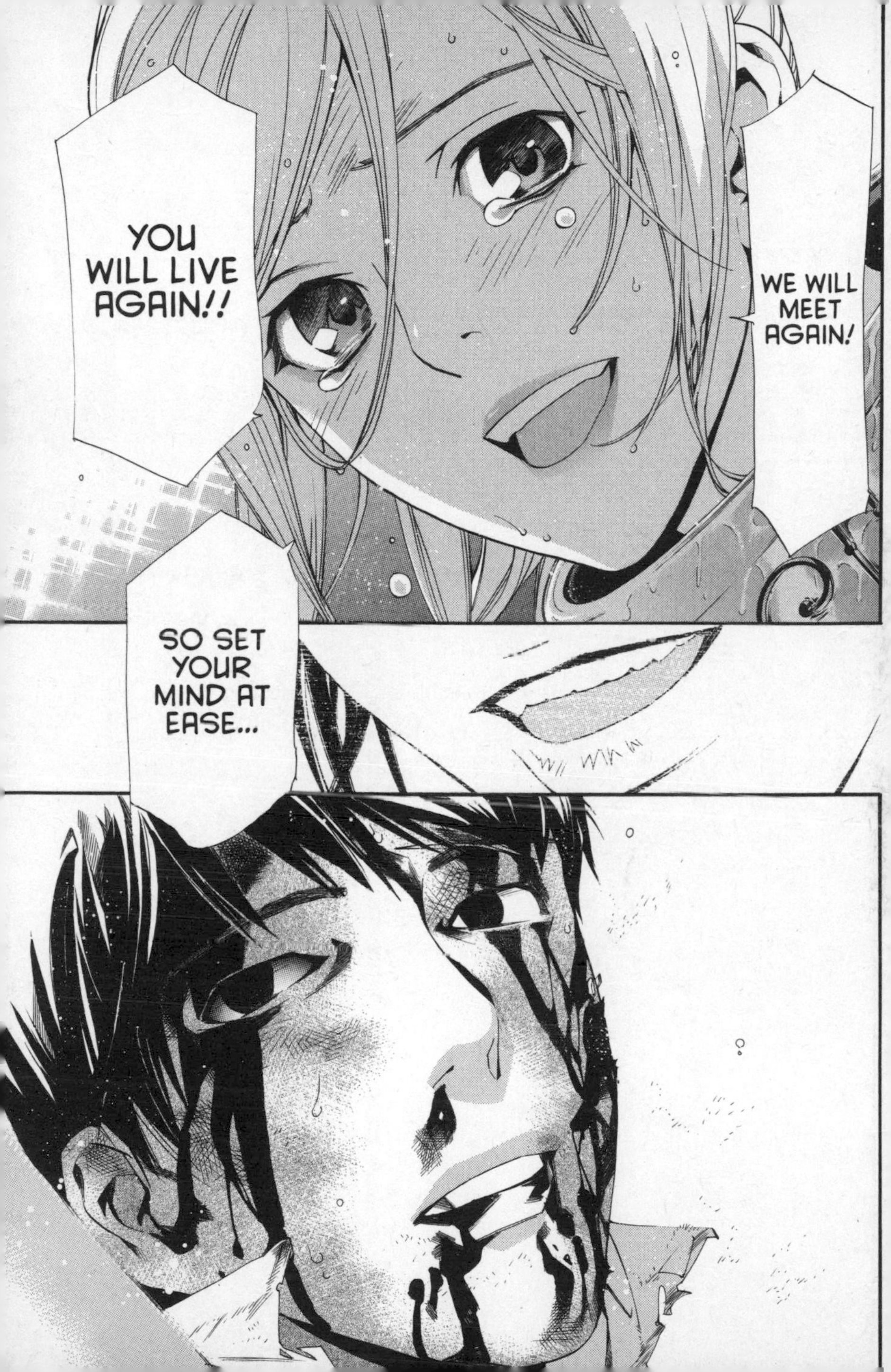
WE WILL MEET AGAIN!
YOU WILL LIVE AGAIN!!
SO SET YOUR MIND AT EASE...

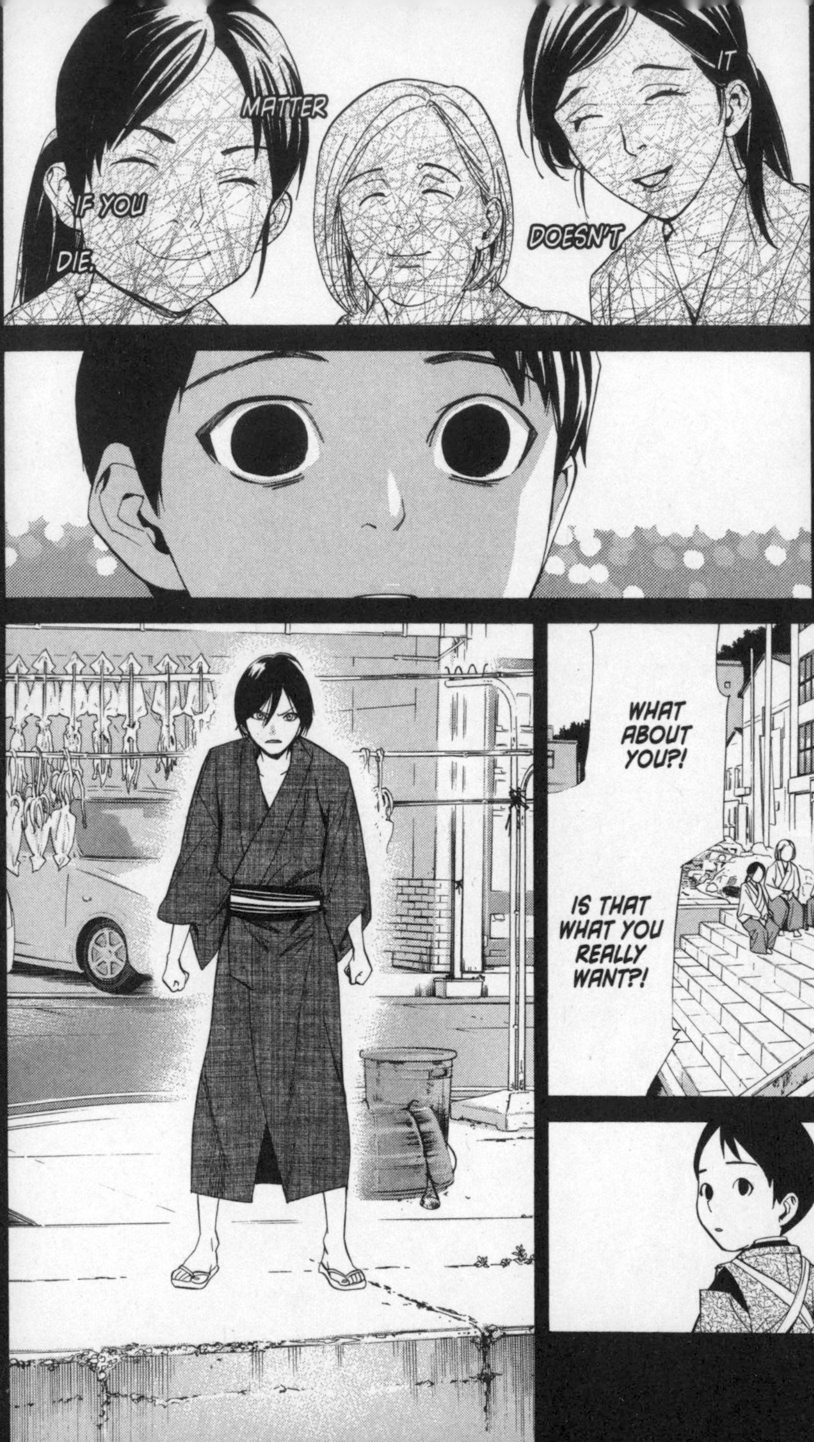
IT
DOESN'T
MATTER
IF YOU
DIE.
WHAT ABOUT YOU?!
IS THAT WHAT YOU REALLY WANT?!

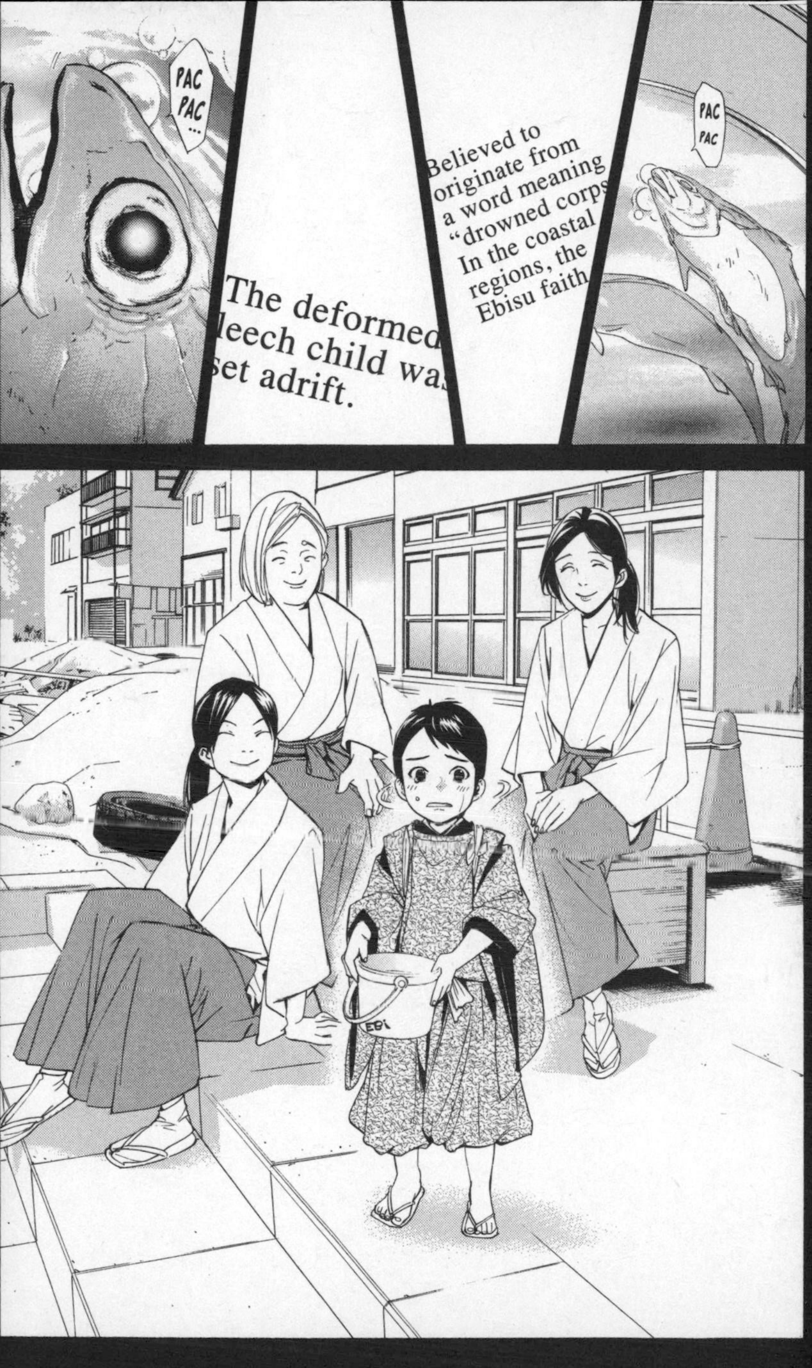
PAC PAC
Believed to originate from a word meaning "drowned corps In the coastal regions, the Ebisu faith
The deformed leech child wa set adrift.
PAC PAC ...
EBI

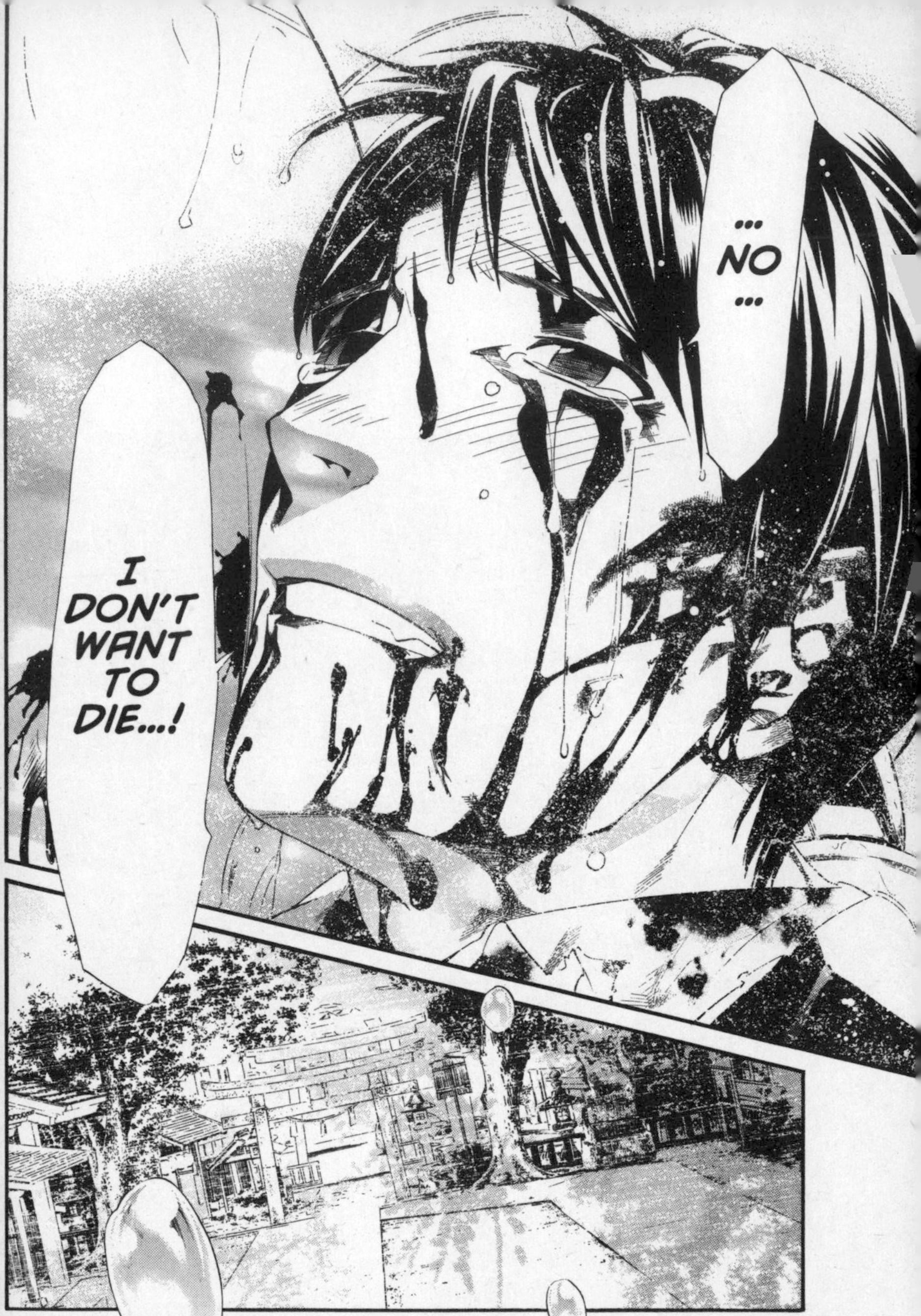
...NO...
I DON'T WANT TO DIE...!

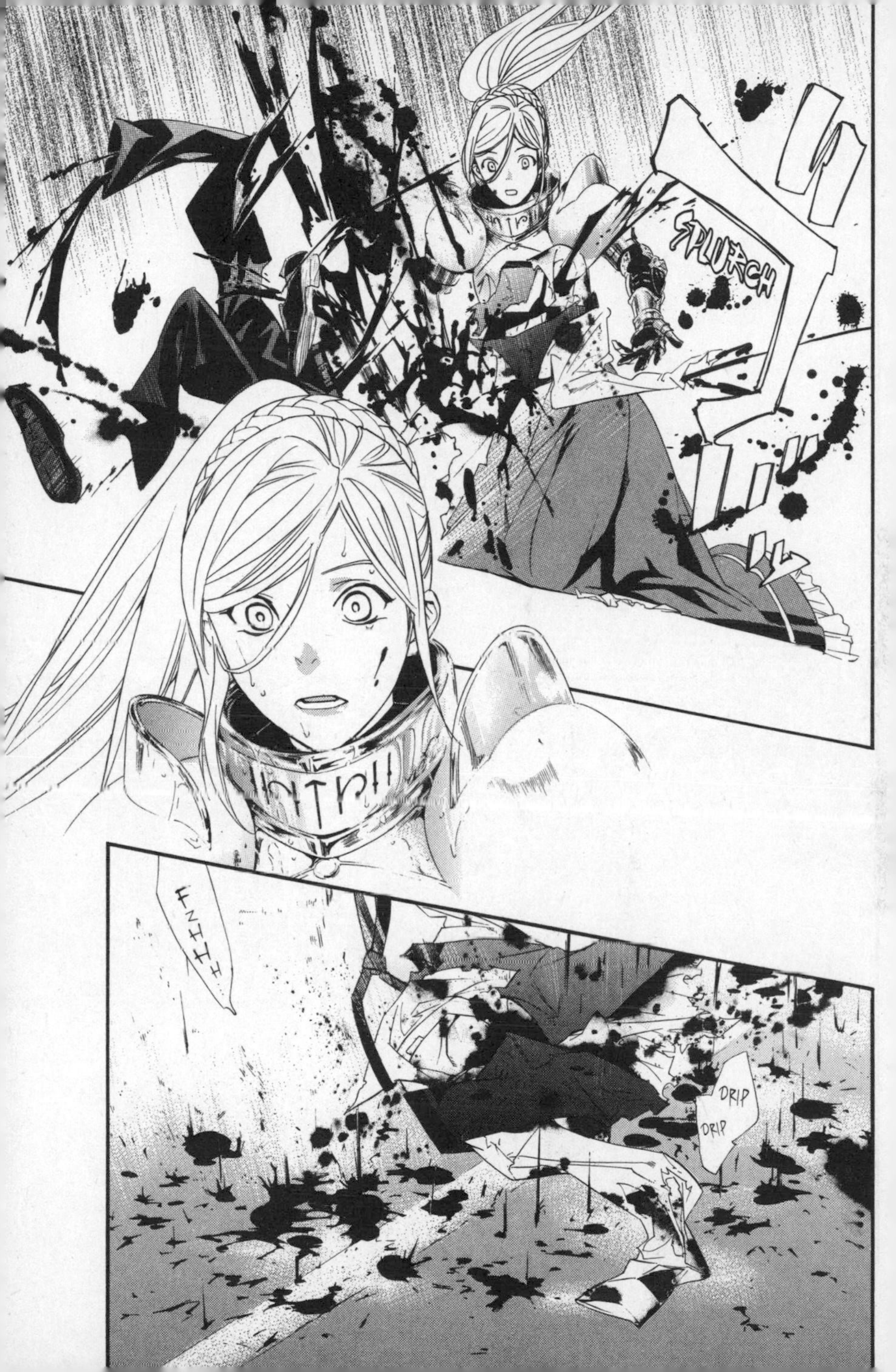
SPLURCH
FZHHH
DRIP
DRIP

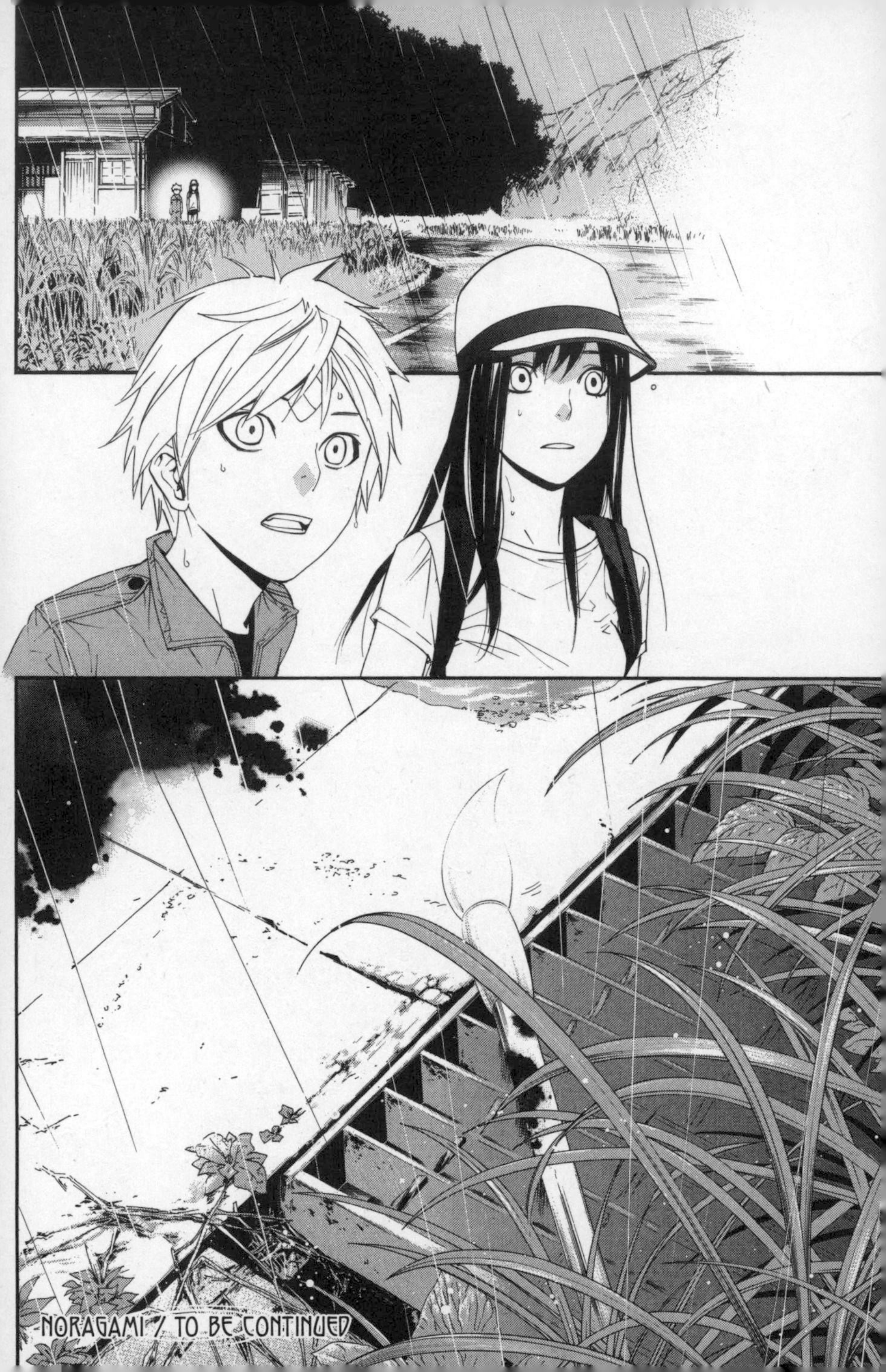
NORAGAMI / TO BE CONTINUED

野

[illegible]

神

ATROCIOUS MANGA

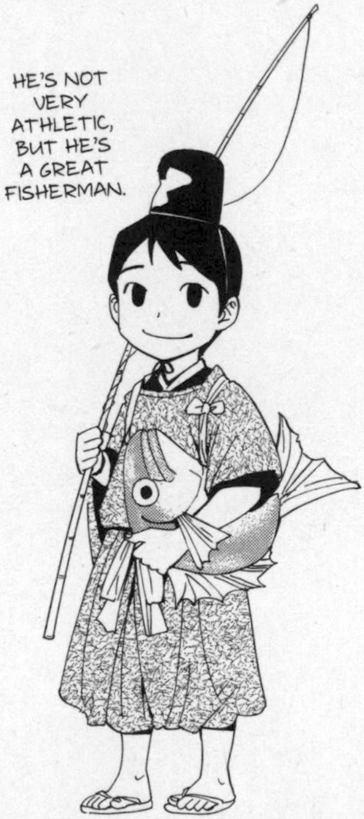
HE'S NOT VERY ATHLETIC, BUT HE'S A GREAT FISHERMAN.

LITTLE EBI

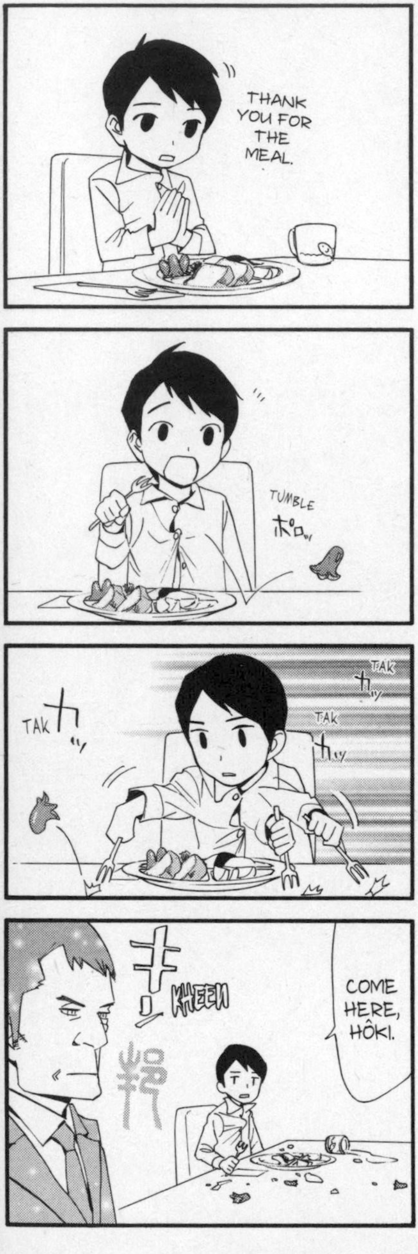
THANK YOU FOR THE MEAL.
TUMBLE
ポロッ
TAK
カッ
TAK
カッ
TAK
カッ
キーン
KHEEN
COME HERE, HÔKI.

MIDDLE-AGED EBI

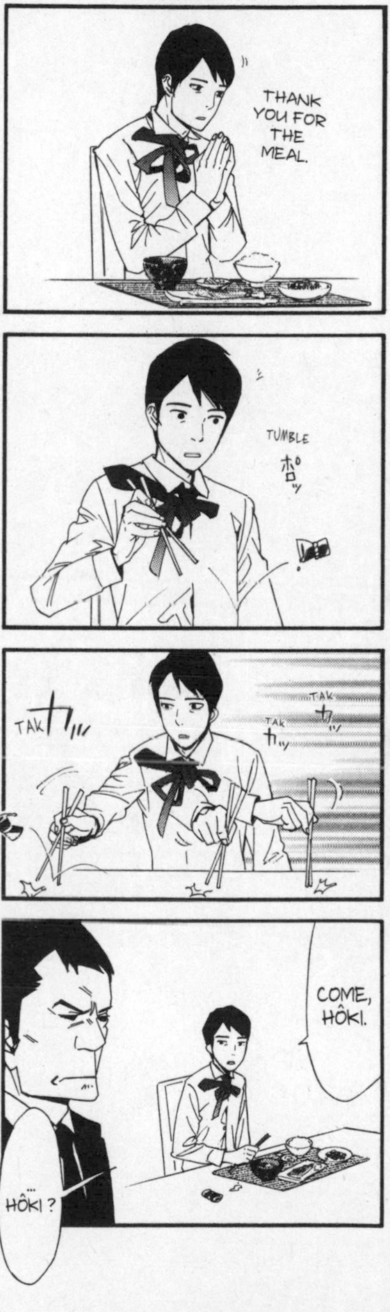

THANK YOU FOR THE MEAL.
TUMBLE
ポロッ
TAK
カッ
TAK
カッ
TAK
カッ
COME, HÔKI.
... HÔKI ?

LIVELY EBI

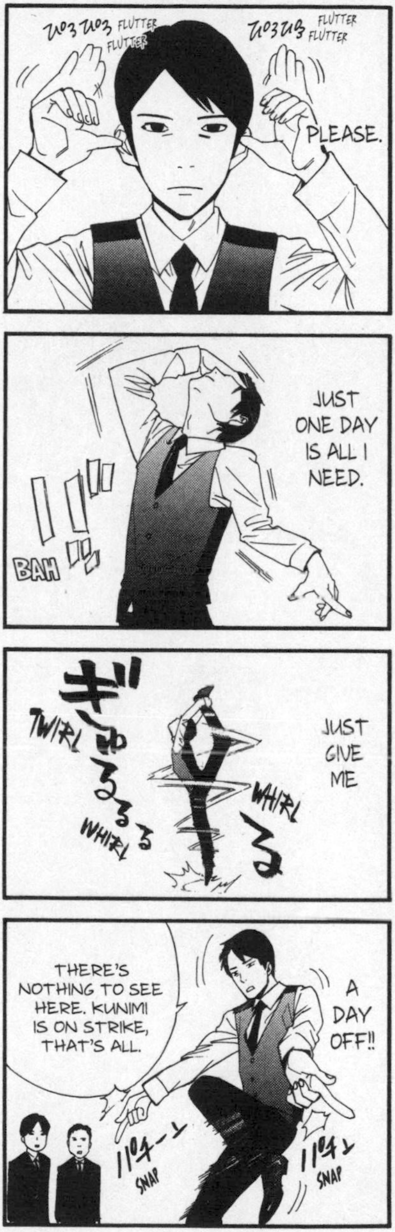

ぴろぴろ FLUTTER FLUTTER
PLEASE.
ぴろぴろ FLUTTER FLUTTER
JUST ONE DAY IS ALL I NEED.
BAH
JUST GIVE ME
ぎゅるるる TWIRL
WHIRL
る WHIRL
A DAY OFF!!
THERE'S NOTHING TO SEE HERE. KUNIMI IS ON STRIKE, THAT'S ALL.
パチン SNAP
パチーン SNAP

DARK EBISU

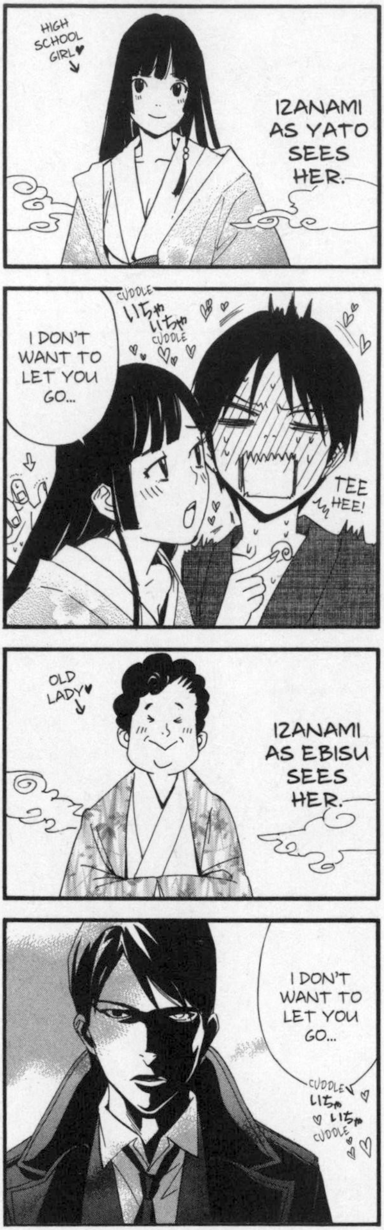
HIGH SCHOOL GIRL♥
IZANAMI AS YATO SEES HER.
I DON'T WANT TO LET YOU GO...
CUDDLE いちゃ いちゃ CUDDLE
TEE HEE!
OLD LADY♥
IZANAMI AS EBISU SEES HER.
I DON'T WANT TO LET YOU GO...
CUDDLE いちゃ いちゃ CUDDLE

VINDICTIVE

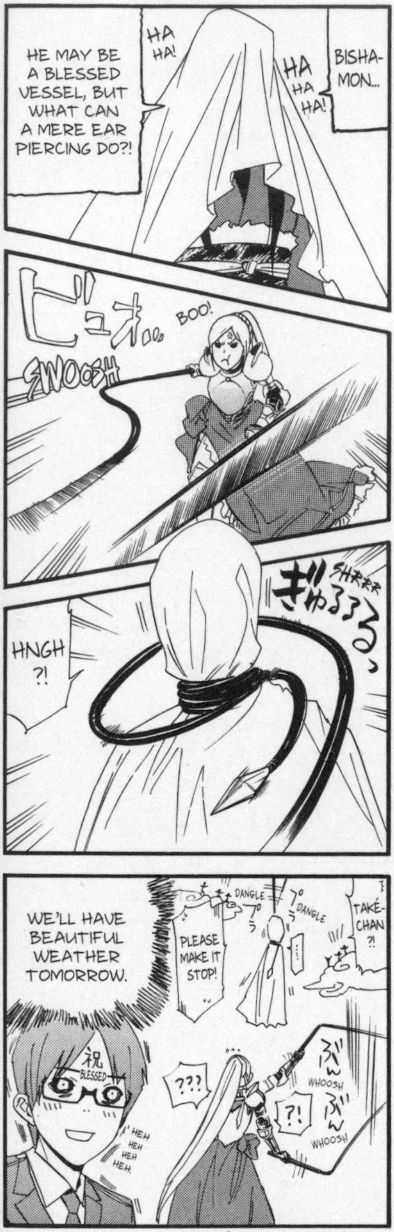
BISHA-MON...
HA HA HA HA!
HA HA!
HE MAY BE A BLESSED VESSEL, BUT WHAT CAN A MERE EAR PIERCING DO?!
ビュオ。。
SWOOSH
BOO!
ぎゅるるる
SHRRR
HNGH ?!
TAKÉ-CHAN ?!
プラ DANGLE
プラ DANGLE
PLEASE MAKE IT STOP!
WE'LL HAVE BEAUTIFUL WEATHER TOMORROW.
ぶぃん WHOOSH
ぶぃん WHOOSH
?!
???
祝 BLESSED
HEH HEH HEH HEH.

Také-chan will come back to life again and again, so don't you worry! But never ever try this at home, kids!
-Kazuma

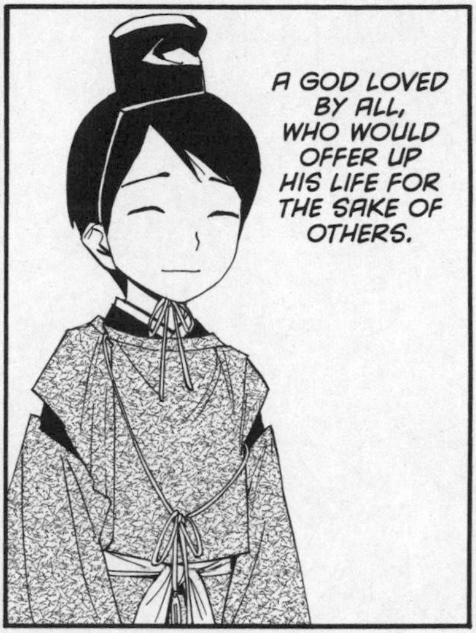
A GOD LOVED BY ALL, WHO WOULD OFFER UP HIS LIFE FOR THE SAKE OF OTHERS.
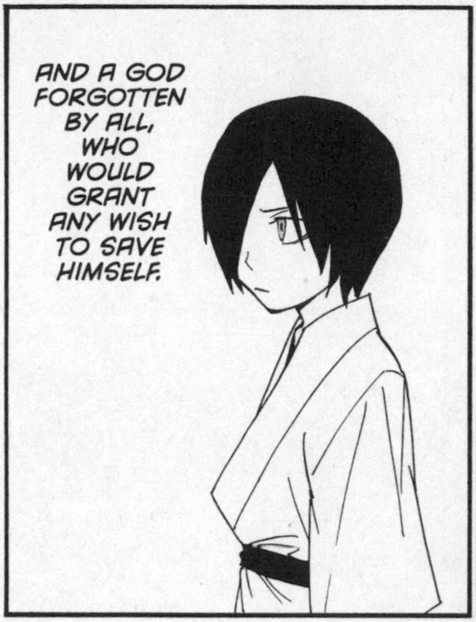
AND A GOD FORGOTTEN BY ALL, WHO WOULD GRANT ANY WISH TO SAVE HIMSELF.
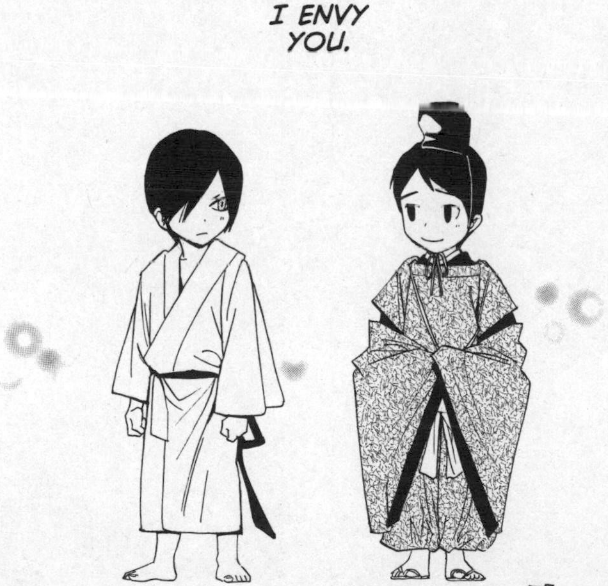
I ENVY YOU.

THANK YOU TO EVERYONE WHO READ THIS FAR!!

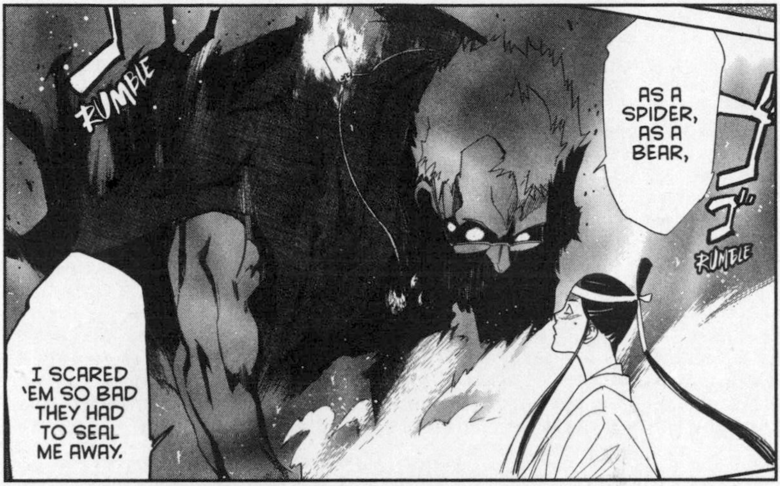
AS A SPIDER, AS A BEAR,
RUMBLE
RUMBLE
I SCARED 'EM SO BAD THEY HAD TO SEAL ME AWAY.

Ôkuninushi opposing the heavens, page 70

Ôkuninushi was the ruler of Izumo, which was the center of the world at that time. Later, he was replaced at the request of the sun goddess Amaterasu by her grandson Ninigi, and retired to Yomi. In some versions of the legend, the transfer of power from the land god Ôkuninushi to the heavenly god Ninigi was less than peaceful. This might be part of where his association with spiders comes into play—as mentioned in a previous note, all those who opposed the Heavenly Emperor were called *kumo*, or spiders. As for what that has to do with bears, the two main shrines in the Izumo region are Izumo Taisha and Kumano Taisha. One of the *kanji* characters in Izumo is *kumo* (this time meaning cloud) and one in Kumano Taisha is *kuma* (bear). Also, *kuma* was alternative pronunciation for *kumo*, so people may not have thought of him as a bear at all—they may have been calling him two different words for "spider." Nevertheless, Ôkuninushi is also associated with local deities in Kumano, and it stands to reason that at least one of these deities would have a bear form.

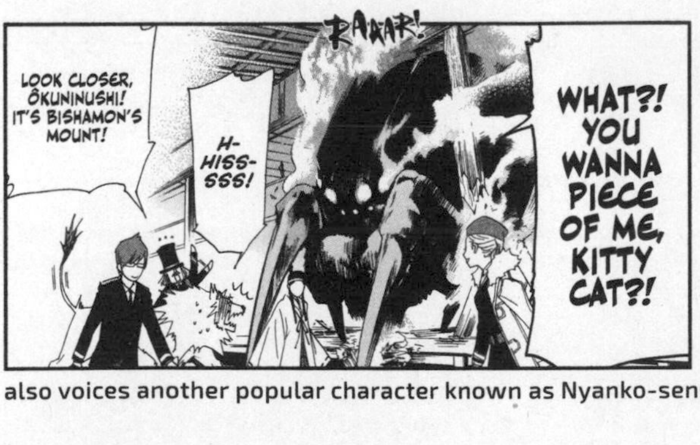
RAAAR!
WHAT?! YOU WANNA PIECE OF ME, KITTY CAT?!
H-HISSS-SSS!
LOOK CLOSER, ÔKUNINUSHI! IT'S BISHAMON'S MOUNT!

Kitty cat, page 73

Here Ôkuninushi faces off against Kuraha, calling him "kitty cat," or *nyanko*. It may be amusing to note that the actor who voices Kuraha in the Japanese version of the *Noragami* anime, Kazuhiko Inoue, also voices another popular character known as Nyanko-sensei.

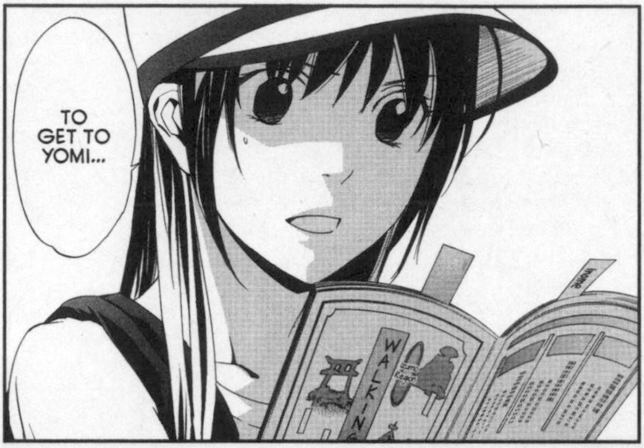
TO GET TO YOMI...

Izumo Region Walking, page 52

Hiyori is using a guide book for people visiting the Izumo Region called *Machi-aruki*, or "walking around town." This is likely the *Noragami* world's version of *Walker*, a series of magazines designed to let people know where all the cool and interesting places to go are. Hiyori is in the Izumo Region because East Izumo is where she will find Yomotsu Hirasaka, which is where the entrance to Yomi is said to be located.

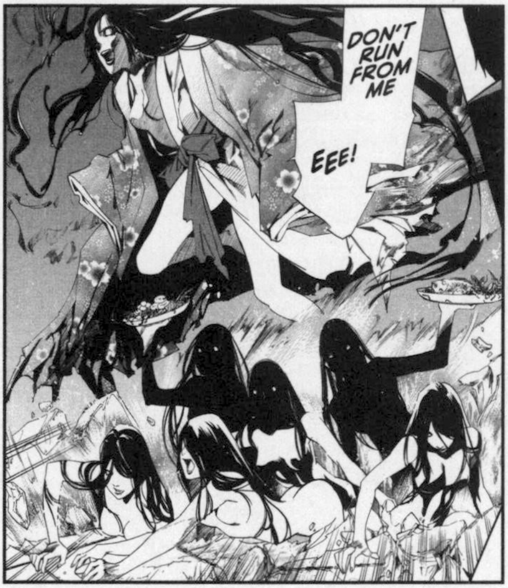
DON'T RUN FROM ME
EEE!

Monster women, page 57

Izanami's minions are the *yomotsu-shikome*, meaning literally "ugly women of the underworld." They helped her to chase Izanagi when he ran from her after beholding her deformity. As mentioned by Ebisu in the previous volume, Izanagi was able to outrun them by distracting them with fruit. Now we see why it was such a bad idea for him to eat the peaches he had brought.

Read him his last rites, page 68

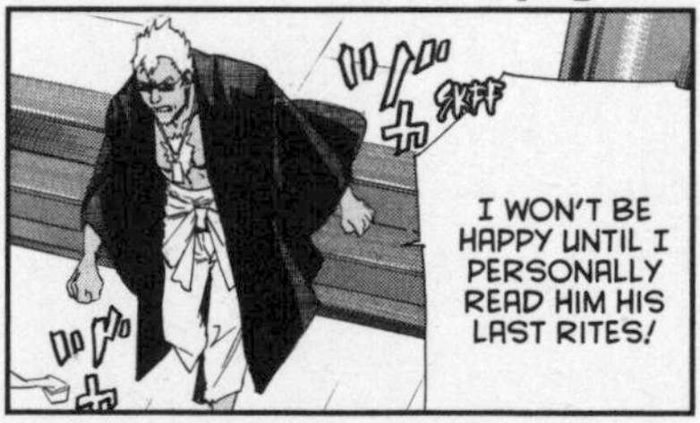
I WON'T BE HAPPY UNTIL I PERSONALLY READ HIM HIS LAST RITES!

The phrase "*indô wo watasu*" literally means "to give guidance," either in life, or in the afterlife, as it is often used to mean "to perform the last rites over the deceased." The phrase can also be used to in reference to giving an ultimatum, as in, "You'd better shape up, or else." In his anger, Ôkuninushi could mean it either way, and probably does mean it both ways.

TRANSLATION NOTES

Japanese is a tricky language for most Westerners, and translation is often more art than science. For your edification and reading pleasure, here are notes on some of the places where we could have gone in a different direction in our translation of the work, or where a Japanese cultural reference is used.

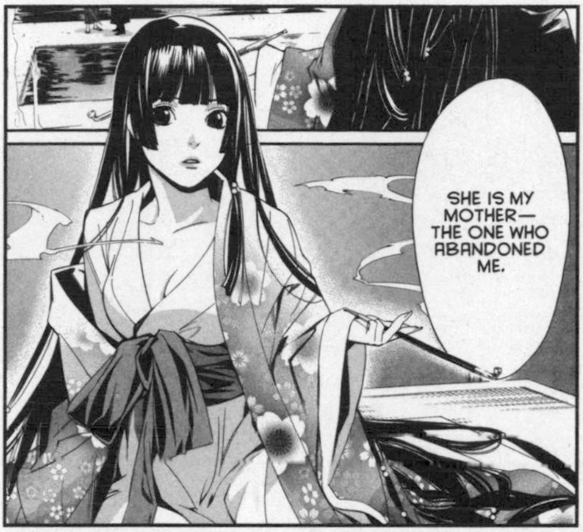
SHE IS MY MOTHER— THE ONE WHO ABANDONED ME.

She Who Invites, page 6

"She who invites" is a translation of the name Izanami, who came to be queen of Yomi after an incident with her Izanagi. She had died giving birth to the fire god, and when Izanagi came to rescue her from the world of the dead, she had already eaten the food there which prevented her from leaving. She went to ask permission to leave from the other residents of Yomi, and told Izanagi not to look at her while he waited for an answer. He grew impatient and looked anyway, seeing that she was no longer her beautiful self, but had transformed into a rotting corpse with foul creatures crawling all over her. He freaked out and ran away from her, and in her wrath she declared that she would destroy a thousand of the living every day, in effect making herself the queen of death.

As for Izanami's relationship to Ebisu, long before the Yomi incident, she and Izanagi wanted to have children, but on their first attempt, they transgressed the marriage ritual and so the two children born of that union were deformed. The first was born with no bones, like a leech, and so was named Hiruko, or "leech child." He was sent floating out to sea in a boat made of reeds. He eventually grew a skeletal structure at the age of three and, according to some legends, later became the god Ebisu. The second child became the island of Awajima.

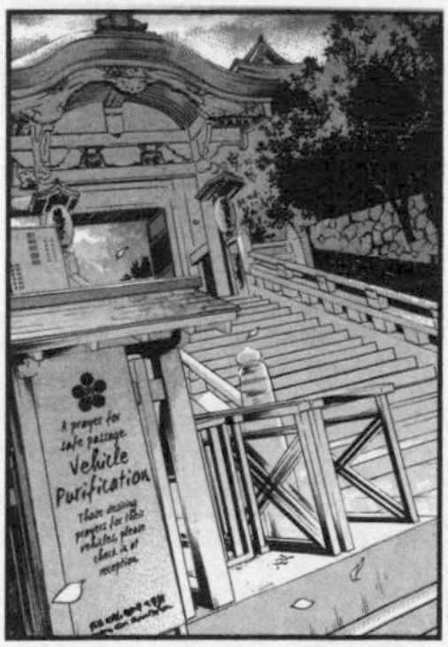
A prayer for safe passage.
Vehicle Purification

Vehicle purification, page 25

The translators believe it would be safe to say that 100% of car accidents in Japan, and possibly the world, involve cars. That being the case, shinto shrines offer vehicle purification, in which a priest will pray over a new car to ward off accidents and promote safe driving in the driver. It's a prayer for good luck and safe travels, similar to the christening of a ship.

Threatened with phalanges, page 27

Phalanges is a fancy word for "fingers." The word actually Kazuma used was hoko, meaning spear. To make sense of this, think back to volume two, when Yato taught Yukiné to create a borderline by pointing his fingers like a spear. In Japanese, the word *hoko*, or rather *hokosaki* (tip of a spear), is often used metaphorically, to mean the direction of an attack, either a physical or verbal one. Because of the metaphorical nature of the word, it works very well to describe a shinki's weapon as such. In English, however, the word "spear" is not used in that way, and is generally used only to describe a specific type of weapon. For this reason, the translators chose to use the word phalanges instead, because it is a literal description of what the shinki are pointing at people, and in addition (to the translators' great fortune), it's the plural of phalanx, a close-knit military unit equipped with...wait for it...spears! Tadah!

Tsuyu, page 31

The translators almost wrote a note for the last volume, because that's when we noticed that, while Tsuyu's name does end in *yu* like Tenjin's shinki's names, it doesn't contain the same *yu* kanji, thus distinguishing her slightly from the *yu* clan. Her name literally means "plum rain," which can be quite fitting if you think of a rain of plum blossom petals... or of plum branches, as the case may be.

Wielder of an Iron Will, page 52

The Japanese title of this chapter is *Ishitsutsui Mochi*, which means "wielder of a stone hammer," or "wielder of a sword with a stone pommel." It is a reference to a song in the *Kojiki*, or "Records of Ancient Matters," which is kind of a mythological history of Japan. The song is used as an order to smite *tsuchigumo*, and the lyrics mention *ishitsutsu*, or swords with stone pommels. The word *tsuchigumo* (earth spider) is a generic term for local people who do not swear allegiance to the divinely appointed emperor, but it is also the name of a spider-like creature from Japanese folklore. As usual, this title has a double meaning: the word *ishi* means "stone" in the original song, but here there is no *kanji* character to restrict it to one meaning, and so it can also mean "will," as in a person's power to choose his or her own actions.

these deities weren't known by any specific name, or they were known by the name of the locale. Then, when certain gods grew to be popular all over the country, they would be adopted into the worship at local shrines. For example, the god of one of the mountains at Kumano may have been designated as Ôkuninushi, and the name of that mountain would then become the name of one of Ôkuninushi's enshrined personas.

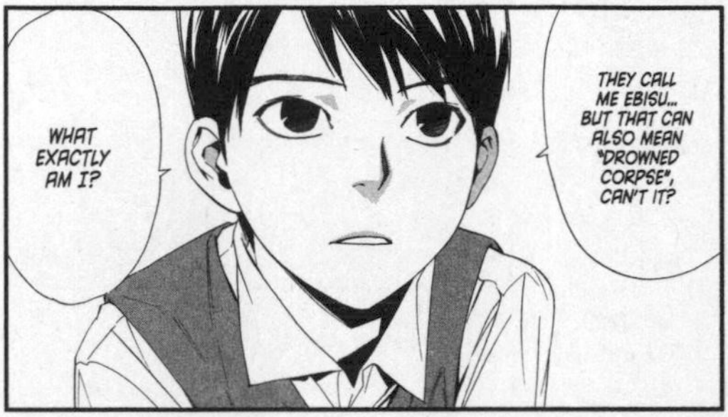
THEY CALL ME EBISU... BUT THAT CAN ALSO MEAN "DROWNED CORPSE", CAN'T IT?
WHAT EXACTLY AM I?

Ebisu = "drowned corpse," page 151

In the fishing community, large animals that washed up dead on the beach, including human corpses, were called *ebisu*. They were considered a sign that there would be a large catch in the near future, and so fisherman would take home any drowned corpses they may find, either on the beach or out at sea, and give them a proper burial.

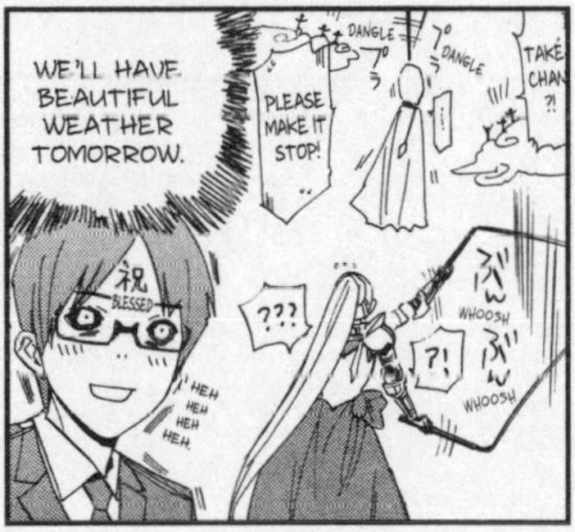
TAKÉ CHAN ?!
DANGLE
DANGLE
PLEASE MAKE IT STOP!
WE'LL HAVE BEAUTIFUL WEATHER TOMORROW.
WHOOSH
WHOOSH
?!
???
祝 BLESSED
HEH HEH HEH HEH.

Beautiful weather tomorrow, page 190

Takemikazuchi is a god of thunder, so if Kazuma has put him out of commission, it seems reasonable to expect fair weather until he recovers. For added good measure, Kazuma has hung up a *teru teru bôzu*, traditionally put up in Japan to ward off rain. *Teru teru bôzu* dolls look like little ghost dolls, or like Takemikazuchi with his head covering and Kinuha around his neck.

Saku-kun, page 124

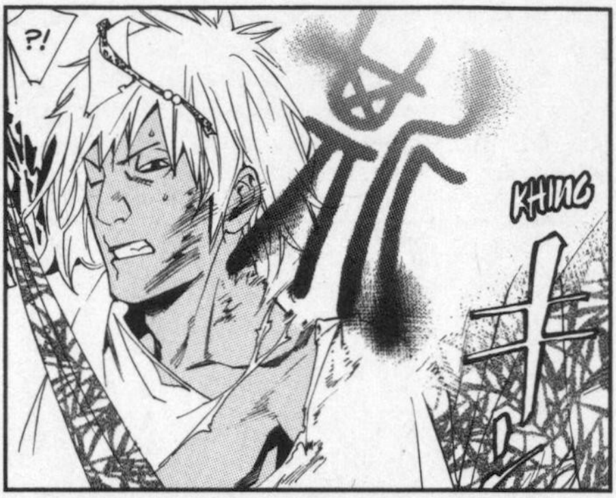
?!
KHING

As you may remember, a shinki is generally given three names: the true name, the instrument name, and the *yobina* (called name). The last name is given to avoid too much repetition of the true name, out of respect to the shinki, because their true name has a degree of sacredness. As is the case with Hiiro and Saku, it would appear that strays are not afforded that same respect, and are simply called by their true names. This may also be because a god would want to avoid including a stray in his or her family of shinki; Tenjin could easily call Saku "Sakuyu," but probably chose not to because of his disdain for strays. It is interesting to note, however, that Ebisu does give all shinki, including strays, the Ebisu family suffix of *mi*.

For the curious, the character for *saku* means "this" or "such," describing something as it is. This is an interesting contrast to the Tenjin's *yu* suffix, which means "metaphor."

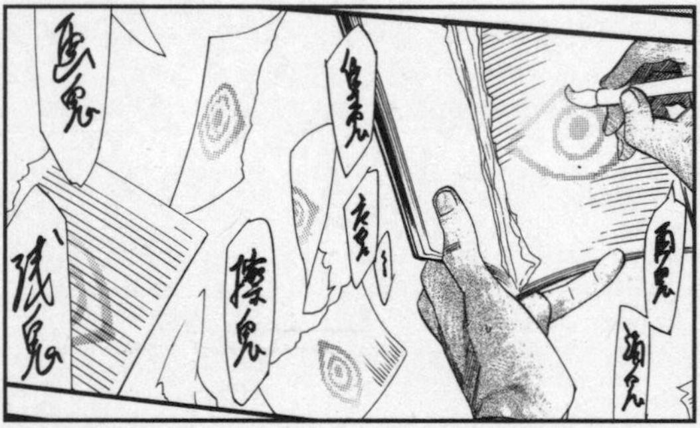

Ayakashi names, page 134

Here Ebisu is hiring a bunch of shinki by naming them. What the names are don't really affect the story, and most of all, the translators can't read all of them, so they elected to leave them in *kanji* here. It may be worth noting that so far all ayakashi names have ended in *ki*, but it is not the same *ki* as in a shinki's instrument name. The *ki* for ayakashi is the same character as *oni*, which can refer to a specific type of supernatural creature, but in this case, like the ayakashi, it appears to be a blanket term for Far Shore beings that are of a more sinister nature than their shinki counterparts.

Names of Ebisu's enshrined personas, page 151

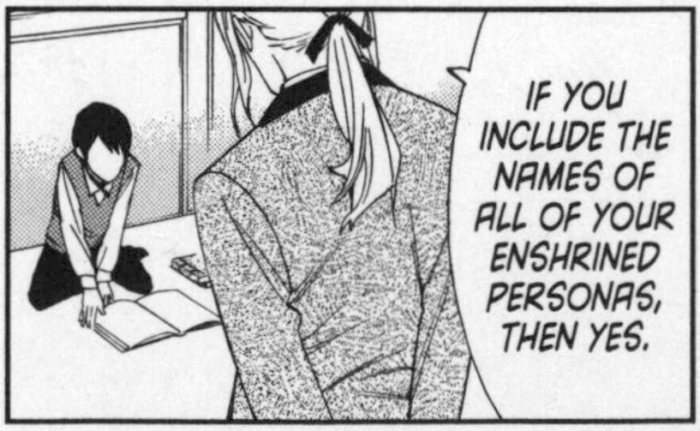
IF YOU INCLUDE THE NAMES OF ALL OF YOUR ENSHRINED PERSONAS, THEN YES.

Specifically, Iwami calls these names Ebisu's *saijin-mei*, which means literally "names of worshiped gods." *Saijin* is the word used to refer to the group of deities worshiped at a single shrine. Originally, many shrines were dedicated to the spirit or deity of something in nature (rivers, mountains, rocks, etc.), and

A Kodansha Comics Trade Paperback Original.

Published in the United States by Kodansha Comics, an imprint of Kodansha USA Publishing, LLC, New York.

Publication rights for this English edition arranged through Kodansha Ltd., Tokyo.

First published in Japan in 2013 by Kodansha Ltd., Tokyo.

ISBN 978-1-63236-128-8

Printed in the United States of America.

www.kodanshacomics.com

9 8 7 6 5 4 3 2 1

Translator: Alethea Nibley & Athena Nibley
Lettering: Lys Blakeslee

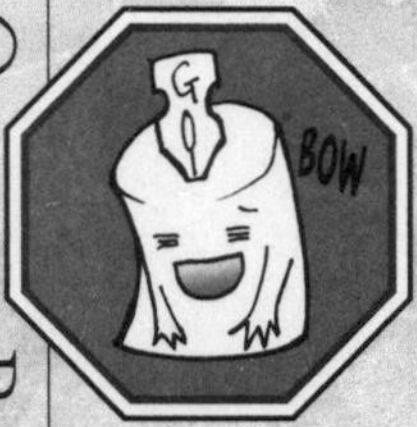
BOW

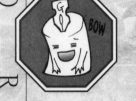

Ebisu is finally showing his true colors, so it's easier to draw him now. It's like I've finally built the muscles needed to draw that character. There are Yato muscles for drawing Yato, background muscles for drawing backgrounds, and tone muscles for laying screentone. Drawing manga is like bodybuilding.

Adachitoka